AI and Fintech

This book explores the transformative intersection of AI and Fintech. It encompasses an in-depth analysis of how AI is reshaping the financial industry, revolutionizing traditional practices, and paving the way for innovative solutions. It provides understanding of the symbiotic relationship between AI and Fintech, offering insights into the current state, future potential, challenges, and ethical considerations within this dynamic landscape. It addresses critical ethical considerations surrounding AI and Fintech, fostering a dialogue on responsible AI integration and data privacy.

Features:

- Explains how AI is being used to automate tasks, improve efficiency, and reduce costs in the financial industry.
- Covers improvement of risk management and fraud detection.
- Includes the development of new financial products and services, such as robo-advisors and cryptocurrency trading platforms.
- Explores the potential impact of AI on the financial industry, both positive and negative.
- Discusses the ethical implications of using AI in the financial sector.

This book is aimed at researchers and professionals in computer engineering, AI, and Fintech.

Computational Intelligence Techniques

Series Editor: Vishal Jain

The objective of this series is to provide researchers a platform to present state-of-the-art innovations, research, and design and implement methodological and algorithmic solutions to data processing problems, designing and analyzing evolving trends in health informatics and computer-aided diagnosis. This series provides support and aid to researchers involved in designing decision support systems that will permit societal acceptance of ambient intelligence. The overall goal of this series is to present the latest snapshot of ongoing research as well as to shed further light on future directions in this space. The series presents novel technical studies as well as position and vision papers comprising hypothetical/speculative scenarios. This book series seeks to compile all aspects of computational intelligence techniques from fundamental principles to current advanced concepts. For this series, we invite researchers, academicians, and professionals to contribute, expressing their ideas and research in the application of intelligent techniques to the field of engineering in handbook, reference, or monograph volumes.

Convergence of IoT, Blockchain and Computational Intelligence in Smart Cities
Edited by Rajendra Kumar, Vishal Jain, Leong Wai Yie, and Sunantha Prime Teyarachakul

Intelligent Techniques for Cyber-Physical Systems
Edited by Mohammad Sajid, Anil Kumar, Jagendra Singh, Osamah Ibrahim Khalaf, and Mukesh Prasad

Big Data Computing: Advances in Technologies, Methodologies, and Applications
Edited by Tanvir Habib Sardar and Bishwajeet Kumar Pandey

Software Defined Network Frameworks: Security Issues and Use Cases
Edited by Mandeep Kaur, Vishal Jain, Parma Nand, and Nitin Rakesh

Machine Learning Hybridization and Optimization for Intelligent Applications
Edited by Tanvir Habib Sardar and Bishwajeet Kumar Pandey

Information Technology Ethics
Hamed Taherdoost

Applications of Blockchain and Computational Intelligence in Environmental Sustainability
Edited by Hamed Taherdoost, Mohsen Saeedi, and Aydin Shishegaran

AI and Fintech: Improving the Financial Landscape
Edited by Jaheer Mukthar K. P., Rosario Mercedes Huerta-Soto, Vishal Jain, and Edwin Hernan Ramirez-Asis

For more information about this series, please visit: www.routledge.com/Computational-Intelligence-Techniques/book-series/CIT

AI and Fintech
Improving the Financial Landscape

Edited by
K. P. Jaheer Mukthar,
Rosario Mercedes Huerta-Soto,
Vishal Jain, and Edwin Hernan Ramirez-Asis

CRC Press
Taylor & Francis Group
Boca Raton London New York

CRC Press is an imprint of the
Taylor & Francis Group, an **informa** business

Designed cover image: Shutterstock

First edition published 2026
by CRC Press
2385 NW Executive Center Drive, Suite 320, Boca Raton FL 33431

and by CRC Press
4 Park Square, Milton Park, Abingdon, Oxon, OX14 4RN

CRC Press is an imprint of Taylor & Francis Group, LLC

ISBN: 9781032825175 (hbk)
ISBN: 9781041085324 (pbk)
ISBN: 9781003645849 (ebk)

DOI: 10.1201/9781003645849

Typeset in Times
by codeMantra

Contents

Preface

The financial industry is undergoing a transformative revolution, driven by the rapid advancements in artificial intelligence (AI) and financial technology (Fintech). The convergence of these two fields is reshaping traditional financial practices, offering new and innovative solutions that are more efficient, secure, and customer-centric. This book, *AI and Fintech: Revolutionizing the Financial Landscape*, aims to provide a comprehensive exploration of this dynamic intersection, offering insights into the current state, future potential, challenges, and ethical considerations of AI in Fintech.

In recent years, AI has emerged as a powerful tool in the financial sector, enabling automation, enhancing risk management, and personalizing financial services. From algorithmic trading and robo-advisors to fraud detection and customer experience enhancement, AI technologies are revolutionizing the way financial institutions operate. This book delves into these critical areas, providing a foundational understanding of the technologies at play and their real-world applications.

Our goal is to present a balanced view of the opportunities and challenges associated with the integration of AI into Fintech. We aim to equip professionals, researchers, policymakers, and students with the knowledge needed to navigate this evolving landscape. This book includes contributions from renowned experts in both academia and industry, offering diverse perspectives on the subject matter. As we explore the transformative potential of AI in Fintech, we also address the ethical implications and regulatory challenges that accompany these advancements. The responsible development and deployment of AI technologies are crucial to ensuring that their benefits are realized while minimizing risks and protecting data privacy.

AI and Fintech: Revolutionizing the Financial Landscape aspires to serve as a definitive reference for those interested in the ongoing transformation of the financial industry. It is our hope that this book will inspire innovation, foster informed decision-making, and contribute to the responsible integration of AI in financial services, ultimately shaping a more efficient, inclusive, and dynamic financial landscape.

About the Editors

K. P. Jaheer Mukthar is a research faculty member in the Department of Economics in Kristu Jayanti College Autonomous, Bengaluru, India. With a strong focus on technology, business, and sustainability, his research contributions have made a significant impact in these areas. His research was recognized and awarded at various international conferences, including the 13th Global Islamic Marketing Conference in Turkey and the 2022 International Conference on Business and Technology in Turkey, among others. He was also awarded the best paper awards from renowned conferences, such as the 6th Equal Opportunity Conference in Bahrain. In addition to his publications and conference contributions, he is also an esteemed guest editor, showcasing his expertise in the field. He also serves as an associate editor and is an editorial review board member for six Scopus-indexed journals.

Rosario Mercedes Huerta-Soto is an experienced economist and academic with a diverse background in both the public and private sectors. She holds a BA and an MA in Business Administration from the National University Santiago Antúnez de Mayolo (UNASAM). Dr Huerta-Soto has held various managerial positions, including roles at Financiera Confianza, Compartamos Financiera, and Agrobanco. She has also been actively involved in academia as a teaching assistant in the Faculty of Economics and Accounting at UNASAM. In addition to her professional pursuits, Dr Huerta-Soto has contributed to academic research, with several articles published in reputable journals.

Vishal Jain is presently working as an associate professor at Department of Computer Science and Engineering, Sharda School of Engineering and Technology, Sharda University, Greater Noida, UP, India. Before that, he worked for several years as an associate professor at Bharati Vidyapeeth's Institute of Computer Applications and Management (BVICAM), New Delhi. He has more than 16 years of experience in academia. He obtained PhD (CSE), MTech (CSE), MBA (HR), MCA, MCP, and CCNA. He has more than 1,350 research citation indices with Google Scholar (h-index score 18 and i-10 index 34). He has authored more than 100 research papers in reputed conferences and journals, including Web of Science and Scopus. He has authored and edited more than 45 books with various reputed publishers, including Taylor and Francis Group. His research areas include information retrieval, semantic web, ontology engineering, data mining, ad hoc networks, and sensor networks. He received a Young Active Member Award for the year 2012–2013 from the Computer Society of India, Best Faculty Award for the year 2017 and Best Researcher Award for the year 2019 from BVICAM, New Delhi.

Edwin Hernan Ramirez-Asis is a senior professor at the Universidad Nacional Santiago Antúnez de Mayolo, Huaraz, Perú. He is currently the Director of the School of Administration at the Faculty of Administration and Tourism at the university. He has his PhD in management. He is a research professor recognized by the National Council of Science, Technology and Technological Innovation, Peru. He has 15 years of experience in teaching and research. He has published ten articles in journals indexed in Scopus and Web of Science. His research interests include information society, innovation in microfinance, and digital marketing.

Contributors

Palagati Anusha
Department of CSE
Guru Nanak Institute of Technology
Hyderabad, India

Gayathri Chakkingal
Department of Commerce
PSGR Krishnammal College for Women
Coimbatore, India

Bharat Chaudhari
Institute of Information and Communication Technology
MGM University
Chh. Sambhajinagar, MH, India

Rashmi Deshmukh
Department of Technology
Shivaji University
Kolhapur, India

Shampa I. Dev
School of Law
CHRIST-Deemed to be University
Bangalore, India

Ahmed A. Elamer
Brunei Business School
Brunei University London
London, United Kingdom

Lina George
Department of Business Studies
University of Technology and Applied Science
Muscat, Oman

Philip George
Department of Robotics
Christ University
Bengaluru, India

R. Esther Hepziba
Department of Business Administration
Madras Christian College
Chennai, India

Majidul Islam
John Molson School of Business (JMSB)
Concordia University
Montreal, Canada

Ajay Kumar Jain
Department of Finance and Accounting
Westminster International University of Tashkent
Tashkent, Uzbekistan

Vishal Jain
Computer Science and Engineering
Sharda University
Greater Noida, India

Mahima Jasniewski
Strategy Manager
Information Resource Inc
Chicago, Illinois

Dilshod Kamilov
Department of Management Studies
Sambhram University
Jizzakh, Uzbekistan

Ganesh Lohar
Department of Technology
Shivaji University
Kolhapur, India

Nishaanth Madathukulam Senthil Kumar
BTech (AI and DS)
Graduate, KGISL Institute of Technology
Coimbatore, India

Thomas Mangara
School of Commerce, Finance and Accountancy
CHRIST-Deemed to be University
Bangalore, India

Rajarajeswari Maniyan
Department of Commerce
PSGR Krishnammal College for Women
Coimbatore, India

M. Narayana Moorthi
Dept of IoT- SCOPE
Vellore Institute of Technology
Vellore, India

Arvind Nath Sinha
Department of Management Studies
GL Bajaj Institute of Technology and Management
Greater Noida, India

Arpita Nayak
Department of Management
KSOM, KIIT DU
Bhubaneswar, India

Kadiri Padmaja
Department of AIML, School of Computing
Mohan Babu University
Tirupati, India

Shreya Pandit
SCOPE
Vellore Institute of Technology
Vellore, India

Pranavsinh Patil
Department of Technology
Shivaji University
Kolhapur, India

Pratik Patil
Department of Technology
Shivaji University
Kolhapur, India

Shreeyash Patil
Department of Technology
Shivaji University
Kolhapur, India

Chokkamreddy Prakash
School of Management Studies
Guru Nanak Institutions Technical Campus
Hyderabad, India

Minakshi Rajput
Institute of Information and Communication Technology
MGM University
Chh. Sambhajinagar, MH, India

Alamelu Mangai Raman
College of Economics and Business Administration
University of Technology and Applied Sciences-Al Musannah
Muladdah, Sultanate of Oman

Sangeetha Rangasamy
School of Business and Management
CHRIST-Deemed to be University
Bangalore, India

Gurramkonda Reddeppa Naidu
Department of Management Studies
Sambhram University
Jizzakh, Uzbekistan

Karthik Reddy
Department of Management Studies
Nitte Meenakshi Institute of Technology
Bengaluru, India

Shravan Salunkhe
Department of Technology
Shivaji University
Kolhapur, India

A. Sankaran
Department of Computer Science and Engineering
Manakula Vinayagar Institute of Technology
Puducherry, India

Ipseeta Satpathy
Department of Management
KSOM, KIIT DU
Bhubaneswar, India

A. Millicent Serena
Department of Business Administration
Madras Christian College
Chennai, India

K. R. Senthilkumar
Librarian
Sri Krishna Arts and Science College
Coimbatore, India

MahabubBasha Shaik
Department of Commerce
International Institute of Business Studies
Bangalore, India

Manisha Singh
VIT Business School
VIT Bhopal University
Bhopal, India

Nivedita Singh
Department of Management Studies
GL Bajaj Institute of Technology and Management
Greater Noida, India

Sonali Srivastava
Jaypee Business School
Jaypee Institute of Information Technology
Noida, India

Sharvari Tamane
Institute of Information and Communication Technology
MGM University
Chh. Sambhajinagar, MH, India

Aashka Thakkar
Department of Business Administration
Parul University
Waghodia, India

S. Vaidheeswaran
Department of Management Studies
Manakula Vinayagar Institute of Technology
Puducherry, India

N. Vanitha
Department of Artificial Intelligence and Machine Learning
Coimbatore Institute of Technology
Coimbatore, India

Nakka Venkatarathnam
Department of Management Studies
Sambhram University
Jizzakh, Uzbekistan

Amit Verma
Department of Commerce
Kalicharan PG College
Lucknow, India

A. B. Mohammed Yousuf
Department of Information Technology
Manakula Vinayagar Institute of Technology
Puducherry, India

1 Artificial Intelligence in Payment Systems

Transforming the Mode of Payment

Arpita Nayak, Ipseeta Satpathy, Vishal Jain, and Majidul Islam

1.1 INTRODUCTION

The world of commerce has experienced profound shifts, transitioning from a predominantly cash-based economy to a fundamentally digital one. Historically, cash was the king of payments. It is palpable, simple, and does not require a middleman. However, it is not without downsides. Cash transactions are inefficient, pose security threats, and lack tracking, which is a major problem for companies and regulators. Banks increasingly use AI and machine learning (ML)-powered big data analytics tools to deliver quicker and more personalized client service. Customers are essential to every service organization, and AI may assist in getting a better knowledge of their wants and behaviors. Consequently, banks use this expertise to customize their goods and services. In addition to customer-facing applications, big data analytics solutions may help banking executives and managers make sound decisions regarding internal company procedures, operations, investments, risks, and resource allocation. Big data analytics and ML have exciting applications, such as identifying fraudulent transactions, optimizing corporate rules, assuring legal and regulatory compliance, safeguarding transactions, and forecasting future occurrences. Therefore, AI technology is sufficiently evolved to be used in the financial industry (Rani & Suresh, 2024). As the payments industry grows and evolves, businesses are looking for new methods to remain competitive and provide value to customers. Artificial intelligence (AI) is one of the most promising technologies in recent years. Integrating AI into payment processes has major benefits for many organizations in the global payments sector. Payment companies, for example, may use AI to automate procedures, cut costs, improve transaction routing, and provide customized goods and services. AI solutions can improve payment processing by automating monotonous processes, eliminating mistakes, and allowing industry actors to concentrate on more important responsibilities. AI technology, by automating operations such as data input, reconciliation, and reporting, may help major merchants and acquirers save time and increase productivity. This enables them to improve the client journey, find new possibilities, and manage risks more efficiently. Using AI in payment processing

DOI: 10.1201/9781003645849-1

can give clients a more efficient, accurate, and timely payment experience (Bygari et al., 2021). AI technology may greatly accelerate payment transactions by providing real-time fraud detection and clearance, decreasing the necessity for manual review and approval methods. AI employs ML algorithms and predictive analytics. AI technologies can analyze enormous amounts of data, detect trends and abnormalities, and alert to probable fraud attempts in real time. Then, payment providers can swiftly and properly approve or refuse transactions (Allahham & Ahmad, 2024). By analyzing customer data with AI technology, businesses may get insights into consumer tastes and behavior, allowing them to personalize their items and improve the overall experience for customers. This can improve client loyalty and retention. Furthermore, AI solutions can assist retailers in simplifying their processes and shorten processing times. This leads to faster and more efficient transactions for customers. For instance, AI-powered chatbots may give clients with real-time guidance and support, lowering wait times and increasing satisfaction. Using AI technology to optimize the customer journey allows merchants to provide a more smooth and engaging experience for their consumers, resulting in higher revenue and growth potential (Lai & Tong, 2022). AI in payment processing uses real-time image recognition that is gradually replacing conventional cash and credit cards. That is why account information is kept electronically, and clients pay for services using the applications for mobile devices such as Google Pay or Apple Wallet Services. Through computer vision, financial institutions are allowing clients to create accounts on the internet, thereby avoiding going to physical financial institutions. Other applications of AI are also quite efficient in identifying fraudulent transactions. AI then forms the payment settings user profiles for pattern recognition starting with the transaction history and previous behaviors. When utilized, AI alerts the bank or customer so that the account can be limited or the transaction confirmed through an SMS, email, or other means of communication. The aforementioned process drastically cuts down the time needed for this operation (Häckel et al., 2022). The following puts down some of the backward payment processes (Tan & Fang, 2019):

- **Cash transactions:** Previously, cash was the king of payments. It is palpable, simple, and does not require a middleman. However, it is not without downsides. Cash transactions are inefficient, pose security threats, and lack traceability, which is a major problem for businesses and regulators.
- **Credit and debit cards:** The advent of credit and debit cards marked a significant improvement in ease and security. Cards reduced the inconvenience of carrying currency and provided a traceable, simple means to transact. They gained popularity notably with the advent of point of sale (POS) technology, which made it easier to make payments at physical retail locations.
- **Bank transfers:** Bank transfers provided an additional degree of ease, particularly for high-value transactions. They give a payment record, and the increased use of Internet banking has made them the preferred alternative for many.

Traditional payment methods are still widely used today, but there are more choices to consider. Some modern payment methods are listed below:

- **Digital wallets:** As cell phones became more widespread, digital wallets evolved as a quick, simple, and secure payment mechanism. Tokenization technology enables consumers to securely retain card information and perform purchases with a single touch through services such as Apple Pay and Google Pay.
- **Contactless payments:** The need for speedy, hassle-free purchases has fueled the growth of contactless payments. These systems leverage technology such as Near Field Communication (NFC) or QR codes to create a frictionless, contactless transaction experience, which has grown in popularity even after the epidemic.
- **Cryptocurrencies:** The rise of cryptocurrencies popularized the notion of decentralized payments. While cryptocurrencies provide benefits such as decreased transaction fees and enhanced anonymity, their volatility and regulatory ambiguity represent barriers to general use.
- **Central bank digital currency (CBDC):** Essentially, the central banks produce and guarantee digital currency. It is the electronic equivalent of a country's conventional currency, which means that rather than producing money, the central bank manages digital accounts or tokens backed by the government's confidence and reputation. As cryptocurrencies and stablecoins acquire worldwide popularity, central banks see the significance of collaborating with digital currencies to remain relevant and competitive.

Some of the key benefits of AI is its forecasting abilities. AI-powered systems, for example, may provide extremely detailed insights into spending habits and trends by assessing, analyzing, and modeling massive amounts of behavioral data. In turn, this data may assist banks and financial institutions in better tailoring their goods and services, resulting in increased profitability, lower operational costs, and improved B2C partnerships. On the opposite side of the 'check-out counter', AI is assisting in the resolution of long-standing consumer complaints. Delays in transaction processing and authorization, as well as the following lag time in updating account balances, are typical complaints among consumers who have grown to demand real-time visibility and transparency in today's hyper-speed, digital economy (Zhang & Chen, 2019). AI's predictive modeling skills have resulted in the development of processing and settlement technologies that can eliminate a wide range of bottlenecks. Transaction authorizations may now be executed even during issuer failures or maintenance downtimes, thanks to AI-powered services. Clearing times may also be reduced using predictive modeling, ensuring that consumers receive timely notifications, alerts, and balance changes (Lowry, 2006). Chatbots and virtual assistants driven by natural language processing are transforming consumer interactions in the payments business. Conversational AI enables payment companies to respond to a wide range of frequent consumer inquiries without the need for human participation. Customers may now receive immediate assistance with account balances, payment due dates, transaction disputes, and other concerns by just speaking with an AI assistant. This has resulted in significantly decreased call centre volumes while boosting 24/7 support accessibility. AI improves payment routing decisions by analyzing transaction volume, cost, and network performance, resulting in more efficient processing. It also automates compliance procedures, monitors transactions for regulatory compliance, and detects questionable activity. This proactive strategy ensures that payment providers meet regulatory standards and successfully manage compliance risks. The use of AI has changed the payment system into a highly successful, secure, and customer-centric ecosystem. Payment providers may use AI-driven technology to create new solutions that increase security, expedite procedures, and improve the entire client experience, allowing them to remain competitive in the payment industry's quickly changing digital market.

1.2 RESEARCH QUESTIONS

- How is AI transforming the payment system that is leading to a new way of payment?
- What are the different components that AI is affecting in the payment process?

1.3 RESEARCH OBJECTIVES

- To understand the implementation of AI in payment systems.
- To comprehend the different benefits of AI in the payment process.

1.4 FRAUD PREVENTION: THE ROLE OF AI IN PAYMENT SYSTEM

AI is crucial for combating fraud in payment systems. AI enables the real-time analysis of enormous amounts of data, which aids in the identification of fraudulent activity including unauthorized transactions and frauds. Businesses may use AI algorithms to improve security measures, execute multi-level security checks, and authenticate consumers successfully. Furthermore, AI-based security intelligence modeling may assist avoid, identify, and manage cyber risks such as authorized push payment (APP) frauds, demonstrating AI's promise in preventing financial crime. With the growth of fast payment systems, real-time fraud detection models driven by AI are becoming increasingly important for enabling the rapid identification and prevention of forged transactions (Siddiqui & Goyal, 2023). AI plays an important role in reducing fraud in e-payment systems by improving verification procedures and detecting fraudulent transactions with ML algorithms. AI, particularly deep learning algorithms, improves credit and debit card verification during payment processing, resulting in more accurate fraud detection. ML algorithms can detect and prevent fraudulent payments by identifying the relationships between data. Professional con artists may swiftly identify and move on to a different merchant when their payments are declined, despite rule-based reasoning used to prevent fraudulent transactions. AI technologies, like deep learning for risk analysis, are projected to significantly affect the payment and commerce industries in the future. AI, blockchain, ML, and cloud computing have significantly disrupted the financial settlement sector. Online payment systems utilize encryption and digital signatures to provide security and prevent fraud.

As e-commerce increases and becomes more secure, the usage of electronic payment methods is expanding, causing a reduction in transactions utilizing checks and cash (Vanini et al., 2023). AI helps to avoid financial fraud by improving the payment system's security procedures, such as client authentication and multi-level security checks. Banks are utilizing AI to detect and prevent banking fraud, such as identity theft and phishing. AI and ML analyze information, content, context, and user behavior to detect dangers and abnormalities in emails, avoiding phishing fraud. AI-based solutions can detect and prevent fraudulent actions through strong consumer authentication and security checks. AI in financial systems has reduced theft and fraud, creating a safer environment for consumers and companies (Mytnyk et al., 2023). AI also helps to detect fraud by analyzing client data such as spending habits and payment histories, hence improving payment system security. To construct client data records, AI algorithms collect information such as spending habits and payment histories. AI algorithms analyze data in real time to detect trends and abnormalities that may suggest fraudulent behavior. AI systems continually learn and enhance their fraud detection skills, resulting in more accurate predictions over time (Rahman et al., 2021). For instance, BlaBlaCar is the world's largest carpooling community, with more than 40 million members. Its massive database had become a popular target for scammers looking to get in and utilize the treasure mine of personal information for illicit reasons. BlaBlaCar contacted DataDome with the following requests: The solution should not degrade the user experience or performance of their websites or mobile apps. Furthermore, no user information could ever be transferred to DataDome via inbound BlaBlaCar traffic. This posed no difficulty for the DataDome solution, which is both lightweight and powerful – and does not require personally identifying information. BlaBlaCar's user accounts are now safeguarded without the need for regular maintenance. The solution can identify and stop both new and old threats (Choi & Lee, 2018). AI-based security intelligence modeling may avoid, identify, and manage cyber risks in payment systems, including APP schemes. Here's how AI can help manage app scams, AI can analyze enormous amounts of data from numerous sources, including transaction records, user behavior patterns, and previous fraud instances, to detect probable fraudulent activity. ML techniques boost AI's capacity to recognize and avoid APP fraud. AI can offer real-time monitoring and notifications, allowing payment service providers to respond quickly when suspicious activity is spotted. Furthermore, AI may help investigate and manage APP fraud by analyzing trends (Ma et al., 2023). AI systems, aided by ML techniques, analyze massive volumes of transaction data to swiftly identify trends and abnormalities that may suggest fraudulent activity. AI systems can successfully distinguish between legal and fraudulent transactions using predictive analytics and anomaly detection, enabling proactive risk mitigation measures. Furthermore, AI-powered fraud detection models are constantly improving and adapting to new threats, increasing their accuracy and efficiency over time. Furthermore, AI offers real-time dynamic risk assessment by assessing numerous contextual aspects such as transaction history, user behavior, and geographic location, assisting payment providers in determining the amount of risk associated with individual transactions. In addition, AI-powered behavioral biometrics and pattern recognition algorithms improve authentication procedures by strengthening security and deterring unauthorized access attempts. AI's complete approach to fraud prevention enables payment systems to respond proactively to developing risks and effectively preserve the integrity of financial transactions (Mustapha et al., 2023). AI techniques remain relevant and beneficial to instant payment systems because they keep the fraud rates low by quickly detecting and preventing fraudulent transactions within the applicable regulatory frameworks. Older modes of fraud detection in financial organizations mainly operate on the use of a set of rules and could take up to several days to audit a transaction. Instant payment systems initiated by the central banks are likely to facilitate quicker authorizations hence requiring real-time fraud checks. Transaction fraud can be detected within the same blink of an eye that is, it is both efficient and secure, due to development in the field of ML and AI technologies. These AI approaches match industry standards for real-world deployment since they allow rapid and precise identification of fraudulent activity, boosting security in immediate payment systems (Said & Hajami, 2022).

In essence, AI is a strong tool for protecting electronic payments and reducing financial risks linked with fraud. Overall, AI plays a critical role in improving payment system security, reducing financial fraud, and protecting consumers' and organizations' money and data.

1.5 MODERNIZING PAYMENT RISK ASSESSMENT WITH AI TECHNOLOGY

AI can help manage risks in payment systems by avoiding and identifying APP scams. AI-based Security Intelligence Modelling helps prevent, identify, and manage cyber risks, including APP frauds. Data-driven AI solutions are experiencing rigorous study and design modifications in their area and can help manage APP fraud by adapting technical solutions depending on local regulations can help industry executives and engineering managers prioritize investment priorities, strategic approaches, and technology solutions for addressing APP fraud (Ma et al., 2023). The financial services sector often deals with massive volumes of data, which has grown in recent years and is anticipated to grow much more in the future. It is anticipated that in 2020, each individual will generate at least 1.7 MB of data every second on average; by 2025, society as a whole is expected to generate 463 exabytes of data each day worldwide. These enormous, complicated data sets include insights that banks may use to build more accurate risk models, make better decisions, and detect suspicious behavior or transactions in real time. However, humans cannot correctly analyze such large amounts of data. As a result, banks are turning to technology to efficiently handle massive volumes of data and find crucial insights that may help them make better decisions, decrease risk, and improve the customer experience. AI uses algorithms to analyze big, complex data sets at scale, identifying patterns and predicting consequences. This enables banks to minimize risk more efficiently by recognizing suspicious or unusual activity that suggests the presence of fraud (Soviany, 2018). Manual fraud detection methods, which rely heavily on human analysts, are no longer a viable or effective way to keep up with the current growth of digital transactions. AI-enabled risk management tools and methodologies provide real-time data analysis, allowing businesses to halt potentially fraudulent transactions or demand verification before advancing. In both loan and transaction fraud detection, the AI or ML model will get cleverer over time. This means that when models process more data, their analytical capabilities improve, allowing them to become more accurate over time and reducing the number of false positives in the system (Rutskiy et al., 2023). Complying with national and international rules is a critical and difficult operation in the financial sector. Large data sets must be evaluated, multiple factors analyzed, and proper documentation presented to the right authorities. ML automates these tasks, ensuring they are executed swiftly and precisely. This results in considerable cost savings for banks in terms of resource optimization and the avoidance of fines or penalties. ML technology may help reduce the frequency of false warnings in the compliance system, ensuring that issues are handled manually by humans only when necessary (Jakšič & Marinic, 2019). AI-powered fraud detection enables high-trust online use cases in the financial services business. Over the last year, we have onboarded some of the world's fastest-growing Fintech and countless Fortune 500 organizations, helping them minimize fraud and make faster choices for their consumers. Intelligent document automation improves the processing time and accuracy of client applications by extracting critical information from documents such as bank statements, transactions, and payslips. We collaborate with customers to decrease manual procedures and connect our user-friendly API to automate document checks, speed up account opening or underwriting processes, and improve compliance (Siddiqui & Goyal, 2023). AI-powered risk management systems can properly anticipate, analyze, and mitigate risks by leveraging predictive analytics, anomaly detection, and behavioral analysis. Furthermore, AI enables real-time risk assessment by considering a variety of contextual data such as transaction history, user behavior, and market trends. This enables payment providers to make more informed decisions and execute proactive risk-mitigation techniques, improving the security and dependability of payment transactions. AI provides continual learning and adaptation, allowing risk management systems to grow and keep up with evolving risks. By leveraging AI capabilities, payment systems may improve their resilience, efficiency, and efficacy in risk management while also providing users with a seamless and safe payment experience. AI not only enhances risk management systems' detection and mitigation capabilities but also increases operational efficiency and cost-effectiveness. By automating laborious procedures and expediting decision-making, AI assists payment providers in optimizing resource allocation, lowering operational costs, and increasing overall efficiency. Furthermore, AI-powered risk management solutions are easily scalable to handle rising transaction volumes and complexity, ensuring that payment systems stay robust and responsive to shifting needs (Sardjono et al., 2021). Applying generative AI in credit can significantly improve the process on how banks analyze clients and their relation with other banks through summarization. Once it has made a credit decision, it can produce both a credit memo and a contract. Several financial institutions use this technology to build credit risk evaluations and extract necessary data of the client from credit memoranda. SAP-based generative AI can also write program codes for credit data acquisition and modeling, which translates the client's risk profile and default/loss probability. AI in credit risk management entails the use of AI and ML techniques for analyzing big data, and patterns and having an accurate prognosis of credit risk. This is because the solutions are AF Since the solutions are automated, large organizations can be provided with faster, more accurate, and more reliable credit risk assessments in comparison with conventional ones. According to the Deloitte (2023) report, insufficient cybersecurity continues to pose significant risks for businesses in all industries. As hacking grows more prevalent, sensitive information is exposed. In 2019, financial services organizations allocated 6%–14% of their IT spend on cybersecurity. Figure 1.1 demonstrates areas where AI implementation might be improved.

Data quality is critical in risk management, particularly when using AI solutions for AML and anti-fraud operations. Financial institutions may efficiently detect and manage possible hazards by screening transactions and external risk indicators. Another area where AI and risk management technologies may have a big influence is stress testing. Organizations can examine their balance sheets' resilience by using complicated simulation models based on hypothetical situations. The 2008 financial crisis is a great illustration of the repercussions of ineffective portfolio risk management caused by a lack of openness and standards. The use of AI in risk management procedures represents a significant shift in how payment systems handle risks and ensure safe transactions. Payment service companies may use AI capabilities to improve security, optimize operations, and give clients a seamless and safe payment experience. With the advent of AI technology, its role in risk management inside payment systems is expected to grow even further, boosting innovation and resilience in digital payments. The ability to incorporate 'what if' scenarios in credit risk management

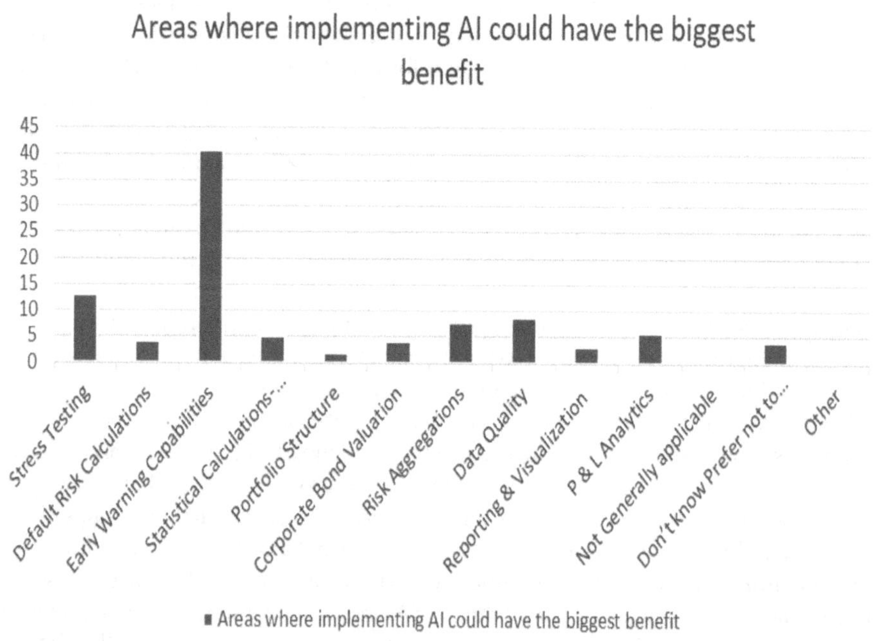

FIGURE 1.1 Areas where implementing AI tools could have the biggest benefit. (Source: https://www.infopulse.com/blog/implementing-ai-financial-risk-management.)

through the early warning systems that are now colloidal with AI is what is going to make a difference for the bankers. All these technologies enable the real-time analysis of internal and external conditions, whether they are financial, behavioral, geographical, or industrial, as well as general perceptions about the organization. This kind of approach tends to capture stress signs that a human specialist would not be able to observe easily. For instance, a working model of an early warning system that applies AI helped in improving the accuracy of potential default rates and disclosed a possible additional €11 million in dodgy credits. Due to their capability of identifying the possible risks earlier and in a more precise manner, such systems are beneficial in enabling the reduction of possible losses and improving decision-making.

1.6 KNOW YOUR CUSTOMER MADE EASY WITH AI

AI automates KYC procedures at financial institutions by utilizing AI and deep learning for E-KYC, increasing efficiency and lowering human error in the payment system. Automation in the KYC process is required to decrease human error and the time required to complete the procedure, particularly in light of the COVID-19 epidemic. The suggested solution automates the E-KYC procedure, often employed in financial institutions, with AI and deep learning. The AI-powered technology extracts information from Aadhaar and PAN cards, including first and last name, number, and date of birth, and presents it in a user-friendly style. This technology greatly decreases the time necessary for document verification, which can take up to three to five business days. The use of AI and deep learning in the KYC process boosts efficiency and accuracy by removing the need for manual data entry and lowering the chance of human mistakes (Bondarde et al., 2023). AI-enabled mobile banking improves KYC compliance in the banking industry by combining human capabilities with AI services. Research done at a private bank in the Middle East revealed that AI banking services can help combat money laundering and ensure compliance with Know Your Customer (KYC) guidelines. Implementing a Socio-economic Approach to Management, combining human capacity with AI banking services, may enhance compliance and raise ROI for AI and KYC deployment. This synchronization of human capacity with AI services assures compliance with anti-money laundering legislation and gives the bank a competitive advantage in the face of financial terrorism (Eid et al., 2022). AI helps to improve security in e-payment systems by allowing KYC processes, which protect personal data and financial resources from misuse and fraud. AI-powered systems may validate consumer information, including IDs and biometrics, throughout the onboarding process algorithms can detect suspicious activity and trends in e-payment systems, preventing fraudulent transactions can continually monitor and analyze client data to detect fraud risks and abnormalities, enabling prompt intervention and prevention. E-payment systems may use AI-powered data analytics to create client profiles and behavior patterns, allowing them to discover and flag any deviations (Lee, 2020). The AI platform uses a user's credit card information to identify the corresponding account.

The first communication channel allows users to submit commands for payment card account functions. The AI platform sends the order to a distant device in the bank's network via the second communication channel.

The remote device on the bank's network gets the command and authenticates the user. Using different communication channels for gathering credit card information and delivering commands improves authentication security (Kacar, 2023). AI-enabled software and hardware can help with risk evaluations in payment systems, thereby enhancing overall payment procedures. AI can analyze enormous volumes of data from a variety of sources, including client profiles, transaction history, and external databases, to detect possible hazards and fraudulent actions. AI can use ML algorithms to adapt to new patterns and trends in payment fraud, leading to more accurate risk assessments. AI can automate client identity verification and KYC procedures to avoid money laundering and ensure regulatory compliance. By simplifying and automating these risk assessment procedures, AI may drastically decrease the time and resources necessary for manual inspections, increasing transaction efficiency. AI can optimize payment system routing to handle transactions efficiently and cost-effectively, resulting in cost savings (Burri et al., 2023). AI improves financial systems by successfully linking merchant identities across channels and optimizing payment routing. AI-enabled software and hardware can lower transaction costs and boost customer trust in purchase choices. AI can improve the efficiency of monetary transactions by optimizing payment routing. Connecting merchant identities across digital payment channels is vital for successful corporate administration and connects several endpoints to a central hub, or 'terminal', in a digital payment system. Using AI, banking systems may easily integrate merchant identities across channels, enhancing transaction efficiency and lowering costs (Weichert, 2017). AI and ML are improving KYC procedures by continuously monitoring and re-KYC. By automating some of these important compliance operations, AI helps financial institutions improve security, decrease risk, increase efficiency, as well as enhance the customer experience. Compliance teams may achieve new levels of efficacy and scalability by collaborating with AI. AI-powered KYC systems use complex algorithms and ML techniques to optimize client verification operations by automating data gathering, analysis, and verification. AI can accurately authenticate customer identities in real time by analyzing large amounts of structured and unstructured data from various sources such as government databases, social media profiles, and financial records, reducing the need for manual intervention and minimizing errors. AI enables dynamic risk assessment by constantly monitoring consumer behavior and transaction patterns, and detecting suspicious activity and potential compliance problems. AI-powered KYC systems may identify high-risk transactions and customers using predictive analytics and anomaly detection, triggering additional inquiry to assure regulatory compliance and reduce financial crime risks. Furthermore, AI enables easy integration with current compliance frameworks and systems, allowing payment companies to respond to changing regulatory needs and market situations (Lopez, 2020). AI-powered KYC solutions provide benefits beyond compliance, such as enhanced customer experience and operational efficiency. AI speeds up client onboarding by automating repetitive KYC procedures and reducing manual participation, leading to less friction and delays in payment processing. AI-driven KYC systems are capable of handling large volumes of client data and transactions, guaranteeing scalability and reliability even in high-volume scenarios. AI enables the automatic authentication of consumer identities by analyzing large datasets from diverse sources, such as government records, biometric data, and internet profiles. This automatic verification procedure reduces the need for manual involvement and speeds up the onboarding process, resulting in a seamless and painless experience for clients (Bhawnra & Singh, 2024). AI-driven KYC systems may detect and highlight suspicious actions or abnormalities in real time, allowing for proactive risk mitigation and fraud prevention. By continually monitoring transactional behavior and trends, AI may identify possible warning indicators and alert compliance teams for additional inquiry, lowering the possibility of financial crimes like money laundering and terrorism funding allows for dynamic risk assessment by combining contextual data like as transaction history, geographic location, and consumer behavior into the study. This contextual knowledge enables KYC systems to adapt and respond to changing risks and regulatory requirements, guaranteeing compliance with AML and KYC standards (Wasserbauer, 2022). The introduction of AI into KYC procedures represents a significant step forward in payment system security and compliance. Payment providers may improve operational performance, simplify compliance processes, and strengthen security measures by using AI-powered KYC solutions. As a result, clients may have a smooth and secure payment experience, while the risks connected with legislation and financial crimes are reduced. As AI advances, its role in KYC systems is projected to rise, encouraging innovation and fortitude in the digital payments sector. AI helps e-payment systems develop strong KYC processes, identify and prevent fraudulent activity, and protect personal and financial data from abuse and fraud.

1.7 GLOBAL COMPANIES IMPLEMENTING AI IN PAYMENT SYSTEMS

The usage of AI and ML in retailers and financial institutions has significantly risen due to the effectiveness of these technologies in solving such issues as cybersecurity and document digitalization. Also, these organizations are implementing AI to manage the payment methods for their clients and consumers more proficiently. These solutions require the implementation into existing payment technology framework; straight through processing or robotic processing automation. Through these advanced technologies, organizations are in a position to reduce cost control and better the consumer experience in payment issues (RPA).

1.7.1 Starbucks

The My Starbucks Barista app, designed for mobile ordering, lets users choose a Starbucks location, place their order via typing or voice directions, and make payments. When a customer enters the store, they simply have to pick up their order. Since its launch in 2009, the app has handled many weekly payments. This success can be attributed to Starbucks' use of Automated Clearing House (ACH) payments, followed by Natural Language Processing (NLP) under the same app. ACH payment systems automate the client company's payment clearance process. This technology allows businesses and financial institutions to transfer funds without utilizing wire transfers, cash, paper checks, or credit card networks. This not only allows for speedier payment processing but also provides a more simplified experience on the mobile app. ACH provides a uniform payment channel that is constantly independent of the customer, making the money transfer procedure easier. Starbucks uses NLP technology to improve the customer experience, from order placing to payment. By adding AI, the app functions as a chatbot service linked to Starbucks' product, price, and payment databases. It is configured to collect extra information about the customer's order and provides customization choices similar to those available from an in-person barista. Furthermore, clients may easily enter their purchase and payment details into their smartphone's microphone. The software will then add the products to their basket, allowing users to check the order for faults or potential changes. Customers will most likely be able to pay using credit, debit, or Starbucks gift cards. Like other mobile ordering applications, the app may allow users to save numerous payment methods (Mejia, 2019).

1.7.2 Stripe

The payments industry has implemented a variety of new AI functions this year, some of which have been created jointly with OpenAI, Microsoft's laboratory behind ChatGPT. Stripe which operates in this industry has partnered with OpenAI to enable the generation of payment for the development laboratory. Stripe's platform currently has a few clients who are using generative AI; among them is Moonbeam – an outfit in the business of assisting content developers to write blog posts, essays, and anything that entails writing among other writing tools, Diagram, a design firm that relies on AI in its operations as well as Runway – a text to video firm.

A recent advancement is the assignment of GPT-4: this is a new kind of chat GPT launched by Stripe to detect service violations such as fraud and assist in expanding the company's support services. The dominance of AI in the operations of the company became the theme of the CNBC interview with David Singleton, Stripe's Chief Technology Officer, where he claimed that Stripe has been relying on AI for many years now. Stripe has employed AI since its formation to identify patterns of malicious conduct and safeguard the millions of businesses that use Stripe, Singleton said. He further noted that although today AI improves the processes of fraud shielding and identification, the mission is to expand these AI services to the other spheres of the company's activity with a focus on the optimization of their product offerings. He also pointed out that the cooperation of people with the help of AI would remain essential in their functioning throughout this and similar processes.

1.7.3 Brex

Brex uses generative AI for the future of corporate spend reporting and payment, especially for travel. In general, the use of AI is incorporated in planning travelling, booking for accommodations, hiring rides and even filling the expense account. It is for this reason that their application to travel, as one of the first uses of generative AI, is a promising and early example based on the field's complexity. As reported by Brex, this new AI feature makes it so much easier to do corporate reimbursement forms, and greatly decreases the amount of work it takes to organize business travels. The firm imagines to have an independent AI agent that will make payments and reimbursements instantly basing its decision on an employee business calendar and organization's data. This agent would help in the easy handling of organization's money related activities and would also help in increasing its efficiency and accuracy in managing corporate travel expenses (Bowden et al., 2021).

1.7.4 Visa

In October, the global producer of payment technologies, Visa, declared a $100 million fund focused on the companies working on generative AI solutions. This strategic initiative seeks to capitalize on the fund, together with Visa's global payment system to generate new language models that could fasten the payment process, reduce fraud, as well as increase value for merchants, issuers, and consumers. Also, it is possible that the fund can contribute to other preparations by Visa which encourage Fintech, for instance a Visa's Fintech Partner Connect – an assembly for fintechs and Visa clients. Generative AI's potential to increase the payment industry is vast, but few business owners incorporate it in their operations. However, consumers do actively interact with AI. Benton also points to milestones of the Salesforce revealing that currently over 50% of the adult population in the United States has been using AI in one way or another. Given this increasing awareness among consumers, there are enormous possibilities of using generative AI in monetary services and creating new methods for efficient and secured payment gateways to curb fraud activities (Gupta et al., 2021).

1.7.5 Amazon

Amazon in late September, it was revealed that Amazon agreed to invest a large sum in Anthropic, the AI company that develops generative AI tools, at least $1. To $2.5-4 billion since 2006 Source: In 2010 alone, non-GMO height profits have been estimated to range between $25 billion and potentially up to $4 billion. This move allows Amazon to acquire a small percentage of Anthropic's shares that is already surrounded by other key market players like Microsoft, Google, and Meta to vie for more clients in the field of AI and secure relationships with finance companies. It is common to find these institutions partnering with such major players in projects calling for cloud technology and other applications.

Anthropic will use Amazon as its main cloud provider, which raises the possibility of Amazon AWS clients connecting to Anthropic's advanced AI tool. This partnership can be seen in the context of Amazon's drive to increase AI and cloud services for its marketplace. AWS Payment Cryptography was unveiled in June and is aimed at allowing payment technologies to be hosted in the cloud. This service is offered similarly to IBM's and Microsoft's, allowing for non-hardware updates of payment systems instead. It also means that the capability can be updated at a faster rate as and when the payments technology changes. Google's direct competitors in the AI services market are numerous, with Amazon, which operates as the world's largest Cloud infrastructure services. AWS has a wide selection of AI and ML services, which is Amazon Recognition for images and video, Amazon Lex for conversation, and Amazon Polly for text-to-speech. Later in 2017, the company introduced SageMaker – a highly effective cloud AI-based ML offering that cemented the company's place in AI and ML. The acquisitions and Anthropic, as well as another incessant investment in AI and ML services, assert Amazon's willingness and intent to keep dominance in a realm that is slowly shifting and drastically progressing. Thus, by integrating Anthropic's AI capabilities into AWS, Amazon wants to provide its numerous clients with improved AI solutions and become a technological leader in terms of AI development for businesses and other organizations that experience rising demand for complex AI applications. One of Amazon's most well-known AI products is Alexa, a virtual assistant. Alexa's integration into Amazon's Echo line of devices provided the corporation with an early advantage in the growing smart speaker business. Notably, Amazon has the largest fleet of mobile robots in its warehouses worldwide and has made significant investments in AI-related mergers and acquisitions. In 2019, it bought Canvas, a warehouse robotics company, and in mid-2020, it purchased Zoox, a well-known autonomous car startup (Shetty, 2019).

1.8 CONCLUSION

AI is the replication of human intellect in machines. It comprises a variety of applications such as speech recognition, language processing, and ML. In terms of payment AI, organizations use these ideas to enhance payment processing, accounting, and finance. AI-powered technologies, like chatbots and virtual assistants, may efficiently address consumer queries during checkout or order fulfilment by utilizing natural language processing. In other words, AI systems mimic human intelligence to handle payment-related issues rapidly and affordably. AI has entirely altered payment systems, radically altering the way transactions are handled. AI has made payment processing quicker, more secure, and extremely efficient by leveraging powerful algorithms and data analytics, significantly enhancing the whole consumer experience. AI has simplified payment operations and dramatically decreased the likelihood of mistakes and security breaches by automating repetitive chores, detecting fraudulent activity, and customizing user interactions. The use of AI technologies in payment processing has various benefits, including the ability to streamline operations by automating repetitive work, reducing mistakes, and allowing industry participants to focus on strategic duties. AI technology transforms into a time-saving and efficient asset by automating data entry, payment reconciliation, and reporting. This enables organizations to optimize the customer journey, find new opportunities, and better manage risks, allowing consumers to have a faster, more efficient, and precise payment experience. Furthermore, AI-powered payment systems have played an important role in the widespread adoption of novel payment methods such as mobile payments, contactless transactions, and biometric verification, making payments easier and smoother. To conclude, AI has become a crucial tool in modern payment systems, promoting innovation, efficiency, and security while transforming the future of commerce.

REFERENCES

M. Allahham and A. Ahmad, "AI-induced anxiety in the assessment of factors influencing the adoption of mobile payment services in supply chain firms: A mental accounting perspective," *Int. J. Data Netw. Sci.*, vol. 8, no. 1, pp. 505–514, 2024.

S. X. Bhawnra and K. B. Singh, "Artificial intelligence for financial inclusion in India." in *Conversational artificial intelligence* (Chapter 33), R. Rawat, R. K. Chakrawarti, S. K. Sarangi, P. Vyas, M. S. Alamanda, K. Srividya, & K. S. Sankaran (Eds.), 2024, pp. 589–606. John Wiley & Sons. https://doi.org/10.1002/9781394200801.ch33

S. Bondarde, P. Ghadge, A. Saldanha, A. Markad, and D. Varpe, "Artificial intelligence-based OCR." In *ICT Systems and Sustainability*, M. Tuba, S. Akashe, & A. Joshi (Eds.), 2023, pp. 329–338. Springer Nature Singapore.

J. Bowden, T. King, D. Koutmos, T. Loncan, and F. S. Lopes, "A taxonomy of fintech innovation," in *Disruptive Technology in Banking and Finance: An International Perspective on FinTech*, T. King, F. S. S. Lopes, A. Srivastav, and J. Williams, Cham: Palgrave Macmillan, 2021, pp. 47–91.

S. R. Burri, A. Kumar, A. Baliyan, and T. A. Kumar, "Transforming payment processes: A discussion of AI-enabled routing optimization," in Proceedings of the *2023 2nd International Conference on Smart Technologies and Systems for Next Generation Computing (ICSTSN)*, Villupuram, India, April 21–22, 2023, IEEE, 2023, pp. 1–7.

R. Bygari, A. Gupta, S. Raghuvanshi, A. Bapna, and B. Sahu, "An AI-powered smart routing solution for payment systems," in *2021 IEEE International Conference on Big Data (Big Data)*, Orlando, FL, December 15–18, 2021.

D. Choi and K. Lee, "An artificial intelligence approach to financial fraud detection under IoT environment: A survey and implementation," *Secur. Commun. Netw.*, vol. 2018, no. 4, pp. 1–15, 2018.

Deloitte, "AI technologies for risk management in financial industry," *Infopulse*, July 3, 2023.

B. Eid, L. Khachan, and M. Bonnet, "KYC principles embedded in AI-enabled mobile banking in the face of money-laundering," *Acad. Manag. Proc.*, vol. 2022, no. 1, pp. 123–130, 2022.

A. Gupta, D. Dovgan, S. Sood, S. Sinha, G. Mahanty, and N. Khoury, "Artificial intelligence (AI) based methods and systems for maximizing credit card revenue," Technical Disclosure Commons, August 13, 2021.

B. Häckel, P. Karnebogen, and C. Ritter, "AI-based industrial full-service offerings: A model for payment structure selection considering predictive power," *Decis. Support Syst.*, vol. 152, no. 113653, p. 113653, 2022.

M. Jakšič and M. Marinč, "Relationship banking and information technology: The role of artificial intelligence and FinTech," *Risk Manag.*, vol. 21, no. 1, pp. 1–18, 2019.

M. Kacar, "Application of AI in customer experience management," in *Marketing and Sales Automation: Basics, Implementation, and Applications*, Cham: Springer International Publishing, 2023, pp. 409–430.

P. C. Lai and D. L. Tong, "An artificial intelligence-based approach to model user behavior on the adoption of E-payment," in *Handbook of Research on Social Impacts of E-Payment and Blockchain Technology*, P. C. Lai (ed.), IGI Global, 2022, pp. 1–15.

J. Lee, "Access to finance for artificial intelligence regulation in the financial services industry," *Eur. Bus. Organ. Law Rev.*, vol. 21, no. 4, pp. 731–757, 2020.

R. P. Lopez, (2020). "Study of user experience design of digital financial services," (Master thesis, Aalto University).

P. B. Lowry, T. M. Wells, G. Moody, S. Humpherys, and D. Kettles, "Online payment gateways used to facilitate E-commerce transactions and improve risk management," *Commun. Assoc. Inf. Syst.*, vol. 17, pp. 1–48, 2006.

K. W. F. Ma, T. Dhot, and M. Raza, "Considerations for using artificial intelligence to manage authorized push payment (APP) scams," *IEEE Eng. Manag. Rev.*, vol. 51, no. 3, pp. 166–179, 2023.

N. Mejia, "Artificial intelligence for payments – Current capabilities and use-cases," *Emerj*, August 28, 2019. https://emerj.com/ai-sector-overviews/artificial-intelligence-for-payments/.

I. B. Mustapha, Y. Vaicondam, A. Jahanzeb, and B. A. Usmanovich, "Cybersecurity challenges and solutions in the fintech mobile app ecosystem," *Int. J. Interact. Mob. Technol.*, vol. 17, no. 22, pp. 100–116, 2023.

B. Mytnyk, O. Tkachyk, N. Shakhovska, S. Fedushko, and Y. Syerov, "Application of artificial intelligence for fraudulent banking operations recognition," *Big Data Cogn. Comput.*, vol. 7, no. 2, p. 93, 2023.

M. Rahman, T. H. Ming, T. A. Baigh, and M. Sarker, "Adoption of artificial intelligence in banking services: An empirical analysis," *Int. J. Emerg. Mark.*, vol. 18, no. 10, pp. 4270–4300, 2021.

N. J. Rani and A. Suresh, "Role of artificial intelligence in bank payment applications," *Cent. Dev. Econ.*, vol. 11, no. 19, pp. 173–182, 2024.

V. Rutskiy, A. Aljarbouh, A. Thommandru, S. Elkin, Y. El Amrani, E. Semina, A. Mishchenko, N. Sorokina, and R. Tsarev, "Prospects for the use of artificial intelligence to combat fraud in bank payments," in *Data Science and Algorithms in Systems*, R. Silhavy, P. Silhavy, and Z. Prokopova (eds.), Cham: Springer International Publishing, 2023, pp. 959–971.

M. A. Said and A. Hajami, "AI methods used for real-time clean fraud detection in instant payment," in *Proceedings of the 13th International Conference on Soft Computing and Pattern Recognition (SoCPaR 2021)*, Springer International Publishing, 2022, pp. 249–257. https://link.springer.com/chapter/10.1007/978-3-030-96302-6_23

W. Sardjono, W. Priatna, M. Tohir, W. Sardjono, W. Priatna, and M. Tohir, "Artificial intelligence as the catalyst of digital payments in the revolution industry 4.0," *ICIC Expr. Lett.*, vol. 12, no. 9, pp. 857–865, 2021.

P. Shetty, "A study on online payment applications in India with reference to Amazon Pay," A Project Submitted to Thakur College of Science and Commerce, 2019.

M. K. Siddiqui and K. K. Goyal, "A study the use of e-payment systems based on artifical intelligence," in *Computing & Intelligent Systems: Artificial Intelligence and Communication Technologies*, S. Hiranwal, and G. Mathur (eds.), 2023, pp. 1063–1076.

C. Soviany, "The benefits of using artificial intelligence in payment fraud detection: A case study," *J. Paym. Strategy Systems*, vol. 12, no. 2, pp. 102–110, 2018.

Y. Tan and M. Fang, "Comparison of traditional payment and blockchain payment methods in the same payment point," in *Proceedings of the 2nd International Symposium on Social Science and Management Innovation (SSMI 2019)*, 2019.

P. Vanini, S. Rossi, E. Zvizdic, and T. Domenig, "Online payment fraud: From anomaly detection to risk management," *Financ. Innov.*, vol. 9, no. 1, p. 66, 2023.

M. Wasserbauer, (2022). "KYC onboarding in financial institutions: A best practice criteria catalogue for selection of video identification frameworks," (Doctoral dissertation, Technische Universität Wien).

M. Weichert, "The future of payments: How FinTech players are accelerating customer-driven innovation in financial services," *J. Paym. Strategy Systems*, vol. 11, no. 1, pp. 23–33, 2017.

Z. Zhang and M. Chen, "Advantages and disadvantages of third party payment method and traditional payment method," in *Proceedings of the 2019 10th International Conference on E-business, Management and Economics*, 2019.

2 Taxonomy of Applications of Artificial Intelligence Techniques for FinTech

N. Vanitha

2.1 INTRODUCTION

FinTech leverages Big Data to increase intuitions after massive amounts of unstructured and structured data sources, enabling more informed decision-making and personalized financial services. With the proliferation of digital transactions, FinTech companies require contact to a wealth of records comprising business proceedings, user behavior patterns, social media interactions, and demographic information. By harnessing Big Data technologies like Hadoop and Spark, FinTech firms can process and analyze this data in real time, uncovering valuable insights that drive business strategies and improve customer experiences. AI-enabled FinTech can discourse problematic business problems and deal bendable provision [1].

The main application of Big Data in FinTech is fraud detection. By examining patterns and abnormalities in operation data, FinTech companies can detect suspicious activities and prevent fraudulent transactions in real time. Advanced algorithms powered by machine learning along with predictive analytics can detect fraudulent behavior with high accuracy, helping financial institutions mitigate risks and protect their customers' assets. Additionally, NLP techniques are used to investigate text facts from numerous causes such as customer reviews, social media posts, and news articles to assess sentiment, identify emerging trends, and enhance customer engagement.

Furthermore, Big Data enables FinTech enterprises to personalize their services and tailor assistances to individual client's needs. By analyzing client data and behavior using predictive analytics and text mining techniques, FinTech firms can gain insights into customers' preferences, financial goals, and risk tolerance levels. This information allows them to compromise targeted product commendations, custom-made investment strategies, and customized financial advice, ultimately improving customer satisfaction and loyalty. Through data-driven understandings and advanced analytics, FinTech companies are transforming the way financial amenities are distributed, manufacture them more available, well-organized, and client-centric. Agreeing to data after the forecast of self-directed investigation artificial intelligence

DOI: 10.1201/9781003645849-2

(AI) tools will permit commercial organizations to decrease their working budgets by 22% by 2030 [2].

Nowadays, FinTech is integrated by IoT with AI to test banks at an actual prompt jump [3].

2.1.1 Applications of Big Data Analytics in Financial Technology

Plenty of applications of Big Data applications are available in the literature studies. AI-enabled chatbots have recognized as a feasible consumer package tool, since they save big business time and cash, they look to be an uncomposable source. The investments are the part and parcel of the finance sector and taking into account of the investments prediction using the AI techniques. This chapter concentrates on the following applications. Figure 2.1 depicts the applications of Big Data analytics in FinTech [4].

2.1.1.1 Predictive Analytics

Predictive analytics is being incorporated into funding to support managerial and strategic decision-making. It involves a range of computational and statistical techniques, such as time series models, clustering, regression, association, and classification. Through the application of these strategies, financial professionals are able to forecast future results by using historical data, which facilitates improved risk management and strategic planning. By offering a thorough overview of

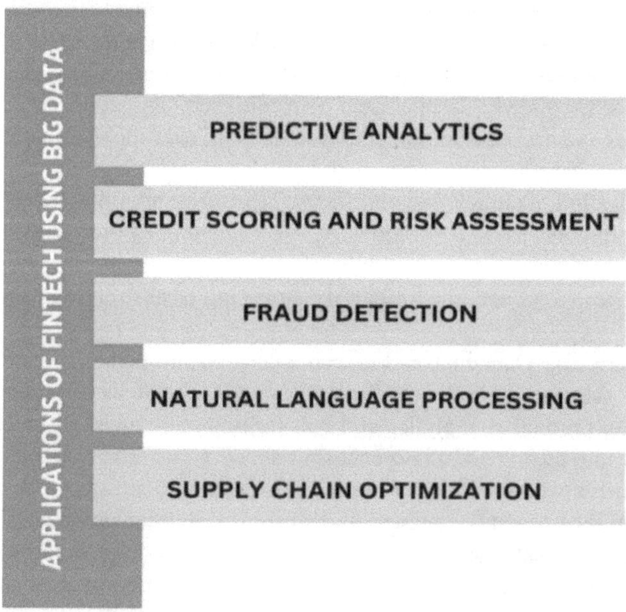

FIGURE 2.1 Applications of Big Data analytics in FinTech.

predictive analytics applications in finance, the work seeks to close the gap between conventional statistical modelling and computational techniques, improving decision support system performance [5].

2.1.1.2 Credit Scoring and Risk Assessment

In the FinTech sector, Big Data is essential to credit scoring and risk evaluation. FinTech companies are able to create credit scoring models that are more accurate and comprehensive by examining an extensive series of data topics, with operation antiquity, credit card usage, repayment habits, work history, and social media activity. These models use predictive analytics and machine learning algorithms to evaluate a person's creditworthiness and probability of loan or credit card default. FinTech companies can reduce lender default risk by combining a variety of data sources and applying cutting-edge analytical algorithms to give underprivileged groups more equitable access to credit. Furthermore, Big Data facilitates ongoing credit portfolio monitoring, enabling proactive risk management and prompt [6].

2.1.1.3 Fraud Detection

Finance can benefit from the practical uses of fraud detection established on memory firmness practice (FDMCM). It improves fraud detection accuracy by utilizing machine learning techniques and resolving imbalanced datasets. The unique nonlinear entrenched machine learning immoral autoencoding coated method is specifically employed to address the problem of unbalanced data. Additionally, it may be trained on datasets of unlabeled financial transactions, making it possible to accurately detect instances of fraud. This technique offers financial institutions a dependable means of reducing fraud threats, protecting themselves from financial losses, and preserving confidence in financial systems, all with a 93% accuracy success rate [7,8].

2.1.1.4 Natural Language Processing

In the FinTech industry, natural language processing (NLP) is an essential apparatus that facilitates improved communication, risk management, regulatory compliance, fraud detection, and customized financial advice. NLP makes it possible for chatbots and virtual assistants driven by AI to provide more personalized recommendations and better customer service. Moreover, by evaluating intricate texts, reducing legal risks, and guaranteeing compliance, NLP helps streamline regulatory procedures. Additionally, through the analysis of transaction data and client communications, NLP algorithms are essential in the detection of fraudulent activity. Global financial services advancement is facilitated by the overall improvement in efficiency, accuracy, and customer happiness that results from the incorporation of NLP into FinTech models [9].

2.1.1.5 Supply Chain Optimization

Big data is utilized in supply chain finance optimization to increase liquidity and efficiency across the whole supply chain. FinTech solutions can give organizations real-time visibility into transaction flows, inventory levels, and supplier performance by utilizing data analytics. This allows firms to maximize working capital and reduce financing expenses. These platforms facilitate dynamic discounting, supply chain financing, and invoice factoring, allowing suppliers to access capital at lower rates based on the strength of their relationships with buyers. Through data-driven insights, supply chain finance optimization helps businesses streamline operations, reduce payment delays, and improve cash flow management, ultimately driving profitability and competitiveness in the global marketplace [10].

2.2 BACKGROUND STUDY

This section deals with the elaborated study on literature studies that provide the applications of AI tools used to deal the Big Data analytics in FinTech.

According to Mirjana Pejić Bach et al. [10], text mining has become increasingly integral within the financial sector, leveraging Big Data technologies to derive insights from textual data sources. This research endeavors to address three fundamental inquiries: Intellectual Core of Text Mining Research: Understanding the foundational concepts and theories in financial text mining is crucial for identifying key trends. Commonly Employed Techniques: With the rise of Big Data, various techniques are used to analyze textual data in finance. Predominant Data Sources and Purposes: Recognizing the primary sources of textual data and their purposes in financial text mining sheds light on the diverse sources of information used. The study employs qualitative analysis methods like literature review and citation analysis, reviewing 123 papers to uncover significant studies, trends, techniques, and data sources in financial text mining. Areas for future research include exploring "grey" literature, developing decision taxonomies, examining organizations implementing text mining, and analyzing internal data sources. Overall, this study enhances understanding of text mining in finance, benefiting both academia and industry [11].

According to Pascal MuamMah et al., the authors aim to discover and showcase the transformative impression of FinTech (Financial Technology) on society and the economy. Key points from the conclusion shed light on the paper's purpose: Acknowledgment of FinTech Innovation: Recognizing FinTech as a significant innovation, the paper highlights its positive impact on humanity through advancements in financial services. Reduction of Dependency and Talent Utilization Enhancement: Emphasizing how FinTech reduces reliance on traditional financial systems, it enables individuals to utilize their talents and skills more effectively through advanced services. Market Analysis and Credit Demand: Discussing how FinTech allows customers to assess market changes and understand how price fluctuations impact credit demand, vital for consumers and suppliers alike. Facilitation of Startups and Funding: Highlighting FinTech's role in facilitating startup funding and development, it provides financial institutions with opportunities to discover new ideas and support innovative ventures. Integration with Modern Technology: Exploring FinTech's integration with various modern technologies, including NLP, it creates utility values and drives digital economics. Through these points, the work targets to showcase the multifaceted influence of FinTech on society and the economy. It underscores the importance of understanding and embracing FinTech innovations to navigate the evolving landscape of financial services effectively [10].

According to Haitham Nobanee et al. [12], the paper explores the thoughtful effect of technology on the banking sector, with particular emphasis on the rising prominence of Big Data analytics. Through a bibliographic review, the study delves into several key themes within the banking industry that are shaped by Big Data, with risk assessment, credit threat, evaluating customer behavior, financial administration, forecasting bankruptcy, implementing anti-fraud measures, tactical outline development, speculation strategies, profit maximization, and competitive analysis. The primary objective is to comprehend the evolving landscape of Big Data in banking and uncover emerging trends and challenges associated with its adoption and implementation. As technology continues to revolutionize the banking sector, institutions are increasingly leveraging Big Data analytics to increase actionable perceptions from huge capacities of structured and unstructured data. These perceptions inform strategic decision-making, enhance risk management practices, and drive innovation in customer-centric services. By examining the juncture of Big Data and banking, the work pursues to offer cherished perceptions for industry practitioners, researchers and policymakers. Understanding the evolving role of Big Data in banking is essential for staying abreast of industry developments and effectively navigating the challenges and opportunities presented by technological advancements [13].

According to Md. Morshadul Hasan [14], the paper adopts a method-based literature review to explore the application of predictive analytics in finance. It delves into various numerical and computational approaches incorporated into decision support methods, surrounding classification, regression, clustering, association, and time series models. The primary objective is to elucidate how these techniques facilitate predictions using financial data and their role in improving results for financial directors and hazard omission specialists. By synthesizing existing literature, the learning ambitions to offer perceptions into the effectiveness and practical consequences of predictive analytics in the finance domain. Understanding the role of predictive analytics in finance is essential for informed decision-making, enhanced risk management practices, and achieving better financial outcomes. Through an examination of different methods and their applications, the paper contributes to advancing knowledge in the field and informs practitioners and researchers around the possible remunerations of leveraging predictive analytics in finance [15].

According to Daniel Broby [15], the paper addresses the transformative impression of Big Data and related technologies like AI and cloud computing on the finance segment. It highlights how these innovations are reshaping various facets of finance, including stock market visions, employment and funds, scam discovery, risk analysis, revenue generation, customer satisfaction, and operational efficiency. In addition to discussing the opportunities presented by Big Data in finance, the paper also delves into the challenges and critical issues associated with its adoption. These include privacy concerns, data quality assurance, compliance with regulatory requirements, and the management of large datasets. Furthermore, the authors propose upcoming enquiry guidelines to address the evolving landscape of Big Data in finance. They emphasize the importance of exploring technical challenges, developing robust data management systems, improving access to Big Data for small firms, mitigating security risks, devising effective implementation strategies, and analyzing the effect of Big Data on commercial markets [12].

Overall, the paper aims to deliver perceptions hooked on the revolutionary effect of Big Data on the finance sector and suggests avenues for further research to capitalize on its potential benefits while addressing associated challenges.

According to Fisnik Doko and Miskovski [13], with an emphasis on strategies, obstacles, and problems, the article seeks to provide an overview of Big Data analytics in the banking industry. Taking into account the vast amounts of transaction data banks handle, it aims to investigate how banks use Big Data and data science to obtain a modest edge, especially in terms of streamlining company operations and procedures. Technological breakthroughs and the spread of digital data have fetched about a dramatic upheaval in the banking business in recent years. Big Data analytics has made it possible for banks to use enormous volumes of both structured and unstructured data to increase operational efficiency, make better decisions, and extract insightful information.

Customer segmentation, risk management, fraud detection, tailored marketing, and product innovation are just a few of the uses of Big Data analytics in banking. Banks may enhance their comprehension of client behavior, recognize market trends, and efficiently manage risks by utilizing sophisticated analytical methods like machine learning and predictive modeling. But there are drawbacks and difficulties with using Big Data analytics in the banking industry. These could include the need for qualified data scientists and analysts, regulatory compliance requirements, sophisticated data integration, and worries about data privacy and security. By offering perceptions into how Big Data analytics is changing in the banking industry, the paper seeks to clarify these points. It aims to pull consideration to the advantages and disadvantages of using Big Data to optimize banking operations and procedures, opening the door for strategic initiatives and well-informed decision-making within the sector. Table 2.1 provides the brief literature review done in this chapter that provides the application of Big Data analytics in finance technology.

2.3 RESEARCH CHALLENGES OF AI IN FINTECH

Some of the research challenges identified are discussed in the following section.

2.3.1 Analysis of NLP in the FinTech Models

In the mid-21st century, NLP plays a crucial role in FinTech models, enabling advanced capabilities such as sentiment analysis, customer support automation, and financial document processing. However, NLP in FinTech encounters significant challenges, including the need for robust language understanding across diverse contexts, the complexities of financial language and terminology, ensuring data privacy and security in processing sensitive financial information, and the incorporation of NLP systems with remaining financial infrastructure and regulatory frameworks. Additionally, the rapid evolution of language and communication patterns necessitates continuous adaptation and innovation in NLP technologies to effectively meet the dynamic needs of the FinTech industry [9,16,17].

TABLE 2.1
Background Study

Year	Authors	Journal Name	Observations & Technologies Used	
2019	Mirjana Pejić Bach [10]	Sustainability	The purpose of the paper is to investigate the landscape of text mining in the financial sector, particularly focusing on the utilization of Big Data technologies and techniques for extracting insights from textual data sources. The study employs a qualitative analysis of literature through a systematic literature review, citation analysis, and co-citation investigation. By reviewing 123 papers, the research aims to provide insights into the most significant studies, research trends, techniques, and data sources in text mining within the financial domain. Additionally, the paper highlights areas for future research, including the exploration of "grey" literature sources, the taxonomy of decisions based on text mining results, examination of organizations implementing text mining, and further analysis of internal data sources for text mining in finance.	Classification and Clustering: These techniques involve organizing textual data into categories or groups based on similarities or patterns. Named Entity Recognition (NER), Information Extraction: Information extraction involves extracting structured information from unstructured text, enabling the transformation of data into useful insights. Sentiment Analysis, Keyword Extraction, Natural Language Processing
2022	Pascal Muam et al.	Journal of Information Technology and Digital World	The purpose of the paper seems to be to explore and highlight the transformative impact of FinTech (Financial Technology) on various aspects of society and economy. The key points from the conclusion that elucidate the purpose of the paper include: Acknowledgment of FinTech Innovation. Reduction of Dependency and Enhancement of Talent Utilization. Market Analysis and Demand for Credit. Facilitation of Startups and Funding, Integration with Modern Technology: The paper discusses how FinTech integrates with various aspects of modern technology, including natural language processing, to create utility values and drive digital economics.	Graphical Representation, Historical Analysis, Application of Economic Concepts: Integration of Financial and Technological Concepts, Natural Language Processing (NLP)

(Continued)

TABLE 2.1 (*Continued*)
Background Study

Year	Authors	Journal Name	Observations & Technologies Used	
2021	Haitham Nobanee et al.	SAGE JOURNALS	The paper aims to explore the significant changes brought about by technology in the banking sector, with a specific focus on the growing trend of Big Data analytics. Through a bibliographic review, the study examines various themes within the banking sector that are influenced by Big Data, including risk assessment, financial management, credit risk, customer analysis, bankruptcy prediction, anti-fraud systems, strategic framework management, investment, profit, and competition. The primary purpose is to understand the evolving landscape of Big Data in banking and identify emerging trends and challenges associated with its implementation.	**Bibliometric analysis:** The study employs bibliometric analysis, which involves quantitative analysis of publications and their citations to identify patterns, trends, and influential contributions in the field of Big Data. **Network analysis:** The research complements bibliometric analysis with network analysis techniques. This involves examining the Citation Rate Analysis Graphical Representation Keyword Selection
2020	Md. Morshadul Hasan et al.	Big Data	The paper aims to highlight how Big Data, along with technologies like machine learning, AI, and cloud computing, is transforming various aspects of the finance sector, such as stock market insights, trade and investments, fraud detection, risk analysis, revenue generation, customer satisfaction, and operational efficiency. Additionally, the paper discusses the challenges and critical issues associated with Big Data in finance, including privacy concerns, data quality, regulatory requirements, and the management of large datasets. The authors also suggest future research directions, emphasizing the need for further exploration into technical challenges, data management systems, access to Big Data for small firms, security risks, implementation strategies, and the impact of Big Data on financial markets. Overall, the paper seeks to provide insights into how Big Data is revolutionizing finance and to propose avenues for future research in this domain.	The authors analyze current trends in the finance industry, particularly regarding the adoption of Big Data, machine learning, AI, and cloud computing. They likely gather data on how these technologies are being implemented by large companies and their impact on various aspects of finance. The paper addresses challenges and critical issues associated with Big Data in finance, such as privacy concerns, data quality, regulatory requirements, and the management of large datasets. The authors likely discuss the implications of these challenges and Based on their analysis, the authors propose future research directions to further explore the impact of Big Data on finance. These may include investigating technical challenges, data management systems, access to Big Data for small firms, security risks, implementation strategies, and the impact of Big Data on financial markets.

(Continued)

TABLE 2.1 (*Continued*)
Background Study

Year	Authors	Journal Name	Observations & Technologies Used	
2020	Md. Morshadul Hasan et al.	Big Data	The paper aims to highlight how Big Data, along with technologies like machine learning, AI, and cloud computing, is transforming various aspects of the finance sector, such as stock market insights, trade and investments, fraud detection, risk analysis, revenue generation, customer satisfaction, and operational efficiency. Additionally, the paper discusses the challenges and critical issues associated with Big Data in finance, including privacy concerns, data quality, regulatory requirements, and the management of large datasets. The authors also suggest future research directions, emphasizing the need for further exploration into technical challenges, data management systems, access to Big Data for small firms, security risks, implementation strategies, and the impact of Big Data on financial markets. Overall, the paper seeks to provide insights into how Big Data is revolutionizing finance and to propose avenues for future research in this domain.	The authors analyze current trends in the finance industry, particularly regarding the adoption of Big Data, machine learning, AI, and cloud computing. They likely gather data on how these technologies are being implemented by large companies and their impact on various aspects of finance. The paper addresses challenges and critical issues associated with Big Data in finance, such as privacy concerns, data quality, regulatory requirements, and the management of large datasets. The authors likely discuss the implications of these challenges and Based on their analysis, the authors propose future research directions to further explore the impact of Big Data on finance. These may include investigating technical challenges, data management systems, access to Big Data for small firms, security risks, implementation strategies, and the impact of Big Data on financial markets.
2019	Fisnik Doko and Miskovski	UBT International Conference	The purpose of the paper is to provide an overview of Big Data analytics in the banking sector, focusing on approaches, challenges, and issues. It aims to explore how banks utilize Big Data and data science to gain a competitive advantage, particularly in areas such as enterprise operations and processes, given the vast amount of transaction data they handle.	The paper utilizes a review of existing research literature, official reports, surveys, and seminars related directly or indirectly to Big Data in banks.

2.3.2 Landscape and Influence of Big Data on Finance

The current scene of Big Data in finance presents several challenges that impact its effective implementation and influence on the industry. One challenge is the complete volume, velocity, and variety of data produced within financial systems, which strains traditional data management and analysis capabilities. Additionally, safeguarding data accuracy, excellence, and consistency residues a substantial challenge, particularly when allocating with large and diverse datasets. Regulatory compliance and data privacy concerns also pose challenges, as financial institutions must navigate complex regulatory frameworks and protect sensitive customer information. Moreover, integrating disparate data sources and legacy systems to extract meaningful insights and drive decision-making present's technical and organizational hurdles. Finally, there is a shortage of skilled professionals with proficiency in Big Data analytics and financial domain knowledge, highlighting the need for talent development and training initiatives to connect the full possible of Big Data in finance. Addressing these challenges is crucial for realizing the transformative possible of Big Data in the financial industry and leveraging it to drive innovation, efficiency, and competitiveness.

2.3.3 Predictive Analytics in Finance

The practice of predictive analytics in finance faces several challenges that can impact its effectiveness and adoption. One experiment is the obtainability and quality of data, as financial datasets may be imperfect, inaccurate, or biased, which can compromise the correctness of predictive models. Additionally, the dynamic nature of financial markets and economic conditions poses challenges for predictive analytics, as historical data may not always be indicative of future trends and behaviors. Regulatory compliance and data privacy concerns also present challenges, as financial institutions must adhere to strict regulations regarding the handling and use of customer data. Moreover, the complexity of financial instruments and transactions requires sophisticated modeling techniques and algorithms, which can be difficult to develop and interpret. Furthermore, there is a need for experts with expertise in both finance and data analytics to effectively implement predictive analytics solutions and interpret the results. Addressing these challenges requires a combination of technological innovation, regulatory compliance measures, and investments in talent development to understand the full possible of predictive analytics in finance and drive informed decision-making [5,18,19].

2.3.4 Exploring Text Mining for Big Data Analysis in Finance

Utilizing text mining for Big Data analysis within the financial division presents several notable challenges. Firstly, financial text data is frequently unstructured and diverse, which complicates the extraction of meaningful insights efficiently. Moreover, the sheer volume and speed at which financial text data is generated pose significant hurdles for processing and analysis. Additionally, the intricate nature of financial language and terminology necessitates advanced NLP techniques to accurately interpret and mine pertinent facts from the data. Ensuring the privacy and security of sensitive financial information during the handling process remains a paramount concern. Furthermore, integrating text mining methodologies with existing financial infrastructure and regulatory frameworks introduces both organizational and technical obstacles. Incapacitating these trials is crucial to completely attach the possible of text mining for Big Data analysis in the financial sector, allowing for the derivation of actionable insights to inform decision-making processes [20].

2.3.5 Big Data Applications the Banking Sector

In exploring Big Data applications in the banking sector through a bibliometric analysis approach, several challenges become apparent. Firstly, the vast volume of data generated by banking activities presents challenges in data management, storage, and processing. Additionally, ensuring the accuracy, reliability, and security of banking data is crucial, especially given the sensitive nature of financial information. Furthermore, integrating disparate data sources and legacy systems within banks poses technical and organizational challenges. Moreover, regulatory compliance requirements add complexity to implementing Big Data applications in banking, requiring adherence to strict guidelines for data protection and privacy. Finally, there is a shortage of skilled professionals with expertise in both banking and Big Data analytics, highlighting the need for talent development and training initiatives. Addressing these challenges is essential to harnessing the potential of Big Data applications in the banking sector and driving innovation, efficiency, and competitiveness [21].

2.3.6 Analytics in Banking: Approaches, Challenges and Issues

Privacy and security: Regulatory restrictions and privacy concerns limit the scalability and flexibility of handling Big Data in the cloud. Ensuring data integrity, privacy, and security is crucial to maintaining public trust and avoiding reputational damage.

Storage and processing issues: The growth of unstructured data, particularly in banking, necessitates the management of large terabyte databases. Conventional data management techniques may not suffice to handle the high volume and velocity of heterogeneous financial datasets, especially when considering real-time analysis and processing.

Technical and architectural challenges: Banks need to adopt appropriate technologies such as Hadoop, NoSQL, and MapReduce to handle vast amounts of complex data effectively. However, the banking industry may lag behind other sectors in implementing these technologies, leading to inefficiencies in data management and analysis.

Analytical challenges: Banks necessitate trained data scientists to control Big Data analytics effectively and discourse authority matters. However, the lack of specialized positions for data scientists in banking, coupled with stringent governance rules may hinder the development of advanced analytical capabilities such as text and sentiment analysis, voice, and video analytics [22–25].

2.3.7 Navigating Challenges in Big Data Analytics for Detecting Fraud in Financial Transaction

Implementing Big Data analytics for fraud detection in financial transactions faces several challenges:

Managing diverse data streams: Gathering and processing vast amounts of data from different sources pose a significant challenge. These data streams may vary in format and structure, requiring sophisticated handling methods.

Real-time processing: Identifying fraudulent activities as they happen demands real-time data processing capabilities. Delays in discovery could prime to severe financial fatalities.

Ensuring data quality and accuracy: Maintaining the integrity and accuracy of data is crucial to avoid both false positives (flagging legitimate transactions as fraudulent) and false negatives (missing actual fraudulent transactions).

Balancing complexity with interpretability: Developing complex fraud detection models is essential for accurate predictions. However, balancing this complexity with the ability to interpret and explain the model's decisions is equally important for trust and transparency.

Adhering to regulations and privacy: Meeting regulatory requirements and safeguarding customer privacy are paramount. Compliance with laws such as GDPR and PCI DSS must be ensured throughout the entire process to protect sensitive information [26–28].

Overcoming these challenges requires advanced analytics technologies, robust data management practices, and strict security measures to effectively detect and prevent fraudulent activities in financial transactions.

2.4 RESEARCH GAPS IDENTIFIED FROM THE BACKGROUND STUDY

From the literature some of the research gaps identified in this chapter were given below

1. **Insufficient depth in real-world application:** Although Big Data consumer analysis is gaining a lot of attention, there isn't enough research done on real-world applications in the literature, such as using Big Data to fight fraud in the banking industry. As a result, there is less analysis of the business elements of these papers, which hinders the development of novel technical articles.
2. **Slow uptake of credit-scoring tools for Big Data:** Although the utilization of Big Data credit-scoring systems has the potential to improve underwriting efficiency and increase accessibility for historically underserved and under banked populations, banks are still trailing behind in its adoption. This disparity emphasizes the need for additional study to identify adoption hurdles and investigate methods for easing the incorporation of new technologies into banking procedures.

3. **Limitation of bibliometric approaches:** The primary source of limitation for current research is the application of bibliometric approaches, which have constraints of their own when it comes to literature analysis. Reliance on databases such as Web of Knowledge may lead to the omission of some studies, highlighting the necessity for different approaches and data sources to guarantee a thorough comprehension of the subject.
4. **Future study directions:** There is a numeral of methods that these holes can be filled in upcoming study. They include looking into "grey" literature sources to get a more current perspective on how text mining is used in finance, creating a taxonomy of decisions based on text mining findings, examining the traits of businesses that have successfully used text mining, and performing more thorough analyses of the data sources used for text mining, with a special emphasis on internal documents. Opportunities to expand knowledge and comprehension in the areas of Big Data and finance exist with these study directions.

2.5 CONCLUSION AND FUTURE WORK

The integration of AI and Big Data analytics into financial services symbols a noteworthy landmark in the advancement of the industry. Its applications span from risk management to customer engagement, promising efficiency and insight previously unattainable. However, challenges such as technological limitations and regulatory hurdles must be overcome to fully realize it's potential. Future work should prioritize advancements in data processing technologies and robust security measures, alongside interdisciplinary collaboration between data scientists, financial experts, and policymakers. By addressing these challenges and fostering innovation, the financial sector can leverage Big Data to drive transformative change and remain competitive in an increasingly data-driven world.

Looking ahead, research efforts should explore innovative applications of Big Data analytics, including real-time fraud detection and personalized financial advice. Embracing evolving technologies like AI and machine learning will be crucial in unlocking deeper insights into customer behavior and market dynamics. Moreover, efforts to enhance transparency and address ethical concerns surrounding data ownership and algorithmic bias are vital to build trust and guarantee the liable use of Big Data in finance. By charting this course and embracing a culture of data-driven decision-making, the financial industry can cover the way for a prospect where Big Data analytics revolutionizes financial services, benefitting both institutions and customers alike.

REFERENCES

1. D. Pillai, A. S. Singh, T. Bhosale and A. Doifode, "A Perspective on the Application of FinTech as a Gateway for Financial Literacy," *2023 International Conference on Information Technology (ICIT)*, Amman, Jordan, August 9–10, 2023, pp. 811–814, doi: 10.1109/ICIT58056.2023.10225810.

2. F. Lacruz and J. Saniie, "Applications of Machine Learning in FinTech Credit Card Fraud Detection," *2021 IEEE International Conference on Electro Information Technology (EIT)*, Mt. Pleasant, MI, USA, May 14–15, 2021, pp. 1–6, doi: 10.1109/EIT51626.2021.9491903.
3. L. R. Paul and L. Sadath, "A Systematic Analysis on FinTech and Its Applications," *2021 International Conference on Innovative Practices in Technology and Management (ICIPTM)*, Noida, India, February 17–19, 2021, pp. 131–136, doi: 10.1109/ICIPTM52218.2021.9388371.
4. A. K. Singh, P. M. Sharma, M. Bhatt, A. Choudhary, S. Sharma and S. Sadhukhan, "Comparative Analysis on Artificial Intelligence Technologies and its Application in FinTech," *2022 International Conference on Augmented Intelligence and Sustainable Systems (ICAISS)*, Trichy, India, November 24–26, 2022, pp. 570–574, doi: 10.1109/ICAISS55157.2022.10010573.
5. K. R Bhavya., A. Dharmara, P. Pareek, M. Ashok Sathe, M. Tiwari and G. Manoharan, "Application of Soft Computing Techniques for Predictive Analytics in Financial Markets," *2023 6th International Conference on Contemporary Computing and Informatics (IC3I)*, Gautam Buddha Nagar, India, September 14–16, 2023, pp. 1756–1760, doi: 10.1109/IC3I59117.2023.10397684.
6. S. Wen, B. Zeng, W. Liao, P. Wei and Z. Pan, "Research and Design of Credit Risk Assessment System Based on Big Data and Machine Learning," *2021 IEEE 6th International Conference on Big Data Analytics (ICBDA)*, Xiamen, China, March 5–8, 2021, pp. 9–13, doi: 10.1109/ICBDA51983.2021.9403128.
7. N. T. Cyriac and L. Sadath, "Is Cyber Security Enough—A Study on Big Data Security Breaches in Financial Institutions," *2019 4th International Conference on Information Systems and Computer Networks (ISCON)*, Mathura, India, November 21–22, 2019, pp. 380–385, doi: 10.1109/ISCON47742.2019.9036294.
8. Ananthu S., N. Sethumadhavan and H. Narayanan AG, "Credit Card Fraud Detection using Apache Spark Analysis," *2021 5th International Conference on Trends in Electronics and Informatics (ICOEI)*, Tirunelveli, India, June 3–5, 2021, pp. 998–1002, doi: 10.1109/ICOEI51242.2021.9453011.
9. K. Patil, M. Badamikar and S. Sonawane, "NLP Based Text Summarization of FinTech RFPs," *2023 International Conference on Sustainable Computing and Data Communication Systems (ICSCDS)*, Erode, India, March 23–25, 2023, pp. 865–869, doi: 10.1109/ICSCDS56580.2023.10104748.
10. P. M. Mah, I. Skalna, J. Muzam and L. K. Song, "Analysis of Natural Language Processing in FinTech Models", AGH University of Science and Technology, Krakow, Poland. https://knowledgecenter.ubt-uni.net/conference/2019/events/270/?utm_source=knowledgecenter.ubt-uni.net%2Fconference%2F2019%2Fevents%2F270&utm_medium=PDF&utm_campaign=PDFCoverPages.
11. M. P. Bach, Ž. Krstić, S. Seljan and L. Turulja. "Text Mining for Big Data Analysis in Financial Sector: A Literature Review," *Sustainability*, vol. 11, no. 5, p. 1277, 2019. https://www.mdpi.com/2071-1050/11/5/1277.
12. H. Nobanee, M. N. Dilshad, M. Al Dhanhani, M. Al Neyadi, S. Al Qubaisi, and S. Al Shamsi, "Big Data Applications the Banking Sector: Bibliometric Analysis Approach," *Sage Open*, vol. 11, 2021. https://journals.sagepub.com/doi/10.1177/21582440211067234.
13. F. Doko and I. Miskovski, "An Overview of Big Data Analytics in Banking," *UBT Knowledge Center.* https://knowledgecenter.ubt-uni.net/conference/2019/events/270/?utm_source=knowledgecenter.ubt-uni.net%2Fconference%2F2019%2Fevents%2F270&utm_medium=PDF&utm_campaign=PDFCoverPages.

14. Md. M. Hasan, J. Popp and J. Oláh, "Current landscape and influence of big data on finance," *Journal of Big Data*, vol. 7: p. 21, 2020. https://journalofbigdata.springeropen.com/articles/10.1186/s40537-020-00291-z
15. D. Broby, "Use of Predictive Analytics in Finance," *The Journal of Finance and Data Science*, vol. 8, pp. 145–161, 2022. https://www.sciencedirect.com/science/article/pii/S2405918822000071?via%3Dihub.
16. Ö. Uğur, T. Kalay, O. Demirel and S. Yıldırım, "Leveraging the power of Natural Language Processing for Financial Intelligence System," *2022 3rd International Informatics and Software Engineering Conference (IISEC)*, Ankara, Turkey, December 15–16, 2022, pp. 1–4, doi: 10.1109/IISEC56263.2022.9998106.
17. M.Rizinski,H.Peshov,K.Mishev,L.T.Chitkushev,I.VodenskaandD.Trajanov,"Ethically Responsible Machine Learning in FinTech," *IEEE Access*, vol. 10, pp. 97531–97554, 2022, doi: 10.1109/ACCESS.2022.3202889.
18. M. Ouahilal, M. El Mohajir, M. Chahhou and B. E. El Mohajir, "A Comparative Study of Predictive Algorithms for Business Analytics and Decision Support Systems: Finance as a Case Study," *2016 International Conference on Information Technology for Organizations Development (IT4OD)*, Fez, Morocco, March 30–April 1, 2016, pp. 1–6, doi: 10.1109/IT4OD.2016.7479258.
19. J. L. C. Sanz and Y. Zhu, "Toward Scalable Artificial Intelligence in Finance," *2021 IEEE International Conference on Services Computing (SCC)*, Chicago, IL, USA, September 5–10, 2021, pp. 460–469, doi: 10.1109/SCC53864.2021.00067.
20. Q. Li, Y. Chen, J. Wang, Y. Chen and H. Chen, "Web Media and Stock Markets: A Survey and Future Directions from a Big Data Perspective," *IEEE Transactions on Knowledge and Data Engineering*, vol. 30, no. 2, pp. 381–399, 2018, doi: 10.1109/TKDE.2017.2763144.
21. A. K. Tiwari and D. Saxena, "Application of Artificial Intelligence in Indian Banks," *2021 International Conference on Computational Performance Evaluation (ComPE)*, Shillong, India, 2021, pp. 545–548, doi: 10.1109/ComPE53109.20
22. A. Kurniawan, N. Iriawan and A. Choiruddin, "A Prescriptive Analytics Framework for Banks' Loan Strategy Development: Indonesian Banks' Case Study," *2023 IEEE International Conference on Computing (ICOCO)*, Langkawi, Malaysia, October 9–12, 2023, pp. 345–350, doi: 10.1109/ICOCO59262.2023.10397847.
23. E. Indriasari, F. L. Gaol and T. Matsuo, "Digital Banking Transformation: Application of Artificial Intelligence and Big Data Analytics for Leveraging Customer Experience in the Indonesia Banking Sector," *2019 8th International Congress on Advanced Applied Informatics (IIAI-AAI)*, Toyama, Japan, July 7–11, 2019, pp. 863–868, doi: 10.1109/IIAI-AAI.2019.00175.
24. A. Srivastava, S. K. Singh, S. Tanwar and S. Tyagi, "Suitability of Big Data Analytics in Indian Banking Sector to Increase Revenue and Profitability," *2017 3rd International Conference on Advances in Computing,Communication & Automation (ICACCA)* (Fall), Dehradun, India, September 15–16, 2017, pp. 1–6, doi: 10.1109/ICACCAF.2017.8344732.
25. B. Cheng and W. Feng, "Analysis of the Application of Big Data in Banking Sector," *2021 IEEE 20th International Conference on Trust, Security and Privacy in Computing and Communications (TrustCom)*, Shenyang, China, October 20–22, 2021, pp. 1397–1401, doi: 10.1109/TrustCom53373.2021.00196.
26. L. R. Maulana, A. N. Fajar and Meyliana, "Extending the Design of Smart Mobile Application to Detect Fraud Theft of E-Banking Access Using Big Data Analytic and SOA," *2021 IEEE 5th International Conference on Information Technology, Information Systems and Electrical Engineering (ICITISEE)*, Purwokerto, Indonesia, November 24–25, 2021, pp. 360–364, doi: 10.1109/ICITISEE53823.2021.9655805.

27. A. Bhowmik, M. Sannigrahi, D. Chowdhury, A. D. Dwivedi and R. RaoMukkamala, "DBNex: Deep Belief Network and Explainable AI based Financial Fraud Detection," *2022 IEEE International Conference on Big Data (Big Data)*, Osaka, Japan, December 17–20, 2022, pp. 3033–3042, doi: 10.1109/BigData55660.2022.10020494.
28. B. K. Jha, G. G. Sivasankari and K. R. Venugopal, "Fraud Detection and Prevention by using Big Data Analytics," *2020 Fourth International Conference on Computing Methodologies and Communication (ICCMC)*, Erode, India, March 11–13, 2020, pp. 267–274, doi: 10.1109/ICCMC48092.2020.ICCMC-00050.

3 Modernizing Finance
The Fintech Revolution Powered by AI

Rajarajeswari Maniyan, Gayathri Chakkingal, Nishaanth Madathukulam Senthil Kumar, and Alamelu Mangai Raman

3.1 INTRODUCTION

3.1.1 Overview of AI and Fintech

With the advent of new artificial intelligence (AI) techniques, finance has become more interactive in recent years [1]. "Artificial Intelligence, or AI, is simply the technology that makes it possible for computers and other devices to mimic human intelligence and problem-solving abilities" [2]. AI is a computational model that enables computers to learn from data and find approximations for difficult problems. Thus, AI has transformed information technology and has simply changed the way people live. AI has been extensively used in many large-scale fields, including the finance sector, because of its flexibility and robustness [3]. As a result, the phrase "Fintech", or financial technology, has become a widely utilized term nowadays [4]. The way AI is integrating with Fintech is changing the way financial services are delivered and used [5].

AI has completely changed the financial technology (Fintech) landscape by promoting efficiency and innovation in several financial industry sectors [6]. Fintech enterprises utilize AI algorithms and machine learning models to examine extensive datasets, facilitating enhanced risk evaluation, fraud identification, and customized customer journeys [7]. These technologies streamline procedures and improve decision-making in real time [8], powering digital lending services, robo-advisors, and algorithmic trading platforms [9]. AI-powered chatbots and virtual assistants improve consumer interactions by offering 24/7 assistance and tailored financial guidance [10]. AI algorithms also support regulatory and compliance tasks, guaranteeing adherence to intricate financial regulations. All things considered, the incorporation of AI into Fintech is transforming conventional banking and investment methods, encouraging increased accessibility, openness, and creativity in the financial services sector [11].

DOI: 10.1201/9781003645849-3

3.1.2 Rationale for Exploring the Intersection of AI and Fintech

Fintech, or financial technology, and AI have a symbiotic relationship that stems from the special skills that each brings to the table as well as the changing demands of the financial sector. The power of AI resides in its capacity to process massive amounts of data quickly and accurately, seeing patterns and insights that human analysts might miss [12]. This translates, in the context of Fintech, into more reliable risk assessment models, automated financial procedures, fraud detection algorithms, and customized financial services catered to specific needs. Fintech enterprises utilize AI to optimize decision-making procedures, optimize operational workflows, and augment customer experiences via chatbots, virtual assistants, and robo-advisors. The goal of all of this is to improve customer satisfaction and regulatory compliance [13,14].

On the other hand, Fintech creates the favorable environment required for AI to flourish. Massive amounts of data are produced by the financial industry from various sources, such as transactions, market trends, and consumer behavior. AI algorithms use this data as fuel, which enables them to continuously learn and adjust to changing conditions. In addition, the financial sector's intense competition encourages innovation, driving AI developers to produce ever more complex solutions to stay ahead of the curve [15].

Both Fintech and AI benefit from their relationship, as Fintech supplies the data and market context that AI needs to thrive, while AI drives fintech's efficiency and innovation. This partnership between AI and Fintech promises to change the financial landscape as both fields develop further, presenting fresh chances for inclusivity, accessibility, and efficiency in the financial services industry.

3.1.3 Objective and Scope

With a focus on Financial Technology (Fintech) and AI, this chapter aims to give readers a thorough understanding of the dynamic intersection of these two fields and how it will impact the financial industry going forward. This chapter aims to clarify the significant effects of AI on banking, investing, insurance, and regulatory compliance, among other areas of the financial industry, through in-depth analysis, case studies, and expert viewpoints. This book intends to provide readers with a deeper understanding of the opportunities and challenges presented by this transformative partnership by exploring the creative applications of AI in Fintech. Within the framework of Fintech innovation, it explores the use of AI algorithms and machine learning techniques in areas like algorithmic trading, risk management, fraud detection, credit scoring, wealth management, and customer service. It also aims to demystify sophisticated AI technologies and their useful applications for consumers, businesses, lawmakers, and financial institutions. In the end, this book aims to inspire readers to imagine the possibilities of a more accessible, effective, and inclusive financial future while also fostering a nuanced conversation about the ethical, regulatory, and societal implications of AI-driven innovations in finance.

3.2 FOUNDATIONS OF AI AND FINTECH

3.2.1 Understanding AI

At its most basic, AI is the study of combining strong datasets with computer science to help solve problems. Its origins can be found in Alan Turing's 1950 groundbreaking work Computing Machinery and Intelligence, which raised the question, "Can machines think?" [16]. The foundation of AI is the idea that human intelligence can be described in a way that makes it simple for a machine to replicate and carry out tasks, from the most basic to the most complicated [17]. The goal of AI, which aims to replicate human intelligence in machines, necessitates exploring the fields of computer science and cognitive psychology.

AI comprises a wide range of technologies and approaches designed to make machines capable of tasks that normally require human-like perception, learning, reasoning, and problem-solving skills [18]. Fundamentally, AI is a forward-looking approach that is based on algorithms and models that analyze large volumes of data to identify trends, forecast outcomes, and produce insights [19]. As a branch of AI, machine learning focuses on creating algorithms that can learn from data and gradually get better at what they do without the need for explicit programming [20]. Deep learning, a more advanced form of machine learning, involves neural networks with multiple layers of interconnected nodes, enabling them to extract complex features from data [21].

To fully understand AI's technical nuances and its wider societal implications, a multidisciplinary approach incorporating concepts from computer science, mathematics, psychology, and ethics is necessary.

3.2.2 Core Concepts in Financial Technology

The terms "financial" and "technology" are combined to form the term Fintech. Despite being a general term with many interpretations, "it generally refers to the development of an industry where new technology use cases are created and implemented to simplify finance functions that appear more traditional". There is a wide range of technologies supporting different Fintech business models. AI, machine learning, blockchain technology, and other big data applications like Robotic Process Automation (RPA) are some examples [22]. The term "Fintech" refers to a broad category of inventions and methods that use technology to improve accessibility, optimize financial services, and improve user experiences. Figure 3.1 showcases these concepts [23,24] as follows:

- **Digital payments:**

  "A digital payment occurs when money is transferred between accounts using a digital device, like a smartphone". This definition includes payments using mobile money, bank transfers, credit, debit, and prepaid cards, among other payment methods. Traditional cash and checks are replaced by electronic transactions, this was made possible by digital payment systems.

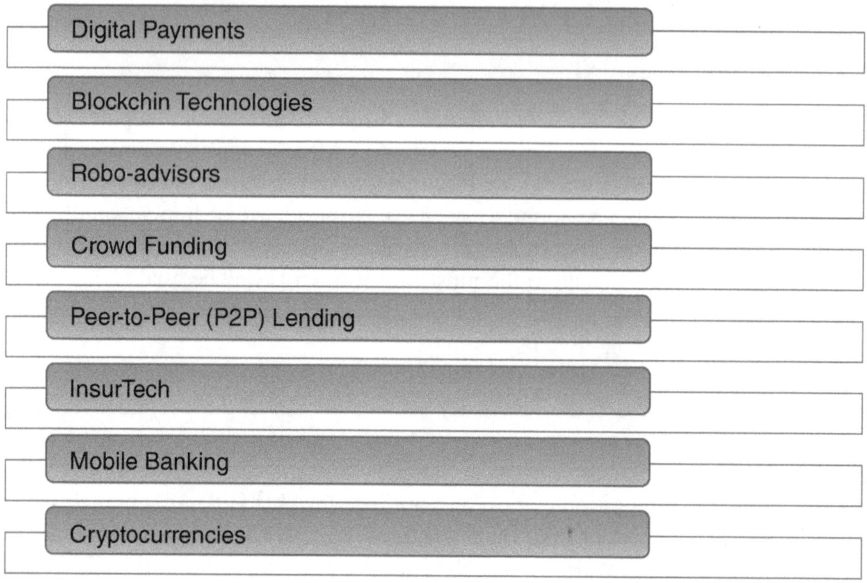

FIGURE 3.1 Key components of financial technology (Fintech) ecosystem.

Peer-to-peer payment networks, contactless payment techniques, and mobile wallets are a few examples of this, which makes financial transactions easier and faster.

- **Blockchain technologies:**

  "Blockchain is a decentralized distributed ledger technology that records transactions securely across multiple nodes. It is stored in the shape of blocks that are joined together to form a chain". Blockchain is an online platform that hosts decentralized digital assets. By applying to supply chain management, identity verification, smart contracts, and cryptocurrency, it ensures transaction records are transparent, immutable, and secure. The digital currency Bitcoin is commonly used in blockchain transactions, and its usage is increasing as more people adopt Fintech.
- **Robo-advisors:**

  To help consumers make informed financial decisions, "robo-advisors are automated investment platforms that employ algorithms to offer individualized investment advice and portfolio management services". To provide affordable investing options, they examine user preferences, risk tolerance, and financial objectives. The use of robo-advisors in the financial sector is expanding, particularly in stock markets and portfolio management, where they enable mobile trading and streamline the trading process.
- **Crowd funding:**

  Through online platforms, crowdfunding platforms help people and companies raise money from a large number of investors or donors. Peer-to-peer lending, reward-based crowdfunding, and equity crowdfunding are some examples of this, which democratizes the process of getting funding for projects and startups. Therefore, "crowdfunding is a means of raising capital through the assistance of close friends, family, clients, and private investors". Many people are enlisted for this strategy through social media and crowd-funding websites, and it leverages their networks to expand reach and visibility. Due to the growth of Fintech, crowdfunding has been steadily rising.

- **Peer-to-Peer (P2P) lending:**

  "Peer-to-peer lending is the process by which average people lend money to each other without the involvement of a financial institution". Therefore, P2P lending platforms do away with the need for conventional financial intermediaries like banks by connecting borrowers and lenders directly. Thus, peer-to-peer (P2P) platforms link lenders and potential borrowers. These platforms, which frequently offer cheaper interest rates and quicker approval procedures, use algorithms to evaluate creditworthiness and streamline loan transactions. Obtaining credit is made simple, quick, and convenient by this method. In P2P lending, customers can buy something now and pay for it later, even in little installments.

- **InsurTech:**

  The goal of InsurTech is to use technology to innovate and simplify procedures in the insurance sector. This covers solutions for risk management, customer interaction, claims processing, and digital underwriting. "Insurtech is the term for the use of financial technology in the insurance industry". Because so many insurance companies are adopting technology, it is now possible to get insurance without ever leaving the house. Furthermore, people can make claims online.

- **Mobile banking:**

  Customers of banks and other financial institutions can conduct a range of transactions through mobile banking by using an app. Through the app, users can access and manage their accounts from any location. An individual can open a new account, check one's balance, send money, and pay bills using mobile banking. More and more customers, particularly those using mobile devices, are looking for simple digital access to their bank accounts. It is projected that 3.6 billion people will use Internet banking globally by 2024 [25].

- **Cryptocurrencies:**

  A cutting-edge type of digital money that functions without the help of centralized organizations or conventional banking systems is represented by cryptocurrencies. Cryptocurrencies, which are based on blockchain technology, control the creation of new units and secure transactions by using cryptographic techniques. The idea of decentralized peer-to-peer transactions was first introduced by Bitcoin, the first and most well-known cryptocurrency, allowing users to transfer money directly to one another without the use of middlemen. Reduced transaction costs, quicker international transactions, and greater financial inclusion are just a few advantages that cryptocurrencies provide, especially for those living in areas with less access to traditional banking services. They do, however, also present difficulties with regard to scalability, security, volatility, and regulatory compliance. Despite these difficulties, institutional investors and consumers alike are beginning to recognize cryptocurrencies as a feasible asset class and means of payment. The development of cryptocurrencies and the technology that underpins them has the power to fundamentally alter the global financial scene by promoting financial services democratization, decentralization, and innovation.

3.2.3 Convergence of AI and Fintech

The environment of the financial sector is drastically changing. Fintech, or financial technology, and AI are powerfully combining to transform the financial industry, which is no longer limited to physical banks and paper statements. This convergence is more than just a technological trend; it is a revolutionary force that is changing the way one handle money, handle our finances, and obtain financial services [26]. AI is the process of imitating human cognitive functions, decision-making, and actions in machines through the simulation of human intelligence. Fintech, on the other hand, is the creative application of technology to provide financial services in ways that are easier to use, more accessible, and efficient.

A new era of opportunities is presented by the convergence of AI and Fintech. The financial sector is changing dramatically as a result of AI's capacity to evaluate enormous datasets, spot trends, and generate accurate forecasts. Making decisions more quickly and intelligently is made possible by a virtual financial expert who can analyze massive volumes of data in a matter of seconds [27]. Furthermore, chatbots and virtual assistants driven by AI are revolutionizing the way the financial sector engages with its customers. These savvy systems can lower operating costs while increasing customer satisfaction and engagement by making tailored recommendations, responding to questions, and helping with transactions. These virtual assistants can comprehend and reply to client inquiries instantly by utilizing natural language processing capabilities, providing a smooth and effective user experience [28]. Furthermore, AI is essential to the financial industry's adherence to regulations. AI-powered solutions are being used by Fintech companies to automate compliance procedures, keep an eye on transactions for questionable activity, and guarantee that regulations are being followed. AI assists financial institutions in better risk mitigation and regulatory compliance by automating compliance tasks and decreasing human error [29].

In general, the financial sector is experiencing previously unheard-of levels of innovation and disruption due to the convergence of AI and Fintech. Fintech firms are revolutionizing traditional banking and investment methods by utilizing AI technologies to provide more effective, transparent, and customer-focused financial services to people and companies across the globe. AI's convergence with Fintech is set to revolutionize the financial industry going forward, opening up new avenues for expansion, inclusivity, and sustainability in the digital era.

3.3 THE CURRENT STATE OF AI IN FINANCE

3.3.1 Application of AI in Traditional Finance

AI is being used in traditional finance in a variety of contexts, including risk management, fraud detection, customer service, and investment strategies. Figure 3.2 shows some important applications of AI [30]:

3.3.2 Impact on Banking, Investment and Insurance

AI is having a significant impact on the banking, investment, and insurance sectors. It is changing established procedures and opening doors for novel approaches. The effects in each sector are broken down as follows:

- **Impact of AI on banking:**
  The inception of chatbots serves customers continuously throughout the day, much like an answering machine. These assist with basic and direct operations, such as opening and closing accounts and transferring money. AI can help banks deliver personalized customer experiences, which will boost customer satisfaction, boost productivity, and foster customer loyalty in several ways. Financial institutions can use AI in banking to gather and evaluate data on the most recent financial activities, market trends, and transactional data to determine the possible risks involved in extending a

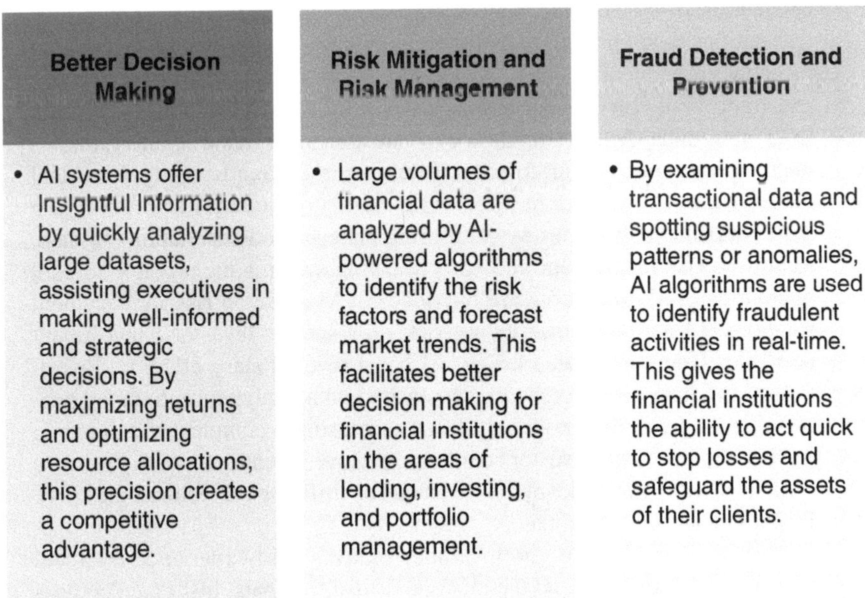

FIGURE 3.2 Role of artificial intelligence in financial decision-making and risk management.

loan. AI guarantees that all policies, regulations, and security measures are sincerely followed during the design and delivery of any financial service by aiding in the maintenance of strict regulatory oversight. AI has significantly decreased customer service costs in finance by automating processes. While AI has brought down the cost of financial services, it has also made obtaining financing very easy. Voice-assisted banking is another technology that AI has brought to the banking sector. Customers can now use voice commands instead of touch screens to access banking services thanks to this technology [31]. AI is spearheading a significant transformation in the banking sector, accelerating changes at an unprecedented rate. Technology is enabling small-value transactions, enhancing cost-effectiveness, and promoting greater integration within the banking system. The efficient use of technology has greatly amplified the growth and development of banks. Consequently, the introduction of AI has attracted more clients and contributed to the expansion of banks [32].

- **Impact of AI on investments:**

  AI is becoming more and more common in the field of investment management, completely changing the way professionals and financial institutions handle risk assessments, portfolio management, and decision-making. The goal of AI integration in investment management is to improve investment strategies and provide higher returns through the use of cutting-edge technologies, data analytics, and sophisticated algorithms. The use of machine learning algorithms to evaluate enormous volumes of financial data, historical market trends, and economic indicators is a crucial application of AI in investment management. AI systems can spot trends, correlations, and anomalies that human analysts might overlook, resulting in better investment choices. AI can adjust to shifting market conditions and improve its investment strategies over time by continuously learning from new data [33]. AI models evaluate portfolio risks, identify investment opportunities, and forecast future market trends using historical data. AI assists investors in forecasting market movements and modifying their investment strategies by examining patterns and correlations in data. Real-time risk assessment and early warning systems for possible market fluctuations and downturns are provided by AI-powered risk management solutions. In addition to reducing risk, this shields investor's investment portfolios from unforeseen losses. AI has a revolutionary effect on investing, giving investors access to sophisticated data analytics, automated processes, and predictive modeling. In an increasingly complex and dynamic market environment, investors can improve investment outcomes, optimize their strategies, and make better decisions by utilizing AI technologies [34].

- **Impact of AI on insurance:**

  Over the next decade, the insurance industry will experience a radical transformation due to rapid technological advancements. Insurance companies that leverage AI to develop innovative products, extract insights from new data sources for cognitive learning, optimize workflows to reduce costs, and exceed client demands for customization and real-time adjustments will emerge as leaders in the AI-driven insurance market. Crucially, insurers in 2030 will thrive if they adopt a mindset that views disruptive technologies as opportunities rather than threats to their current operations [35]. AI has a significant impact on the insurance sector, changing many facets of the insurance value chain as well as how insurers function and engage with clients. Through the analysis of massive amounts of data, such as customer demographics, health records, and behavioral data, AI helps insurers evaluate risks more precisely. Tasks related to claims processing, such as assessment, fraud detection, and settlement computations, are automated and streamlined by AI. Algorithms examine transactional data to spot suspicious trends or anomalies that might point to fraud. Early fraud claim detection helps insurers minimize losses, safeguard their financial position, and uphold their credibility and confidence with policyholders. Chatbots and virtual assistants driven by AI offer individualized insurance advice, help with policy inquiries, and provide support throughout the customer journey. AI systems can predict the needs and preferences of their users by evaluating their data and interactions, which results in more personalized and interesting user experiences [36,37].

3.3.3 Trends and Market Dynamics

AI in Fintech is a dynamic field that is constantly changing due to regulatory changes, consumer preferences, and technology advancements. The following are some significant market factors and trends influencing the state of AI in Fintech:

- **Increased usage of AI:**
  AI-powered solutions are becoming more and more popular among Fintech businesses and established financial institutions as a way to boost customer satisfaction, increase operational effectiveness, and obtain a competitive edge. The need to adapt to shifting market conditions, the increasing accessibility of AI technologies, and the development of machine learning algorithms are the main forces behind this trend [38].
- **AI assistants and robo-advisors:**
  These customer-focused solutions are typically integrated into a more sophisticated online banking app, though they can also exist as standalone mobile or web applications. These Fintech AI assistants make it possible to use tailored strategies to enhance customer satisfaction and address a wide range of important topics, including financial advice and account security [39].
- **Automated fraud detection:**
  To deter fraud, the majority of Fintech businesses would rather announce that they have deployed AI solutions. Fintech businesses use this strategy to draw in partners and customers while deterring possible criminal activity [39].
- **AI-powered regulatory compliance:**
  AI is being used by Fintech companies to automate regulatory compliance procedures and guarantee adherence to intricate financial regulations. Financial institutions can lower their operational costs and compliance risks

by using AI-powered solutions that can monitor transactions for suspicious activity, analyze regulatory requirements, and produce reports that demonstrate compliance [39].

- **Focus on ethical AI and responsible innovation:**
  Transparency, responsible innovation, and ethical AI practices are becoming more and more important as AI is used in Fintech. To maintain fairness, accountability, and consumer protection in the application of AI technologies, regulators are becoming more aware of AI-powered financial services and are enforcing rules and regulations in this area [39].

3.4 REVOLUTIONIZING TRADITIONAL PRACTICES

3.4.1 Algorithmic Trading and Investing Strategies

Algorithms, also known as Algos, are a collection of guidelines designed to perform particular tasks. To automate trading and produce profits at a frequency that is unattainable for a human trader, algorithms are introduced. Known as algorithmic trading, the procedure establishes rules according to timing, quantity, pricing, and other mathematical models [40]. When it comes to trading in financial markets, investors and financial institutions employ a wide variety of strategies that are collectively referred to as algorithmic trading. These tactics make use of computer algorithms to evaluate market data, spot trading opportunities, and carry out orders with little assistance from a human [41].

The strategies to adopt for algorithm trading are the following [42]:

- **Trend following strategy:**
  Trend following, one of the most popular trading strategies, is based on trend analysis, which includes price level movements, breakouts, and moving averages.
- **Index fund rebalancing strategy:**
  Periodically, index funds are rebalanced to bring them into line with benchmark indices. These rebalancing events present opportunities that algorithmic traders take advantage of.
- **Mathematical model-based strategy:**
  This strategy relies heavily on mathematical models, like delta-neutral, to enable trading of both underlying securities and options. Delta-neutral strategies include positions that maintain a balance between positive and negative deltas, which represent the change in asset price to its derivative.
- **Mean revision:**
  The mean reversion strategy is based on the idea that short-term high and low asset prices typically return to the mean value over time. Its main objective is to define and identify price ranges that can be implemented algorithmically.
- **Volume-weighted average price (VWAP):**
  The VWAP approach uses past volume profiles to divide large orders into smaller portions.

Its objective is to execute orders as close as possible to the volume-weighted average price (VWAP).

- **Time-weighted average price (TWAP):**
  The TWAP strategy divides large orders into smaller portions within specified time slots, which span from start to finish. Within the allotted time, it seeks to execute orders at an average price.
- **Percentage of Volume (PoV):**
  With the PoV strategy, the algorithm sends partial orders in accordance with the market volume traded and a predetermined participation ratio. Orders are executed using this strategy in proportion to the total market volume traded.

3.4.2 The Role of Robo-Advisors in Wealth Management

"A robo-advisor is an online platform that offers automated, algorithmic financial planning and investing services with minimal to no human oversight". By combining technology and financial knowledge to democratize access to investment services, robo-advisors have become disruptive forces in the wealth management space. Their ability to use automation and algorithms to deliver individualized investment advice and portfolio management services underpins their multifaceted role in wealth management [43].

The ability of robo-advisors to provide individualized investment advice based on the goals and profiles of specific investors is essential to their function. Robo-advisors use complex algorithms to build individualized investment portfolios by taking into account variables like time horizons, investment goals, and risk tolerance [44]. Additionally, robo-advisors give investors automated portfolio rebalancing and ongoing monitoring. Robo-advisors make sure that investment portfolios stay in line with investors' goals and risk tolerance by monitoring market trends and doing real-time performance analyses. By taking a proactive approach to portfolio management, investors can minimize the need for manual intervention while maintaining alignment with their financial objectives [45].

Robo-advisors, in short, are essential to contemporary wealth management because they fuse technological innovation with individualized financial advice. In addition to democratizing access to professional investment services through their accessibility, affordability, and transparency, their automated portfolio management and personalized approach also enable investors to more confidently and effectively reach their financial goals. Robo-advisors are positioned to continue playing a significant role in reshaping the future of wealth management as the Fintech scene develops [46].

3.4.3 AI in Credit Assessment and Risk Management

With its cutting-edge tools and processes to improve decision-making and reduce risks, AI has completely transformed credit assessment and risk management in the financial sector. This shift is primarily driven by the use of AI algorithms to examine enormous volumes of data from various sources, such as credit reports, transaction histories, financial records, and other data sources. To find patterns, trends, and correlations in the data, these algorithms use machine learning techniques. This allows for more thorough and accurate evaluations of creditworthiness. Many advantages are provided by it, such as increased precision, quicker decision-making, lower risk, and cost savings [47].

AI's real-time monitoring and predictive analytics capabilities also play a significant part in risk management. AI algorithms constantly monitor consumer behavior, market trends, and economic indicators to identify early warning signs of financial distress and evaluate potential risks. AI-driven risk management systems allow financial institutions to proactively mitigate risks and implement targeted interventions to prevent unfavorable outcomes by identifying anomalies and deviations from expected patterns [48]. Additionally, by quickly and accurately spotting suspicious activity and fraudulent transactions, AI-powered fraud detection systems improve risk management. These systems use real-time fraud detection and high-risk transaction flagging by utilizing machine learning algorithms and sophisticated data analytics [49]. AI assists financial institutions in minimizing losses and safeguarding customers and stakeholders from financial harm by automating the detection and prevention of fraudulent activities.

3.4.4 Machine Learning and Deep Learning for Future Applications

"Machine learning (ML) is a subfield of computer science and AI, that focuses on using data and algorithms to make AI more accurate over time by mimicking human learning" [20]. Whereas, "Deep Learning (DL) is a branch of machine learning that mimics the intricate decision-making capabilities of the human brain using multilayered neural networks, or deep neural networks" [21]. Although they are both forms of AI, machine learning, and deep learning are not the same. While deep learning is a subset of machine learning that uses artificial neural networks to simulate how the human brain learns, machine learning is AI that can adapt automatically with little assistance from humans [50].

Future applications of machine learning and deep learning have the potential to completely change the technology and industry landscape [51]. In the realm of healthcare, these technologies have the potential to transform disease diagnosis and treatment by analyzing medical images and patient data and provide more individualized and accurate care [52]. These technologies enhance trading strategies, detect fraud, and assess credit risk in the financial domain, leading to more dependable financial operations and risk management. The application of ML and DL in the retail industry will boost sales through tailored recommendations, optimize inventory management, and improve customer experiences. In the meantime, ML and DL are enhancing industrial operation's efficiency and minimizing downtime in manufacturing by improving production processes and predictive maintenance. Furthermore, ML and DL are propelling the development of autonomous cars, giving them the ability to understand and navigate complicated environments on their own. This will change transportation systems and increase road safety. Additionally, these technologies are spurring innovation in a wide range of fields, including climate science, retail personalization, energy optimization, and many more, with the potential to create new opportunities and resolve challenging issues in the years to come [53].

3.5 INNOVATIVE SOLUTIONS IN FINTECH

3.5.1 Fraud Detection and Prevention

AI-driven innovative solutions are revolutionizing fraud prevention and detection in a variety of industries. AI-based fraud prevention systems can identify intricate patterns of fraudulent behavior, detect fraudulent activities in real time, and mitigate risks more successfully than traditional methods because they can leverage sophisticated machine learning algorithms and data analytics techniques [54]. A novel strategy is anomaly detection, in which AI systems examine vast amounts of transactional data to spot departures from typical patterns and highlight possibly fraudulent transactions for additional scrutiny. Predictive modeling is another intriguing approach, in which AI algorithms examine past data to forecast future fraud patterns and proactively put preventive controls in place to reduce risks [55]. Additionally, combining AI with cutting-edge biometric authentication technologies—like voice and facial recognition—improves security protocols and lowers the possibility of account takeover and identity theft [56]. Overall, proactive and intelligent approaches to preventing and detecting fraud are provided by AI-driven solutions, which help organizations preserve trust and integrity in the digital age while protecting their assets and customers.

3.5.2 Customer Experience Enhancement Through AI

AI is spearheading a paradigm shift in industry-wide customer experience enhancement by providing creative answers to changing consumer demands and preferences. Businesses can provide individualized, seamless, and proactive experiences that encourage customer satisfaction, loyalty, and advocacy by utilizing AI-powered tools and technologies [57].

Personalized interactions are one important way that AI improves the customer experience. AI-powered chatbots and virtual assistants interact with clients in real time, offering prompt help and support at multiple points of contact. By analyzing massive volumes of customer data to predict unique needs and preferences, AI makes hyper-personalization possible. This degree of customization improves customer satisfaction and raises engagement, conversion, and retention rates [58,59]. AI also improves customer service capabilities by automating repetitive tasks and optimizing workflows. AI solutions can process transactions, respond to routine questions, and offer self-service options, freeing up human agents to work on more intricate and valuable interactions. This increases overall customer satisfaction and loyalty by increasing efficiency, cutting down on wait times, and guaranteeing consistent service delivery [60].

In general, AI-driven improvements to customer experiences are revolutionizing how companies engage with their clientele, resulting in increased value, efficiency, and personalization. Businesses that use AI technologies can differentiate their brand in a crowded market, create lasting relationships based on loyalty, trust, and satisfaction, and create memorable and impactful experiences that resonate with customers.

3.5.3 Regulatory Implication of AI in Finance

As legislators and regulatory bodies struggle to handle the opportunities and challenges posed by AI-driven technologies, the regulatory environment surrounding the use of AI in finance is changing quickly. Regulators are concentrating on making sure that AI applications are used sensibly, morally, and in accordance with current laws as they become more common in the financial services industry.

The need for explainability and transparency is one of the main regulatory implications of AI in finance. Concern over the transparency of AI decision-making processes is growing as these algorithms get more complex and sophisticated, especially in areas like algorithmic trading, credit scoring, and risk management (Figure 3.3). To ensure accountability and consumer protection, regulators are calling for increased explainability and transparency in AI systems, requiring financial institutions to record and disclose the reasoning behind AI-driven decisions [61]. Furthermore, bias and discrimination are concerns raised by the application of AI in finance. In training data, AI algorithms may unintentionally reinforce or magnify pre-existing biases, producing unfair or discriminatory results, especially in the lending and insurance industries. To reduce these risks and guarantee equity and fairness in decision-making processes, financial institutions must put in place safeguards and mechanisms. For this, regulators are closely examining AI systems for possible bias and discrimination. The widespread use of AI in finance also presents issues with cybersecurity and data privacy. To train and function properly, AI algorithms require enormous volumes of sensitive data, which raises questions regarding data security, consent, and privacy [62].

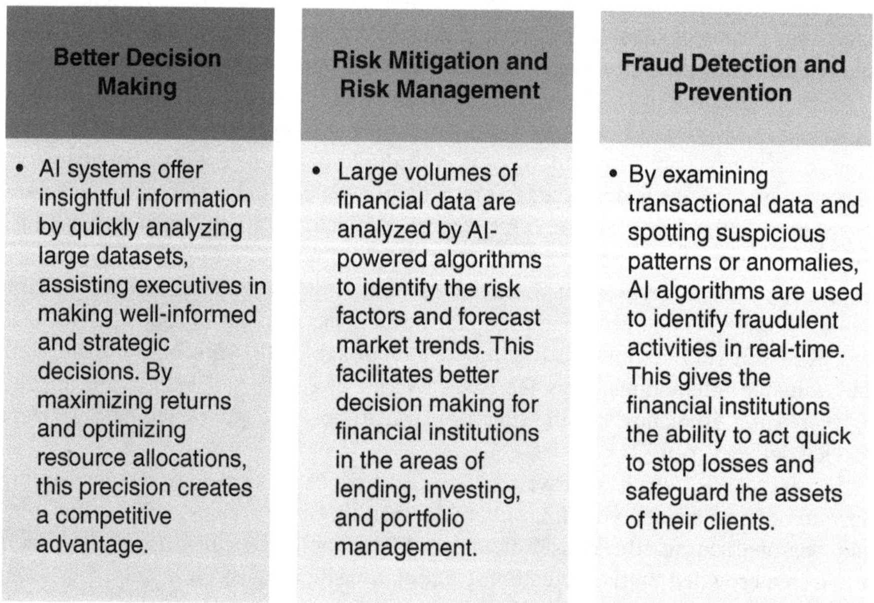

FIGURE 3.3 Applications of artificial intelligence in financial services.

Strengthening internal governance within financial institutions and requiring personal responsibility to include humans in the process are two ways to address this weakness. This strategy is based on the managerial responsibility frameworks that were developed in the wake of the 2008 Global Financial Crisis and the seemingly unending wave of unethical behavior in the finance industry worldwide. These frameworks ought to be aware of and compatible with human-in-the-loop and broader data privacy strategies outside of finance [63].

3.6 REAL-WORLD APPLICATION AND CASE STUDIES

3.6.1 Show Case of Successful AI-Driven Fintech Initiatives

One of the biggest banks, JPMorgan Chase, has led the way in implementing AI and ML technologies to improve the banking experiences of its customers. They have put machine learning algorithms into place to provide their clients with customized product recommendations and financial advice. Additionally, to improve customer service and provide individualized banking experiences globally, BBVA, a multinational banking group based in Spain, has embraced AI and ML. To improve its capacity to identify possible fraudulent transactions, HSBC has also used AI and ML. The bank's AI systems can detect patterns and anomalies that could point to fraudulent activity by analyzing enormous amounts of transaction data in real time. This greatly lowers the risk of financial losses for the bank and its clients [64]. Square, a payment processing company, is helping sellers automate tasks, optimize workflows, and save time by leveraging generative AI capabilities. Bank of America's use of generative AI to identify fraudulent credit card transactions is one of the real-world applications of generative AI in banking. Wells Fargo automates the process of creating financial statements for its clients by utilizing generative AI. The bank can provide its clients with accurate financial information more quickly by streamlining this task [65].

3.6.2 Impact on Efficiency, Risk Management and Profitability

It takes more than just having the best policies to stay ahead of the curve in today's intensely competitive market. It's all about maximizing profits in an industry that is vulnerable to even the smallest changes in the dynamics of the market. AI is being used more and more to hone this competitive edge because AI has the potential to redefine industry standards and operational efficiency [66].

AI has the potential to drastically transform a business's daily operations, a fact that is increasingly recognized across various industries. AI and machine learning (ML) are now closely linked with risk management, as they enhance productivity and efficiency while reducing costs. The technology's capacity to handle and analyze massive amounts of unstructured data quickly and with a significant reduction in human intervention has made this possible. In addition to enabling banks to make accurate credit decisions, technology has also allowed banks and other financial institutions to reduce operational, regulatory, and compliance costs. Furthermore, businesses can forecast future market conditions and make well-informed decisions to minimize risks and maximize returns with the aid of AI-powered predictive analytics. AI also increases profitability through maximizing pricing strategies, enhancing customer targeting and engagement, and spotting cost-saving opportunities. Businesses can boost customer loyalty and sales by personalizing marketing campaigns, making relevant product or service recommendations, and improving the overall customer experience through data-driven insights (Figure 3.3). As a result, AI/ML solutions can produce vast amounts of timely, accurate data, which enables financial institutions to become experts in customer intelligence, facilitating the effective execution of plans and reducing possible losses [67].

3.6.3 Lessons Learned and Best Practices

AI has been incorporated into Fintech, and this has produced important lessons and best practices that will influence the sector going forward. This includes [68,69]:

- **AI-driven personal finance apps:**
  AI has transformed personal finance by enabling the creation of complex apps that meet user's specific financial requirements. These applications examine user's spending patterns, income trends, and financial objectives using machine learning algorithms. By processing this data, AI-driven personal finance apps provide tailored insights, budget recommendations, and savings strategies.
- **Virtual financial advisors:**
  AI-powered virtual financial advisors are a major advancement in the provision of individualized financial advice. These virtual assistants comprehend user's financial circumstances, risk tolerance, and investment objectives through machine learning. Real-time investment advice, portfolio optimization, and retirement planning are all possible with virtual financial advisors because of their constant learning and adaptability to user's changing situations.
- **Automated credit risk assessment:**
  Assessing the creditworthiness of people with unusual financial profiles is made more difficult by the fact that traditional credit scoring models frequently rely on standard criteria and historical data. Automated credit risk assessment models are one way AI tackles this problem. This produces a more complex assessment of a person's creditworthiness, increasing access to financial services for a larger group of people.
- **AI-powered trading strategies:**
  AI-powered algorithmic trading has emerged as a key component of contemporary financial markets. Large volumes of historical and current market data are analyzed by AI algorithms to find trends, patterns, and trading signals. These algorithms take advantage of opportunities and inefficiencies in the market by executing trades at frequencies and speeds faster than those of a human. The efficiency and potential returns of trading are increased when one can instantly adjust to shifting market conditions.
- **AI-driven invoice verification:**
  Through automated verification systems, AI has simplified and increased the accuracy of invoice processing. Invoices can be swiftly analyzed by

machine learning algorithms, which cross-reference them with delivery receipts and purchase orders. This speeds up the entire invoicing process and lowers the possibility of errors and discrepancies. AI-driven invoice verification contributes to more effective financial operations for businesses by improving financial transparency, lowering manual workload, and lowering the possibility of fraudulent activity.

3.7 A COMPREHENSIVE GUIDE FOR PROFESSIONALS AND POLICYMAKERS

3.7.1 Navigating the AI—Fintech Landscape

At its core, AI in Fintech encompasses a diverse array of applications, such as algorithmic trading, robo-advisory services, fraud detection, credit scoring, and customer service automation. To effectively navigate this landscape, stakeholders must keep up with emerging trends, creative solutions, and regulatory developments, as well as assess the potential risks and opportunities associated with AI-driven technologies [70]. Navigating the AI Fintech landscape requires a thorough understanding of the intersection of AI and financial technology, along with the technological, regulatory, and market dynamics shaping this rapidly evolving ecosystem.

The field of AI technology is vast. It includes generative AI, robotics, machine learning, and big language models. But what becomes clear is that there are three key areas where people believe these variables have the greatest influence on risk management and compliance:

1. Risk assessment and transaction tracking
2. Screening and profiling of individuals and entities
3. Streamlining manual tasks and increasing productivity

Knowing the laws governing the application of AI in financial services is essential to navigating the AI Fintech scene. Global regulatory bodies are debating the effects of AI-driven technologies and have released policies and guidelines to guarantee consumer protection, equity, and transparency [71].

Moreover, navigating the AI Fintech landscape requires a keen awareness of technological advancements and market trends. The Fintech industry's business environment is changing following years of rapid expansion and upheaval. Financial institutions and fintechs alike will need to steer clear of these obstacles with a strategic plan. Firms that want to succeed need to recognize and adjust to the major trends that are going to change their markets [72].

3.7.2 Opportunities and Challenges for Industry Professionals

AI is rapidly becoming a disruptive force, transforming many aspects of daily life and the modern workplace. It presents both opportunities and challenges, significantly impacting how we live and work [73].

3.7.2.1 Challenges

- **Ethical considerations:**
  Making ethical decisions with AI is one of the main issues. As AI systems grow more independent, concerns about privacy, bias, and responsibility surface. It is still crucial to make sure AI functions equitably and responsibly.
- **Job disruption:**
  Automation driven by AI has the potential to change the nature of work. It raises concerns about job displacement though it offers prospects for better efficiency. In an AI-driven workplace, industry experts must adjust to shifting job roles and responsibilities. It is necessary to take proactive steps to upskill and reskill the workforce because the shift may result in job displacement.
- **Data transparency:**
  It might be difficult to comprehend how complex AI systems arrive at particular judgments or suggestions since they frequently lack transparency. This opacity might give rise to worries about biases, particularly in vital fields like criminal justice or healthcare.
- **Data privacy and security:**
  High-quality data is essential for AI algorithm training and decision-making. Industry experts need to tackle issues concerning privacy, security, and data quality to guarantee the integrity and dependability of AI systems [74].

3.7.2.2 Opportunities

- **Personalization:**
  AI technology facilitates customized client experiences. Industry experts may use AI to customize goods, services, and advertising campaigns to each individual's preferences, increasing client loyalty and satisfaction.
- **Enhanced decision-making:**
  AI systems can evaluate large volumes of data and offer insightful analysis. This increases performance and results by enabling organizations and individuals to make data-driven decisions which improves results and develops stronger company plans.
- **Increased automation, efficiency and productivity:**
  AI frees humans to concentrate on more intricate and creative work by automating monotonous chores. Workflows are streamlined, accuracy is increased, and efficiency is improved, enabling enterprises to reach better productivity levels [73,75].

3.7.3 Policy Consideration for Regulators and Policy Makers

For AI and ML to be successfully integrated into the banking and financial services sector, effective regulation is essential. Regulators and legislators need to find a balance between encouraging innovation and safeguarding the stability of the financial system and consumers. Regulators may promote ethical AI and ML adoption and foster industry confidence by offering clear rules and frameworks [76,77].

- **Risk management and fraud detection:**
  Financial firms should be required by regulators to put in place strong risk management and compliance procedures before using AI. This entails carrying out risk analyses, keeping an eye on AI systems to ensure they comply with legal specifications, and developing procedures for dealing with mistakes and malfunctions.
- **Ensuring consumer protection:**
  It is recommended that policymakers create consumer protection frameworks to prevent predatory tactics and guarantee that financial products and services powered by AI adhere to regulatory requirements. Regulations about costs, interest rates, and terms of service for financial products driven by AI may fall under this category.
- **Data privacy and security regulations:**
  To safeguard the private financial information of consumers, regulators should enact strict laws about data privacy and security. This covers actions including requiring user consent, encrypting data, and establishing policies for sharing and storing data.
- **Monitoring and evaluation:**
  The financial system, consumer welfare, and market competition are all areas where regulators should set up systems for monitoring and evaluating the effects of AI. This includes gathering statistics on the use of AI, reviewing regulatory frameworks regularly, and getting input from relevant parties [78].

Regulators are also human, and even they can make mistakes. However, the most important thing will be to learn from mistakes and attempt to lessen the effects of such errors. Like the proper application of AI, effective regulation necessitates vision, focus, and the ability to adapt and learn. For that machine learning needs to be understood as a continual process of improvement if regulation is to be successful.

3.8 ETHICAL CONSIDERATIONS IN AI AND FINTECH

3.8.1 Responsible AI Integration

AI is both a major contributor to and a beneficiary of the rapid advancement of technology, which is creating a plethora of options and has already had many positive social and human effects. AI technology assists healthcare providers in enhancing diagnosis, treatment, and preventative protocols. They are useful for agricultural operations, environmental monitoring and preservation initiatives, and the planning and administration of infrastructure, cities, and businesses. They support mobility and transportation networks that are safer and more effective. They provide efficient tools for information querying and multilingual and multimodal interaction. But there are also justifiable worries about hazards, disruptive consequences, and societal stresses associated with these quick technological advancements, which call for careful consideration and resolution. This aims to reduce dangers, look into ethical concerns, and use advancements in AI for the benefit of society [79].

An all-encompassing strategy that places ethical considerations, justice, accountability, and transparency at the forefront of the process is required for responsible

AI integration. The first step in implementing ethical guidelines for AI research, implementation, and use is to establish unambiguous frameworks. And for that, principles like justice, accountability, openness, privacy, and human rights must all be upheld by these systems [80]. In practical terms, this means putting policies in place to detect and reduce biases in AI algorithms and datasets, guaranteeing decision-making processes are transparent and explicable, and setting up systems for accountability and governance [81]. Data security and privacy are critical, necessitating strong safeguards like encryption, anonymization, and user permission procedures to safeguard people's private data [82]. As long as human oversight and intervention capabilities are retained to handle complicated decision-making activities, ongoing monitoring, and evaluation will be necessary to guarantee AI systems function as intended and follow ethical and legal requirements. In the end, responsible AI integration is a cooperative effort that necessitates a continuous dedication to moral standards, openness, and responsibility to guarantee that AI technologies are applied in a way that maximizes advantages to society and minimizes dangers and negative effects [83].

3.8.2 Data Privacy and Security

Ensuring strong data privacy and security safeguards is crucial in the AI Fintech industry to build user confidence and protect sensitive financial data. Adherence to strict data protection protocols is fundamental to responsible AI integration in Fintech. This means protecting people's financial information by implementing access controls, anonymization techniques, and encryption methods to prevent unauthorized access or security breaches [84].

3.8.3 Budding Ethical AI—Fintech Practices

The development of ethical AI practices is gaining attention from stakeholders as the Fintech sector uses AI technologies more and more. To ensure justice, accountability, transparency, and consumer protection during the development and implementation of AI-driven financial solutions, ethical AI Fintech practices comprise a set of principles and guidelines [85,86].

- **Comply with moral principles:**
  To ensure that a responsible AI framework is implemented, organizations must be extremely clear about the laws, regulations, and behavior patterns (of applications) that they deem to be morally and fairly defined.
- **Introduction of accountability:**
  An established and up-to-date organizational structure is necessary for the governance of AI. To establish accountability during and after the AI development process, it is recommended that individuals at all organizational levels be assigned specific roles and responsibilities within it.
- **Reduce risk and boost resilience:**
  A technical system is considered robust if it can withstand disturbances. AI systems need to be created to behave consistently, accurately delivering results, and overcoming outside threats.

- **Recognize and address bias:**
  For AI to be ethical, stakeholders need to have faith that the system makes morally righteous and equitable decisions, rather than just following the law or guidelines outlined in a code of conduct. One significant part of this is that AI behavior and decisions are perceived as impartial, meaning they don't unfairly favor penalize particular individuals over others.
- **Ensure transparency:**
  Human oversight is insufficient on its own. For AI to be deemed responsible, it is necessary to have a fundamental degree of transparency regarding its development, its decision-making process and decisions, as well as its behavior. Transparency is essentially about communication, explainability, and traceability.

3.9 PERSPECTIVE FROM EXPERTS

Figure 3.3 presents a comprehensive overview of various expert perspectives on the topic. It includes contributions from industry practitioners, who offer practical insights based on real-world experience; insights from academic researchers, providing evidence-based analysis and theoretical frameworks; and perspectives from regulatory authorities, highlighting regulatory considerations and guidelines (Figure 3.4). Together, these viewpoints provide a well-rounded understanding of the subject from multiple angles.

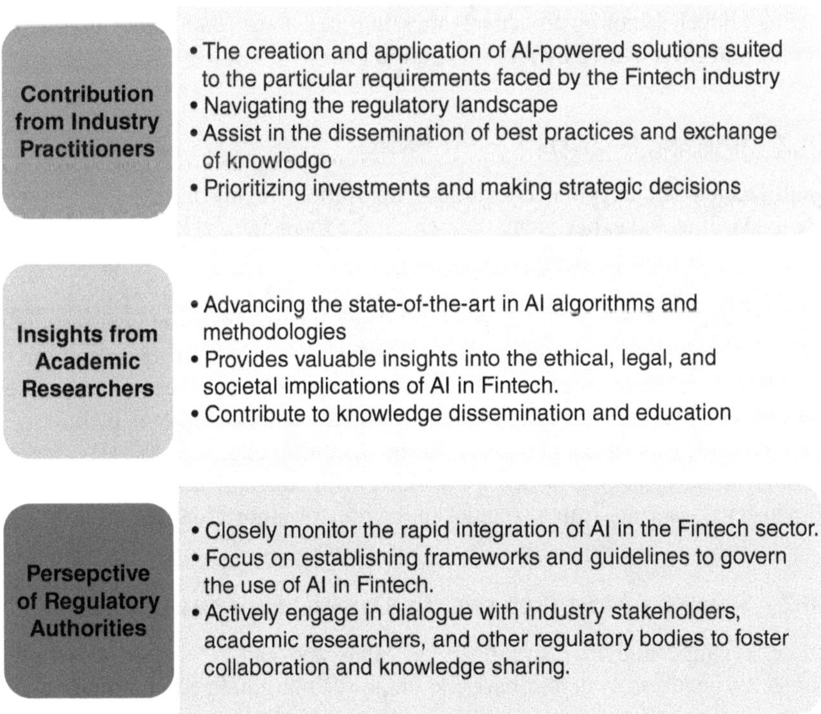

FIGURE 3.4 Stakeholder perspectives on AI integration in Fintech.

3.10 THE PATH FORWARD TOWARD A RESPONSIBLE FUTURE

3.10.1 Balancing Opportunities and Challenges

Harnessing the full potential of these technologies while minimizing risks and guaranteeing responsible innovation requires striking a balance between the opportunities and challenges that AI in Fintech presents. On the one hand, AI presents unprecedented possibilities to transform the financial services industry by boosting productivity, streamlining decision-making, and increasing accessibility to financial goods and services. Financial institutions stand to gain from the potential of AI-powered solutions in the form of reduced costs, enhanced customer satisfaction, fraud detection, risk management, and investment strategy optimization [87].

But these opportunities also bring with them important considerations and challenges. Data security, ethical concerns, legal compliance, and algorithm interpretability are a few examples. Financial institutions need to take a strategic, all-encompassing approach to AI in Fintech to successfully balance these opportunities and challenges [88]. Clear governance frameworks must be created, moral standards and guidelines for the responsible application of AI must be established, talent and capabilities must be invested in, cooperation with regulators and industry stakeholders must be prioritized, and accountability, fairness, and transparency must be given top priority in AI-driven decision-making processes. Financial institutions can stimulate innovation, build confidence and trust among stakeholders and customers, and open up new growth and competitiveness opportunities in the quickly changing Fintech sector by proactively tackling these issues and taking advantage of the opportunities provided by AI [89] (Figure 3.4).

3.10.2 Inspiring Innovation in AI Fintech

A multifaceted strategy that encourages innovation, teamwork, and a culture of ongoing learning and experimentation within the financial services sector is needed to inspire innovation in AI-fintech. By fostering interdisciplinary cooperation and assembling varied teams of data scientists, engineers, financial specialists, and domain experts to take on challenging tasks and investigate novel prospects at the nexus of AI and finance, organizations can foster innovation. Organizations can foster a culture of experimentation and risk-taking that empowers teams to investigate novel concepts, technologies, and business models without the fear of failure. By utilizing outside expertise and gaining access to cutting-edge technologies, adopting open innovation principles—such as working with startups, academic institutions, and industry consortia—can also quicken the pace of innovation [90].

3.10.3 Shaping a More Inclusive and Dynamic Financial Landscape

A more dynamic and inclusive financial landscape can be shaped by applying AI-fintech to address systemic barriers, empower marginalized communities, and foster prosperity and economic growth for all. An effective strategy is to leverage AI to increase the underprivileged population's access to financial services, including the unbanked and underbanked. Furthermore, by facilitating the creation of cutting-edge goods and services catered to the requirements of marginalized communities, AI-fintech can be a key component in advancing financial inclusion [91].

In conclusion, the financial landscape needs to become more dynamic and inclusive by leveraging AI-fintech to improve access to financial services, develop innovative solutions for underserved communities, and allow individuals and businesses to fully participate in the financial system. It is possible to create a more equitable, robust, and prosperous financial ecosystem that benefits everyone, regardless of socioeconomic status or location, by emphasizing financial inclusion, encouraging innovation, and utilizing the transformative power of AI.

3.11 CONCLUSION

3.11.1 Summary of Key Findings

The main conclusions highlight how AI can drastically change the financial landscape, with profound effects on inclusivity, accessibility, and efficiency. AI in finance has the potential to improve decision-making, automate repetitive work, and optimize operations in several financial industry sectors, including banking, insurance, investment management, and regulatory compliance. Furthermore, AI-driven innovations have the potential to increase financial literacy, give underprivileged populations greater access to financial services, and enable people and companies to take a more active role in the financial ecosystem. However, there are still issues with addressing regulatory complexities, ensuring the ethical use of AI, and reducing the risks associated with algorithmic bias, data privacy, and systemic vulnerabilities. Developing a more inclusive, dynamic, and sustainable financial landscape will require sustained cooperation between industry players, legislators, and academics to fully utilize AI's advantages.

3.11.2 Call to Action for the Future

In terms of the future, the financial sector is calling for action to fully embrace the transformative potential of AI in Fintech. To transform financial services, promote global financial inclusion, and accelerate economic growth, all stakeholders must unite and take advantage of this opportunity. To foster an ecosystem of innovation, knowledge sharing, and responsible AI adoption, cooperation between financial institutions, technology companies, regulatory agencies, and academic institutions is crucial.

It will take a concentrated effort to invest in talent development and skills training if Fintech is to fully benefit from AI. To successfully navigate the complexities and challenges ahead, it will be essential to arm the workforce with the requisite knowledge of AI technologies and data science. Organizations can make sure that their teams are equipped to use AI responsibly and successfully by promoting a culture of ongoing learning and adaptation.

Furthermore, when implementing AI-driven solutions, it is critical to give regulatory compliance and ethical considerations a top priority. To mitigate the risks associated with algorithmic bias, data privacy, and systemic vulnerabilities, proactive measures must be implemented. In this context, regulatory bodies are crucial, and cooperation between industry players and legislators is necessary to create strong frameworks that support innovation while defending consumer rights and preserving the integrity of the market.

In conclusion, Fintech's use of AI has a bright future ahead of it, but everyone involved must be committed to the effort and work together. Through a commitment to collaboration, talent development, and ethical considerations, the financial industry can effectively utilize AI to establish a financial ecosystem that is more dynamic, inclusive, and long-lasting for future generations.

REFERENCES

1. L. Cao, Q. Yang and P. S. Yu, "Data science and AI in FinTech: an overview," *International Journal of Data Science and Analytics*, vol. 12, pp. 81–99, 2021.
2. "What is artificial intelligence (AI)," *IBM*, [Online]. Available: https://www.ibm.com/topics/artificial-intelligence.
3. A. Elbeltagi, N. L. Kushwaha, A. Srivastava and A. T. Zoof, "Artificial intelligent-based water and soil management," in *Deep Learning for Sustainable Agriculture*, Ramesh Chandra Poonia, Vijander Singh, Soumya Ranjan Nayak (eds.), Academic Press, 2022, pp. 129–142.
4. B. Nicoletti, *The Future of Fintech*, Palgrave Macmillan, 2017.
5. S. Ahmadi, "A comprehensive study on integration of big data and AI in financial industry and its effect on present and future opportunities," *International Journal of Current Science Research and Review*, vol. 7, no. 1, pp. 66–74, 2024.
6. V. Kaushik, "AI in FinTech: 7 ways AI is revolutionizing finance industry," *techahead*, 20 October 2023. [Online]. Available: https://www.techaheadcorp.com/blog/ai-in-fintech/#:~:text=AI%20is%20revolutionizing%20the%20FinTech%20industry%20by%20automating%20financial%20processes,AI%20automation%20is%20financial%20transactions.
7. A. Kazakevich, "Benefits and use cases for Artificial Intelligence (AI) and Machine Learning (ML) in FinTech," *HQSoftware*, 20 November 2023. [Online]. Available: https://hqsoftwarelab.com/blog/benefits-use-cases-ml-ai-in-fintech/#:~:text=According%20to%20research%2C%20about%2056,behavior%2C%20and%20even%20customer%20profiles.
8. G. Phillips-Wren and L. C. Jain, "Artificial intelligence for decision making," in *Knowledge-Based Intelligent Information and Engineering Systems, 10th International Conference*, Bournemouth, UK, October 9–11, 2006.
9. R. Tao, C. Su, Y. Xiao, K. Dai and F. Khalid, "Robo advisors, algorithmic trading and investment management: wonders of the fourth industrial revolution in financial markets," *Technological Forecasting and Social Change*, vol. 163, no. 3, p. 120421, 2020.
10. M. Tiutiu and D. Dabija, "Improving customer experience using artificial intelligence in online retail," in *Proceedings of the International Conference on Business Excellence*, Bucharest, Romania, March 23–25, 2023.
11. E. Feyen, J. Frost, L. Gambacorta, H. Natarajan and M. Saal, "Fintech and the digital transformation of financial services: implications for market structure and public policy," *BIS Papers*, vol. 117, 2021. pp. 1–53.
12. "Artificial intelligence: what it is and why it matters," *sas*, [Online]. Available: https://www.sas.com/en_in/insights/analytics/what-is-artificial-intelligence.html#:~:text=Artificial%20intelligence%20(AI)%20makes%20it,learning%20and%20natural%20language%20processing.

13. “AI revolution in the fintech industry,” *AMLEGALS*, 1 March 2024. [Online]. Available: https://amlegals.com/ai-revolution-in-the-fintech-industry/.
14. K. L. Siau, F. H. Nah, Y. Qian, B. L. Eschenbrenner and L. Chen, “Artificial intelligence in financial technology,” in *15th China Summer Workshop on Information Management (CSWIM 2022)*, Ningbo, China, June 25–26, 2022.
15. Blomstein, “AI hitting on competition?,” *Lexology*, 28 April 2023. [Online]. Available: https://www.lexology.com/library/detail.aspx?g=e369f176-4cfb-49de-a41d-89561128d4cc.
16. E. Mancilla, “Understanding artificial intelligence: the basics of AI,” *invgate*, 4 July 2022. [Online]. Available: https://blog.invgate.com/artificial-intelligence.
17. “Artificial Intelligence (AI): what it is and how it is used,” *Investopedia*, 4 December 2023. [Online]. Available: https://www.investopedia.com/terms/a/artificial-intelligence-ai.asp.
18. N. Laskowski and L. Tucci, “Artificial intelligence (AI),” *TechTarget*, [Online]. Available: https://www.techtarget.com/searchenterpriseai/definition/AI-Artificial-Intelligence#:~:text=What%20is%20artificial%20intelligence%20(AI,speech%20recognition%20and%20machine%20vision.
19. P. Kumari, “What is AI analytics?: redefining decision-making and innovation | Integration of data analytics, AI, and business intelligence in business operation,” *LinkedIn*, 20 November 2023. [Online]. Available: https://www.linkedin.com/pulse/what-ai-analytics-redefining-decision-making-innovation-jha-s9i3f#:~:text=AI%20Analytics-,1.,on%20data%20patterns%20and%20probabilities.
20. “What is machine learning (ML)?,” *IBM*, [Online]. Available: https://www.ibm.com/topics/machine-learning.
21. “What is deep learning?” *IBM*, [Online]. Available: https://www.ibm.com/topics/deep-learning.
22. “Fintech (Financial Technology),” *CFI*, [Online]. Available: https://corporatefinanceinstitute.com/resources/wealth-management/fintech-financial-technology/.
23. A. Mostafa, “Obstacles of FinTech in Egyptian bank sector under social distancing,” *Scientific Journal for Financial and Commercial Studies and Researches*, vol. 2, no. 1, pp. 426–454, 2021.
24. H. Alhosseiny, “Fintech: concept, opportunities and challenges, and Egypt’s fintech landscape,” *Journal of Organizational Culture Communications and Conflict*, vol. 27, no. 1, pp. 1–18, 2023.
25. J. Lindner, “Online banking usage statistics,” *Gitnux*, 16 December 2023. [Online]. Available: https://gitnux.org/online-banking-usage-statistics/#:~:text=As%20of%202021%2C%20around%2073,worldwide%20use%20online%20banking%20services.
26. B. Burke, “The convergence of fintech & AI,” *LinkedIn*, 24 January 2024. [Online]. Available: https://www.linkedin.com/pulse/convergence-fintech-ai-bruce-burke-zdnfe?trk=public_post.
27. “AI in Fintech: how artificial intelligence is transforming financial services,” Rebeldot, [Online.. Available: https://www.rebeldot.com/blog/ai-in-fintech-how-artificial-intelligence-is-transforming-financial-services.
28. H. Jiang, Y. Cheng, J. Yang and S. Gao, “AI-powered chatbot communication with customers: dialogic interactions, satisfaction, engagement, and customer behavior,” *Computers in Human Behavior*, vol. 134, p. 107329, 2022.
29. B. Bayam-Trojanowska, “Use the excellence of artificial intelligence (AI) to improve your compliance posture,” *Nordcloud*, [Online]. Available: https://nordcloud.com/blog/how-ai-can-help-you-obtain-regulatory-compliance/.
30. “AI in finance: applications, use cases, and future prospects,” *ediiie*, [Online]. Available: https://www.ediiie.com/blog/ai-in-finance-applications-use-cases-and-future-prospects/.

31. L. Puri, "A study of applications of artificial intelligence in banking and finance sector," *International Journal For Innovative Research in Multidisciplinary Field*, special no. 20, pp. 35–37, 2020.
32. S. Shetty, C. Spulbar, R. Birau and R. Filip, "Impact of artificial intelligence in banking sector with reference to private banks in India," *Annals of the University of Craivo*, Physics, vol. 32, pp. 59–75, 2022.
33. P. Karthika, A. Anburaj and S. Raja, "Artificial intelligence in investment management, asset management and warehouse management," *i-Manager's Journal on Data Science & Big Data Analytics*, vol. 1, no. 1, pp. 40–46, 2023.
34. A. Gupta, "Assessing the impact of artificial intelligence on investment portfolio management," *LinkedIn*, 25 October 2023. [Online]. Available: https://www.linkedin.com/pulse/assessing-impact-artificial-intelligence-investment-portfolio-gupta-ndk6f#:~:text=Artificial%20intelligence%20(AI)%20is%20having,for%20human%20investors%20to%20see.
35. R. Balasubramanian, A. Libarikian and D. McElhaney, "Insurance 2030—the impact of AI on the future of insurance," *McKinsey & Company*, 12 March 2021. [Online]. Available: https://www.mckinsey.com/industries/financial-services/our-insights/insurance-2030-the-impact-of-ai-on-the-future-of-insurance.
36. "Impact of artificial intelligence on the insurance industry," *Acko*, 17 January 2024. [Online]. Available: https://www.acko.com/articles/general-info/impact-of-artificial-intelligence-on-the-insurance-industry/.
37. P. Ladva and A. Grasso, "Benefits and use cases of AI in insurance," *Swiss Re*, 17 April 2023. [Online]. Available: https://www.swissre.com/risk-knowledge/advancing-societal-benefits-digitalisation/opportunities-ai-insurance.html.
38. "IBM global AI adoption index 2023," *IBM*, 10 January 2024. [Online]. Available: https://newsroom.ibm.com/2024-01-10-Data-Suggests-Growth-in-Enterprise-Adoption-of-AI-is-Due-to-Widespread-Deployment-by-Early-Adopters#:~:text=Advances%20in%20AI%20tools%20that,top%20factors%20driving%20AI%20adoption.
39. "AI in FinTech: role, opportunities and use cases," *intellectsoft*, 22 November 2023. [Online]. Available: https://www.intellectsoft.net/blog/ai-in-fintech/#:~:text=AI%20in%20the%20FinTech%20market%20is%20widely%20used%20for%20more,with%20a%20favorable%20business%20climate.
40. T. Vipond, "Algorithms (Algos)," *CFI*, [Online]. Available: https://corporatefinanceinstitute.com/resources/career-map/sell-side/capital-markets/what-are-algorithms-algos/#:~:text=the%20stock%20price.-,Strategies%20for%20Algorithmic%20Trading,cost%20reduction%2C%20and%20pairs%20trading.
41. S. Seth, "Basics of algorithmic trading: concepts and examples," *Investopedia*, 14 December 2023. [Online]. Available: https://www.investopedia.com/articles/active-trading/101014/basics-algorithmic-trading-concepts-and-examples.asp.
42. A. Banerjee, "What is algo trading in India? Best strategies, risks, and benefits of Algo Trading," *Smallcase*, 22 September 2023. [Online]. Available: https://www.smallcase.com/learn/what-is-algo-trading/.
43. "What is a robo-advisor?," *Investopedia*, 26 February 2024. [Online]. Available: https://www.investopedia.com/terms/r/roboadvisor-roboadviser.asp#:~:text=level%20of%20risk.-,The%20Bottom%20Line,manage%20and%20rebalance%20their%20portfolios.
44. Perficient, "Impact of robo-advisors in wealth management," [Online]. Available: https://www.perficient.com/-/media/files/guide-pdf-links/impact-of-robo-advisors-in-wealth-management.pdf.
45. K. Phoon and F. Koh, "Robo-advisors and wealth management," *The Journal of Alternative Investments*, vol. 20, no. 3, pp. 79–94, 2017.

46. Wipro, "Future of robo-advisors in investment and wealth management," [Online]. Available: https://www.wipro.com/content/dam/nexus/en/industries/securities-and-capital-markets/latest-thinking/future-of-robo-advisors-in-investment-and-wealth-management.pdf.
47. B. Johnson, "AI in credit risk management for large enterprises: what it is, how it works, challenges, and solutions," *highradius*, 29 December 2023. [Online]. Available: https://www.highradius.com/resources/Blog/ai-in-credit-risk-management/.
48. M. Ramaswamy, "The evolving role of artificial intelligence in credit risk management," Indiaai, 9 March 2023. [Online]. Available: https://indiaai.gov.in/article/the-evolving-role-of-artificial-intelligence-in-credit-risk-management.
49. R. N. Satyala, "Fraud detection and risk management: harnessing the power of AI to safeguard the financial industry," *LinkedIn*, 1 July 2023. [Online]. Available: https://www.linkedin.com/pulse/fraud-detection-risk-management-harnessing-power-ai-industry-satyala.
50. C. Staff, "Deep learning vs. machine learning: a beginner's guide," *coursera*, 9 February 2024. [Online]. Available: https://www.coursera.org/articles/ai-vs-deep-learning-vs-machine-learning-beginners-guide.
51. "Deep learning and the future of artificial intelligence," *altexsoft*, 22 October 2021. [Online]. Available: https://www.altexsoft.com/blog/deep-learning/.
52. C. Habehh and S. Gohel, "Machine learning in healthcare," *Current Genomics*, vol. 22, no. 4, pp. 291–300, 2021.
53. S. Reddy, "Impact of machine learning on various industries," *Pranathi*, 6 October 2023. [Online]. Available: https://www.pranathiss.com/blog/machine-learning-industries/.
54. "AI in the banking sector: how fraud detection with AI is making banking safer," *Infosys BPM*, [Online]. Available: https://www.infosysbpm.com/blogs/bpm-analytics/fraud-detection-with-ai-in-banking-sector.html.
55. "Understanding AI fraud detection and prevention strategies," *DigitalOcean*, [Online]. Available: https://www.digitalocean.com/resources/article/ai-fraud-detection.
56. D. Balroop, "AI and biometrics: advancements in security and identity verification," *LinkedIn*, 19 December 2023. [Online]. Available: https://www.linkedin.com/in/dave-balroop-techunity?trk=article-ssr-frontend-pulse_publisher-author-card.
57. M. Daqar and A. Smoudy, "The role of artificial intelligence on enhancing customer experience," *International Review of Management and Marketing*, vol. 9, no. 4, pp. 22–31, 2019.
58. E. Castillo, "How can artificial intelligence improve customer experience?," *Pathmonk*, 30 November 2023. [Online]. Available: https://pathmonk.com/artificial-intelligence-improve-customer-experience/.
59. K. J. Jaby, "10 excellent ways AI will improve customer experience in 2024," *Survey Sparrow*, 29 February 2024. [Online]. Available: https://surveysparrow.com/blog/ai-customer-experience/.
60. "How AI can improve your customer experience in 2023," *Adobe Experience Cloud*, 8 October 2023. [Online]. Available: https://business.adobe.com/blog/basics/ai-customer-experience
61. T. Ehret, "Know your AI: compliance and regulatory considerations for financial services," *Thompson Reuters*, 19 December 2023. [Online]. Available: https://www.thomsonreuters.com/en-us/posts/corporates/ai-compliance-financial-services/.
62. B. Quinn, "How will artificial intelligence affect financial regulation?," *Economics Observatory*, 18 October 2023. [Online]. Available: https://www.economicsobservatory.com/how-will-artificial-intelligence-affect-financial-regulation#:~:text=This%20could%20result%20in%20biased,sensitive%20financial%20information%20is%20paramount.
63. R. P. Buckley, D. A. Zetzsche, D. W. Arner and B. W. Tang, "Regulating artificial intelligence in finance: putting the human in the loop," *Sydney Law Review*, vol. 43, no. 1, pp. 43–81, 2021.

64. N. Zagha, "27 real examples of AI implementation in fintech and banking," *LinkedIn*, 11 March 2024. [Online]. Available: https://www.linkedin.com/pulse/27-authentic-examples-ai-implementation-fintech-nasser-sami-qtxee?trk=organization_guest_main-feed-card_reshare_feed-article-content.
65. L. Rosencrance, "Top 5 generative AI use cases in fintech in 2024," *Techopedia*, 18 March 2024. [Online]. Available: https://www.techopedia.com/top-generative-ai-use-cases-in-fintech.
66. Simplifai, "Profitability through innovation: the impact of AI in insurance," *LinkedIn*, 11 January 2024. [Online]. Available: https://www.linkedin.com/pulse/profitability-through-innovation-impact-ai-insurance-simplifai-6tzaf.
67. "Artificial intelligence in risk management," *KPMG*, [Online]. Available: https://kpmg.com/ae/en/home/insights/2021/09/artificial-intelligence-in-risk-management.html#:~:text=In%20risk%20management%2C%20AI%2FML,lower%20degrees%20of%20human%20intervention.
68. A. Ryzhokhin, "AI in fintech: use cases and best practices," *Ardas*, 2 January 2024. [Online]. Available: https://ardas-it.com/ai-in-fintech-use-cases-and-best-practices.
69. P. Francis, "AI in FinTech in 2024: 7 ways AI is revolutionizing the industry," *Uvik*, 17 August 2023. [Online]. Available: https://uvik.net/blog/ai-in-fintech/.
70. "FinTech explained," *ai-jobs.net*, 6 December 2023. [Online]. Available: https://ai-jobs.net/insights/fintech-explained/.
71. "Navigating the AI landscape insights from compliance and risk management leaders," Moody's Analytics, [Online]. Available: https://www.moodys.com/web/en/us/site-assets/ma-kyc-navigating-the-ai-landscape-report.pdf.
72. S. Conahan, "Navigating the evolving fintech landscape in 2024," *Finextra*, 19 January 2024. [Online]. Available: https://www.finextra.com/blogposting/25561/navigating-the-evolving-fintech-landscape-in-2024.
73. K. Chauhan, "Artificial intelligence: challenges and opportunities in the modern workplace and daily life," *Times of India*, 6 June 2023. [Online]. Available: https://timesofindia.indiatimes.com/readersblog/theintersection/artificial-intelligence-challenges-and-opportunities-in-the-modern-workplace-and-daily-life-54814/.
74. Z. Roberts, "The impact of AI on industries: opportunities and challenges," *LinkedIn*, 15 February 2023. [Online]. Available: https://www.linkedin.com/pulse/impact-ai-industries-opportunities-challenges-zack-roberts.
75. *Thomson Reuters*, "Future of professionals report—how AI is the catalyst for transforming every aspect of work," *Thomson Reuters*, August 2023. [Online]. Available: https://www.thomsonreuters.com/content/dam/ewp-m/documents/thomsonreuters/en/pdf/reports/future-of-professionals-august-2023.pdf.
76. J. Giordani, "The role of regulators and policymakers in driving AI and machine learning adoption in the banking and financial services industry," *LinkedIn*, 6 July 2023. [Online]. Available: https://www.linkedin.com/pulse/role-regulators-policy-makers-driving-ai-machine-banking-john-giordani#:~:text=Regulators%20and%20policymakers%20have%20a,sector%20are%20transparent%20and%20explainable.
77. "Fintech policy tool kit for regulators and policy makers in asia and the pacific," March 2022. [Online]. Available: https://www.adb.org/sites/default/files/publication/780806/fintech-policy-tool-kit-regulators-policy-makers.pdf.
78. C. Coglianese, "How to regulate artificial intelligence," *The Regulatory Review*, 15 January 2024. [Online]. Available: https://www.theregreview.org/2024/01/15/coglianese-how-to-regulate-artificial-intelligence/.
79. M. Ghallab, "Responsible AI: requirements and challenges," *AI Perspectives*, vol. 1, no. 3, pp. 1–7, 2019.
80. V. Dignum, "Responsible artificial intelligence: designing AI for human values," *ITU Journal: ICT Discoveries*, no. 1, pp. 1–8, 2017.

81. V. Prabhakaran, M. Mitchell, T. Gebru and I. Gabriel, “A human rights-based approach to responsible AI,” *Computers and Society*, 2022. https://arxiv.org/pdf/2210.02667
82. “Responsible AI and privacy,” *tsaaro consulting*, [Online]. Available: https://tsaaro.com/reports/responsible-a-i-and-privacy/.
83. H. Keshyap, “Here’s everything you need to know about responsible AI,” inc42, 12 March 2024. [Online]. Available: https://inc42.com/glossary/responsible-ai/.
84. “Data privacy implications in the fintech ecosystem,” *Amlegals Legal Strategists*, 19 January 2024. [Online]. Available: https://amlegals.com/data-privacy-implications-in-the-fintech-ecosystem/#%20.
85. M. Sullivan, “Key principles for ethical AI development,” *Transcend*, 20 October 2023. [Online]. Available: https://transcend.io/blog/ai-ethics.
86. K. Kanev, “Responsible AI: how to make your enterprise ethical, so that your AI is too,” DXC Technologies, [Online]. Available: https://dxc.com/in/en/insights/perspectives/paper/responsible-ai#:~:text=For%20AI%20to%20be%20considered,itself%20and%20how%20it%20behaves.
87. K. Mehta, “The dual nature of AI: striking a balance between opportunities and challenges for the financial sector,” *Express Computer*, 23 January 2024. [Online]. Available: https://www.expresscomputer.in/guest-blogs/the-dual-nature-of-ai-striking-a-balance-between-opportunities-and-challenges-for-the-financial-sector/108452/.
88. Fenige, “Artificial intelligence in fintech: challenges, opportunities, and ethics,” LinkedIn, 8 November 2023. [Online]. Available: https://www.linkedin.com/pulse/artificial-intelligence-fintech-challenges-opportunities-ethics-sfyzf#:~:text=Artificial%20Intelligence%20in%20fintech%20offers,regulatory%20compliance%2C%20and%20ethical%20aspects.
89. C. Maple, L. Szpruch, G. Epiphaniou, K. Staykova, S. Singh, W. Penwarden, Y. Wen, Z. Wang, J. Hariharan and P. Avramovic, *The AI Revolution: Opportunities and Challenges for the Finance Sector*, The Alan Turing Institute, 2023.
90. Think Evolve Consultancy, “Unleashing the power of AI: inspiring innovations transforming healthcare, sustainability, and fintech,” *LinkedIn*, 14 June 2023. [Online]. Available: https://www.linkedin.com/pulse/unleashing-power-ai-inspiring-innovations-transforming.
91. Evolve Venture Capital, “Fintech for financial inclusion: empowering underserved communities,” *LinkedIn*, 26 February 2024. [Online]. Available: https://www.linkedin.com/pulse/fintech-financial-inclusion-empowering-underserved-communities-oe6hc.

4 A Comprehensive Review on Exploring the Impact of Machine Learning and Deep Learning in FinTech

Chokkamreddy Prakash, Palagati Anusha, Kadiri Padmaja, and Mahima Jasniewski

4.1 INTRODUCTION TO MACHINE LEARNING AND DEEP LEARNING IN FINTECH

4.1.1 Understanding the Basics

Artificial intelligence (AI) is made up of AI, and machine learning (ML) and deep learning (DL) are parts of that AI, but ML is a part of AI and DL is a subset of ML [1]. ML denotes the development of systems that learn from experience without being programmed explicitly [2], conversely, DL uses artificial neural networks which are algorithms designed to resemble brain functions for interpretation of complex information [3]. These technologies have been adopted in Fintech industries where they have found relevance in areas including but not limited to fraud protection, reducing costs as well as enhancing efficiencies [4]. Interestingly, though used interchangeably many times whenever mentioned, still there exist some differences between ML and DL. For instance, DL requires large datasets with more computational power than traditional ML methods thus removing the need for feature engineering because it can automatically find the required features needed for detecting them [5,2]. Furthermore, implementing these approaches in FinTech comes with its set of challenges such as addressing moral issues or creating regtech to manage intelligent data use [6].

4.1.2 Evolution of ML in Digital Financing

The growth of ML in FinTech is a critical element for the industry's growth and change. These financial companies have used AI as one of its branches, ML, to develop different financial services like loans, transfers or insurance [7]. In addition, this was made possible by integration with other disruptive technologies such as big data and blockchain. This occurred mainly after the 2008s global financial recession [8]. Stupendously enough even though there has been progress over time as well as

 DOI: 10.1201/9781003645849-4

importance resulting from the use of ML on Fintech it also creates an environment where traditional financiers can hardly keep pace with Fintech firms that employ them for fraud protection, cost minimization and efficiency improvement [4]. Also, when it comes to enhancing patentability value within companies on Fintech is done through the introduction of ML while blockchain proves to be most valuable for this purpose [9]. ML has been at the heart of Fintech evolution which consequently enabled it to generate new market segments and improve financial services. The adoption of ML by FinTech companies has not only fostered innovation but has also posed challenges for traditional financial institutions, necessitating adaptation to remain competitive [7,4]. The impact of ML on FinTech is profound, with its value reflected in the increased valuation of companies that innovate with these technologies [9].

4.1.3 Rise of DL in Financial Applications

There has been a recent increase in research and development activities in the field of DL within finance which indicates its rising application. DL is increasingly being applied to various financial tasks among them include time series analysis, asset allocation and risk management [10-12]. Financial markets are noisy and dynamic among others, DL can learn complex patterns in data that will be useful for it amongst other things. However, there are also negative aspects as well as limitations of DL on FinTech noted by authors. For instance, some studies have identified algorithmic biases and lack of essential empirical research as pitfalls that may arise in ML and AI algorithms used for finance [13]. It is also argued that combining blockchain with DL could make financial transactions more stable thereby providing substantial advantages for the banking industry [14].

4.2 APPLICATION OF ML IN FINTECH

A lot of Fintech companies have adopted ML to perform different tasks, thus creating the disruption in the banking industry. The use of ML algorithms involves many activities such as credit scoring, fraud detection and making finance services automatic [15]. Some improvements have been made with regard to ML techniques like logistic regression and autoencoders that can catch cases of credit card fraudulent transactions [16]. It is also projected to decrease the operational cost by 22% by 2030 for banks [16]. However, it has taken a surprising turn from being just a back-office operation within the banks into a digital payments, portfolio management and stock trading facility for its clients [17]. This is not without a kickback because online transaction security has recently become highly debated due to cybercrimes that can be used in engaging fraudsters [18]. However, incorporating ML into FinTech despite criticism is seen as an innovation promoter and efficiency booster in the financial sector.

4.2.1 Fraud Detection and Prevention

To address the impact of Environmental, Social, and Governance (ESG) norms on the financial performance of Small Finance Banks (SFBs) in India that are not directly addressed in the provided papers, broader research on ESG impacts on financial performance in the Indian context can help. In fact, return on equity among Nifty 50 companies has been negatively impacted by ESG practices that include environmental and governance pillars [19]. This is confirmed by [20], which indicates a negative correlation between ESG risk levels and financial performance among Indian financial firms. Alternatively, some such as [21] argue that ESG performance is positively associated with firm performance only at its upper quantiles of the distribution of company results for top Indian companies. However, while [22] does show a positive link between environmental and social performance and emerging market banks financial success; this does not hold for corporate governance ratings. On the other hand, Tobins Q which gives it governance pillar for Indonesian banking corporations was reported in a study [23].

4.2.2 Personalized Suggestions and Consumer Segmentation

E-commerce and marketing embrace personalized recommendations and customer segmentation. Individualized recommendations are tailored to the buyer's preferences, enabling them to be more satisfied and loyal [24]. Alternatively, customer segmentation refers to dividing customers according to diverse criteria for better marketing targeting towards these segments [25,26]. However quite interestingly, unlike personalized recommendations that may be considered as individual-based approaches; segmentation can boost personalization through identifying similar behavioral/needs-based customer groups [27,28]. Moreover, depending on the diversity of recommended products, such recommender systems can offer improved results by using their social media links [29]. Nonetheless, it is worth mentioning that personalization sometimes backfires with some customers rather than satisfying them because it annoys or disappoints them [30].

4.2.3 Risk Management and Scoring

For financial institutions, Credit Risk Management and credit scoring are two key approaches aimed at measuring borrowers' capabilities. The assessments rely on various patterns and methodologies that employ the applicant's financial records and personal details to make a forecast of defaulting [31]. Notably, it has emerged that despite conventional methods like logistic regression and discriminant analysis being used widely, ML techniques such as Random Forests and Classification Restricted Boltzmann Machines introduced higher prediction accuracy levels characterized by higher abilities to handle complex non-linear relationships [32]. Moreover, some models adopt novel tools including intelligent-agent-based fuzzy group decision-making or Ant Colony Systems that enhance interpretability and precision of credit scoring models [33]. These advances are meant to achieve integrated holistic models capable of handling both quantitative and qualitative data adequately at the same time [34].

4.3 DL Benefits within Fintech Sector

DL has some tough benefits for Fintech such as the ability to process and learn large volumes of complex data. In particular, DL algorithms have proven helpful in dealing with time series data, predicting market movements and offering better trading algorithms [10]. Moreover, it is evident that there has been a role of DL in FinTech that facilitated performance in asset allocation such as the Black-Litterman model. The instruments have outperformed those from investment portfolios. However, DL is also promising. For instance, its applications in automated financial management especially with respect to asset allocation may still be unknown compared to other Fintech domains [11]. This proposes an idea that the research on results but a complete horizon of processes and consequences of methodical learning towards Financial Technologies are new areas so far.

4.3.1 Improved Algorithmic Trading

There are some different approaches that make algorithmic trading more effective and among them is the use of neural networks and reinforcement learning methods for improved trade management [35]. These developments have led to the emergence of more complicated trading strategies, which become outdated over time. They are flexible in their approach besides they also enable better risk management [36]. Algorithmic trading on the other hand focuses on increasing its efficiency rather than reducing effects emotions [37]. Nevertheless, there have been concerns about market safety and trustworthiness raised by algorithmic trading. Meanwhile, multilevel objective optimization combined with real-time optimization of design variables within genetic algorithms can be employed for ad-hoc and adaptive trading systems [38]. In addition, these systems handle the trade-off between various performance metrics, such as profit and risk, while they continuously adapt to changes in market conditions.

4.3.2 Natural Language Processing Innovations Enables Seamless Communication with Customers.

The natural language processing technology effectively facilitates customer engagement, with systems creating an interaction experience. The integration of NLP with ML and DL advancements has enhanced the capabilities of language processing enabling interactions between individuals and computers across industries. Despite progress in sentiment analysis and emotion interpretation challenges remain in interpreting verbal cues crucial for customer interactions. Understanding human language complexity poses difficulties for NLP systems as computers struggle to grasp nuances. Recognizing the importance of developing solutions that meet performance requirements without data, time, storage or power consumption is, on the rise.

4.4 PROBLEMS AND ELEMENTS THAT MIGHT APPEAR WHILE PLACING ML AND DL INTO FINTECH

ML and DL are increasingly being embraced by the FinTech sector. However, the adoption of these AI technologies demonstrates a number of challenges. An example is that there are many challenges including the increased data volume, extensive computational power, and the issues of cybersecurity and data privacy [39]. Moreover, the integration of AI and ML in financial services systems raises a number of ethical, regulatory and competitive issues concerning AI and the effects that AI may have on traditional financial institutions. The rise of finance ML and DL is likely to allow a new breed of FinTech to rise, although the issues are not necessarily new as they relate to the successful deployment of AI. For instance, in the context of FinTech, the use of AI is causing concerns about the ability of traditional financial institutions to match the speed of FinTech, which can enable FinTech firms to take advantage of AI efficiencies more effectively [4]. In addition, the interrelation between big data, AI and ML in the context of FinTech raises some interesting questions about the dark side of this interrelation, including the emergence of challenges such as those related to AI ethics and the use of smart data [6].

4.4.1 Amidst Data Privacy and Security Concerns

In the age of the cloud, big data, and social network services (SNSs), data privacy and security issues become more conspicuous, i.e. the ones who store information in the cloud or use OSNs. The literature states that the risks are complex, including risks to children, their well-being, data security and availability, privacy concerns, and the need to have robust strategies to mitigate such risks [40]. The security attributes of confidentiality, integrity, availability of data, privacy-preservability and accountability are recognized as vital, to overcome the problems associated with this application. Similarly, highlighting data privacy complexity in cloud technologies with a view to put emphasis on preventing data from being stolen by attackers through the utilization of encryption or other privacy methods is indicated. Intuitively, on one hand, the cloud computing enriches our daily life with multiple advantages; but simultaneously, it supplies a well-known and grave problem, namely the insider threats, data breaches and complete protection of user's data from a legal perspective. Under the banner of Internet of Things, consumer purchasing behavior is plagued by presumed data privacy risks which are reported by a majority of responders to be the single biggest reason why an online transaction could be nixed. In this specific setup, what we should make sure of is to also understand that the privacy protection tools and algorithms are left by the groups to individuals, hence we have to direct more awareness of these applications.

4.4.2 Mechanism of Decisions and Concerns About Approval and Regulation and Ethical Problems

Interpreting the ML models is one of the important things, which has a relationship with regulatory compliance and moral concerns. A plenitude of papers reports that despite the demand for interpretable models such as long-term cognitive network (LTCN) that has been proposed for class pattern [41], the task is still to ensure a trade-off between the model interpretability and performance. The compliance with regulations is further bound up by the dual use of AI technologies, but they are only being used for clinical pharmacology and the spread of the wars by means of bioweapons [42]. The employment of AI systems is additionally packed with ethical issues for the emphasized aspect of transparency, accountability and privacy which very much inspire AI practitioners and lawmakers. Interestingly, efforts for making the models interpretable include the recognition that AI systems are complex and the accountability is a key requirement for their implementation. This is something that also appears in the application of fuzzy sets with rough fuzzy sets and logistic regression that show up in model interpretability [43]. Furthermore, an LLM ethical decision-making process in the self-driving vehicle domain similarly opens a door to ethical dilemmas regarding the alignment of such technologies with the human ethical frames. Ethics in healthcare must be critical events, especially when we set palliative care to follow the ethical principle that professionals find their way in compassionate care of patients at the end of their life [44]. The construction of structures such as InterNRL which aspires to both accuracy and interpretability is an indication of the continuity of the efforts in the struggle to solve these matters in real clinical use. The far-stretched usage of ML in healthcare has now fronted the ethical considerations on patients' data security and the transparency that is required in the algorithms. Nevertheless, the area of AI ethics may use an integrated framework (XAI), to allow for a systematic process of handling these issues, [45].

4.5 OUTLOOK FOR FUTURE TRENDS AND VISION FOR ML AND DL FOR FINTECH

The probabilities of ML and DL's positive influence on the financial technology (FinTech) business are good due to their dependence on various aspects of their sector. AI predicts the success of ML and DL in the field of FinTech through the enhancement of predictive analytics, risk management, fraud detection, and customer support among other processes and areas. An expansion of ML and DL algorithms along with the growing opportunity to access financial data, that probably going to be the source of these innovations. By the same measure, the possibility is big but latent challenges abound following the requirement for interpretability of ML models, managing computational costs, and high prediction accuracy. The unpredictability of the black boxes of many ML models, especially the generality apparent in DL, is the chief reason and the scariest factor standing in the way of the implementation of the outlined ML models in the highly regulated FinTech market. Thus, topics of both improving these models and enabling users to understand how they work are essential [46]. Nonetheless, issues such as the quality of data, and the computational resources necessary to achieve good results with sophisticated models are noteworthy for incorporation [47].

4.5.1 Blockchain Implementation

The integration of blockchain into various sectors is a wide-ranging process consisting of the adoption of new regulating technologies, special traits of the system, and different applications in numerous industries. The application of blockchain technology is a vital element of the plan, allowing for decentralization architecture and automation of operational processes, including digital record-keeping [48]. The Scientific heritage of the technology from a digital platform to a complex framework to tackle different applications has the potential to run multiple fields in sciences such as finance, health, and transportation [49]. On the other hand, the processes contain several issues and particularities, which have to be addressed. For instance, high fluidity of transport vehicles in transportation networks requires real-time shared data, what can be ensured through blockchain security and traceability. But is that much data will mean that edge computing is really needed as to solve the computational burden [50]. On the other hand, the cybersecurity advantage of blockchain might be arguable when it is applied to specific system demanding alternative solutions [51]. Adoption of the mentioned approach in Internet of Things networks is constrained by the functional capacities of the nodes so that the emergence of a string of blockchain solutions of reduced weight is required. The implementation of blockchain to the defense industry mark platform should incorporate aspects like throughput, latency, and interoperability issues [44].

4.5.2 Growth of Robotic and Tech-Driven Advisory Services and the Development of New Interactive Systems for Instant DecisionMaking

Among the subjects which are the focus of the latest research is the growing popularity of automated financial advisor and the next gen systems, which run on real-time intelligence. The literature highlights how AI and automation are incorporated into the business operations of financial services and there is also evidence of the trading performance of robo-advisors during downturns in the market conditions. Developments like these may be the causes of a trend because these approaches are more streamlined and data-driven. Not surprisingly, learned FAs reduce the losses during crises though the bigger implications of such automated technologies lie in diverse areas of practice. To illustrate, the big data packages used in intelligent systems of financial decision-making have set a new standard in business decision accuracy and efficiency [52]. Subsequently, the cryptomanagement concept involves a whole new model of management that consists of a blockchain network for real-time, true-to-life decision-making [53].

4.5.2.1 Major Findings

1. ML and DL are crucial in FinTech, with applications including fraud detection, personalised recommendations, and risk assessment.
2. Implementation issues include data privacy, model interpretability, and regulatory compliance.
3. FinTech's future will be shaped by important themes such as blockchain integration and robot financial advisors.
4. Developing and deploying ML and DL models in FinTech requires ethical considerations and transparent methods.

4.6 CONCLUSION

ML and DL offer substantial prospects for innovation in FinTech, propelling advances in predictive analytics, risk management, and customer service. However, resolving issues of data privacy, interpretability, and regulatory compliance is critical for the proper integration of these technologies. Looking ahead, the incorporation of blockchain and the proliferation of automated financial advisors are expected to significantly disrupt the FinTech scene, emphasising the importance of ethical issues in technology development and implementation.

REFERENCES

1. Lalitha, R. (2021). Ai vs. machine learning vs. deep learning. In *Artificial Intelligence (AI)*, 1st ed., (pp. 73–82). CRC Press. https://doi.org/10.1201/9781003005629
2. Yarali, A. (2022). Applications of Artificial Intelligence, ML, and DL. In *Intelligent Connectivity: AI, IoT, and 5G*, (pp. 279–297). Wiley-IEEE Press. https://doi.org/10.1002/9781119685265.ch16
3. Akila, D., Jeyalaksshmi, S., Padmapriya, D., Prithika, P., & Elangovan, V. R. (2022). Significance of machine learning and deep learning in development of artificial intelligence. In *Multi-Criteria Decision Models in Software Reliability*, Ashish Mishra, Nguyen Thi Dieu Linh, Manish Bhardwaj, Carla M. A. Pinto (eds.), (pp. 25–44). CRC Press.
4. Sharbek, N. (2022). How traditional financial institutions have adapted to artificial intelligence, machine learning and FinTech?. *Proceedings of the International Conference on Business Excellence*, 16(1), 837–848.
5. Mishra, C., & Gupta, D. L. (2017). Deep machine learning and neural networks: An overview. *IAES International Journal of Artificial Intelligence*, 6(2), 66.
6. Nguyen, D. K., Sermpinis, G., & Stasinakis, C. (2023). Big data, artificial intelligence and machine learning: A transformative symbiosis in favour of financial technology. *European Financial Management*, 29(2), 517–548.
7. Gupta, R., Kukreja, G., Gupta, A., & Tyagi, L. (2021). Artificial intelligence fostering fintech: Emerging trends and use cases. In *Cybersecurity in Emerging Digital Era: First International Conference, ICCEDE 2020*, Greater Noida, India, October 9–10, 2020, Revised Selected Papers 1 (pp. 61–73). Springer International Publishing.
8. Alam, N., Gupta, L., Zameni, A., Alam, N., Gupta, L., & Zameni, A. (2019). Fintech emergence and global evolution. In *Fintech and Islamic Finance: Digitalization, Development and Disruption* (pp. 11–35). Palgrave. https://doi.org/10.1007/978-3-030-24666-2
9. Kabulova, J., & Stankevičienė, J. (2020). Valuation of fintech innovation based on patent applications. *Sustainability*, 12(23), 10158.
10. Chen, J. F., Chen, W. L., Huang, C. P., Huang, S. H., & Chen, A. P. (2016). Financial time-series data analysis using deep convolutional neural networks. In *2016 7th International Conference on Cloud Computing and Big Data (CCBD)*, Macau, China, November 16–18, 2016 (pp. 87–92). IEEE.
11. Day, M. Y., Lin, J. T., & Chen, Y. C. (2018). Artificial intelligence for conversational robo-advisor. In *2018 IEEE/ACM International Conference on Advances in Social Networks Analysis and Mining (ASONAM)* (pp. 1057–1064). IEEE. https://doi.org/10.1109/ASONAM.2018.8508269
12. Milojević, N., & Redzepagic, S. (2021). Prospects of artificial intelligence and machine learning application in banking risk management. *Journal of Central Banking Theory and Practice*, 10(3), 41–57.
13. Biju, A. K. V. N., Thomas, A. S., & Thasneem, J. (2023). Examining the research taxonomy of artificial intelligence, deep learning & machine learning in the financial sphere—a bibliometric analysis. *Quality & Quantity*, 58, 1–30.
14. Zhao, B., Wang, R., Cai, Y., & Zhao, E. (2020). Block chain financial transaction using artificial neural network deep learning. *IOP Conference Series: Materials Science and Engineering*, 740(1), 012161.
15. Lestari, N. I., Hussain, W., Merigo, J. M., & Bekhit, M. (2022). A survey of trendy financial sector applications of machine and deep learning. In *EAI International Conference, BigIoT-EDU* (pp. 619–633). Cham: Springer Nature.
16. Lacruz, F., & Saniie, J. (2021). Applications of machine learning in fintech credit card fraud detection. In *2021 IEEE International Conference on Electro Information Technology (EIT)*, Mt. Pleasant, MI, May 14–15, 2021 (pp. 1–6). IEEE.
17. Dabbeeru, R., & Rao, D. N. (2021). Fintech applications in banking and financial services industry in India. Available at SSRN 3881967.

18. Stojanović, B., Božić, J., Hofer-Schmitz, K., Nahrgang, K., Weber, A., Badii, A., … & Runevic, J. (2021). Follow the trail: Machine learning for fraud detection in Fintech applications. *Sensors*, 21(5), 1594.
19. Rao, A., Dagar, V., Sohag, K., Dagher, L., & Tanin, T. I. (2023). Good for the planet, good for the wallet: The ESG impact on financial performance in India. *Finance Research Letters*, 56, 104093.
20. Saini, M., Dhingra, B., & Yadav, M. (2023). ESG risk and financial performance of the Indian financial firms. *International Journal of Governance and Financial Intermediation*, 1(4), 304–314.
21. Maji, S. G., & Lohia, P. (2023). Environmental, social and governance (ESG) performance and firm performance in India. *Society and Business Review*, 18(1), 175–194.
22. Shakil, M. H., Mahmood, N., Tasnia, M., & Munim, Z. H. (2019). Do environmental, social and governance performance affect the financial performance of banks? A cross-country study of emerging market banks. *Management of Environmental Quality: An International Journal*, 30(6), 1331–1344.
23. Gutiérrez-Ponce, H., & Wibowo, S. A. (2023). Do sustainability activities affect the financial performance of banks? The case of Indonesian Banks. *Sustainability*, 15(8), 6892.
24. Luping, S., Lijun, Z., & Ping, W. (2016). A literature review of online personalized recommendations and prospects. *Foreign Economics & Management*, 38(6), 82–99.
25. Das, P., & Singh, V. (2022). Knowing your customers using customer segmentation. In *Computational Methods and Data Engineering: Proceedings of ICCMDE 2021*, Asari, V. K., Singh, V., Rajasekaran, R., & Patel, R. B. (eds.) (pp. 437–451). Singapore: Springer Nature Singapore.
26. Panuš, J., Jonášová, H., Kantorová, K., Doležalová, M., & Horáčková, K. (2016). Customer segmentation utilization for differentiated approach. In *2016 International Conference on Information and Digital Technologies (IDT)*, Rzeszow, Poland, July 5–7, 2016 (pp. 227–233). IEEE.
27. Ballestar, M. T., Grau-Carles, P., & Sainz, J. (2018). Customer segmentation in e-commerce: Applications to the cashback business model. *Journal of Business Research*, 88, 407–414.
28. Derevitskii, I., Severiukhina, O., & Bochenina, K. (2019). Clustering interest graphs for customer segmentation problems. In *2019 Sixth International Conference on Social Networks Analysis, Management and Security (SNAMS)*, Granada, Spain, October 22–25, 2019 (pp. 321–327). IEEE.
29. He, X. (2022). Does utilizing online social relations improve the diversity of personalized recommendations?. *International Journal of Strategic Decision Sciences (IJSDS)*, 13(1), 1–15.
30. Shen, A. (2014). Recommendations as personalized marketing: Insights from customer experiences. *Journal of Services Marketing*, 28(5), 414–427.
31. Analide, F. S. C. (2011). Information asset analysis: Credit scoring and credit suggestion. *International Journal of Electronic Business*, 9(3), 203–218.
32. Tomczak, J. M., & Zięba, M. (2015). Classification restricted Boltzmann machine for comprehensible credit scoring model. *Expert Systems with Applications*, 42(4), 1789–1796.
33. Yu, L., Wang, S., & Lai, K. K. (2009). An intelligent-agent-based fuzzy group decision making model for financial multicriteria decision support: The case of credit scoring. *European Journal of Operational Research*, 195(3), 942–959.
34. Caruso, G., Gattone, S. A., Fortuna, F., & Di Battista, T. (2021). Cluster analysis for mixed data: An application to credit risk evaluation. *Socio-Economic Planning Sciences*, 73, 100850.
35. Aloud, M. E., & Alkhamees, N. (2021). Intelligent algorithmic trading strategy using reinforcement learning and directional change. *IEEE Access*, 9, 114659–114671.

36. Pathak, S., Pawar, A., Taware, S., Kulkarni, S., & Akkalkot, A. (2023). A survey on machine learning algorithms for risk-controlled algorithmic trading. *International Journal of Scientific Research in Science and Technology*, 10, 1069–1089.
37. Jia, X., & Lau, R. Y. K. (2018). The control strategies for high frequency algorithmic trading. In *2018 IEEE 4th International Conference on Control Science and Systems Engineering (ICCSSE)*, Wuhan, China, August 21–23, 2018 (pp. 49–52). IEEE.
38. Lee, J., & Sabbaghi, N. (2020). Multi-objective optimization case study for algorithmic trading strategies in foreign exchange markets. *Digital Finance*, 2(1), 15–37.
39. Badr, Y. (2021). On the integration of artificial intelligence and blockchains 3.0: Prospects and challenges. In *2021 IEEE 18th International Conference on Software Architecture Companion (ICSA-C)*, Stuttgart, Germany, March 22–26, 2021 (pp. 120–120). IEEE.
40. Malik, V., & Singh, S. (2020). Big data computing: Privacy risks management. *Journal of Computational and Theoretical Nanoscience*, 17(5), 2248–2253.
41. Nápoles, G., Salgueiro, Y., Grau, I., & Espinosa, M. L. (2022). Recurrence-aware long-term cognitive network for explainable pattern classification. *IEEE Transactions on Cybernetics*, 53, 6083–6094.
42. Rubinic, I., Kurtov, M., Rubinic, I., Likic, R., Dargan, P. I., & Wood, D. M. (2023). Artificial intelligence in clinical pharmacology: A case study and scoping review of large language models and bioweapon potential. *British Journal of Clinical Pharmacology*, 90(3), 620–628.
43. Kang, Y., Yu, B., & Xu, Z. (2023). Interpretable multi-attribute predictive analysis model based on rough fuzzy sets and logistic regression. IEEE Transactions on Fuzzy Systems, 31, 3522–3532.
44. Cerchione, R., Centobelli, P., & Angelino, A. (2023). Blockchain-based IoT model and experimental platform design in the defence supply chain. *IEEE Internet of Things Journal*. https://doi.org/10.1109/JIOT.2023.3240288
45. Vainio-Pekka, H., Agbese, M. O. O., Jantunen, M., Vakkuri, V., Mikkonen, T., Rousi, R., & Abrahamsson, P. (2023). The role of explainable AI in the research field of AI ethics. *ACM Transactions on Interactive Intelligent Systems*, 13(4), 1–39.
46. Gao, L., & Guan, L. (2023). Interpretability of machine learning: Recent advances and future prospects. IEEE MultiMedia, 30, 105–118.
47. Kuttan, G. O., & Elayidom, M. S. (2023). Review on computer aided breast cancer detection and diagnosis using machine learning methods on mammogram image. *Current Medical Imaging*, 19(12), 1361–1371.
48. Darshan, M., Amet, M., Srivastava, G., & Crichigno, J. (2023). Cross-chain interoperability for next-gen blockchain systems. *IEEE Internet of Things Journal*. https://doi.org/10.1109/JIOT.2023.3279693
49. Zantalis, F., Koulouras, G., & Karabetsos, S. (2023). Blockchain technology: A framework for endless applications. *IEEE Consumer Electronics Magazine*, 13, 61–71.
50. Chavhan, S., Kumar, S., Tiwari, P., Liang, X., Lee, I. H., & Muhammad, K. (2023). Edge-enabled blockchain-based V2X scheme for secure communication within the smart city development. *IEEE Internet of Things Journal*, 10, 21282–21293.
51. Djenouri, Y., Yazidi, A., Srivastava, G., & Lin, J. C. W. (2023). Blockchain: Applications, challenges, and opportunities in consumer electronics. *IEEE Consumer Electronics Magazine*, 13, 36–41.
52. Tong, D., & Tian, G. (2023). Intelligent financial decision support system based on big data. *Journal of Intelligent Systems*, 32(1), 20220320.
53. Wang, G., Li, J., Wang, X., Li, J., Yuan, Y., & Wang, F. Y. (2022). Blockchain-based crypto management for reliable real-time decision-making. *IEEE Transactions on Computational Social Systems*, 10, 3333–3342.

5 Synergy in Finance
Humans and AI Reshaping Fintech

Arvind Nath Sinha and Nivedita Singh

> Ignoring technological change in the financial system based upon technology is like a mouse starving to death because someone moved their cheese
>
> **Chris Skinner**
> *Digital Transformation and Fintech Expert*

5.1 INTRODUCTION

Top managements are used to being in the hot seat. Only the most difficult issues come across their desks, and an organization's destiny is frequently determined by how those issues are resolved. One of these pivotal occasions could be the way in which leaders decide to use generative AI. Putting money into this novel technology wisely could give you a competitive edge that yields enormous returns. However, placing the incorrect wagers could lead to issues with data privacy, legal ramifications, and a plethora of other ethical dilemmas.

Artificial intelligence is shaping the blueprint of the evolving Fintech industry. The financial technology sector, or Fintech, is undergoing a revolution unlike any it has seen before. This transformation is driven by the ever-growing influence of Artificial Intelligence (AI). AI is no longer a futuristic concept in Fintech; it's rapidly becoming an integral part of the industry, permeating everything from automating mundane back-office tasks to personalizing customer interactions in real time. Employees and customers constitute the majority of the human spectrum for Fintech industry. This chapter delves into the evolving relationship between humans and AI within the Fintech industry. We will explore how this dynamic collaboration is reshaping the way people work and how customers experience financial services.

AI's infiltration into Fintech is multifaceted, significantly impacting both the workforce and customer experience. Repetitive tasks like data entry, reconciliation, and basic customer service inquiries are being automated, streamlining workflows, freeing human resources for complex tasks requiring judgement and analysis [1–3]. This not only allows for faster processing times but also fosters a superior customer experience through personalized financial products, 24/7 support via AI-powered chatbots, and enhanced security with AI-driven fraud detection.

DOI: 10.1201/9781003645849-5

However, the impact of AI extends beyond mere automation. AI acts as a powerful tool for augmenting human capabilities within the Fintech industry. AI algorithms can analyze vast datasets to identify trends, patterns, and insights that would be difficult, if not impossible, for humans to detect on their own [4,5]. These data-driven insights provide valuable information to financial professionals, allowing them to make more informed decisions in areas like risk assessments, fraud detection, and personalized recommendations for customers.

The transformation of the Fintech workforce is a direct consequence of this human-AI collaboration. As AI takes over repetitive tasks, the skillsets required for success in the industry are changing. While some roles may be completely replaced by automation, many more will require adaptation and collaboration with AI tools. This necessitates a new approach to talent development within Fintech organizations. Upskilling and reskilling initiatives are crucial for equipping existing employees with the necessary skills to thrive in this evolving technological landscape. Additionally, fostering a culture of continuous learning and adaptation is essential for employees to embrace the changing nature of work and work effectively alongside AI colleagues [6,7]. Clear communication plans should also be implemented to address employee concerns about job displacement and provide transparency about the future of work in the Fintech sector.

On the customer experience side of the equation, AI is revolutionizing how people interact with financial services. We are witnessing the rise of intelligent self-service portals, virtual assistants powered by AI, and chatbots that can handle basic customer inquiries and requests around the clock [8,9]. These AI-driven solutions offer several advantages for customers, including 24/7 availability, faster resolution times, and the potential for more personalized interactions. For instance, AI-powered chatbots can personalize responses based on a customer's past interactions and financial profile, offering a more tailored and relevant experience.

However, it is important to acknowledge that AI-driven customer service is not without its drawbacks. One potential concern is the lack of empathy inherent in AI interactions. While AI chatbots can provide quick and efficient solutions, they may struggle to understand the nuances of human emotions and provide the same level of empathy as a human customer service representative. Additionally, data privacy remains a critical consideration in the age of AI-powered customer experiences [10,11]. As AI algorithms gather and analyze vast amounts of customer data, ensuring the security and responsible use of this data is paramount.

AI improves how corporations communicate with customers very simply outlined by chatbots and virtual assistants to supply the comfort of 24/7 client support and offer a level of personalization and treatments to the overall query whereas at a similar instance operational around key challenges like getting the ability to promptly learn from empathetic behaviors of human client assistance members. The chapter continues to analyze hyper-personalization in Financial Services, Robo-Advisory, and securing transactions using AI (Figure 5.1).

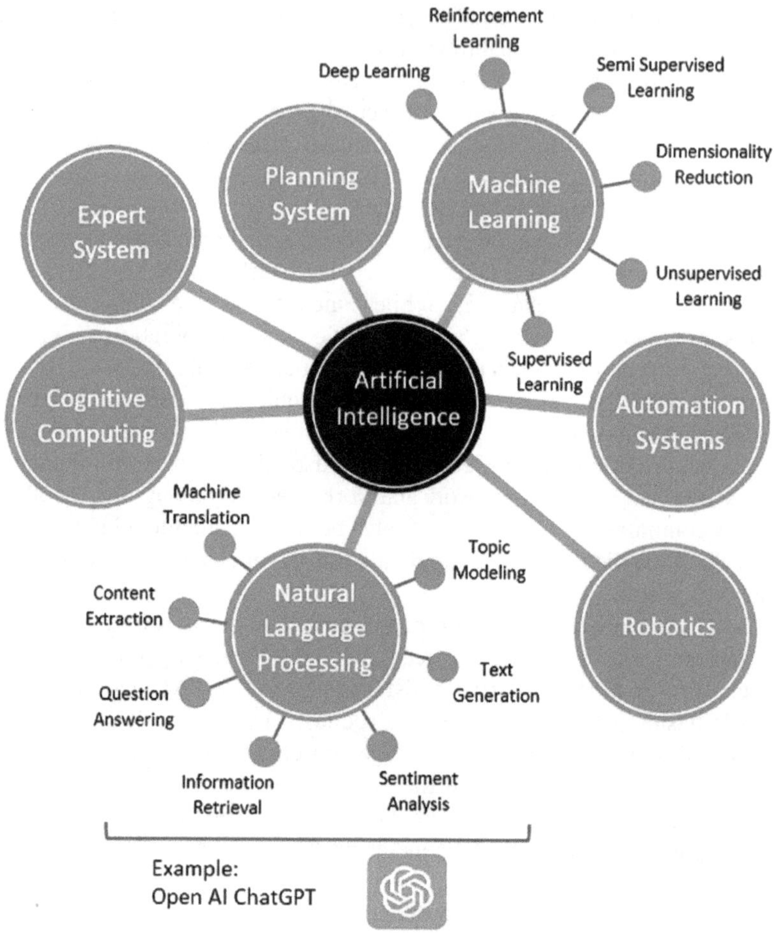

FIGURE 5.1 What is artificial intelligence? (Source: Khosravi, T., Al Sudani, Z.M., & Oladnabi, M. (2023). To What Extent Does ChatGPT Understand Genetics? *Innovations in Education and Teaching International*, 1–10. https://doi.org/10.1080/14703297.2023.2258842.)

5.1.1 Key Considerations for Using Artificial Intelligence

The tech experts encourage F&A decision makers to keep these considerations in mind when applying this new technology:

- **Be responsible custodians of these financial insights:** Maintain engagement as AI models become active contributors in analyzing and crafting narratives regarding financial performance. The importance of human oversight will grow significantly, particularly given the rapid adoption of technology by certain finance and accounting teams, whether as standalone models or integrated into routine financial processes. Ensuring a human layer of validation and final approval for each transaction or report generated will be essential. Anticipate and prepare to address inquiries from stakeholders regarding AI-generated content.

- **Utilize the perspective of controllership:** In finance and accounting, risk management and controls are essential. Although the accuracy of these solutions is constantly enhancing, it's vital for operators to consistently apply the controllership perspective to each evaluated use case. They must assess risks, materiality, and potential financial exposure that may affect their operations. Operators should verify and validate the accuracy and completeness of both inputs and outputs. As with any emerging technology, it's important to align use cases with key control matrices to foresee its effects.
- **Establishing internal business partnerships is crucial:** Analysis and reporting are among the most affected domains, with a surge in self-service solutions expected across enterprises. This might entice certain business leaders to exclusively depend on novel and seemingly intelligent AI-powered advisors for decision-making (and some may circumvent the F&A department or presume that the information provided has already undergone Finance's scrutiny). Building alliances between Finance and other business units can pose challenges, so it's important to identify the internal stakeholders who will be affected and strategize to foster trust and collaboration from the outset.

5.1.2 Patterns of Artificial Intelligence

From autonomous vehicles, predictive analytics applications, facial recognition, to chatbots, virtual assistants, cognitive automation, and fraud detection, the breadth of AI applications is vast. However, irrespective of the specific application, there's a common thread among all of them. Organizations with extensive experience in implementing numerous AI projects have come to understand that despite the diversity in application, AI use cases can be categorized into one or more of seven common patterns as discussed in a report by Forbesi.e. hyper-personalization implying treating each customer as an individual; autonomous system to reduce manual work; using past and existing behaviors to predict future outcomes by deploying machine learning and other cognitive approaches; more and more human-like conversation like communication and interactions between humans and machines; enhanced capabilities to identify outliers and anomalies in existing data with AI; use of deep learning to have accurate recognition of image, video, audio or objects; goal-driven system pattern or enhanced ability to solve puzzles. Any tailored strategy for AI implementation necessitates unique programming and pattern development. However, regardless of how these trends are combined, they all adhere to a fairly standard set of rules. These seven patterns are then individually applied or combined in different permutations based on the specific solution for which AI is being utilized.

5.2 REDEFINING THE FINTECH WORKFORCE: HUMANS AND AI – A COLLABORATIVE FUTURE

The evolving human-AI relationship in Fintech is significantly impacting the way people work within the industry. AI is not simply replacing human workers; it's reshaping the roles and responsibilities of the Fintech workforce. This section delves into the concept of automation and task augmentation, exploring how AI is transforming various tasks and workflows. We will examine real-life case studies that illustrate the practical applications of AI in Fintech and their impact on the workforce.

5.2.1 Automation and Task Augmentation: AI's Growing Role in Fintech Operations

One of the most significant effects of AI in Fintech is the automation of repetitive and rules-based tasks. These tasks, often manual and time-consuming, can be efficiently handled by AI algorithms, freeing up human resources to focus on higher-level cognitive functions. A study by McKinsey & Company estimates that up to 80% of activities in financial services could be automated by 2030, with significant implications for workforce composition.

Fraudulent transactions pose a major threat to financial institutions and their customers. Traditionally, fraud detection relied on rule-based systems that monitored for specific patterns in transactions. However, with the increasing sophistication of fraud tactics, these systems often struggled to keep pace. **Capital One**, a leading financial services company, implemented a machine learning-based fraud detection system in 2018. This system analyzes real-time transaction data to identify anomalies and suspicious patterns. By leveraging AI, Capital One has significantly reduced fraudulent transactions while minimizing false positives. This case study exemplifies how AI can automate the task of fraud detection, allowing human analysts to focus on investigating complex cases and improving the overall fraud detection system.

5.2.1.1 Beyond Automation: AI as a Powerful Augmentation Tool

While automation is a crucial aspect of AI's impact, it's important to understand that AI is not simply replacing human workers. Instead, AI acts as a powerful tool for augmenting human capabilities within the Fintech industry. AI algorithms excel at analyzing vast datasets and identifying trends and patterns that would be difficult, if not impossible, for humans to detect on their own. This allows financial professionals to make more informed decisions in various areas, such as:

- **Risk assessment:** AI can analyze credit history, financial statements, and other data points to create more accurate risk profiles for loan applications and investments. This allows financial institutions to make better lending decisions and manage risk more effectively [9].
- **Investment strategies:** AI algorithms can analyze market trends, news feeds, and social media data to identify potential investment opportunities. While human expertise remains crucial for portfolio management, AI can provide valuable insights to inform investment decisions [8].

- **Personalized recommendations:** AI can analyze customer data to personalize financial products and services. For instance, AI-powered tools can recommend personalized investment portfolios or credit cards based on a customer's financial goals and risk tolerance [12].

5.2.1.2 AI-Powered Wealth Management at Morgan Stanley

Morgan Stanley, the leading investment bank, has implemented a suite of AI-powered tools to enhance its wealth management services. These tools utilize machine learning algorithms to analyze customer data and market trends, providing financial advisors with personalized insights and recommendations for their clients. This allows advisors to spend less time on data analysis and more time building relationships and providing tailored financial advice to their clients.

The caselet above highlights how AI is automating routine tasks and augmenting human decision-making within Fintech. As AI continues to evolve, we can expect its impact on the Fintech workforce to deepen. However, this doesn't necessarily translate to job displacement. With proper training and reskilling initiatives, human workers can learn to collaborate effectively with AI tools, leveraging their unique capabilities to achieve optimal results.

5.2.1.3 Moving Forward: The Importance of Upskilling and Reskilling

The transformation of the Fintech workforce necessitates a proactive approach from organizations. Upskilling and reskilling initiatives are crucial for equipping existing employees with the necessary skills to thrive in this evolving technological landscape. These initiatives may focus on areas like:

- **Data analysis:** Understanding how to interpret data visualizations and extract insights from AI-generated reports.
- **Machine learning fundamentals:** Gaining a basic understanding of machine learning concepts and how AI algorithms work.
- **Problem-solving and critical thinking:** Developing strong analytical and problem-solving skills to collaborate effectively with AI tools.

By embracing automation and task augmentation through AI, Fintech organizations can streamline operations, increase efficiency, and enhance customer experiences. However, maximizing the benefits of AI requires a workforce equipped with the skills to collaborate effectively with these intelligent systems. The future of the Fintech workforce lies in fostering a human-AI partnership, where humans and AI leverage their unique strengths to drive innovation and success in the financial services industry.

5.2.2 Areas of Fastest and Deepest AI Impact: Reshaping Fintech Job Roles

As AI continues to evolve, its impact on the Fintech workforce will vary across different functions and roles. Some areas within Fintech are experiencing a faster and deeper adoption of AI, leading to significant automation and reshaping of job roles.

Let's explore some of the functions most susceptible to AI disruption and examine the potential consequences for specific job titles.

1. **Back-office operations: Streamlining processes with AI automation**

   Back-office operations within Fintech institutions encompass a wide range of administrative tasks such as loan processing, account management, and regulatory compliance. These tasks are often repetitive, data-driven, and rule-based, making them prime candidates for automation with AI.

   Avant, a leading online lending platform, implemented a suite of AI-powered tools to automate loan processing. This system utilizes machine learning algorithms to analyze customer data and assess creditworthiness. By automating loan processing steps like document verification and eligibility checks, Avant has significantly reduced processing times and improved efficiency.

   The automation of back-office tasks through AI is likely to impact roles like loan processors, underwriters, and data entry clerks. While some of these positions may be eliminated completely, others will require adaptation. For instance, loan processors may transition to roles focused on managing complex loan applications or handling customer inquiries related to AI-generated decisions.
2. **Data analysis: From manual interpretation to AI-driven insights**

   Financial data analysis plays a critical role in various Fintech functions, including risk management, fraud detection, and investment research. Traditionally, this analysis relied on human analysts sifting through vast amounts of data to identify trends and patterns. However, AI algorithms are revolutionizing data analysis by enabling faster processing, deeper insights, and the ability to handle complex datasets that would be overwhelming for human analysts.

   A 2023 report by PwC titled "Artificial Intelligence in Risk Management" highlights the growing adoption of AI in financial institutions for risk assessment. The report mentions that AI can analyze vast amounts of financial data, including credit histories, market trends, and social media sentiment, to predict potential risks with greater accuracy.

   The rise of AI in data analysis will likely impact roles like financial analysts, risk analysts, and quantitative analysts. While the demand for these skills may not disappear entirely, the focus will likely shift towards interpreting AI-generated insights and using them to inform decision-making. Additionally, new roles may emerge that specialize in working with AI tools and extracting maximum value from their data analysis capabilities.
3. **Algorithmic trading: AI-powered decisions at high speed**

   Algorithmic trading, also known as high-frequency trading (HFT), utilizes computer programs to execute trades on financial markets at lightning speeds. While algorithmic trading has been around for decades, AI is introducing a new level of sophistication. AI algorithms can analyze market data in real time, identify complex patterns, and execute trades based on these insights much faster than human traders.

AlphaGo Zero poses a suitable example of Algorithmic Trading. In 2016, DeepMind's AI program AlphaGo Zero defeated the world champion in the complex game of Go. This event showcased the power of AI in learning and making strategic decisions. While AlphaGo Zero itself isn't directly used in trading, its underlying technology and advancements in deep learning are inspiring the development of AI-powered trading algorithms that can analyze market dynamics and make investment decisions with remarkable speed and accuracy.

The increasing role of AI in algorithmic trading is likely to impact roles like high-frequency traders and quantitative analysts focused on short-term trading strategies. However, human expertise will likely remain crucial in areas like overall portfolio management, risk management, and setting trading parameters for AI algorithms.

5.2.2.1 Beyond Automation: The Evolving Landscape of Fintech Jobs

While AI is automating tasks across various Fintech functions, it's important to remember that this doesn't necessarily translate to widespread job displacement. Instead, AI is creating a new landscape where human and machine capabilities are combined for optimal results. New roles are emerging that require a blend of technical skills, data analysis expertise, and the ability to collaborate effectively with AI tools. Here are some examples:

- **AI specialists:** These professionals will possess expertise in AI technologies, machine learning algorithms, and their applications within the Fintech industry. They may be responsible for developing and maintaining AI systems, ensuring data quality, and troubleshooting technical issues.
- **Human-AI collaboration specialists:** These roles will focus on bridging the gap between human and AI capabilities. They will need strong communication skills to explain complex AI-generated insights to stakeholders and ensure that AI systems are used ethically and responsibly.
- **Data storytellers:** This role will involve translating complex financial data and AI-generated insights into clear and actionable narratives

5.2.3 New Skillsets, Reskilling, and Smoothening the Transition: Equipping the Workforce for the Future

The transformation of the Fintech workforce driven by AI necessitates a proactive approach from organizations. While some job roles may be automated, many more will require adaptation and collaboration with AI tools. The World Economic Forum's "Future of Jobs Report 2020" highlights the importance of clear communication and collaboration between employers and employees during automation transitions. The report emphasizes the need for proactive reskilling and upskilling initiatives to prepare the workforce for the future.

By fostering a culture of continuous learning, open communication, and investment in upskilling and reskilling initiatives, Fintech organizations can empower their workforce to adapt and thrive in the AI era. This collaborative approach will ensure a smooth transition towards an AI-powered future where human and machine capabilities complement each other for accelerated performance.

To ensure a smooth transition and equip employees with the skills needed to thrive in this evolving landscape, Fintech organizations need to invest in upskilling and reskilling initiatives. Additionally, fostering a culture of continuous learning and open communication is crucial for managing anxieties around job displacement and building trust in the future of work.

5.2.3.1 Upskilling and Reskilling Programs: Equipping Employees for the AI Age

Upskilling and reskilling initiatives focus on equipping existing employees with the necessary skills to adapt to the changing demands of their roles. These programs can provide employees with the knowledge and expertise to work effectively alongside AI tools and contribute meaningfully in an AI-driven environment. Figure 5.2 depicts some key areas where upskilling and reskilling efforts can be targeted:

Data analysis and interpretation: As AI generates vast amounts of data and insights, the ability to interpret data visualizations, extract meaningful information, and translate it into actionable strategies becomes crucial. Training programs can equip employees with essential data analysis skills, including using data visualization tools and understanding statistical concepts.

- **Machine learning fundamentals:** A basic understanding of machine learning concepts and how AI algorithms work empowers employees to collaborate effectively with these intelligent systems. Training programs can introduce employees to machine learning terminology, common algorithms used in Fintech, and potential biases to be aware of.
- **Problem-solving and critical thinking:** AI excels at automating tasks, but human expertise remains essential for tackling complex problems, identifying unexpected situations, and making high-stakes decisions. Upskilling initiatives can focus on enhancing problem-solving and critical thinking skills to allow employees to leverage their unique strengths alongside AI.
- **Communication and soft skills:** The ability to clearly explain complex financial concepts and build trust with clients remains paramount, even in

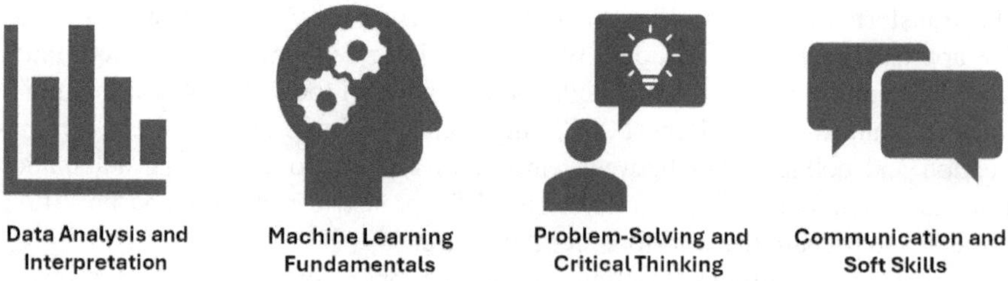

FIGURE 5.2 Key areas for upskilling and reskilling. (Created by authors.)

an AI-driven environment. Refining communication skills and fostering empathy becomes even more critical as human interaction takes on a more advisory role.

Barclays Bank, a leading financial institution, launched its AI Skills Academy in 2020. This program offers employees training modules on various AI-related topics, including machine learning, data science, and responsible AI practices. By equipping its workforce with the necessary skills, Barclays aims to empower employees to embrace AI and contribute to its successful integration within the organization.

5.2.3.2 Fostering a Culture of Continuous Learning: Embracing Lifelong Learning

The pace of technological change within Fintech is rapid, necessitating a culture of continuous learning within organizations. This culture encourages employees to stay updated on the latest advancements in AI and related technologies. Here are some strategies to promote continuous learning:

- **Internal knowledge sharing sessions:** Organizing regular workshops and seminars led by internal AI specialists can foster knowledge sharing and keep employees informed about the latest AI trends and applications within Fintech.
- **Encouraging participation in external training programs:** Providing financial assistance or flexible work arrangements to support employees pursuing external training programs or certifications in AI-related fields demonstrates an organization's commitment to continuous learning and employee development.
- **Building learning communities:** Creating online forums or communities of practice dedicated to AI and Fintech can provide a platform for employees to discuss challenges, share resources, and learn from each other's experiences.

5.2.3.3 Transparency and Communication: Addressing Employee Concerns

The rise of AI can understandably lead to anxieties among employees about potential job losses. To manage these concerns and build trust, organizations need to implement clear communication plans. These plans should address the following aspects:

- **The role of AI:** Clearly communicate how AI will be used within the organization and its intended impact on various job roles. Emphasize AI's role as a collaborative tool rather than a replacement for human workers.
- **Reskilling and upskilling opportunities:** Outline the organization's commitment to providing employees with the necessary training and support to adapt and thrive in the changing environment.
- **Career development pathways:** Offer guidance and support to employees seeking to transition to new roles within the organization as a result of AI implementation.

5.3 REIMAGINING CUSTOMER EXPERIENCES

It proves without question that the COVID-19 pandemic has accelerated the need for Artificial Intelligence (AI) in the customer service industry as organizations around the world look for real-time information access to their customers. AI is transforming the way companies interact with people – both internally and externally.

5.3.1 AI-Powered Customer Service

The rise of AI in Fintech is not only transforming internal operations but also revolutionizing customer experiences. Traditional customer service models, often reliant on phone calls and limited operating hours, are evolving to embrace the power of AI-powered solutions. Chatbots, virtual assistants, and intelligent self-service portals are increasingly becoming the first line of defence for customer inquiries within the Fintech industry.

5.3.1.1 AI-Powered Chatbots: Always Available, Always Helpful

Chatbots are computer programs that simulate conversation with human users. Within Fintech, AI-powered chatbots are transforming customer service by offering 24/7 availability, immediate responses to basic inquiries, and the ability to handle multiple conversations simultaneously.

JPMorgan Chase, a leading financial institution, has implemented an AI chatbot named "KAI" to assist customers with various banking tasks. KAI can answer frequently asked questions, troubleshoot technical issues, and even schedule appointments. By providing 24/7 support and automating basic inquiries, KAI has helped JPMorgan Chase streamline customer service operations and improve customer satisfaction.

5.3.1.2 Virtual Assistants: Personalized Guidance at Your Fingertips

Virtual assistants take AI-powered interaction a step further, offering a more personalized customer experience. These intelligent assistants can leverage customer data and past interactions to provide tailored support and recommendations.

Charles Schwab, a prominent investment firm, utilizes an AI-powered virtual assistant that goes beyond answering basic questions. This virtual assistant can analyze a customer's investment portfolio and offer personalized advice based on their financial goals and risk tolerance. By leveraging AI, Charles Schwab empowers customers with personalized guidance, fostering a deeper level of engagement.

5.3.1.3 Intelligent Self-Service Portals: Empowering Customers with Self-Reliance

AI is also transforming self-service portals within Fintech. These portals are no longer static repositories of information; they are becoming intelligent platforms that can anticipate customer needs and guide them through complex tasks.

For instance, an AI-powered self-service portal can walk a customer step-by-step through the loan application process, highlighting relevant information and addressing potential concerns proactively. This empowers customers to resolve issues independently while still providing access to human support when needed.

5.3.1.3.1 The Benefits of AI-Powered Customer Service

The implementation of AI-powered customer service solutions within Fintech offers several advantages:

- **24/7 availability:** Customers can receive assistance with their inquiries anytime, anywhere, regardless of time zone or business hours.
- **Faster resolution times:** AI chatbots and virtual assistants can address basic questions and resolve simple issues quickly, improving customer satisfaction and reducing wait times.
- **Personalized interactions:** AI-powered tools can leverage customer data to offer tailored support and recommendations, fostering a more engaging customer experience.

5.3.1.3.2 Addressing the Drawbacks: The Human Touch Still Matters

While AI-powered customer service offers significant benefits, there are also potential drawbacks to consider.

- **Lack of empathy:** AI systems can struggle to understand the nuances of human emotions and respond with empathy in complex situations.
- **Need for human oversight:** AI chatbots and virtual assistants may not be able to handle all customer inquiries effectively. In such cases, it's crucial to have human agents readily available to provide assistance.

The key lies in striking a balance between AI automation and the human touch. By leveraging AI for its strengths in efficiency and availability, while ensuring human oversight for empathy and complex issues, Fintech organizations can create a seamless and positive customer experience [10,11].

5.3.2 AI for Personalization and Financial Advisory Services

5.3.2.1 Hyper-Personalization Through AI: Tailored Solutions for Every Customer

Beyond offering efficient customer service, AI is revolutionizing how Fintech institutions approach customer relationships. By leveraging vast amounts of customer data, AI algorithms can personalize financial products and recommendations to an unprecedented degree. This hyper-personalization allows Fintech companies to cater to individual needs and preferences, fostering deeper customer engagement and loyalty.

5.3.2.1.1 Understanding Customer Needs with AI Analytics

AI algorithms can analyze a wide range of customer data points, including transaction history, financial goals, risk tolerance, and even social media behavior (with consent). By analyzing these data sets, AI can create a comprehensive customer profile, enabling a deeper understanding of individual financial needs and aspirations.

5.3.2.1.2.1 Example Nubank's AI-Powered Credit Card Recommendations Nubank, a leading digital bank in Brazil, utilizes AI to personalize credit card recommendations for its customers. Their AI system considers a customer's financial history, spending habits, and income to suggest the most suitable credit card with optimal rewards and interest rates. This hyper-personalized approach has contributed to Nubank's remarkable customer growth and high satisfaction rates.

5.3.2.1.2 AI-Powered Recommendations: From Generic to Personalized

Traditionally, financial institutions offered a limited set of products and services. With AI, recommendations can be tailored to each customer's unique financial situation. For instance, an AI system may recommend a high-yield savings account to a customer with a significant emergency fund, or suggest robo-advisory services to someone interested in automated investment strategies.

5.3.2.1.2.1 Benefits of Hyper-Personalization in Fintech Hyper-personalization through AI offers several benefits for both customers and Fintech institutions:

- **Increased customer satisfaction:** By receiving financial products and recommendations tailored to their needs, customers are more likely to be satisfied and feel valued by their financial institution.
- **Improved customer engagement:** Personalized communication and offerings can lead to deeper customer engagement, fostering long-term loyalty.
- **Enhanced revenue opportunities:** By recommending relevant products and services, Fintech companies can potentially increase revenue streams.

5.3.2.1.3 Challenges and Considerations

While hyper-personalization offers significant advantages, there are also challenges to consider:

- **Data privacy concerns:** It's crucial for Fintech institutions to ensure responsible data collection practices and obtain explicit customer consent for using their data for personalization purposes.
- **Algorithmic bias:** There is a potential for AI algorithms to perpetuate biases based on the data they are trained on. It's essential to implement robust data governance and fairness checks to mitigate this risk.

By addressing these challenges and using AI responsibly, Fintech institutions can leverage hyper-personalization to create a customer-centric experience that fosters trust, loyalty, and sustainable growth.

5.3.2.2 Robo-Advisory and AI-Powered Financial Advice: Democratizing Wealth Management

The rise of AI in Fintech has significantly impacted the world of wealth management. Robo-advisors, automated platforms that utilize AI algorithms to manage investments, are making financial planning more accessible and affordable for a wider range of individuals.

5.3.2.2.1 *AI-Powered Investment Strategies*

Robo-advisors leverage AI algorithms to analyze market trends, assess risk tolerance, and create personalized investment portfolios for their clients. These algorithms can process vast amounts of data in real time, allowing them to identify investment opportunities and make adjustments to portfolios based on changing market conditions.

Betterment, a leading robo-advisor, utilizes AI through its "Smart Saver" feature. This AI tool analyzes a customer's income and spending habits to automatically transfer funds into a savings account, helping them achieve their financial goals faster. Betterment's AI capabilities demonstrate how robo-advisors are going beyond basic portfolio management and providing holistic financial planning assistance.

5.3.2.2.2 *Robo-Advisory: A Boon for Millennial Investors*

The affordability and accessibility of robo-advisors are particularly attractive to younger generations like millennials. Many millennials may not have the resources to hire a traditional human financial advisor, and robo-advisors offer a lower-cost alternative with a user-friendly interface.

5.3.2.2.2.1 Benefits of AI-Powered Wealth Management AI-powered wealth management through robo-advisors offers several advantages:

- **Reduced costs:** Robo-advisors typically charge lower fees compared to traditional human advisors, making wealth management more accessible to a wider audience.
- **Automated portfolio management:** AI algorithms can handle routine tasks like rebalancing portfolios and managing risk, freeing up clients to focus on their long-term financial goals.
- **Data-driven investment decisions:** AI-powered analysis allows for objective and unbiased investment decisions based on market data and client risk tolerance.

5.3.2.2.2.2 Addressing Concerns: Data Privacy and the Human Touch Despite the benefits, some concerns surround AI-powered wealth management:

- **Data privacy:** Robo-advisors rely on significant amounts of client data to personalize investment strategies. It's crucial for these platforms to implement robust security measures and ensure transparent data privacy practices.
- **The human touch:** While AI excels at data analysis and automation, complex financial situations may still require the expertise and nuanced judgment of a human advisor.

5.3.2.3 The Future: A Collaborative Approach

The future of wealth management likely lies in a collaborative approach between AI and human advisors. Robo-advisors can handle automated tasks and provide data-driven insights, while human advisors can offer personalized guidance, emotional intelligence, and address clients' unique needs and concerns.

5.3.3 Frictionless Transactions and Increased Security: A Winning Combination

AI is not only personalizing interactions but also streamlining financial transactions within Fintech. By leveraging biometric authentication, voice recognition, and predictive analytics, AI is contributing to a future of frictionless and secure financial experiences.

5.3.3.1 Biometric Authentication: Convenience and Security

Biometric authentication utilizes unique physical characteristics like fingerprints, facial recognition, or iris scans to verify a user's identity. This technology, powered by AI, offers a more secure and convenient alternative to traditional password-based authentication methods.

Axis Bank, a leading Indian private bank, has implemented an AI-powered "Happy Hours" feature within its mobile banking app. This feature utilizes facial recognition technology to allow customers to log in and perform secure transactions without entering a password during designated hours. This innovative approach demonstrates how AI can enhance convenience while maintaining robust security measures.

5.3.3.2 Voice Recognition: Conversational Banking at Your Fingertips

AI-powered voice assistants are transforming how customers interact with their finances. These assistants can be used to check account balances, transfer funds, and even pay bills simply through voice commands.

HDFC Bank, another major Indian financial institution, offers a virtual assistant named "EVA" powered by AI. EVA can answer customer queries about account information and transactions and even provide personalized financial recommendations using natural language processing. This voice-based interface allows for a more conversational and convenient banking experience.

5.3.3.3 Predictive Analytics: Preventing Fraud Before It Happens

AI algorithms excel at analyzing vast amounts of data to identify patterns and predict potential threats. In the context of Fintech, AI-powered fraud detection systems can analyze transaction data in real-time to identify suspicious activity and prevent fraudulent transactions.

For instance, AI can analyze spending habits and flag transactions that deviate significantly from a customer's normal spending patterns. This proactive approach to fraud detection helps safeguard both customers and financial institutions.

5.3.3.3.1 The Future of Secure Transactions: A Symbiotic Relationship

As AI continues to evolve, we can expect even more sophisticated methods for secure and frictionless transactions. The future likely lies in a symbiotic relationship between AI and human expertise. While AI excels at data analysis and real-time threat detection, human oversight remains crucial for investigating complex fraud cases and implementing appropriate security protocols.

By leveraging AI for its strengths in automation and data analysis, Fintech institutions can create a secure and convenient financial experience for their customers, fostering trust and loyalty in the digital age.

5.4 THE CHANGING LANDSCAPE FOR SPECIFIC ROLES: NAVIGATING THE HUMAN-AI COLLABORATION

The rise of AI within Fintech is impacting specific job roles across the industry. While some tasks may become automated, these changes are prompting an evolution in skillsets and a shift towards human-AI collaboration. Let's delve deeper into how specific roles are adapting to this evolving landscape.

5.4.1 Financial Analysts: From Data Crunchers to Data Interpreters

Traditionally, financial analysts have spent a significant amount of time gathering and analyzing financial data. AI can automate these tasks, freeing up financial analysts to focus on higher-order functions like interpreting complex data sets, identifying trends, and providing strategic insights to inform business decisions [3,13]

- **Evolving skillset:** Financial analysts of the future will need a strong foundation in data science and machine learning to effectively utilize AI-generated reports and translate data insights into actionable recommendations.

5.4.2 Loan Officers: Streamlined Processes and Personalized Risk Assessment

AI can significantly streamline the loan application process by automating tasks like document verification and initial creditworthiness checks. Loan officers can then leverage AI powered risk assessment tools to make faster and more informed lending decisions while focusing on building relationships with potential borrowers and providing personalized guidance throughout the loan process [14,15]. A range of studies have explored the use of AI-powered risk assessment tools in lending decisions. Lee (2012) and Thiel (2019) both highlight the potential for these tools to improve the speed and accuracy of lending processes, with Thiel specifically noting the superiority of AI models over traditional ones. Wu (2022) further supports this, demonstrating the effectiveness of the random forest technique in predicting loan default. Taremian (2011) introduces a Hybrid Intelligent Decision Support System for credit risk assessment, which combines neural networks and genetic algorithms to enhance precision and sensitivity in evaluating high-risk customers and high-value loans. These studies collectively underscore the potential of AI-powered tools to enhance lending decisions, particularly in terms of speed, accuracy, and personalized guidance.

- **Evolving skillset:** Loan officers will need strong communication and interpersonal skills to build rapport with clients. Additionally, the ability to explain complex financial concepts and navigate AI-powered risk assessments will be crucial.

5.4.3 Wealth Managers: From Portfolio Management to Holistic Financial Planning

AI-powered robo-advisors can handle automated portfolio management tasks. This allows human wealth managers to shift their focus towards providing holistic financial planning services, tailoring investment strategies to clients' unique needs and goals, and offering guidance on areas like retirement planning and estate planning [12,16].

- **Evolving skillset:** Wealth managers will require expertise in behavioral finance and financial planning strategies in addition to traditional investment knowledge. Strong emotional intelligence and client communication skills will also be essential for building trust and long-term relationships with clients.

5.4.3.1 Continuous Learning: The Key to Success

Regardless of specific roles, continuous learning and upskilling will be paramount for all Fintech professionals to thrive in the AI-powered future. Organizations should offer training programs in data analysis, machine learning fundamentals, and human-AI collaboration to equip their workforce with the necessary skillsets.

5.4.3.2 The Future: A Symphony of Human Expertise and AI Capabilities

The evolving landscape of Fintech does not necessitate a complete replacement of human roles by AI. Instead, we are witnessing a shift towards a collaborative environment where humans and AI work together to achieve optimal results. By embracing upskilling initiatives, fostering collaboration, and focusing on human strengths, Fintech professionals can navigate the changing landscape and contribute to a more innovative and successful future for the industry.

5.5 THE FUTURE OF WORK IN FINTECH: A HUMAN-AI COLLABORATION LANDSCAPE

While AI is automating tasks and reshaping job roles in Fintech, a more nuanced picture emerges when considering the long-term trends. The future of work in this sector is likely to be characterized by a collaborative landscape where humans and AI work together to achieve optimal results. Here, we explore some potential long-term trends and the emergence of new job opportunities within this evolving ecosystem.

5.5.1 The Rise of Human-AI Collaboration

AI excels at tasks requiring data analysis, pattern recognition, and repetitive processes. However, human expertise remains crucial in areas like complex decision-making, creative problem-solving, and building trust with clients. The future of Fintech work lies in fostering a collaborative environment where humans and AI leverage each other's strengths [17–19].

- **Human expertise in the AI lifecycle:** Humans will be essential throughout the AI lifecycle, from defining business problems and selecting appropriate datasets to validating AI outputs and ensuring ethical considerations are addressed.
- **Focus on soft skills and emotional intelligence:** As AI handles routine tasks, human roles will increasingly emphasize soft skills like communication, empathy, and the ability to build strong relationships with clients.

5.5.2 New Job Opportunities in the Evolving Fintech Landscape

While some jobs may be automated, the rise of AI is also creating new opportunities within Fintech. Here are some potential areas for future job growth:

- **AI specialists:** As AI adoption increases, there will be a growing demand for specialists who develop, maintain, and troubleshoot AI systems within Fintech institutions [4,20].
- **Data storytellers:** The ability to translate complex data insights generated by AI into clear and actionable narratives will be a valuable skill for communicating with various stakeholders.
- **Human-AI collaboration specialists:** These professionals will bridge the gap between humans and AI, ensuring effective communication and collaboration for optimal decision-making.
- **Cybersecurity experts:** As Fintech becomes more reliant on AI and data, robust cybersecurity measures will be paramount. Cybersecurity experts will be crucial for safeguarding sensitive information and protecting against cyber threats.

5.5.3 The Importance of Continuous Learning and Adaptability

The future of work in Fintech will require a workforce that embraces continuous learning and adaptation. Upskilling and reskilling initiatives will be essential for existing employees to remain relevant in the evolving job market. Additionally, fostering a culture of lifelong learning will ensure that the Fintech workforce can adapt to new technologies and stay ahead of the curve.

5.5.4 A Collaborative Future Built on Human Potential

The future of Fintech work is not about humans being replaced by machines, but rather about humans and AI working together to create a more efficient, secure, and customer-centric financial experience. By embracing upskilling, fostering collaboration, and focusing on human strengths, the Fintech industry can leverage the power of AI to build a thriving and innovative workforce for the years to come.

5.6 ETHICAL CONSIDERATIONS IN HUMAN-AI COLLABORATION: FOSTERING TRUST IN THE FINTECH REVOLUTION

The integration of AI into Fintech presents immense opportunities for efficiency, personalization, and innovation. However, alongside these benefits lie critical ethical considerations that require careful attention. Here, we explore some key concerns surrounding AI implementation in Fintech and discuss the importance of responsible development and deployment practices.

5.6.1 Potential Biases in AI Algorithms

AI algorithms are only as good as the data they are trained on. Biased data sets can lead to biased algorithms, perpetuating discrimination in areas like loan approvals, credit scoring, and investment recommendations [21,22].

For mitigating bias the Fintech institutions must implement robust data governance practices to ensure training data is fair and representative. Techniques like data cleansing and algorithmic audits can help identify and mitigate potential biases.

5.6.2 The Importance of Data Privacy

The increasing reliance on customer data for AI-powered solutions necessitates strong data privacy practices. Transparency about data collection, storage, and usage is crucial for building trust with customers [23,24]. Therefore, upholding data privacy stands utmost priority. Fintech institutions should obtain explicit consent from customers regarding data collection and ensure compliance with data privacy regulations like GDPR (General Data Protection Regulation) and CCPA (California Consumer Privacy Act).

5.6.3 Transparency and Fairness in Customer Interactions

As AI plays a more prominent role in customer interactions, ensuring transparency and fairness is essential. Customers should be informed about the use of AI in decision-making processes and have the option to interact with a human representative when necessary [25,26]. Developing "explainable AI" systems that can provide clear explanations for AI-driven decisions is crucial for building trust and ensuring fairness.

5.6.4 The Need for Human Oversight

While AI excels at automation and data analysis, complex ethical dilemmas and exceptional circumstances may require human judgment and intervention. Robust human oversight mechanisms should be in place to ensure responsible AI applications [27,28]. A "human-in-the-loop" approach, where humans oversee key decision-making processes and intervene, when necessary, can help mitigate ethical risks and ensure responsible AI usage.

5.6.5 Building a Responsible AI Future in Fintech

By proactively addressing these ethical considerations, Fintech institutions can foster trust with customers, regulators, and society as a whole. A commitment to responsible AI development, deployment, and ongoing monitoring practices is essential for ensuring that AI serves as a force for positive change within the Fintech industry.

5.7 THE HUMAN FACTOR: IRREPLACEABLE SKILLS AND VALUES

While AI is transforming the Fintech landscape, the human factor remains irreplaceable. Certain skills and values inherent to humans play a crucial role in driving success in this evolving ecosystem. Here, we explore some key human attributes that complement AI capabilities and contribute to effective decision-making and problem-solving within Fintech.

5.7.1 Creativity and Innovation: Pushing the Boundaries

AI excels at analyzing existing data and optimizing processes. However, it lacks the human capacity for creative problem-solving and generating original ideas. Human creativity will be vital for Fintech institutions to stay ahead of the curve, develop innovative financial products and services, and navigate unforeseen challenges [4,29].

- **Human expertise in ideation and strategy:** While AI can analyze data and identify patterns, humans are better equipped to translate insights into actionable strategies and develop innovative solutions for complex financial problems.

5.7.2 Critical Thinking and Ethical Decision-Making

AI can process large amounts of data, but it cannot replicate the human ability for critical thinking and ethical reasoning. Human judgment remains essential for analyzing complex situations, making ethical choices, and ensuring responsible AI implementation that aligns with societal values [30,31].

- **Human oversight for ethical considerations:** As AI plays a more prominent role in decision-making processes, humans will be responsible for overseeing ethical considerations, ensuring fairness, and mitigating potential biases in AI algorithms.

5.7.3 Emotional Intelligence: Building Trust and Empathy

Fintech is not just about numbers and algorithms; it's about people and their financial well-being. Emotional intelligence, the ability to understand and manage one's own emotions, and empathize with others, is a crucial human skill in building trust and rapport with clients [32,33].

- **Human touch in customer interactions:** Even with AI-powered chatbots and virtual assistants, human customer service representatives with strong emotional intelligence skills will be essential for building trust, offering personalized support, and mitigating customer concerns.

5.7.4 Leadership: Guiding the Future of Fintech

Effective leadership is paramount for navigating the changing landscape of Fintech. Leaders with a clear vision, the ability to inspire and motivate teams, and the capacity to make strategic decisions that leverage both human and AI capabilities will be crucial for the success of Fintech institutions [34,35].

- **Human-centric leadership for the AI age:** Leaders in Fintech will need to foster a culture of human-AI collaboration, empowering employees to leverage their unique skills alongside AI tools for effective problem-solving and innovation.

5.7.4.1 The Synergy of Human and AI Capabilities

The future of Fintech lies not in replacing humans with AI, but in harnessing the power of both. By capitalizing on human creativity, critical thinking, emotional intelligence, and leadership skills, Fintech institutions can leverage AI for its strengths in automation, data analysis, and efficiency. This synergy between human and AI capabilities will be essential for building a thriving and innovative Fintech sector for the years to come.

5.8 REGULATORY LANDSCAPE AND IMPLICATIONS: NAVIGATING THE EVOLVING FRONTIER

The rapid integration of AI into Fintech necessitates a dynamic and adaptable regulatory landscape. Governments and financial authorities worldwide are scrambling to develop regulations that address the unique challenges and opportunities presented by AI technologies. Here, we explore the evolving regulatory landscape and its implications for the Fintech industry.

5.8.1 A Global Focus on Data Security and Privacy

As AI relies heavily on customer data, data security and privacy are paramount concerns for regulators across the globe. Regulations like the General Data Protection Regulation (GDPR) in Europe, the California Consumer Privacy Act (CCPA) in the United States, and the Indian Privacy Protection Bill (still under consideration) establish guidelines for data collection, storage, and usage. These regulations aim to empower consumers with control over their personal information [36–38].

- **Compliance across borders:** Fintech institutions operating globally must ensure compliance with relevant data privacy regulations in each jurisdiction they serve. This includes obtaining explicit customer consent for data collection, implementing robust security measures to safeguard sensitive information, and offering clear mechanisms for data access and rectification requests.

5.8.2 Addressing Algorithmic Bias and Fairness

Algorithmic bias can perpetuate discrimination in areas like loan approvals, credit scoring, and investment recommendations. Regulatory bodies are developing frameworks to ensure fairness and transparency in AI-powered decision-making processes within Fintech [21,39].

- **Mitigating bias on a global scale:** The European Commission's "Ethics Guidelines for Trustworthy AI" emphasize fairness, transparency, and accountability in AI development, offering a potential framework for international collaboration [40]. Similarly, Indian regulatory bodies may implement similar frameworks to ensure fair and unbiased AI use in Fintech. Additionally, promoting diversity and inclusion within the Fintech workforce across all regions can help mitigate the risk of bias in algorithm development.

5.8.3 Consumer Protection in an AI-Powered Future

Regulations are being developed to ensure consumer protection in the age of AI-powered financial services. This includes ensuring transparency about the use of AI in customer interactions, providing clear complaint resolution mechanisms for instances where AI-based decisions are disputed, and safeguarding against potential manipulation or exploitation through AI-powered financial products [41,42].

- **Transparency and explainability across regions:** Fintech institutions should be transparent about the use of AI in customer interactions, regardless of location. This includes explaining how AI influences decisions and providing options for customers to opt out of AI-driven processes if desired. Additionally, regulations like India's proposed "Algorithmic Accountability Framework" and similar initiatives in the US and Europe may mandate explainable AI systems that can provide clear explanations for AI-driven decisions.

5.8.4 The Need for International Regulatory Collaboration

The global nature of Fintech necessitates collaboration between regulatory bodies across different countries to ensure a consistent and effective regulatory framework for AI implementation [43].

- **Harmonization of regulations:** International collaboration can help establish global standards for data privacy, algorithmic fairness, and consumer protection in the context of AI-powered Fintech services. This would create a more predictable environment for Fintech businesses operating across borders and fostering innovation within the global Fintech ecosystem.

5.9 THE PATH FORWARD – A COLLABORATIVE APPROACH FOR A SUSTAINABLE FUTURE

The future of Fintech and AI presents a landscape rich with opportunities yet rife with challenges that require careful navigation. On one hand, advancements in AI offer unprecedented potential for innovation and efficiency in financial services. AI-driven algorithms can streamline operations, enhance customer experiences, and provide more accurate risk assessments. Moreover, the proliferation of Fintech start-ups demonstrates the appetite for disruptive technologies in the industry. Innovation in AI Fintech holds immense promise for revolutionizing financial services, offering greater efficiency and personalized experiences.

However, alongside these opportunities, significant challenges exist. Concerns over data privacy and security remain paramount as AI systems increasingly handle sensitive financial information. Additionally, there are worries about job displacement as automation replaces traditional roles in finance. Furthermore, regulatory frameworks struggle to keep pace with the rapid evolution of Fintech and AI, leading to uncertainty and potential compliance issues.

The regulatory landscape is constantly evolving to keep pace with AI advancements in Fintech. By working collaboratively with stakeholders and regulators around the world, Fintech institutions can navigate these evolving requirements and ensure responsible AI development and implementation. A focus on data security, algorithmic fairness, consumer protection, and responsible AI development practices will be crucial for building trust with customers and fostering a sustainable and responsible AI-powered future for the Fintech industry.

5.10 CONCLUSION

Artificial Intelligence is revolutionizing how financial institutions operate and fueling businesses. It has constantly proved itself to be that one leading tool which has revolutionized the whole banking and finance industry. The perfect blend of such modern technologies has accorded the Fintech companies around the globe with surplus opportunities to comply with every demand of their customers without compromising their security and convenience.

AI models execute trades with unprecedented speed and precision, taking advantage of real-time market data to unlock deeper insights and dictate where investments are made. By analyzing intricate patterns in transaction data sets, AI solutions allow financial organizations to improve risk management. This enables more personalized interactions with customers, faster and more accurate customer support, credit scoring refinements and innovative products and services. Overall, the integration of AI in finance is creating a new era of data-driven decision-making, efficiency, security and customer experience in the financial sector.

Convincingly, the future of Fintech hinges on collaborative contributions between humans and AI. Embracing this partnership can unlock unprecedented potential for innovation, efficiency, and customer-centricity in financial services. However, to realize these benefits fully, stakeholders must prioritize ethical AI development, address data privacy concerns, and navigate regulatory complexities. Moreover, fostering a culture of collaboration and knowledge-sharing will be crucial for nurturing talent and driving continuous improvement in the industry. By working together harmoniously, humans and AI can shape a future where Fintech serves as a force for positive change, empowering individuals and businesses alike to thrive in the digital economy.

REFERENCES

1. Arora, A., Gupta, S., Devi, C., & Walia, N. (2023). Customer Experiences in the Era of Artificial Intelligence (AI) in Context to FinTech: A Fuzzy AHP Approach. *Benchmarking: An International Journal*, 30(10), 4342–4369. https://doi.org/10.1108/BIJ-10-2021-0621.
2. Tad, M.C., Mohamed, M.S., Samuel, S.F., & Deepa, M.J. (2023). Artificial Intelligence and Robotics and Their Impact on the Performance of the Workforce in the Banking Sector. *Revista de Gestão Social e Ambiental*, 17. e03410. https://doi.org/10.24857/rgsa.v17n6-012.
3. Pothumsetty, R. (2020). Implementation of Artificial Intelligence and Machine Learning in Financial Services. *International Journal of Engineering and Technology*, 7(3), 3186.
4. Pandey, M.K., & Sergeeva, I. (2022). Artificial Intelligence Impact Evaluation: Transforming Paradigms in Financial Institutions. *World of Economics and Management*, 22(1), 147–164.
5. Mehrotra, A. (2019). Artificial Intelligence in Financial Services – Need to Blend Automation with Human Touch. *2019 International Conference on Automation, Computational and Technology Management (ICACTM)*, Amity University, London, WC, April 24–26, 2019, 342–347.
6. Jaiswal, A., Arun, C.J., & Varma, A. (2021). Rebooting Employees: Upskilling for Artificial Intelligence in Multinational Corporations. *The International Journal of Human Resource Management*, 33, 1179–1208.
7. Morandini, S., Fraboni, F., Angelis, M.D., Puzzo, G., Giusino, D., & Pietrantoni, L. (2023). The Impact of Artificial Intelligence on Workers' Skills: Upskilling and Reskilling in Organisations. *Informing Science The International Journal of an Emerging Transdiscipline*, 26, 39–68.
8. Saroj Mithra, A., Charan Duddukuru, V., & Manu, K.S. (2023). How Artificial Intelligence is Revolutionizing the Banking Sector: The Applications and Challenges. *Asian Journal of Management*, 14(3), 2321–5763.
9. Biallas, M.O., & O'Neill, F. (2020). Artificial Intelligence Innovation in Financial Services. *Research Papers in Economics.*
10. Castillo, D., Canhoto, A.I., & Said, E. (2020). The Dark Side of AI-Powered Service Interactions: Exploring the Process of Co-destruction from the Customer Perspective. *The Service Industries Journal*, 41, 900–925.
11. Zhao, T., Cui, J., Hu, J., Dai, Y., & Zhou, Y. (2021). Is Artificial Intelligence Customer Service Satisfactory? Insights Based on Microblog Data and User Interviews. *Cyberpsychology, Behavior and Social Networking*, 25(2), 110–117.
12. Brenner, L., &Meyll, T. (2020). Robo-Advisors: A Substitute for Human Financial Advice? *Journal of Behavioral and Experimental Finance*, 25, 100275. http://doi.org/10.2139/ssrn.3414200

13. Gomes, P., Verçosa, L.F., Melo, F.J., Silva, V.F., Filho, C.J., & Bezerra, B.L. (2022). Artificial Intelligence-Based Methods for Business Processes: A Systematic Literature Review. *Applied Sciences*, 12(5), 2314.
14. Wu, Q. (2022). Real-Time Predictive Analysis of Loan Risk with Intelligent Monitoring and Machine Learning Technique. *2022 IEEE 4th International Conference on Power, Intelligent Computing and Systems (ICPICS)*, 852–856. 29–31 July 2022, Shenyang, China. http://doi.org/10.1109/ICPICS55264.2022.9873618.
15. van Thiel, D., & van Raaij, W.F. (2019). Artificial Intelligent Credit Risk Prediction: An Empirical Study of Analytical Artificial Intelligence Tools for Credit Risk Prediction in a Digital Era. *Journal of Risk Management in Financial Institutions*, 12(3), 268–286. https://doi.org/10.69554/NLZL1152
16. *Day, M., Cheng, T., & Li, J. (2018). AI Robo-Advisor with Big Data Analytics for Financial Services. 2018 IEEE/ACM International Conference on Advances in Social Networks Analysis and Mining (ASONAM)*, 1027–1031. https://doi.org/10.1109/ASONAM.2018.8508854
17. Wang, D., Churchill, E.F., Maes, P., Fan, X., Shneiderman, B., Shi, Y., & Wang, Q. (2020). From Human-Human Collaboration to Human-AI Collaboration: Designing AI Systems That Can Work Together with People. *Extended Abstracts of the 2020 CHI Conference on Human Factors in Computing Systems*. 1–6, 25 April, 2020. IBM Research. https://research.ibm.com/publications/from-human-human-collaboration-to-human-ai-collaboration-designing-ai-systems-that-can-work-together-with-people
18. McCaffrey, T. (2018). Human-AI Synergy in Creativity and Innovation. In *Artificial Intelligence – Emerging Trends and Applications*. IntechOpen, pp. 144–160. https://doi.org/10.5772/intechopen.75310
19. Pitso, T. (2019). Shared Futures: An Exploration of the Collaborative Potential of Intelligent Machines and Human Ingenuity in Cocreating Value. In: Brito, S. M. (ed.), *Toward Super-Creativity – Improving Creativity in Humans, Machines, and Human – Machine Collaborations*. IntechOpen, pp 1–23. https://doi.org/10.5772/intechopen.85054
20. Alekseeva, L., Azar, J., Giné, M., Samila, S., & Taska, B. (2021). The Demand for AI Skills in the Labor Market.. *Labour Economics*,71. https://doi.org/10.1016/j.labeco.2021.102002
21. Schmidt, N., & Stephens, B.E. (2019). An Introduction to Artificial Intelligence and Solutions to the Problems of Algorithmic Discrimination. *ArXiv*, abs/1911.05755.
22. Nelson, G.S. (2019). Bias in Artificial Intelligence. *North Carolina Medical Journal*, 80, 220–222.
23. Themistocleous, C. (2018). Customer Data: Contemporary Issues of Privacy and Trust. In: Vrontis, D., Weber, Y., Thrassou, A., Shams, S., Tsoukatos, E. (eds), *Innovation and Capacity Building*. Palgrave Studies in Cross-disciplinary Business Research, in association with EuroMed Academy of Business. Cham: Palgrave Macmillan, pp. 167–185. https://doi.org/10.1007/978-3-319-90945-5_9
24. Flikkema, P.G., and Cambou, B. F. (2017) "When things are sensors for Cloud AI: Protecting privacy through data collection transparency in the age of digital assistants" in *Proceedings of the 2017 Global Internet of Things Summit* (GIoTS), Geneva, Switzerland, June 6–9, 2017, pp. 1–4.
25. MoDastoni, D.A. (2023). Exploring Methods to Make AI Decisions More Transparent and Understandable for Humans. *Advances in Engineering Innovation*, 3, 32–36
26. Hois, J., Theofanou-Fuelbier, D., & Junk, A.J. (2019). How to Achieve Explainability and Transparency in Human AI Interaction. In Stephanidis, C. (eds.), *HCI International 2019 – Posters. HCII 2019. Communications in Computer and Information Science*. Cham: Springer. https://doi.org/10.1007/978-3-030-23528-4_25

27. Eitel-Porter, R. (2020). Beyond the Promise: Implementing Ethical AI. *AI and Ethics*, 1, 73–80.
28. Naik, N., Hameed, B.M., Shetty, D.K., Swain, D., Shah, M.J., Paul, R., Aggarwal, K., Ibrahim, S., Patil, V., Smriti, K., Shetty, S., Rai, B.P., Chłosta, P., & Somani, B.K. (2022). Legal and Ethical Consideration in Artificial Intelligence in Healthcare: Who Takes Responsibility? *Frontiers in Surgery*, 9, 862322.
29. Kruse, L., Wunderlich, N., & Beck, R. (2019). Artificial Intelligence for the Financial Services Industry: What Challenges Organizations to Succeed. Proceedings of 52nd *Hawaii International Conference on System Sciences*, Maui, Hawaii, USA, pp. 6408–6417.
30. Lepri, B., Oliver, N., & Pentland, A. (2021). Ethical Machines: The Human-Centric Use of Artificial Intelligence. *iScience*, 24, 102249.
31. De Cremer, D., & Kasparov, G. (2021). The eEhical AI – Paradox: Why Better Technology Needs More and Not Less Human Responsibility. *AI and Ethics*, 2, 1–4.
32. Dhar, V., & Stein, R.M. (2016). FinTech Platforms and Strategy. *Communications of the ACM*, 60, 32–35.
33. Patrick, B.K. (2009). The Importance of Emotional Intelligence. In *Proceedings of the 37th annual ACM SIGUCCS fall conference: communication and collaboration (SIGUCCS '09)*. Association for Computing Machinery, New York, NY, 15–18. https://doi.org/10.1145/1629501.1629506
34. Campbell, T., Knox, M.W., Rowlands, J., Cui, Z.A., & DeJesus, L. (2021). Leadership in FinTech: Authentic Leaders as Enablers of Innovation and Competitiveness in Financial Technology Firms. Fostering Innovation and Competitiveness with FinTech, RegTech, and SupTech, pp. 250–270. IGI Global.
35. Leandro, D.J., & Umana, D.M. (2021). The Impact of Transformational Leadership on the Self-Creative Efficacy and Intrinsic Motivation in FINTECH Organizations. *International Journal of Business and Management Research*, 9(4), 448–456.
36. Davis, M. (2021). Consumer Privacy Regulations: Considerations in the Age of Globalization and Big Data. In I. Management Association (ed.), *Research Anthology on Privatizing and Securing Data*. IGI Global Scientific Publishing, pp. 1844–1860. https://doi.org/10.4018/978-1-7998-8954-0.ch089.
37. Vegh, L. (2018). Privacy and Security Concerns for the Internet of Things in the GDPR Era – A Survey. *Journal of Military Technology*, 1(2), 5–10.
38. Bhasin, M.L. (2012). Online Privacy Protection: Privacy Seals and Government Regulations in Select Countries. *International Journal of Finance and Accounting*, 1, 148–161.
39. Lepri, B., Oliver, N., Letouzé, E., Pentland, A., & Vinck, P. (2017). Fair, Transparent, and Accountable Algorithmic Decision-making Processes. *Philosophy & Technology*, 31, 611–627.
40. Floridi, L. (2019). Establishing the Rules for Building Trustworthy AI. *Nature Machine Intelligence*, 1, 261–262.
41. Lee, J. (2019). Access to Finance for Artificial Intelligence Regulation in the Financial Services Industry. *European Business Organization Law Review*, 21, 731–757.
42. Treleaven, P.C., & Batrinca, B. (2017). Algorithmic Regulation: Automating Financial Compliance Monitoring and Regulation Using AI and Blockchain. *Journal of Financial Transformation*, 45, 14–21.
43. Maldonado Narváez, M.I. (2020). Necessity of a Fintech Global Regulation. *Juridicas CUC*, 17, 65–86.

Cases/Reports Links

Axis Bank. (2023, March 22). Axis Bank Launches 'Happy Hours' Feature with Facial Recognition Technology. https://cardinsider.com/blog/get-upto-50-off-at-select-restaurants-with-the-axis-bank-dining-festival-offer/.

Barclays. (2021, September 22). Barclays AI Skills Academy. https://home.barclays/news/2024/01/how-Barclays-is-harnessing-AI/.

Betterment. (2023, March 1). Betterment Smart Saver. https://www.betterment.com/cash-reserve.

Capital One. (2020, February 11). How Machine Learning Is Fighting Fraud at Capital One. https://www.ciodive.com/news/capital-one-ML-fraud-democratization/649017/.

Charles Schwab. (2023, January 19). Schwab Intelligent Assistant. https://intelligent-client.schwab.com/.

Iansiti, M., & Lakhani, K. R. (2020, January–February). Competing in the age of AI: How machine intelligence changes the rules of business. *Harvard Business Review*. https://hbr.org/2020/01/competing-in-the-age-of-ai

Azagury, J., Fang Grant, K., Moore, M., Ashraf, M., & Wright, O. (2024). *Reinvention in the age of generative AI*. Accenture. https://www.accenture.com/content/dam/accenture/final/accenture-com/document-2/Accenture-Reinvention-in-the-age-of-generative-AI-Report.pdf

Gharbawi, M., Ward, E., Bratt, E., Diver, L., Mueller, H., Quartu, R., & Robinson, H. (2024). *Artificial intelligence in UK financial services*. Bank of England. https://www.bankofengland.co.uk/report/2024/artificial-intelligence-in-uk-financial-services-2024

Searle, D. (2019, September 17). The seven patterns of AI. *Forbes*. https://www.forbes.com/sites/cognitiveworld/2019/09/17/the-seven-patterns-of-ai/?sh=5d73281d12d0

Manyika, J., Lund, S., Chui, M., Bughin, J., Woetzel, L., Batra, P., Ko, R., & Sanghvi, S. (2017). *Jobs lost, jobs gained: What the future of work will mean for jobs, skills, and wages*. McKinsey Global Institute. https://www.mckinsey.com/~/media/mckinsey/industries/public%20and%20social%20sector/our%20insights/what%20the%20future%20of%20work%20will%20mean%20for%20jobs%20skills%20and%20wages/mgi-jobs-lost-jobs-gained-executive-summary-december-6-2017.pdf

Ministry of Electronics and Information Technology. (2018). *A free and fair digital economy: Protecting privacy, empowering Indians*. Government of India. https://www.meity.gov.in/data-protection-framework

World Economic Forum. (2023). *The future of jobs report 2023*. https://www.weforum.org/publications/the-future-of-jobs-report-2023/

World Economic Forum. (2023). *The Presidio recommendations on responsible generative AI*. https://www3.weforum.org/docs/WEF_Presidio_Recommendations_on_Responsible_Generative_AI_2023.pdf

JPMorgan Chase. (2020, August 12). JPMorgan Chase Announces Enhancements to Award-Winning Digital Banking Platform with Focus on AI-Powered Solutions. https://www.jpmorgan.com/technology/artificial-intelligence.

McKinsey & Company. (2020, January). Jobs Lost, Jobs Gained: Workforce Transitions in a Time of Automation. https://www.mckinsey.com/~/media/BAB489A30B724BECB5DEDC41E9BB9FAC.ashx.

Pw C. (2023, June). Artificial Intelligence in Risk Management. https://www.pwc.com/gx/en/issues/data-and-analytics/publications/artificial-intelligence-study.html.

World Economic Forum. (2020, October). The Future Agenda: Jobs and Skills in the Age of Automation. https://www.weforum.org/agenda/2023/09/ai-automation-augmentation-workplace-jobs-of-tomorrow/.

6 Enhancing Financial Document Digitization

Handwritten Text Conversion to Digital Using Convolution Neural Networks

Rashmi Deshmukh, Shravan Salunkhe, Pratik Patil, Ganesh Lohar, Shreeyash Patil, and Pranavsinh Patil

6.1 INTRODUCTION

In today's digital age, financial companies are increasingly relying on automation and digitization to streamline their operations and improve efficiency. However, one significant challenge faced is the transformation of manually written financial texts into digital formats. Handwritten character poses a unique obstacle due to its variability in style, size, and orientation, making accurate transcription and recognition challenging.

Handwritten text recognition (HTR) is a multidisciplinary field containing various domains such as ML, image processing and NLP. It encompasses a wide range of applications, from digitizing historical documents and transcribing handwritten notes to enabling efficient data entry in mobile devices and automating postal services.

Handwriting stands as the predominant and widespread method employed by humans for communication. Additionally, it serves as a proficient and successful means of documenting information, even amidst the integration of modern technologies such as the SwiftKey keyboard, voice commands, etc. A handwriting recognition system typically refers to a method utilized to identify human handwriting in various languages, whether from a digital image or drawn on any electronic media, known respectively as offline and online handwriting recognition. Moreover, its usage spans across three main categories: numerals, characters, and cursive writing. This technology finds extensive application in various domains including language translation, banking for check processing, and facilitating keyword searches, etc.

The standard procedures of a manual text recognition system encompass various steps like obtaining visual data, pre-processing, partitioning of image, extracting characters, and categorization of image. The initial phase involves acquiring images, which is the primary step in obtaining a handwritten form suitable for scanning. Pre-processing aims to eliminate distortion from the scanned image for

DOI: 10.1201/9781003645849-6

subsequent processing. Among the pre-processing techniques, thresholding converts the scanned image into a binary form. Subsequently, segmentation divides each word into sub-images, a crucial step particularly for continuous handwriting, facilitating feature extraction from each character image. Feature extraction follows, capturing all distinctive characteristics from each image, which are instrumental for classification in the final stage.

Numerous classification methods like convolution neural networks (CNNs), Neural Networks, and support vector machines (SVMs), adopt distinct approaches to image recognition. Typically, researchers evaluate system performance primarily through classification accuracy assessment. While extensive research exists on manually written text recognition, the utilization of CNNs is relatively nascent. CNNs have emerged as potent tools for image recognition and pattern detection tasks, capitalizing on their capability to learn hierarchical data representations. They present promising avenues for converting handwritten text into digital formats, particularly in financial document digitization. Consequently, this work focuses on designing offline HTR using CNNs.

In this work, we opted for two widely used databases, MNIST and EMNIST, due to their provision of clean data. Consequently, the chosen algorithms commence with feature extraction. Here, we utilize image pixels as inputs for the classifier, leveraging CNN's capability to handle both feature extraction and classification. The project's performance evaluation relies on the confusion matrix to determine classification accuracy.

The work explores the application of CNNs in enhancing financial document digitization by converting handwritten text to digital formats. We know and try to solve the challenges associated with HTR, including variability in handwriting styles and the need for robust recognition algorithms. Further, this work discusses how CNNs can be trained to accurately transcribe handwritten text, leveraging their ability to extract meaningful features from images and learn complex patterns.

Utilizing CNNs enables financial companies to automate the transformation of manual financial texts into digital formats with precision and effectiveness. This not only streamlines document management processes but also facilitates data analysis and information retrieval in financial operations.

6.2 LITERATURE REVIEW

V. V. Mainkar et al. (2020) explored a range of pre-processing techniques applicable to character recognition across various types of images, encompassing simple handwritten documents as well as those with coloured backgrounds and diverse intensities. The central objective of the study revolves around devising a system or approach for identifying handwritten characters and transforming them into editable text. The paper delves into several pre-processing methodologies, including detecting and rectifying skew, expanding the dynamic range of contrast, error elimination techniques, and standardization and dividing the image into distinct parts, as well as structural analysis of image techniques.

N. Saqib et al. (2022) aimed to achieve superior accuracy in recognizing offline handwritten digits compared to prior studies. Unlike previous systems limited to recognizing single digits, this system is designed to recognize multiple numbers simultaneously. Therefore, the author emphasized efficient segmentation to isolate individual digits.

Y. B. Hamdam and S. Prof (2021) demonstrated the superior effectiveness in accurately recognizing characters across all types of OCR systems. The main focus lies in constructing a model for recognizing handwritten characters using statistical SVM techniques. This research establishes a framework for recognizing a variety of stylish characters, resulting in improved recognition rates and accuracy. By incorporating a procedure for recognizing stylish characters, the proposed framework achieves enhanced accuracy. The handwriting style may vary, encompassing distorted strokes and variations in the size of texts. The SVM-based HCR method proposed in this study achieves a recognition accuracy of 94%, outperforming existing methods.

H. Zhao et al. (2020) used the integration of deep learning method in HTR focuses on deciphering Chinese text from prehistoric texts. The primary goal includes addressing uncertainty inherent in Chinese characters and the challenges associated with annotating large amount of manually written text information. To tackle this problem, a multilayer NN is constructed.

J. C. Aradillas et al. (2021) tackled the problem of HTR in old documents; especially when there is limited labelled information that may contain noise in the training dataset. The paper presents three key elements. Firstly, it explores the application of TL from a large database to comparatively smaller database, investigating which layers of the model require fine-tuning. Secondly, it examines different ways to effectively integrate transfer learning and augmentation of data to enhance recognition accuracy.

K. Dergachov et al. (2021) study introduces a contemporary approach to enhancing the performance of optical recognition systems by offering a range of pre-processing algorithms that users can select according to their preferences. It presents a series of novel algorithms designed to improve the quality of optical text recognition systems. The research demonstrates the effectiveness of these technical solutions, indicating that with source data pre-processing, nearly 100% accuracy in text recognition can be achieved.

G. Muehlberge et al.'s (2019) study utilizes the Transkribus platform. This technology adopts a line-oriented methodology, wherein the source consists of digitized text along with the accurately transcribed text for it.

A. M. Ozbayoglu et al. (2020) discussed a wide range of financial applications where deep learning has been applied successfully. These include stock price prediction, portfolio management, fraud detection, credit scoring, algorithmic trading, and risk management. The paper concludes by summarizing the key findings and emphasizing the potential of deep learning to transform the finance industry by improving decision-making processes, risk management, and overall efficiency.

T. T. Alemayoh et al. (2022) focused on the utilization of IMU and force sensors to capture handwriting motion data and the implementation of DL techniques for character-recognition from the captured data. Also, it shows potential applications in fields such as gesture recognition, handwriting analysis, and human-computer interaction.

S. Mahadevkar et al. (2024) introduced AI-based hybrid approach to enhance HTR and showed the integration of multiple artificial intelligence techniques to improve accuracy and robustness. The paper focuses on the possible implications across different applications, including document digitization, text analysis, and the automation of tasks related to handwritten text processing.

N. Saqib et al. (2022) presented a CNN-based approach for HTR, emphasizing the utilization of massive multisource data. Its main focus lies in exploring the efficacy of CNN techniques in handling diverse datasets for improved recognition accuracy. The paper concludes that leveraging abundant multisource data enhances the performance of CNN models, showing promising results for handwritten character recognition tasks, thus focusing on CNN-based approaches in this domain.

S. Ahlawat et al. (2019) concentrated on enhancing handwritten digit recognition utilizing convolutional neural networks (CNN). Through experimentation, the authors demonstrated significant improvements in handwritten digit recognition accuracy by employing CNN-based techniques. The paper explores various architectural configurations and training methodologies to optimize performance. The study concludes that CNNs offer a robust method for improving HTR systems. The findings underscore the importance of CNNs in pattern recognition tasks and suggest their potential for broader applications beyond digit recognition.

W. AlKendi et al. (2023) provided a comprehensive survey of advancements and challenges in HTR, aiming to consolidate existing knowledge and identify areas for future research. The authors identified recent advancements in HTR techniques, including the adoption of deep learning models, integration of contextual information, and advancements in pre-processing methods. The paper also highlights ongoing challenges such as handling variability in handwriting styles, addressing computational complexity, and improving accuracy on noisy datasets.

S. Ali et al. (2019) focused on proposing an enhanced way for HTR utilizing CNNs. The author presented a better scheme for achieving enhanced accuracy and efficiency in handwritten digit recognition tasks compared to existing methods. The paper explores various architectural designs, training strategies, and optimization techniques to achieve these results.

A. Alajaji et al. (2022) investigated domain adaptation methods tailored for human context recognition tasks, specifically addressing the challenge of transitioning from laboratory settings to real-world field environments. The authors concluded that adapting models trained in controlled lab environments to real-world field conditions is critical for achieving robust and accurate human context recognition. The findings are in bridging the gap between controlled settings and practical deployment scenarios, enabling the development of more reliable and effective context-aware systems.

Z. Hashim et al. (2022) presented a comparative study evaluating various machine learning techniques for handwritten signature verification. Through experimentation and analysis, the authors assessed the performance of different methods and identify strengths and weaknesses in each approach. The findings aim to present machine learning techniques in signature verification tasks and inform the selection of appropriate methods for practical applications.

E. Vidal et al. (2023) focused on providing page-level assessment scheme for measuring the performance of HTR systems. The authors proposed and evaluated a comprehensive methodology for assessing the accuracy of HTR at the page level. The author demonstrated the effectiveness of their approach in providing holistic evaluations, capturing both character-level and contextual errors. The findings aim to contribute to the development of robust evaluation frameworks for HTR systems, facilitating advancements in this field.

A. F. D. Sousa Neto et al. (2022) investigated the development and evaluation of a robust handwritten recognition system designed to operate effectively under various data restriction scenarios. It aims to address challenges related to limited training data availability and variations in data distribution, focusing on enhancing the system's adaptability and performance across different conditions. The paper suggests that the system's adaptability and reliability make it a valuable tool for real-world handwritten recognition tasks across different contexts and conditions. The authors emphasized the system's ability to achieve robust performance, demonstrating its potential for practical applications where data availability may be constrained.

B. Ji and T. Chen (2019) explored the application of generative adversarial networks (GANs) for generating handwritten text. The authors demonstrated the feasibility of using GANs to generate realistic handwritten text samples. They investigated various architectures and training methodologies to achieve convincing results. The study shows the application of generative models for text generation tasks.

G. Katiyar and S. Mehfuz (2016) presented a method integrating multiple techniques including neural networks, Hidden Markov Models (HMMs) and SVM. Experimental outcomes showcase the efficacy of the proposed system in attaining elevated accuracy levels in character recognition tasks. These results underscore the promise of hybrid methodologies in augmenting the accuracy and resilience of systems designed for recognizing handwritten characters. The research concludes that the amalgamation of neural networks, HMMs, and SVMs in a hybrid recognition system yields enhanced performance in offline handwritten character recognition, surpassing the capabilities of standalone methods.

A. A. A. Ali and S. Mallaiah (2022) suggested a hybrid strategy that merges CNN architectures with SVM classifier enhanced by dropout regularization for intelligent handwritten recognition. Results from experiments indicate that this hybrid model outperforms individual CNN or SVM classifiers, underscoring the efficacy of combining CNN and SVM techniques. This work suggests a method which elevates both accuracy and resilience of handwritten recognition systems.

M. S. Akter et al. (2022) explored a deep learning approach for manual word recognition, focusing on a novel method for generating handwritten words. The main findings of the paper are it demonstrates the effectiveness of deep learning approach in accurately recognizing handwritten words. The author introduced a novel method for generating handwritten words, which contributes to improving the system. The paper suggests that a proposed approach offers promising results for handwritten word recognition tasks, showing potential for various applications in document processing and text analysis. The study concludes that the deep learning approach, coupled with the novel method for generating handwritten words, presents a viable solution for handwritten word recognition. The authors highlighted the significance of harnessing deep learning methods to improve manual text recognition systems. The paper suggests that the used approach can facilitate advancements in the domain of handwritten word recognition.

M. Karthi et al. (2019) introduced an innovative method for detecting content within handwritten English letters. Through experimentation, the proposed method demonstrates effective detection and recognition of handwritten letter content. This method offers promising results for various applications like document processing, text analysis, and handwriting recognition. The authors proposed a new method for detecting content in handwritten English letters, designed specifically for this purpose. The paper evaluates the effectiveness of their method through experimentation and analysis, demonstrating high accuracy and robustness in detecting and recognizing handwritten letter content. The findings suggest that the proposed approach offers significant advancements in HTR systems, showcasing its potential for practical applications in document digitization and text analysis tasks. The paper concludes that the new method is presented for written English characters. The authors emphasized the effectiveness and versatility of their method in accurately identifying and interpreting handwritten letter content, underscoring its potential for enhancing document processing and text analysis capabilities. The paper suggests that the proposed approach can facilitate advancements in HTR systems, enabling improved accuracy and efficiency in various real-world applications.

S. S. Ahmed et al. (2023) introduced an innovative method for recognizing handwritten digits through the utilization of deep learning. The proposed technique demonstrates superior performance in accurately recognizing handwritten digits compared to existing methods. The authors explored various deep learning architectures and training strategies to optimize recognition accuracy, achieving promising results across different datasets and scenarios. The paper conducts comprehensive evaluations to assess the robustness, scalability, and efficiency of their technique, highlighting its effectiveness in real-world applications. The research findings suggest that the newly developed method for recognizing handwritten digits using deep learning represents a notable advancement in the domain of pattern recognition. The author presented deep learning models for improving the accuracy and performance of the system. The paper suggests that this technique can facilitate the development of more reliable and versatile digit recognition systems, enabling various applications in fields such as document processing, optical character recognition (OCR), and biometrics. Additionally, the paper discusses potential avenues for future research, such as exploring novel architectures, incorporating additional features or modalities, and addressing scalability and deployment challenges. Overall, the paper underscores the potential of deep learning techniques in advancing handwritten digit recognition and highlights the importance of continued innovation in this area.

J. A. P. Lopes et al. (2022) presented an offline system for verifying handwritten signatures, employing deep neural networks as its foundation. The system aims to authenticate handwritten signatures by comparing them against reference signatures stored in the database. Through experimentation, the proposed system demonstrates robust performance in accurately verifying handwritten signatures, offering potential applications in security and authentication systems. The main objective of the paper is to create a signature verification system for offline manual signatures, leveraging deep neural networks. The authors aimed to address the challenge of accurately authenticating handwritten signatures in various contexts, including document verification, financial transactions, and access control. The study concludes that the system based on deep neural networks offers promising results in accurately verifying handwritten signatures. The authors emphasized the efficiency of employing deep learning methods to capture and analyze signature characteristics, resulting in enhanced accuracy and reliability in verification. The paper emphasizes the importance of leveraging deep neural networks for enhancing security and authentication systems, particularly in scenarios where handwritten signatures play a critical role. The authors suggested exploring enhancements to the proposed system, such as incorporating additional features or modalities for signature analysis, optimizing model architectures and training methodologies for improved performance, and conducting extensive evaluations on larger and more diverse datasets. The paper also proposes investigating the integration of the verification system into practical applications, such as document management systems or financial transaction platforms, to assess its real-world utility and scalability. Overall, the authors highlighted the possibilities for future exploration and advancement in the utilization of deep neural networks.

L. G. Hafemann et al. (2017) gave a detailed literature review and surveyed various methods and approaches proposed in the research community for authenticating handwritten signatures. The review seeks to offer understanding regarding the latest techniques, obstacles, and patterns in the verification of handwritten signatures conducted offline. The authors identified and analyzed a wide range of techniques and methodologies used in offline handwritten signature verification. The paper discusses key aspects such as feature extraction, classification algorithms, dataset characteristics, and performance evaluation metrics. The findings reveal the evolution of signature verification systems over time, highlighting advancements in feature representation, machine learning algorithms, and dataset collection and annotation methods. The paper concludes with the significance of the reviewed literature in advancing the understanding and development of offline handwritten signature verification techniques, while also identifying directions for future research and practical implementation.

L. G. Hafemann et al. (2017) proposed a novel approach using deep CNNs. It explores the use of CNNs to train discriminative features from signature images, eliminating the need for handcrafted feature extraction. The experimental findings showcase the efficiency of the suggested method in precisely verifying handwritten signatures, surpassing conventional approaches and achieving top-tier performance on established datasets. The authors extensively experimented to assess the effectiveness of their proposed technique for verifying handwritten signatures conducted offline. The paper uses standard benchmark datasets, such as the MCYT-100 and the Brazilian PUC-PR datasets, to train and test their CNN-based signature verification system. Experimental evaluations include performance factors such as model accuracy, model precision, model recall, and model-F1-score, as well as comparisons with existing approaches to find the superiority of the system. Additionally, the author studied to analyze the contribution of different components of the CNN architecture to the overall performance. The experimental outcomes indicate that the CNN-based method is highly effective and superior in accurately verifying handwritten signatures, showcasing top-tier performance on established datasets.

M. M. Hameed et al. (2021) surveyed the literature to summarize existing approaches, techniques, and methodologies for verifying handwritten signatures using machine learning algorithms. The review seeks to offer an understanding of the latest techniques, obstacles, and developments in verifying signatures conducted offline. Based on the systematic review, the authors highlighted several key findings and observations like wide variety of machine learning algorithms used in offline signature verification, including SVMs, NNs, RF, and LR etc. The paper focuses on the challenges associated with variability in signature styles, dataset bias, and the limited availability of annotated data for training and testing.

A. Rexit et al. (2022) presented a multilingual system for recognizing handwritten signatures, which relies on fusion of high-dimensional features. It proposes a novel approach that combines multiple feature sets extracted from signature images to improve recognition accuracy and robustness across different languages. The experimental findings illustrate the efficacy of the proposed technique in precisely recognizing handwritten signatures across multiple languages, outperforming baseline methods and achieving top-tier performance on established datasets. The main findings of the paper are that proposed multilingual handwritten signature recognition system offers a promising solution for recognizing signatures in diverse languages, addressing the challenge of language-dependent variations in signature styles. Experimental assessments showcase the advancement of the proposed technique compared to current methods, emphasizing its efficacy in precisely identifying signatures across different scripts and writing styles. The authors probably conducted extensive experimentation to assess the performance on multilingual manual signs. Experimental evaluations include training and testing the system on benchmark datasets containing signatures in different languages and scripts. Moreover, the paper has compared the proposed method with baseline methods and cutting edge methods to showcase its superiority. Overall, these analyses validate the effectiveness of the multilingual handwritten signs finding system across various languages and writing styles.

X. Y. Zhang et al. (2017) presented a comprehensive study that aims to investigate various aspects of Chinese character recognition, including feature representation, classification algorithms, dataset characteristics, and performance evaluation metrics. Additionally, the paper introduces a new benchmark dataset containing Chinese words. The paper examines both online and offline approaches and draws attention to the distinctions and similarities between these two modalities. Experimentation shows different feature showing techniques, such as stroke-based and image-based features, in capturing the distinctive characteristics of handwritten Chinese characters. The authors investigated various classification methods like ML methods and DL models, to assess their performance in recognizing handwritten Chinese characters. The introduction of a new benchmark dataset establishes a standardized platform for evaluating various Chinese character recognition systems, enabling equitable comparisons across different studies. The paper concludes that online and offline manual Chinese text finding system poses unique problems because of the complexity and variability of Chinese characters. Also feature representation and classification algorithms play crucial roles in determining the performance of Chinese character recognition systems.

D. Chauhan et al. (2022) focused on manual character-finding system with the use of a Siamese-network design. These networks are mainly used for the comparison tasks, making them suitable for tasks like signature verification, fingerprint matching, and text finding. The primary goal of the work is to investigate how Siamese networks perform in recognizing handwritten characters and to assess their effectiveness in comparison to alternative methods. The paper concludes with Siamese network design showing promise for hand-written character recognition tasks, achieving competitive or superior performance compared to existing approaches and the effectiveness of Siamese networks in capturing the similarity between handwritten characters demonstrates their potential for various similarity-based tasks beyond character recognition.

A. Fateh et al. (2021) focused on the recognition of handwritten numerals across multiple languages, employing a strong deep network in conjunction with transfer learning techniques. Multilingual recognition systems aim to recognize numerals written in different languages or scripts, providing flexibility and adaptability across diverse linguistic contexts. The main focus of the study is to showcase DL methods for multilingual numeral recognition, leveraging transfer learning to enhance model performance across languages and datasets. The experimental findings indicate that the proposed method achieves notable accuracy and resilience in recognition, surpassing baseline techniques and achieving leading performance on established datasets. The paper finds that the robust deep network architecture, combined with transfer learning techniques, demonstrates effectiveness in accurately recognizing handwritten numerals across multiple languages. The paper concludes that the proposed approach offers a scalable and adaptable solution for multilingual numeral recognition, with potential applications in document processing, OCR systems, and digital humanities research. Transfer learning enables the model to leverage knowledge learned from one language or dataset to improve performance on other languages or datasets, demonstrating the potential for knowledge transfer in multilingual recognition tasks.

N. Aneja and S. Aneja (2019) focused on employing transfer learning alongside CNNs for recognizing handwritten Devanagari characters. Transfer learning involves refining a model trained on one task to enhance performance on a related task, leveraging acquired features. The primary aim is to assess the efficacy of transfer learning with CNNs in recognizing Devanagari characters, which are utilized in several South Asian languages like Hindi, Marathi, and Nepali. Experimental evaluations show that fine-tuning of CNN model with small set of data containing Devanagari characters significantly improves recognition performance compared to training from scratch. The paper finds that transfer learning offers leverage features trained from the images like ImageNet and adapts to the specific method of recognition of Devanagari characters, avoiding the requirement of a huge database and the proposed method offers a scalable and efficient solution for Devanagari character recognition, with potential applications in document processing, OCR systems, and processing of natural language. The paper concludes the effectiveness of TL highlights the importance of trained features with related tasks for enhancement of the performance on specific tasks.

H. Davoudi and A. Traviglia (2023) focused on the acquisition of discrete representations for recognizing handwritten text. Representation learning is a fundamental task in machine learning where data is transformed into a suitable representation for a particular task. In the context of HTR, discrete representation learning involves encoding handwritten text into a structured, discrete form that facilitates recognition. The primary objective of the paper is to explore how discrete representation learning techniques can enhance the accuracy and resilience of systems designed for recognizing handwritten text. Experimental results demonstrate that encoding handwritten text into a structured, discrete form enables more effective feature extraction and representation, leading to improved recognition performance. Discrete representation learning techniques offer a scalable and efficient solution for HTR, with potential applications in document processing, OCR systems, and natural language processing tasks. The proposed approach provides a novel perspective on representation learning for HTR, offering insights into the effectiveness of discrete encoding methods compared to traditional continuous representations.

J. Memon et al. (2020) conducted a thorough and systematic examination of literature pertaining to handwritten OCR. The focus is on synthesizing existing research in the field to provide a systematic study of methodologies and advancements in handwritten OCR systems. The review encompasses various aspects such as classification, languages, feature extraction, and deep learning approaches used in handwritten OCR. Analysis of the literature reveals trends and challenges in handwritten OCR, such as the impact of language diversity, the accuracy of extraction of specific character improvements achieved through deep learning approaches. The review identifies key research directions and potential areas for further exploration in handwritten OCR, such as the development of language-specific models, enhancement of feature extraction techniques, and integration of domain-specific knowledge for improved recognition accuracy. The paper highlights the importance of benchmark datasets, evaluation protocols, and standardization efforts in advancing the field of handwritten OCR and fostering reproducible research.

6.3 SYSTEM ARCHITECTURE

The system design, comprising crucial stages like image capture, pre-processing steps, partitioning of image, finding of specific features, and image classification, highlights the complexity and thoroughness required for accurate HTR. The use of popular databases such as MNIST and EMNIST ensures that the system is trained on clean data, necessary to achieve high classification accuracy.

The process starts with an input image containing characters (such as handwritten or printed text). The input image goes through pre-processing steps to improve its quality. These steps include noise reduction, contrast adjustment, and resizing. Next, elements are extracted from the pre-processed image. These features represent relevant information about figures, such as edges, corners, and texture patterns. The extracted features are scaled or normalized to provide consistent input for subsequent stages. The heart of the system is CNN. This deep learning model is trained to recognize characters based on the extracted features. It consists of layers such as convolution, pooling and fully connected layers. CNN classifies input features into specific character classes (e.g. letters, numbers, and symbols). The output is the recognized character. In short, the system takes an input image, processes it, extracts features, scales the data, and uses a CNN for character recognition.

- **Input data (manuscript)**: This is the stage where handwritten text samples are provided for recognition. The samples can come from different sources and represent the raw data for the recognition system.
- **Pre-processing Unit**: Currently, the source image goes through several pre-processing steps, such as resizing for standard resolution, converting to grayscale to simplify processing, noise reduction typically using filters such as Gaussian blur, binarization to increase contrast between characters and background, and possibly stroke extraction handwriting, wing table, normalization and, if necessary, segmentation of characters or regions.
- **Feature extraction unit:** Relevant features such as edges and shapes are extracted from pre-processed images. Now a CNN is employed, convolution layers capture local patterns and features, followed by pooling to reduce spatial dimensions and flattening or global average pooling to create a feature vector for classification. Additional feature extraction techniques could be used to capture more high-level features.
- **Classification unit:** This unit involves selecting or training a model such as CNNs or RNNs to recognize characters or text. The feature vector is fed into the model, which then makes predictions based on the training it has undergone.
- **Data set unit:** This unit manages the training and test datasets necessary for model development, including data collection, pre-processing, partitioning into training dataset, validation of data, and test subsets, and when necessary, augmenting the data to increase the diversity of the datasets.
- **Output (recognized text):** The final output is the recognized text from the input manuscript. This stage may include post-processing and editing the presentation to guarantee that the text conforms to the appropriate format and is adaptable for a range of applications such as transcription and data input.

The system architecture is shown in detail in Figure 6.1

6.4 METHODOLOGY

The development of an offline HTR system using CNNs represents a significant advance in the field of human-computer interaction. Preserving the timeless tradition of handwritten communication in the digital age, the study explores an untapped application of CNNs in image recognition, specifically in the context of converting handwritten content into machine-readable text.

In HTR systems, CNNs typically work as follows (a simplified diagrammatic explanation would show these steps in sequence):

- The input image (handwritten text) is processed through various layers.
- Convolutional layers extract local features by applying filters.
- Rectified Linear Unit (ReLU) layers used to grasp intricate patterns.
- Fully connected layers analyse the features to perform classification, recognizing individual characters or words.

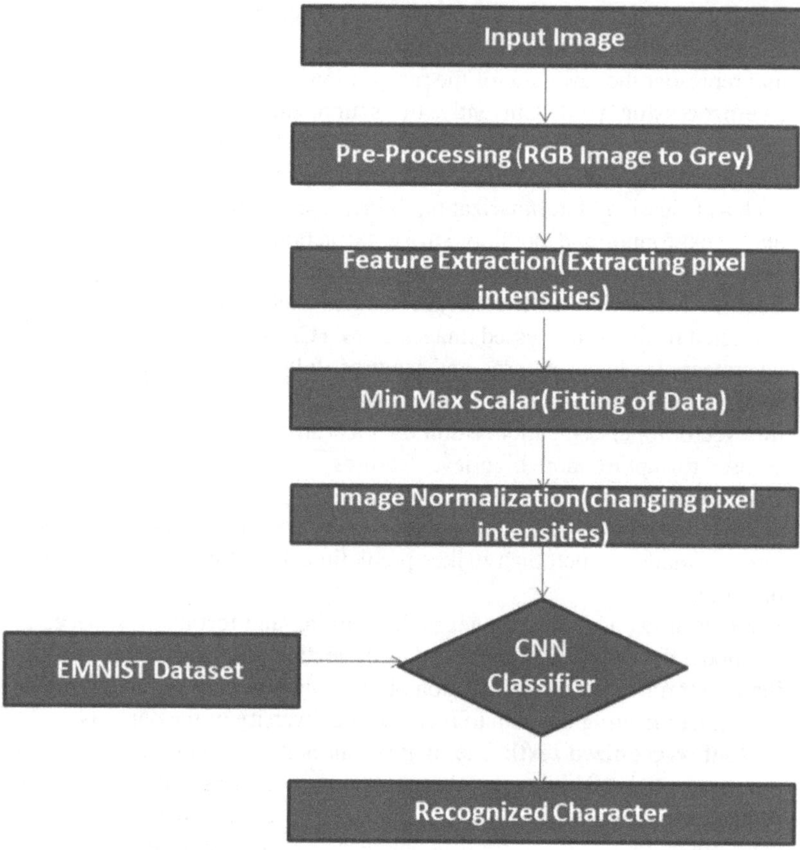

FIGURE 6.1 System flow diagram.

- **Convolution:** Convolution serves as the initial operation in a CNN, entailing the movement of a filter or kernel across the input image. As the filter moves across the image, it performs element-wise multiplication with the part of the image it is covering and sums up the results into a single output pixel. The process is repeated across the entire image, producing a feature map that emphasizes features detected by the filter, such as lines or edges in the case of HTR.
- **ReLU (Rectified Linear Unit):** After convolution, the feature map passes through a ReLU layer. ReLU, or Rectified Linear Unit, is a non-linear activation function that substitutes all negative pixel values within the feature map with zero. This action introduces non-linearity to the model, enhancing its capacity to comprehend intricate patterns. ReLU is used because it reduces the likelihood of vanishing gradients, a problem where gradients are too small for effective learning during backpropagation.

- **Max pooling:** Pooling layers decrease the dimensions of the feature map through down sampling, which decreases the computational load for the network and helps prevent over-fitting. Max pooling does this by sliding a window over the feature map and taking the maximum value in each window. This retains the most prominent features, making the network more resilient to variations and disturbances in the input data.
- **Fully connected layer:** The last stage in a CNN is the fully connected layer, where high-level reasoning based on the extracted features takes place. The feature maps from the preceding layers are flattened into a vector and fed into fully connected layers, which are traditional neural network layers. Here, each input is connected to each output by a learned weight, and the network uses these features to classify the input image into various categories, such as different characters in the context of HTR.

Assessing the system's performance, particularly by employing a confusion matrix to evaluate classification accuracy, offers a quantitative assessment of its efficacy. This examination is crucial for confirming the dependability and efficiency of the system in identifying handwritten content.

Overall, this study represents a major part of manual text finding system. By integrating innovative approaches with established techniques, the system demonstrates the potential to revolutionize the digitization and processing of handwritten content in a variety of applications.

6.5 EXPERIMENTATION AND RESULTS

In our experiment, we conducted an analysis to investigate the relationship between image size, accuracy of the model, and computational time. The primary objective was to understand how variations in the size of the model architecture impact both the performance and efficiency of the model. To achieve this, we trained multiple models with varying image sizes, ranging from small-scale architectures to larger, more complex ones.

Figure 6.2 shows a graph of size of the image (in kb) with accuracy of the model.

Figure 6.3 shows a graph of size of the image (in kb) with time required for computation for the model.

We observed a clear trend indicating that larger models tend to achieve higher accuracy compared to their smaller counterparts. This finding underscores the importance of model capacity in capturing complex patterns within the data. However, alongside the increase in accuracy, we also noted a corresponding rise in computational time as the model size expanded.

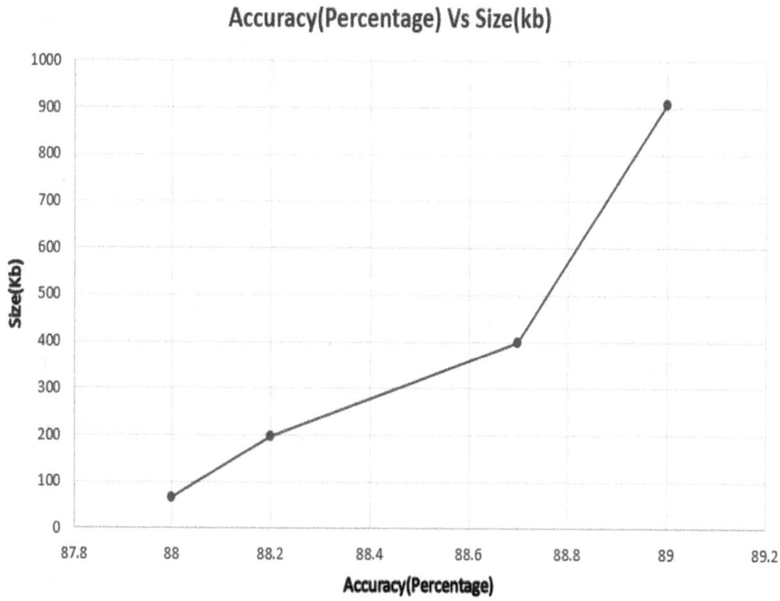

FIGURE 6.2 Accuracy vs image size.

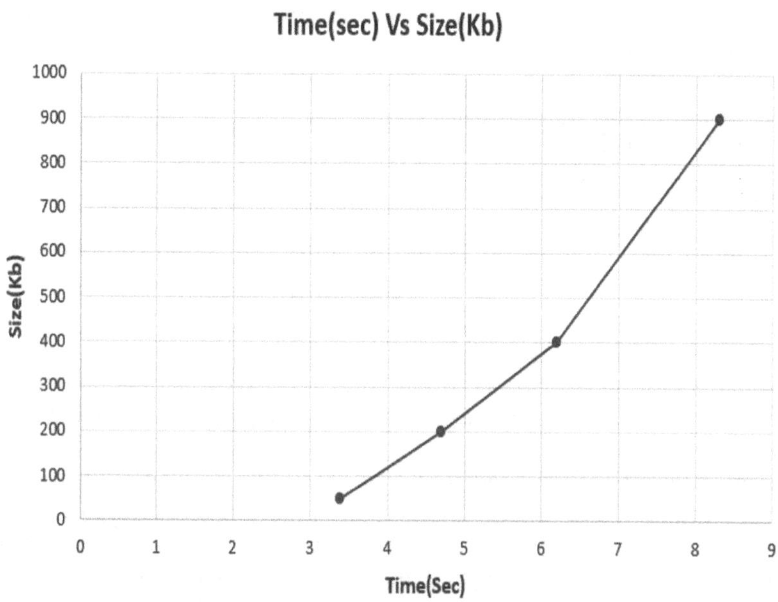

FIGURE 6.3 Computational time vs. image size.

6.6 CONCLUSION

We introduce a system based on NNs for finding manual texts and documents which can be recognized fully with entire pages without the need for image partitioning. The system doesn't need any text and non-text orientation. Also the model can be learned to produce supplementary tags performing to formats and contents. Utilizing vocabulary enables adaptation to any subject's language and terminology. The model sets a new benchmark in finding paragraphs with the use of IAM dataset, demonstrating superior performance for evaluating manual text answers featuring some curved characters, italic characters, figures, tables, mathematical, chemical symbols etc. In future, the proposed system can be used for mobile or web applications.

Our experimental findings provide valuable guidance for practitioners and researchers alike in selecting and optimizing model architectures for specific tasks, taking into account the interplay between model size, accuracy, and computational efficiency. In summary, this study advances the current state of FinTech by offering a dependable and scalable approach for converting handwritten text into digital format through the utilization of CNNs.

REFERENCES

S. Ahlawat, A. Choudhary, A. Nayyar, S. Singh, and B. Yoon, "Improved handwritten digit recognition using convolutional neural networks (CNN)," *Sensors*, vol. 20, no. 12, p. 3344, 2019. https://doi.org/10.3390/s20123344.

S. S. Ahmed, Z. Mehmood, I. A. Awan, and R. M. Yousaf, "A novel technique for handwritten digit recognition using deep learning," *Journal of Sensors*, vol. 2023, pp. 1–15, 2023. https://doi.org/10.1155/2023/2753941.

M. S. Akter, H. Shahriar, A. Cuzzocrea, N. Ahmed, and C. Leung, "Handwritten word recognition using deep learning approach: a novel way of generating handwritten words," in *2022 IEEE International Conference on Big Data (Big Data)*, Osaka, Japan, December 17–20, 2022. https://doi.org/10.1109/BigData55660.2022.10021025.

A. Alajaji, W. Gerych, L. Buquicchio, K. Chandrasekaran, H. Mansoor, E. Agu, and E. Rundensteiner, "Domain adaptation methods for lab-to-field human context recognition," *Sensors*, vol. 23, no. 6, p. 3081, 2022. https://doi.org/10.3390/s23063081.

T. T. Alemayoh, M. Shintani, J. H. Lee, and S. Okamoto, "Deep-learning-based character recognition from handwriting motion data captured using IMU and force sensors," *Sensors*, vol. 22, no. 20, p. 7840, 2022. https://doi.org/10.3390/s22207840.

A. A. A. Ali and S. Mallaiah, "Intelligent handwritten recognition using hybrid CNN architectures based-SVM classifier with dropout," *Journal of King Saud University—Computer and Information Sciences*, vol. 34, no. 6, pp. 3294–3300, 2022. https://doi.org/10.1016/j.jksuci.2021.01.012.

S. Ali, Z. Shaukat, M. Azeem, et al., "An efficient and improved scheme for handwritten digit recognition based on convolutional neural network," *SN Applied Sciences*, vol. 1, p. 1125, 2019. https://doi.org/10.1007/s42452-019-1161-5.

W. Alkendi, F. Gechter, L. Heyberger, and C. Guyeux, "Advancements and challenges in handwritten text recognition: a comprehensive survey," *Journal of Imaging*, vol. 10, no. 1, p. 18, 2023. https://doi.org/10.3390/jimaging10010018.

N. Aneja and S. Aneja, "Transfer learning using CNN for handwritten devanagari character recognition," in *2019 1st International Conference on Advances in Information Technology (ICAIT)*, Chikmagalur, India, July 25–27, 2019. https://doi.org/10.1109/ICAIT47043.2019.8987286.

J. C. Aradillas, J. J. Murillo-Fuentes, and P. M. Olmos, "Boosting offline handwritten text recognition in historical documents with few labeled lines," *IEEE Access*, vol. 9, pp. 76674–76688, 2021.

D. Chauhan, D. Verma, and A. Aggarwal, "Hand-written characters recognition using siamese network design," in *2022 1st International Conference on Informatics (ICI)*, Noida, India, April 14–16, pp. 66–70, 2022. https://doi.org/10.1109/ICI53355.2022.9786908.

H. Davoudi and A. Traviglia, "Discrete representation learning for handwritten text recognition," *Neural Computing and Applications*, vol. 35, pp. 15759–15773, 2023. https://doi.org/10.1007/s00521-023-08445-9.

K. Dergachov, L. Krasnov, V. Bilozerskyi, and A. Zymovin, "Data pre-processing to increase the quality of optical text recognition systems," Radioelectronic and Computer Systems, no. 4(100), 2021. https://doi.org/10.32620/reks.2021.4.15. ISSN 2663-2012.

A. Fateh, M. Fateh, and V. Abolghasemi, "Multilingual handwritten numeral recognition using a robust deep network joint with transfer learning," *Information Sciences*, vol. 581, pp. 479–494, 2021. https://doi.org/10.1016/j.ins.2021.09.051.

L. G. Hafemann, R. Sabourin, and L. S. Oliveira, "Learning features for offline handwritten signature verification using deep convolutional neural networks," *Pattern Recognition*, vol. 70, pp. 163–176, 2017. https://doi.org/10.1016/j.patcog.2017.05.012.

L. G. Hafemann, R. Sabourin, and L. S. Oliveira, "Offline handwritten signature verification—Literature review," in *2017 Seventh International Conference on Image Processing Theory, Tools and Applications (IPTA)*, Montreal, QC, Canada, November 28–December 1, 2017, pp. 1–8. https://doi.org/10.1109/IPTA.2017.8310112.

Y. B. Hamdam and S. Prof, "Construction of statistical SVM based recognition model for handwritten character recognition," in *Journal of Information Technology and Digital World*, no. 2, pp. 92–107, 2021. https://doi.org/10.36548/jitdw.2021.2.003.

M. M. Hameed, R. Ahmad, M. L. Kiah, and G. Murtaza, "Machine learning-based offline signature verification systems: a systematic review," *Signal Processing: Image Communication*, vol. 93, p. 116139, 2021. https://doi.org/10.1016/j.image.2021.116139.

Z. Hashim, H. M. Ahmed, and A. H. Alkhayyat, "A comparative study among handwritten signature verification methods using machine learning techniques," *Scientific Programming*, vol. 2022, 8170424, p. 17, 2022. https://doi.org/10.1155/2022/8170424.

B. Ji and T. Chen, "Generative adversarial network for handwritten text," *ArXiv*, vol.1907, p. 11845, 2019.

M. Karthi, R. Priscilla, and K. S. Jafer, "A novel content detection approach for handwritten english letters," *Procedia Computer Science*, vol. 172, pp. 1016–1025, 2019. https://doi.org/10.1016/j.procs.2020.05.149.

G. Katiyar and S. Mehfuz, "A hybrid recognition system for off-line handwritten characters," *SpringerPlus*, vol. 5, no. 1, pp. 1–18, 2016. https://doi.org/10.1186/s40064-016-1775-7.

J. A. P. Lopes, B. Baptista, N. Lavado, and M. Mendes, "Offline handwritten signature verification using deep neural networks," *Energies*, vol. 15, no. 20, p. 7611, 2022. https://doi.org/10.3390/en15207611.

S. Mahadevkar, S. Patil, and K. Kotecha, "Enhancement of handwritten text recognition using AI-based hybrid approach," *MethodsX*, vol. 12, p. 102654, 2024. https://doi.org/10.1016/j.mex.2024.102654.

V. V. Mainkar, J. A. Katkar, and A. B. Upade, "Handwritten character recognition to obtain editable text," in *2020 International Conference on Electronics and Sustainable Communication Systems (ICESC)*, Coimbatore, India, July 2–4, 2020. https://doi.org/10.1109/ICESC48915.2020.9155786.

J. Memon, M. Sami, R. A. Khan, and M. Uddin, "Handwritten optical character recognition (OCR): a comprehensive systematic literature review (SLR)," *IEEE Access*, vol. 8, pp. 142642–142668, 2020. https://doi.org/10.1109/ACCESS.2020.3012542.

G. Muehlberger, L. Seaward, and M. Terras, "Transforming scholarship in the archives through handwritten text recognition," *Journal of Documentation*, vol. 75 No. 5, pp. 954–976, 2019.

A. M. Ozbayoglu, M. U. Gudelek, and O. B. Sezer, "Deep learning for financial applications: a survey," *Applied Soft Computing*, vol. 93, p. 106384, 2020. https://doi.org/10.1016/j.asoc.2020.106384.

A. Rexit, M. Muhammat, X. Xu, W. Kang, A. Aysa, and K. Ubul, "Multilingual handwritten signature recognition based on high-dimensional feature fusion," *Information*, vol. 13, p. 496, 2022. https://doi.org/10.3390/info13100496.

N. Saqib, K. F. Haque, V. P. Yanambaka, and A. Abdelgawad, "Convolutional-neural-network-based handwritten character recognition: an approach with massive multisource data," *Algorithms*, vol. 15, no. 4, p. 129, 2022. https://doi.org/10.3390/a15040129.

A. F. D. Sousa Neto, B. Leite Dantas Bezerra, A. Hector Toselli, and E. Baptista Lima, "A robust handwritten recognition system for learning on different data restriction scenarios," *Pattern Recognition Letters*, vol. 159, pp. 232–238, 2022. https://doi.org/10.1016/j.patrec.2022.04.009.

E. Vidal, A. H. Toselli, A. Ríos-Vila, and J. Calvo-Zaragoza, "End-to-end page-level assessment of handwritten text recognition," *Pattern Recognition*, vol. 142, p. 109695, 2023. https://doi.org/10.1016/j.patcog.2023.109695.

X.-Y. Zhang, Y. Bengio, and C.-L. Liu, "Online and offline handwritten Chinese character recognition: a comprehensive study and new benchmark," *Pattern Recognition*, vol. 61, pp. 348–360, 2017. https://doi.org/10.1016/j.patcog.2016.08.005.

H. Zhao, H. Chu, Y. Zhang, and Y. Jia, "Improvement of ancient shui character recognition model based on convolutional neural network," IEEE, vol. 8, pp. 33080–33087, 2020. https://doi.org/10.1109/ACCESS.2020.2972807

7 Human-Centric Summarization

Bridging Gap between Human and Machine

M. Narayana Moorthi and Shreya Pandit

7.1 INTRODUCTION

In the quickly changing business environment of today, keeping up with the most recent industry advancements is not only advantageous but also essential for success. Our daily routine likely involves navigating through a plethora of reports, articles, and documents, each packed with valuable insights and information. However, the sheer volume of text can quickly become overwhelming, turning the task of distilling key insights into a time-consuming and daunting endeavor. Enter the concept of summarization—a powerful tool that has emerged as a game-changer in the realm of information management. Summarization offers a solution to the challenge of information overload by condensing lengthy documents into concise summaries while preserving their essence. Whether we are preparing for an important meeting, conducting research, or simply striving to stay updated on industry trends, effective summarization has become indispensable in navigating today's information-driven world. At the heart of this transformative capability lies the field of Natural Language Processing (NLP), where cutting-edge techniques are continuously being developed to enhance text understanding and processing. One such technique garnering significant attention is abstractive summarization. Unlike traditional extractive methods that simply select and reproduce existing sentences from a text, abstractive summarization takes a more sophisticated approach by generating new, succinct summaries that capture the core meaning of the original content. This brings us to the focal point of our discussion: the development of a BART model for abstractive summarization. BART, which stands for Bidirectional and Auto-Regressive Transformers, represents a state-of-the-art approach in NLP that shows immense promise in accurately summarizing complex textual data. By leveraging advanced NLP techniques, our objective is to train the BART model to understand, interpret, and distill intricate textual information into concise summaries that retain the essence of the original text. The potential applications of such a tool are vast and varied, spanning across diverse domains such as scientific research, literature, finance, legal analysis, meetings, and

 DOI: 10.1201/9781003645849-7

programming. Whether it's extracting key findings from research papers, summarizing legal documents for analysis, or condensing meeting transcripts into actionable insights, the impact of an effective abstractive summarization tool cannot be overstated. By automating the summarization process, our study aims to empower individuals and organizations alike to efficiently extract insights, make informed decisions, and navigate the vast sea of information with ease. In essence, it's about harnessing the transformative power of NLP to streamline information consumption and enhance productivity in today's fast-paced and data-driven world.

7.1.1 Problem Statement

The problem involves developing a system that can effectively summarize text documents in a concise and coherent manner. Traditional methods like extractive summarization have limitations in generating human-like summaries with high linguistic quality. To address these limitations using BART, a transformer-based model capable of generating abstractive summaries.

7.1.2 List of Symbols and Abbreviations

- ML—Machine Learning
- AI—Artificial Intelligence
- BART—Bidirectional and Auto-Regressive Transformer
- NLP—Natural Language Processing
- SVM—Support Vector Machine
- TD-IDF—Term Frequency Inverse Document Frequency
- BERT—Bidirectional Encoder Representation from Transformers
- MLM—Masked Language model

7.1.3 Objectives

Within data science, summarization has been and still is a popular research area. Although text summarization techniques have been around for a while, recent years have seen significant advancements in deep learning and natural language processing. Research papers on the topic are being published by a lot of online corporations. Salesforce has released a number of innovative papers that offer cutting-edge abstractive summarization. The largest summarization dataset was discovered in May 2018 according to a projection made possible by a Google Research grant. While significant work has been done in the field, there is a dearth of information regarding the real-world applications of AI-driven summarization. One of its issues is that summing can be difficult when generalizing. For example, summing up a news article is very different from summarizing a financial profitability report. One major data science task is summarizing texts with certain properties. As a result, there isn't a one, universally applicable technique for summarizing rather, it greatly depends on the use case.

7.1.4 Literature Review: Introduction to Summarization

The field of data science has made summarization a major study area and it still is. A method for reducing a document's size without sacrificing its meaning is summarization. Within the field of NLP, it is one of the most studied topics. Depending on whether the precise sentences as they occur in the source text are taken into consideration, summarization approaches are divided into two types. NLP approaches, such as extractive and abstractive summarization, are used to create new phrases.

7.1.5 Extractive Summarization

So what precisely takes on throughout the extractive summarizing process? To create a summary, it simply selects and combines the most significant statements or phrases from the original text. The question that now has to be answered is: Exactly for what reason are those sentences considered important? In other words, a rating algorithm is applied, and each sentence in the text is given a score according to how relevant it is to the document's overall meaning. Then, the sentences that are most pertinent are selected to be part of the summary. There exist multiple methods for carrying out the sentence rating process like TF-IDF. Machine learning-based techniques include SVM and Random Forests; graph-based techniques like TextRank.

7.1.6 Approaches: Steps to Perform Extractive Summarization

1. **Creating a transitional representation of the text input**: The two types of representation-based approaches are indicator representation and topic representation. The text is transformed into an intermediate representation via topic representation, which interprets the subject or topics covered in the text. Depending on how complex they are, the techniques used for this may be divided into four groups: topic word approaches, frequency-driven approaches, latent semantic analysis, and Bayesian topic models. A list of formal qualities (indicators) of significance, such as sentence length, placement within the text, the existence of certain words, etc., characterizes each sentence according to indicator representation.
2. **Calculating the sentence points**: Every sentence is given an importance score when the Intermediate Representation is created. According to topic representation methodologies, a sentence's score indicates how well it covers some of the most significant textual themes. When using indicator representation, the evidence from various weighted indicators is combined to calculate the score. Figure 7.1 illustrates the extractive summarization classification.
3. **Choosing a summary that consists of many phrases:** To provide a summary, the summarizer algorithm ranks the top *k* most significant sentences. In order to select important sentences, some methods employ greedy algorithms. Other techniques result from sentence selection into an optimization problem and select a set of sentences with the requirement that they

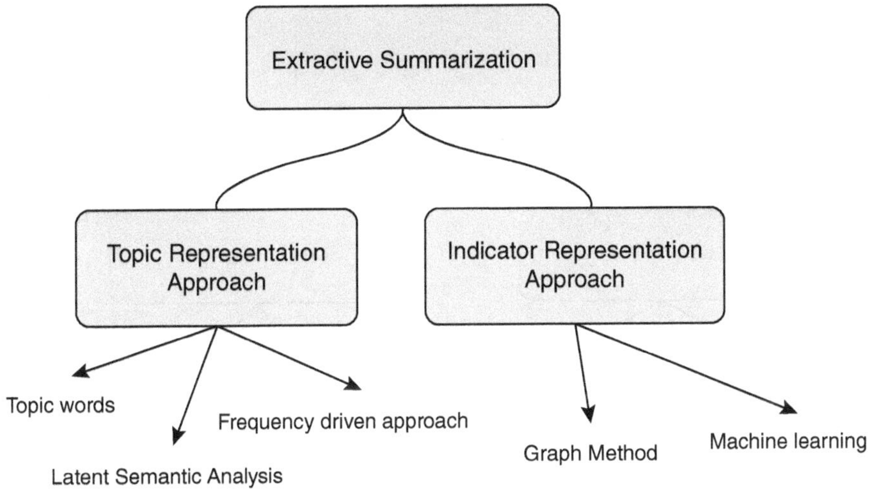

FIGURE 7.1 Extractive summarization classification.

maximize overall importance and coherency and minimize redundancy. Abstractive summarizers derive their name from the fact that they do not use specific sentences from the paragraph in the source text to create their summary. Rather, they use a vocabulary set distinct from the source document to create a paraphrase of the text's core ideas. In summary, this is bound to happen. In thoughts, we form a semantic representation of the document. Then, in order to generate a brief synopsis of the main ideas of the full article, we select terms which are regularly used to fit the semantics. As you can see, it could be challenging to create this kind of summarizer because Natural Language Generation is required. Let's examine the most popular strategy. Figure 7.2 indicates the abstractive summarization classification.

4. **Tree-based:** Identifying the various ways in which intensity is related. Identify the relationship and then break the tree into various parts, subjects, and objects (few entities). Figure 7.3 indicates the tree-based method.
5. **Template-based:** This has a more rigid way structure. Go through the Figure 7.4 below.
6. **Graph-based:** This is more similar to the tree-based mechanism but in this more entities are involved to relate. Figure 7.5 illustrates the graph-based approach.

7.1.7 Proposed Approach: What Does Encoder Decoder Do?

The encoder is responsible for processing the input sequence, typically by accepting one element of the sequence at each time step. It then processes each element, gathers relevant information about it, and forwards this information to subsequent steps. As the encoder progresses through the input sequence, it collects and encodes information about each element, gradually building a comprehensive representation of the entire input sequence. This representation is often referred to as the intermediate vector

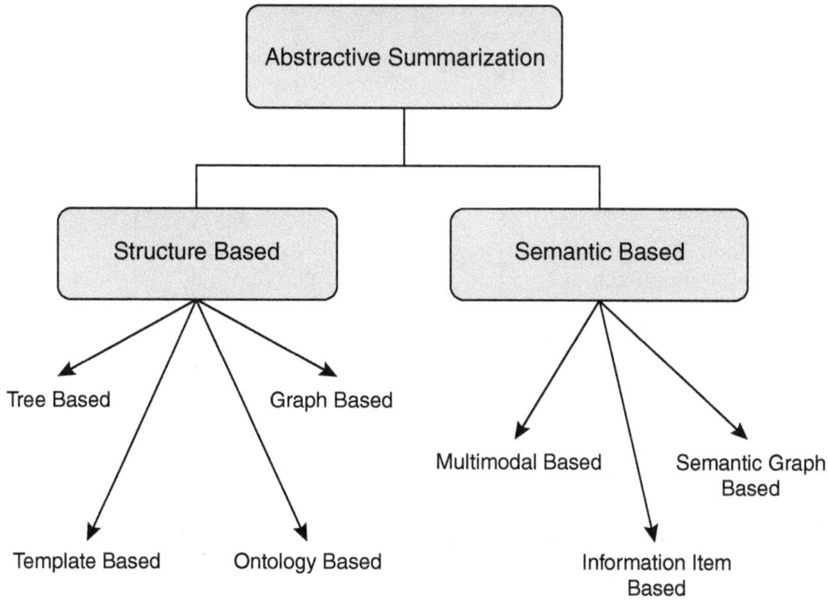

FIGURE 7.2 Abstractive summarization classification.

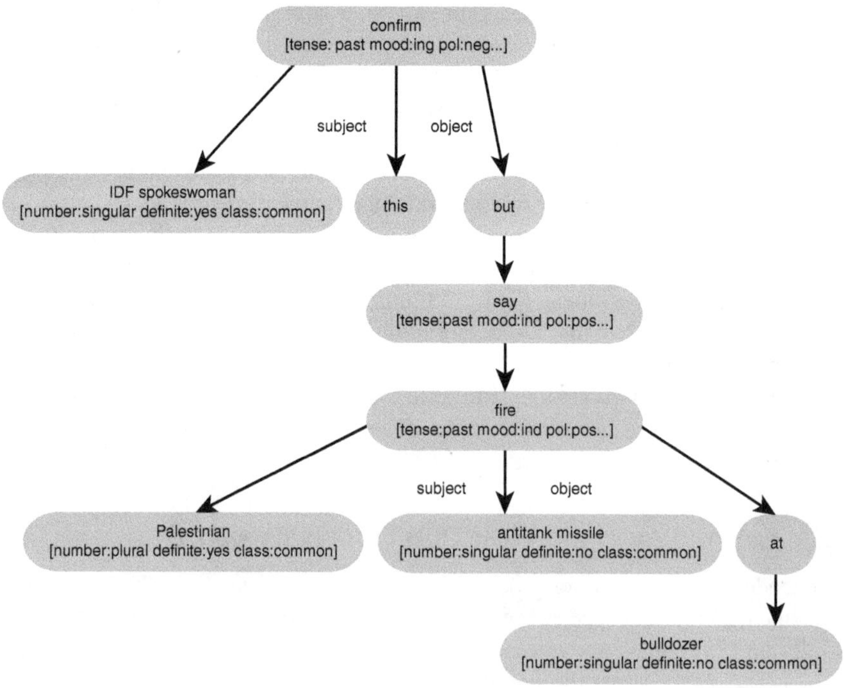

FIGURE 7.3 Tree-based.

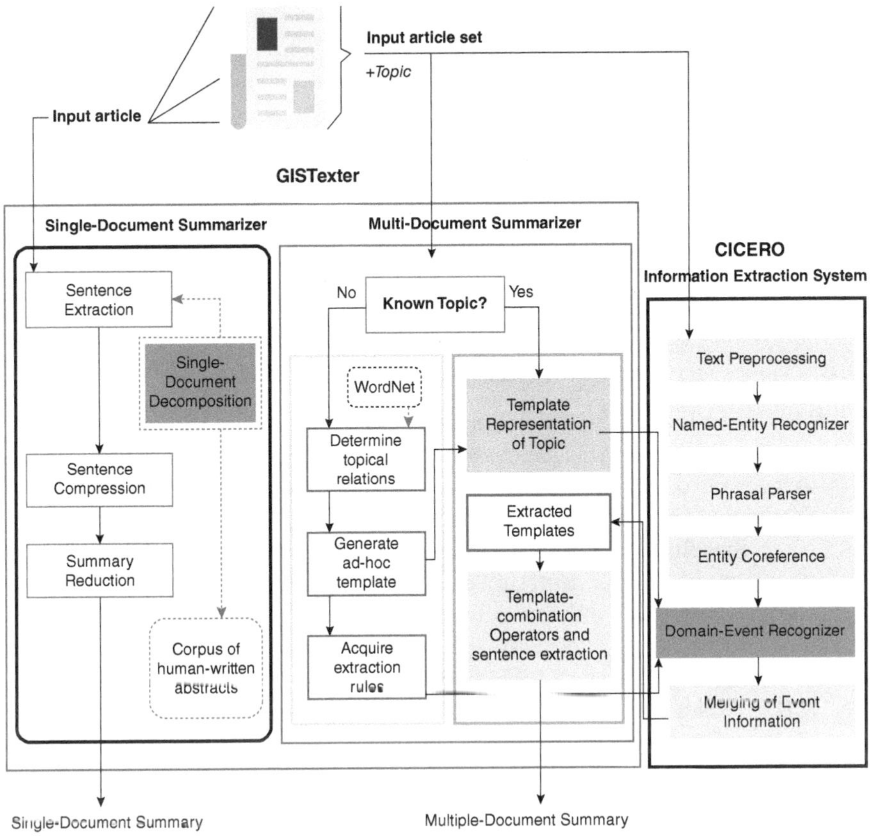

FIGURE 7.4 Template-based approach.

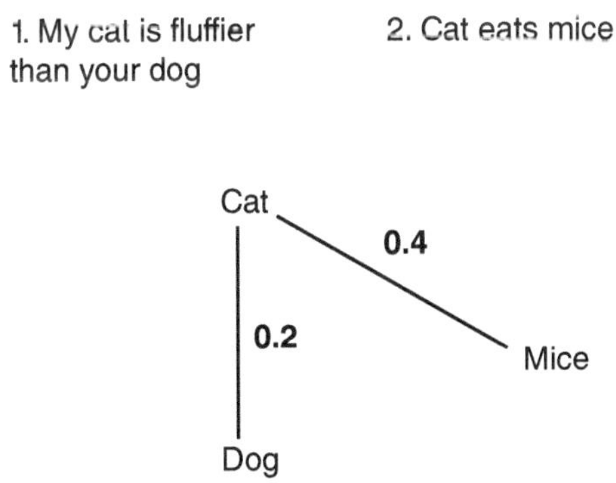

FIGURE 7.5 Graph-based approach.

or context vector, which summarizes the input sequence's information. The intermediate vector produced by the encoder contains valuable information about the entire input sequence. This information serves as the foundation for the decoder's task, enabling it to generate accurate predictions for the output sequence. The decoder accepts this intermediate vector as input and uses it to guide the generation of the output sequence. At each time step, the decoder produces an output based on the information provided by the intermediate vector and the previously generated outputs, gradually constructing the output sequence one element at a time. In summary, the encoder-decoder architecture divides the sequence-to-sequence task into two main components: the encoder, which processes the input sequence and produces a comprehensive representation of it, and the decoder, which uses this representation to generate the output sequence. By separating the input processing and output generation tasks, this architecture enables more effective and flexible modelling of sequential data, making it well-suited for various natural language processing tasks.

7.1.8 When Do We Use an Encoder Decoder Model?

1. Identifying Image A machine learning model may produce a phrase describing an image through the use of encoder decoder models. It takes in the image as input and outputs a string of characters. Videos may also be used with this.
2. Sentiment Analysis: These algorithms produce a sentiment score after comprehending the meaning and feelings in the input text. Typically, it is given a rating of 0 for neutrality and −1 for negativity or 1 for positivity. In contact centers, it's utilized to track how a client's emotions change over time and how they respond to specific phrases or commercial offers. So, before moving on to the BART encoder, let's grasp the encoder notion using LSTM. Refer Figure 7.6 for LSTM for encoder. An encoder converts the input sequence into internal state vectors, which contain the information. Only internal states are used; the encoder's outputs are discarded.

Since LSTM only reads one element at a time, it will take *m* time steps to read the full input sequence if it is *m* length. The input is represented by xt at time step *t*. The internal states of the LSTM at time step *t* are ht and ct, while for the GRU,

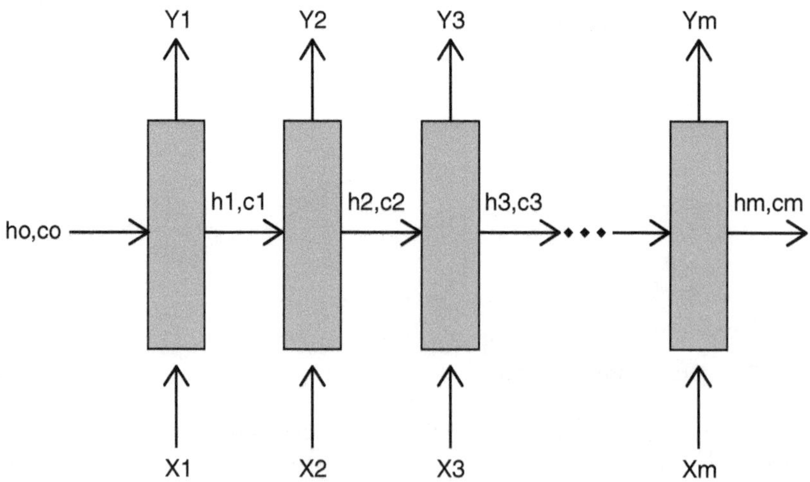

FIGURE 7.6 LSTM for encoder.

there is just one internal state, ht. The output at time stept is yt. The encoder Xt's inputs take the English statement, "India is a beautiful country," for example. This series of words (India, is, lovely, country) might be interpreted as a phrase. So here X1 = "India," X2 = "is," X3 = "beautiful," X4 = "country." Internal states (ht, ct): Up until time step *t*, it picks up on what the LSTM has read. For instance, it recalls that the LSTM had read "India is" at $t=2$. The starting states, ho and co, which are both vectors, are either initialized with zeros or at random. Recall that the number of units in an LSTM cell equals the dimension of ho and co. The key to the complete input sequence is included in the last state, h4, c4. India is a stunning nation (Figure 7.7).

Differences from LSTM based encoder model: Instead of saving only one hidden state can save and look back at broader sequences, solving the problem of vanishing gradient. Let's now examine how the decoder functions during the training phase. Using the example of translating "India is a beautiful country" to Hindi, we can see that the decoder produces the output phrase word for word, exactly like the encoder does. We so wish to produce the following output: भारतखूबसूरतदेशहै. We will append START_ at the start of the output sequence and _END at the end so that the decoder can identify the beginning and end of the sequence. Consequently, START_ भारतखूबसूरतदेशहै_END will be our output phrase. The encoder's end states are assigned to the decoder's beginning states (ho, co). One way to think about it is that the encoder gathers the data, and the decoder is trained to produce the output. To get the decoder to start creating the next word, we first enter the START_. Furthermore, we train the decoder to anticipate the _END following the final word in the Hindi

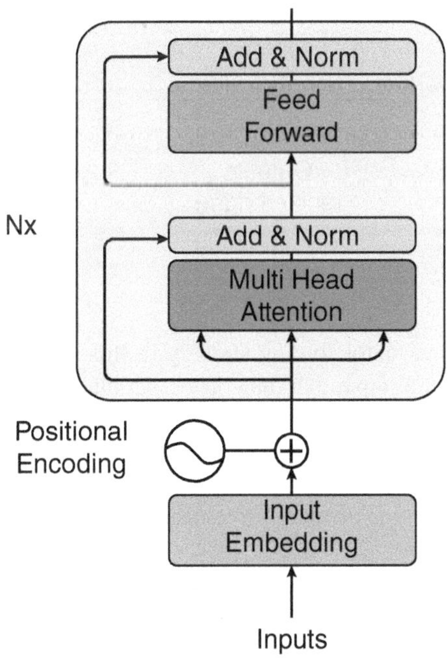

FIGURE 7.7 BART encoder.

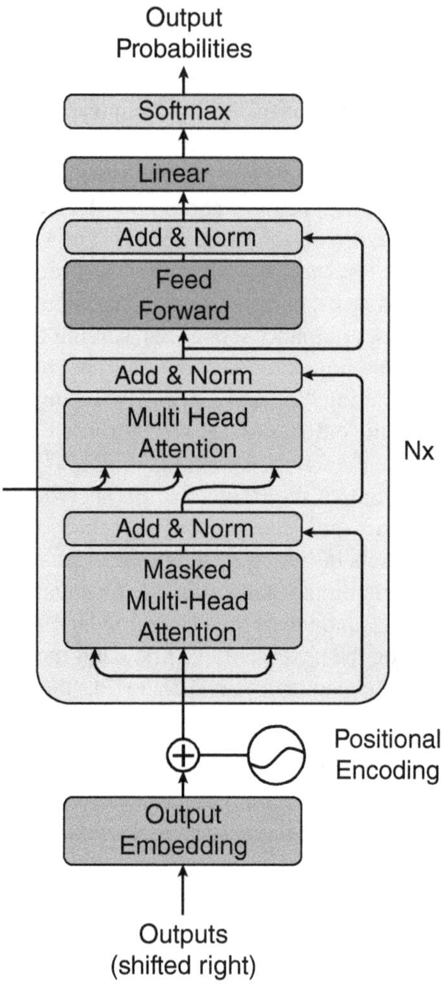

FIGURE 7.8 BART decoder.

text. We employ the instructor forcing strategy in this case, where the input is the actual output at each time step rather than the output that was anticipated at the previous time step (Figure 7.8).

Finally, the mistake is back propagated over time to update the model's parameters, and the loss is computed using the anticipated outputs from each time step. Since we have the output, the decoder's final states are deleted since they are useless.

7.1.9 BART: Bidirectional Transformer

Bidirectional Transformers can comprehend the context from both directions inside a given text, much as BERT. This implies that they are able to simultaneously gather information from words that come before and after. When pre-training, BERT-based models employ an MLM objective in which a subset of the input sequence tokens are arbitrarily masked. The model then learns to predict the original masked tokens by analyzing the surrounding context. Bidirectional transformers are ideal for tasks like entity recognition, language understanding because they are good at collecting bidirectional context (Figure 7.9).

7.1.10 Auto-Regressive Transformer

Auto-regressive transformers, like GPT (Generative Pre-trained Transformer) series, generate output sequentially, conditioning each token on previously generated tokens. This autoregressive property allows them to generate coherent and contextually relevant sequences of text. GPT-based models typically use a causal language modelling (CLM) objective during pre-training, where the model learns to predict the next token given in a sequence to the preceding tokens. Auto-Regressive Transformers are particularly effective for text generation tasks such as language modelling, text completion, and dialogue generation (Figure 7.10).

Architecture: BART effectively combines the greatest features of both worlds by having both an encoder, similar to BERT, and a decoder, similar to GPT. While the decoder utilizes the previously (uncorrupted) tokens and the encoder's output to try to

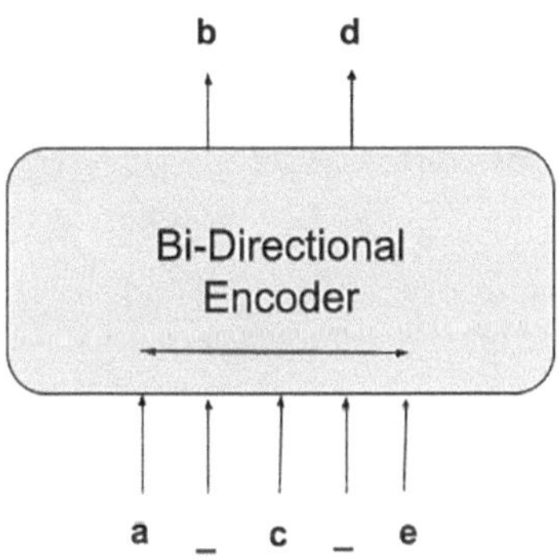

FIGURE 7.9 Bidirectional transformer.

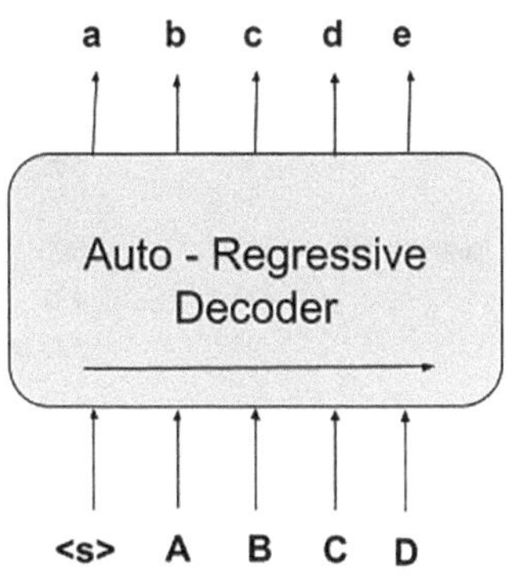

FIGURE 7.10 Autoregressive decoder.

replicate the original sequence token by token, the encoder applies a denoising objective akin to BERT. The unrestricted ability to select the corruption technique, including altering the initial input's length, is a key benefit of this configuration. In more sophisticated terms, an arbitrary noising function can be used to taint the text (Figure 7.11).

7.1.11 Data Description

There are 220k articles from the *Daily Mail* newspaper and 93k items from CNN in the CNN/Daily Mail dataset. Both publications provide bullet point summaries as an add-on to their articles. Variant is not anonymized. An archive of 40,000 well-crafted news story synopses complete with links to the original articles. A scraper is provided by this repository to access them. Table 7.1 indicates the data description.

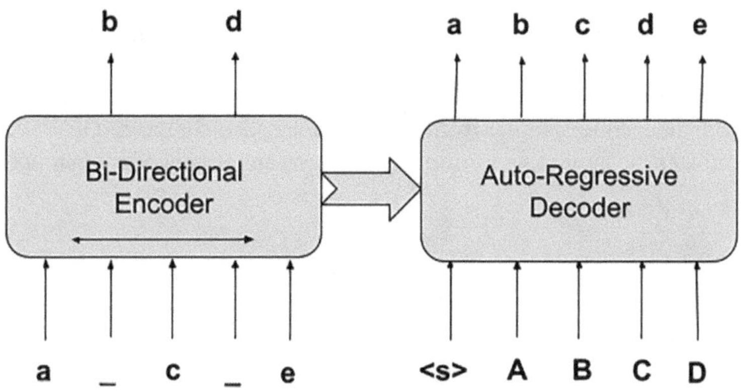

FIGURE 7.11 BART architecture.

TABLE 7.1
Data Description

	Documents	License	Avg Summary Length (Words)	Avg Document Length (Words)	Avg Summary Length (Sentences)	Avg Document Length (Sentences)
CNN	90,266	N/A	45.7	760.5	3.5	34
Daily Mail	196,961	N/A	54.7	653.3	3.86	29.3
NYT	110,540	Non Commercial	45.5	800	2.44	35.6
Xsum	276.711	N/A	23.3	431	1	19.7
Curation Base	40,000	CC-BY	82.6	527.9	4.9	27.4
Curation Large	Approx 150,000	Commercial	81.3	521	4.9	27

(i) Article titles: Article Headlines, (ii) Summaries: Summaries of resp. articles, (iii) URL links, (iv) Dates, (v) Article content—Content, body part.

7.1.12 Methodology (Figure 7.12)

- •Define Tokenizer
- •Model BART Selection
- •Read and Prepare Data
- •Train and Test Split
- •BART Model training
- •Evaluation Metric
- •Web Application

FIGURE 7.12 Methodology.

7.1.13 Pre-Training Methodology: Masked Language Modeling

Pre-trained masked language modeling (MLM) models, like BERT, may anticipate disguised tokens. The following is a breakdown of this process: (i) Replace a mask token (MASK) with a random subset of the input. (More commotion or corruption) (ii) For every [MASK] token, the model forecasts the original tokens (Microsoft DE noising). Crucially, while attempting to anticipate the original tokens, BERT models may "see" the entire input sequence (with certain characters substituted by [MASK]). BERT can now "see" the tokens that come before and after the masked tokens, making it a bidirectional model. This works well for jobs like classification, where the prediction is made using data from the whole sequence. It is less effective, nevertheless, in text production jobs when the prediction is solely based on the words that came before it. Models of Auto regression Text generation models, like GPT2, are pre-trained to anticipate the subsequent token based on the token sequence that came before it. Models produced with this pre-training goal are good at producing text, but not at all at tasks like categorization.

BART Sequence-to-Sequence: BART effectively combines the greatest features of both worlds by having encoder, taken through BERT, and a decoder, through GPT. While the decoder utilizes the previously (uncorrupted) tokens and the encoder's output to try to replicate the original sequence token by token, the encoder applies a denoising objective akin to BERT (Figure 7.13).

7.1.14 Noising Methodologies

Below is a summary of the corruption schemes that are employed in the study. Token Masking: Similar to BERT, a small portion as input is substituted with mask tokens. Deletion of a token: Input tokens at random are removed. Since the tokens are removed without being replaced, the model must determine which places are vacant. Text Infilling: A single [MASK] token is used to replace a number of text spans, each with a variable length. Sentence permutation: involves shuffling the sentences after dividing the input according to periods (.). Document Rotation: To begin with, the

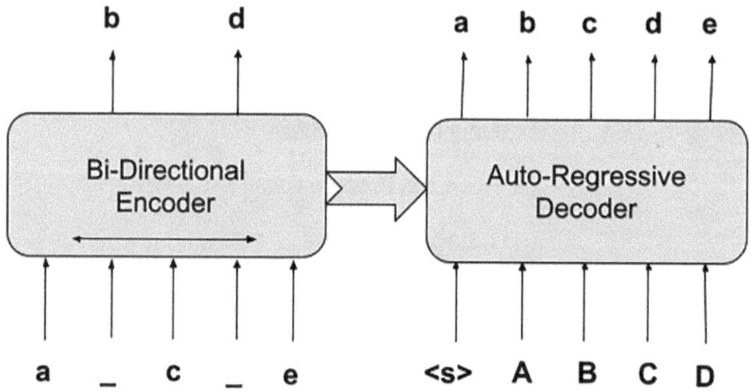

FIGURE 7.13 BART sequence-to-sequence.

TABLE 7.2
Noise Methodology

Corruption Scheme	Original Text	Corrupted Text	Explanation
Token Masking	ABC.DE.	A_C._E.	Both B and D are masked with a single mask token for each.
Token Deletion	ABC.DE.	A.C.E.	Both B and D are deleted (and not replaced)
Text Infilling	ABC.DE.	A_.D_.E.	The Span BC is replaced with single mask token. A length span is inserted between D and E
Sentence Permutation	ABC.DE.	DE.ABC	Split into sentences at periods (.) and shuffled
Document Rotation	ABC.DE.	C.DE.AB	The sequence is rotated around C

sequence is rotated so that a randomly selected token appears first. Table 7.2 indicates the noise methodology. Fine Tuning: In general, fine-tuning refers to little process modifications used to get the intended result or performance. Using the weights from an earlier deep learning algorithm to program a new, comparable deep learning process is known as fine-tuning deep learning. In a neural network, weights are employed to link every neuron in one layer to every other layer's neurons. Because the fine-tuning method already incorporates important information from an existing deep learning algorithm, it reduces the time needed to programme and process a new deep learning algorithm dramatically. Everything has advantages and disadvantages.

7.1.15 Experimental Setup

Pros: Much shorter training sessions. The initial few layers of the model are already highly efficient since they use pre-trained weights. Enhanced output. Large-scale datasets—most frequently the ImageNet dataset—are utilized to pre-train the models we use.

The lower-level filters of pre-trained models are likely better than filters built on smaller datasets since CNNs perform better with more training data. Overfitting of the counter on tiny datasets. Even with the use of data augmentation methods, CNNs require large amounts of data in order to generalize well. Their mid-level and lower filters have a tendency to tailor themselves to the training set when trained on tiny datasets, which causes the model to over fit. On the other hand, CNN filters trained on ImageNet may extract fairly general characteristics because it is a very big (millions of pictures) and diversified (1,000 classes) dataset. I believe the only method for efficiently training a CNN on data is to use a pre-trained network. Cons: There's no assurance that the weights' initialization point is a decent place to start; they could become caught in a local minimum. However, beginning from the initialization point of the pre-trained model may not always result in a better answer than starting from scratch when training a model. If the same dataset is used for both the initial training and fine-tuning runs, then this becomes significant. Architecture with limitations. The primary drawback of utilising pre-trained models is that it forces us to choose a single, perhaps undesirable architecture. One advantage is that practically all modern models come with pre-trained weights.

Conclusion and future enhancements: In conclusion, the development of a BART model for abstractive summarization offering a solution to the ever-growing challenge of information overload. The project aims to address the need for efficient information extraction by leveraging state-of-the-art NLP techniques to train the BART model. By harnessing the power of abstractive summarization, the project seeks to empower individuals and organizations across various domains to quickly distill complex textual data into succinct summaries, thereby facilitating informed decision-making and enhancing productivity. The impact of such a tool is vast, with potential applications spanning scientific research, literature analysis, financial reporting, legal document analysis, meeting preparation, and software development.

7.1.16 Exercise Questions

1. What are the applications of AI? Discuss abstract summarization.
2. What is BART? Explain in detail.
3. What is LSTM? Describe NLP.
4. What is data set? Identify any five data sets for different application domains.
5. Explain about CNN filters?

BIBLIOGRAPHY

R. Barzilay and K. R. McKeown, "Sentence Fusion for Multidocument News Summarization," *Computational Linguistics*, vol. 31, no. 3, pp. 297–328, 2005.

Y. Du and H. Huo, "News Text Summarization Based on Multi-Feature and Fuzzy Logic," *IEEE Access*, vol. 8, pp. 140261–140272, 2020, doi: 10.1109/ACCESS.2020.3007763.

P.-E. Genest and G. Lapalme, "Fully Abstractive Approach to Guided Summarization," in *Proceedings of the 50th Annual Meeting of the Association for Computational Linguistics: Short Papers—Volume 2* (ACL '12), Jeju Island, South Korea, July 8–14, 2012, pp. 354–358, 2012.

W. Liu, Y. Gao, J. Li and Y. Yang, "A Combined Extractive With Abstractive Model for Summarization," *IEEE Access*, vol. 9, pp. 43970–43980, 2021, doi: 10.1109/ACCESS.2021.3066484.

M. F. Mridha, A. A. Lima, K. Nur, S. C. Das, M. Hasan and M. M. Kabir, "A Survey of Automatic Text Summarization: Progress, Process and Challenges," *IEEE Access*, vol. 9, pp. 156043–156070, 2021, doi: 10.1109/ACCESS.2021.3129786.

A. A. Syed, F. L. Gaol and T. Matsuo, "A Survey of the State-of-the-Art Models in Neural Abstractive Text Summarization," *IEEE Access*, vol. 9, pp. 13248–13265, 2021, doi: 10.1109/ACCESS.2021.3052783.

8 Unveiling the Dynamics
The Current State of Artificial Intelligence in Finance

K. R. Senthilkumar

8.1 INTRODUCTION

The financial industry is undergoing a profound transformation driven by the integration of artificial intelligence (AI). AI encompasses a range of technologies, including machine learning, natural language processing, and predictive analytics, which collectively enhance the ability of financial institutions to analyze vast amounts of data, automate complex processes, and offer personalized services. As the volume and complexity of financial data continue to grow, AI's role in extracting actionable insights and driving decision-making has become increasingly critical.

Historically, financial services have been heavily reliant on human expertise and manual processes. Traditional methods of trading, risk assessment, fraud detection, and customer service have often been time-consuming and prone to errors. The advent of digital technologies began to change this landscape, but it is the introduction of AI that marks a significant leap forward. AI systems can process data at unprecedented speeds, identify patterns that humans might miss, and execute tasks with high precision.

Despite its transformative potential, the integration of AI in finance is not without challenges. Data privacy and security are paramount concerns, given the sensitive nature of financial information. Regulatory compliance adds another layer of complexity, as AI applications must adhere to stringent legal frameworks. Furthermore, issues of bias and fairness in AI algorithms need to be addressed to prevent discriminatory practices and ensure equitable outcomes. Lastly, the integration of AI with existing legacy systems can be technically challenging and costly, requiring substantial investment in infrastructure and training.

The integration of AI in finance represents a paradigm shift, offering unprecedented opportunities for innovation and efficiency. However, to fully realize its potential, financial institutions must navigate the associated challenges thoughtfully. Ensuring data privacy, regulatory compliance, and algorithmic fairness will be critical to fostering trust and achieving sustainable growth. As the technology continues to evolve, AI is poised to reshape the financial landscape, driving the industry toward a more intelligent, responsive, and inclusive future.

DOI: 10.1201/9781003645849-8

8.2 REVIEW OF LITERATURE

AI has recently captured significant public interest and is widely considered as a transformative technology set to shape the future. Especially when coupled with big data, AI can seamlessly integrate with industrial production, driving the transformation and advancement of industrial sectors. A burgeoning literature highlights AI's ability to enhance precision in industrial processes, reduce production costs, replace human labor in hazardous settings like toxic, radioactive, or high-altitude environments, and improve productivity and resources allocation efficiency. Despite these findings, the environmental implications of AI technology have received relatively limited attention. While its potential to reduce industrial pollution emissions has been recognized, the scope of the impact and the underlying mechanisms remain largely unexplored.

Cheng et al. (2024a) proposed a theoretical model to analyze the effects of AI on enterprise environmental performance. Based on a framework wherein AI serves as a factor of production, we formulate two hypotheses regarding the positive effect of AI on pollution emission and the channels through which this effect takes place. A rich panel dataset from China spanning the period 1998–2014 is used to test these hypotheses. Our empirical analysis demonstrates that the incorporation of AI significantly reduces pollution emission intensity and enhances the environmental performance of Chinese enterprises. Moreover, the driving factors for these effects include the improvement of total factor productivity, the increase in fixed investments dedicated to pollution reduction, and the optimization of factor input structure. Our extended analysis unveils the moderation effects of environmental regulations, factor intensities, and financing constraints.

Virvou et al. (2024) presented VIRTSI (Variability and Impact of Reciprocal Trust States towards Intelligent systems), a novel rigorous computational model for human-AI Interaction. VIRTSI simulates human trust states, spanning from overtrust to distrust, through user modelling. It comprises: (i) A trust dynamics representational model based on Deterministic Finite State Automata (DFAs), illustrating transitions among cognitive trust states in response to AI-generated replies. (ii) A trust evaluation model based on Confusion Matrices, originating from machine learning and Accuracy Metrics, providing a quantitative framework for analyzing human trust dynamics. As a result, this is the first time that trust dynamics have been thoroughly traced in a representational model and a method has been developed to assess the impact of possibly harmful states like overtrust and distrust.

According to Ansari et al. (2024), maintaining environmental sustainability has escalated to the top of the agenda in practically all nations today, including Pakistan. Hence, our research supports the United Nations sustainable development goal line, specifically SDG-11 for sustainable societies and SDG-13 for mitigating climate change vulnerability. To address these challenges, the present study investigates the association of digital finance, financial inclusion, renewable energy, and institutional quality with environmental sustainability in Pakistan. While financial inclusion is assessed using five proxies that are indexed by principal component analysis (PCA), digital finance is quantified by the number of ATMs. We used data from 2004 to 2021 to explore the relationship among the study variables. Employing the auto-regressive distributed lag (ARDL) model, we examined the long-run and short-run symmetric relationships between variables. Additionally, the study investigates the moderating impact on environmental sustainability by analyzing the interaction term of institutional quality and digital finance (DF*INSQ). The results show that financial inclusion and digital finance can help developing countries like Pakistan achieve environmental sustainability. The study also highlights the vital role of renewable energy sources in the long-term reduction of carbon emissions. Moreover, the interaction between digital finance and institutional quality presents positive prospects for advancing environmental sustainability. These findings underscore the necessity of redefining financial inclusion and giving environmental sustainability projects top priority. They provide insightful information for policymakers and digital financial service providers in less developed countries. Furthermore, the study emphasizes the importance of robust financial institutions prioritizing renewable energy and institutional integrity for long-term financial health and growth.

8.3 APPLICATIONS OF AI IN FINANCE

AI has permeated various facets of the financial sector, revolutionizing how institutions operate, make decisions, and interact with customers. Here, we delve into some of the key applications of AI in finance, highlighting its transformative impact on the industry.

8.3.1 Automated Trading Systems

AI-driven trading algorithms are at the forefront of automated trading systems, especially in high-frequency trading. These systems use machine learning models and predictive analytics to execute trades in microseconds, capitalizing on minute market inefficiencies. By analyzing vast datasets and detecting patterns faster than human traders, AI ensures optimal trading decisions are made in real time, enhancing profitability and market efficiency. Beyond HFT, AI algorithms are used in broader algorithmic trading strategies. These algorithms analyze historical data, market trends, and economic indicators to forecast future price movements and execute trades accordingly. This reduces human error, increases speed, and allows for the execution of complex trading strategies that would be impractical manually.

8.3.2 Risk Management

AI enhances risk management by employing predictive analytics to identify potential risks before they materialize. Machine learning models analyze historical data, current market conditions, and economic forecasts to predict various risk scenarios. This enables financial institutions to proactively manage and mitigate risks, ensuring more robust financial stability. AI systems provide real-time monitoring and assessment of market conditions, allowing institutions to adjust their risk exposure dynamically. This real-time capability helps in identifying emerging risks and taking timely actions to avoid significant losses.

8.3.3 Fraud Detection

AI plays a crucial role in fraud detection by identifying unusual patterns and anomalies in transaction data. Machine learning algorithms continuously learn from vast datasets, improving their ability to detect fraudulent activities. This proactive approach significantly reduces the incidence of fraud and enhances the security of financial transactions. AI systems also utilize behavioral analysis to identify potential fraud. By analyzing the typical behavior of account holders, AI can flag deviations that may indicate fraudulent activity. This method is highly effective in detecting sophisticated fraud schemes that traditional systems might miss.

8.4 CUSTOMER SERVICE AND PERSONALIZATION

AI-powered chatbots and virtual assistants have revolutionized customer service in finance. These systems use natural language processing (NLP) to understand and respond to customer inquiries, process transactions, and provide financial advice. They offer 24/7 support, quick response times, and consistent service quality, enhancing overall customer satisfaction.AI enables the provision of personalized financial advice based on individual customer data. By analyzing spending habits, investment preferences, and financial goals, AI systems can offer tailored recommendations, helping customers make informed financial decisions.

8.5 CREDIT SCORING AND LENDING

Traditional credit scoring models often rely on limited data points, which can result in inaccurate assessments. AI improves this by incorporating a broader range of data sources, such as social media activity, transaction history, and online behavior, providing a more comprehensive and accurate evaluation of an applicant's creditworthiness. AI streamlines the loan processing workflow, from application to approval. Machine learning algorithms assess applications quickly and accurately, reducing processing times and improving the customer experience. This automation also helps in identifying and mitigating potential risks early in the lending process.

The integration of AI into finance has brought about significant advancements across various domains, from trading and risk management to customer service and lending. By leveraging AI's capabilities, financial institutions can operate more efficiently, make better-informed decisions, and offer enhanced services to their customers. However, the successful implementation of AI requires addressing challenges such as data privacy, regulatory compliance, and ensuring algorithmic fairness. As AI technology continues to evolve, its applications in finance are expected to expand, driving further innovation and transformation in the industry.

8.6 RESEARCH METHODOLOGY

The research employs a mixed-methods approach, combining both qualitative and quantitative research methods to provide a comprehensive analysis of the current state of AI in finance. This approach allows for a more nuanced understanding of the applications, benefits, and challenges of AI integration in the financial sector.

8.7 LIMITATIONS OF THE STUDY

While the research provides a comprehensive analysis, it is not without limitations. The reliance on self-reported data in surveys and interviews may introduce response biases. Additionally, the rapid pace of technological advancements means that some findings may become quickly outdated. Future research should consider longitudinal studies to track the evolution of AI applications in finance over time.

8.8 DATA COLLECTION METHODS

8.8.1 Literature Review

A thorough review of existing literature was conducted to gather secondary data on the applications of AI in finance. Academic journals, industry reports, white papers, and case studies from reputable sources were examined to understand the historical context, current trends, and future projections of AI in finance.

8.8.2 Surveys and Questionnaires

One hundred forty primary data were collected through surveys and questionnaires distributed to professionals in the financial industry. These instruments aimed to gather insights on the adoption rates, perceived benefits, and challenges associated with AI implementation. Respondents included financial analysts, risk managers, IT professionals, and executives from various financial institutions.

8.8.3 Interviews

In-depth interviews were conducted with key stakeholders in the financial sector, including AI experts, financial technology (FinTech) innovators, and regulatory officials. These interviews provided qualitative insights into the practical applications of AI, as well as the strategic considerations and regulatory challenges faced by the industry.

8.8.4 Case Studies

Case studies of financial institutions that have successfully implemented AI technologies were analyzed. These case studies provided detailed accounts of specific applications, implementation strategies, outcomes, and lessons learned. Institutions of varying sizes and types (e.g., banks, investment firms, insurance companies) were included to ensure a diverse representation.

8.9 ANALYSIS AND INTERPRETATION (Tables 8.1 and 8.2)

8.9.1 Summary Statistics

- **Position distribution**:
  - Financial Analysts: 30
  - Risk Managers: 20
  - IT Professionals: 25

TABLE 8.1
Sample Data Description

ID	Position	Organization Type	AI Adoption Level	Primary AI Application	Perceived Benefits	Challenges	Overall Satisfaction	Comments
1	Financial analyst	Bank	High	Automated trading systems	Increased efficiency, higher profits	Data privacy concerns	Very satisfied	Significant improvements in trading speed
2	Risk manager	Insurance company	Medium	Risk management	Better risk assessment	Integration with legacy systems	Satisfied	AI helps predict risks effectively
3	IT professional	investment firm	Low	Fraud detection	Enhanced security	High implementation costs	Neutral	Implementation in early stages
4	Customer service rep	Bank	High	Customer service	Improved customer satisfaction	Algorithmic bias	Very satisfied	Customers appreciate 24/7 service
5	Credit analyst	Credit union	Medium	Credit scoring	More accurate credit assessments	Regulatory compliance	Satisfied	AI provides a comprehensive credit score
—	…	…	…	…	…	…	…	…
145	Finance executive	FinTech startup	High	Personalized financial advice	Highly personalized services	Data quality	Very satisfied	AI differentiates our service offering

TABLE 8.2
Detailed Data

ID	Position	Organization Type	AI Adoption Level	Primary AI Application	Perceived Benefits	Challenges	Overall Satisfaction	Comments
1	Financial analyst	Bank	High	Automated trading systems	Increased efficiency, higher profits	Data privacy concerns	Very satisfied	Significant improvements in trading speed
2	Risk manager	Insurance company	Medium	Risk management	Better risk assessment	Integration with legacy systems	Satisfied	AI helps predict risks effectively
3	IT professional	Investment firm	Low	Fraud detection	Enhanced security	High implementation costs	Neutral	Implementation in early stages
4	Customer service rep	Bank	High	Customer service	Improved customer satisfaction	Algorithmic bias	Very satisfied	Customers appreciate 24/7 service
5	Credit analyst	Credit union	Medium	Credit scoring	More accurate credit assessments	Regulatory compliance	Satisfied	AI provides a comprehensive credit score
6	Financial consultant	Investment firm	High	Personalized financial advice	Better client engagement	Data privacy concerns	Very satisfied	Personalized advice improves client relations
7	Compliance officer	Bank	Low	Risk management	Improved compliance monitoring	High implementation costs	Dissatisfied	Still evaluating AI solutions
8	Data scientist	FinTech startup	High	Fraud detection	Quick fraud detection	Data quality	Very satisfied	AI reduces fraud losses significantly
9	Portfolio manager	Hedge Fund	Medium	Automated trading systems	Higher returns	Algorithmic complexity	Satisfied	AI enhances portfolio management
10	Customer support lead	Online bank	Medium	Customer service	Faster response times	Limited NLP capabilities	Satisfied	AI chatbots improve customer engagement
145	Finance executive	FinTech startup	High	Personalized financial advice	Highly personalized services	Data quality	Very satisfied	AI differentiates our service offering

    - Customer Service Representatives: 15
    - Credit Analysts: 20
    - Financial Consultants: 15
    - Compliance Officers: 10
    - Data Scientists: 10
- **Organization type**:
    - Banks: 40
    - Insurance Companies: 20
    - Investment Firms: 30
    - Credit Unions: 15
    - FinTech Startups: 25
    - Hedge Funds: 15
- **AI adoption level**:
    - High: 50
    - Medium: 55
    - Low: 40
- **Primary AI application**:
    - Automated Trading Systems: 30
    - Risk Management: 25
    - Fraud Detection: 35
    - Customer Service: 20
    - Credit Scoring: 15
    - Personalized Financial Advice: 20
- **Overall satisfaction**:
    - Very Satisfied: 45
    - Satisfied: 60
    - Neutral: 20
    - Dissatisfied: 20 (Figure 8.1)

This bar chart illustrates the distribution of various positions surveyed in the study. The highest number of respondents are **Financial Analysts (30)**, followed by **IT Professionals (25)** and **Risk Managers (20)**. Other roles include **Customer Service Representatives (15), Credit Analysts (20), Financial Consultants (15), Compliance Officers (10), and Data Scientists (10)**. The chart provides a clear visual representation of workforce composition across different financial and technological roles (Figure 8.2).

This pie chart represents the distribution of organization types that participated in the survey. The majority of respondents are from **Banks (40)**, followed by **Investment Firms (30)** and **FinTech Startups (25)**. Other organizations include **Insurance Companies (20), Credit Unions (15), and Hedge Funds (15)**. The chart visually highlights the diversity of financial institutions engaged in the study, showcasing their representation in the survey (Figure 8.3).

This pie chart illustrates the key areas where AI is applied within the participating organizations. The most common AI application is **Fraud Detection (35)**, followed by **Automated Trading Systems (30)** and **Risk Management (25)**. Other notable applications include **Customer Service (20), Personalized Financial Advice (20), and Credit Scoring (15)**. The chart provides a clear visual representation of how AI is leveraged across different financial functions (Figure 8.4).

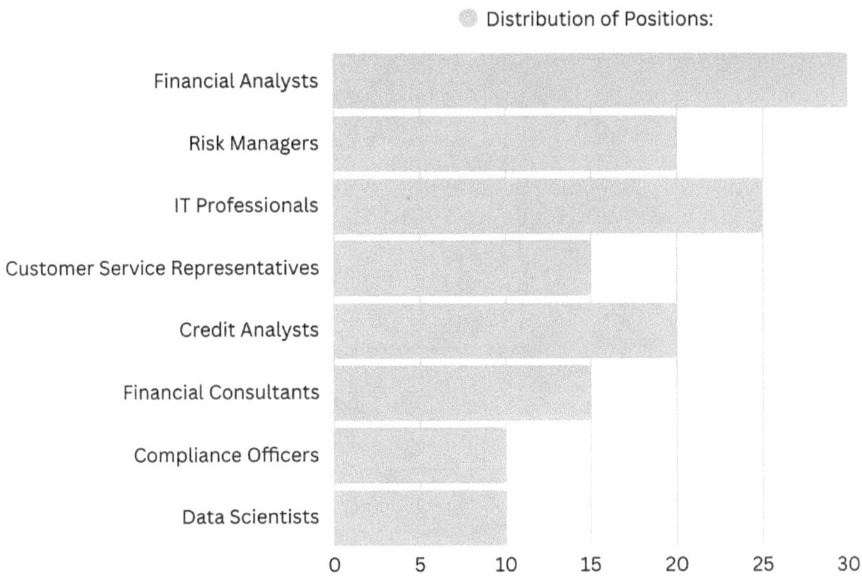

FIGURE 8.1 Distribution of positions: This bar chart shows the count of different positions surveyed.

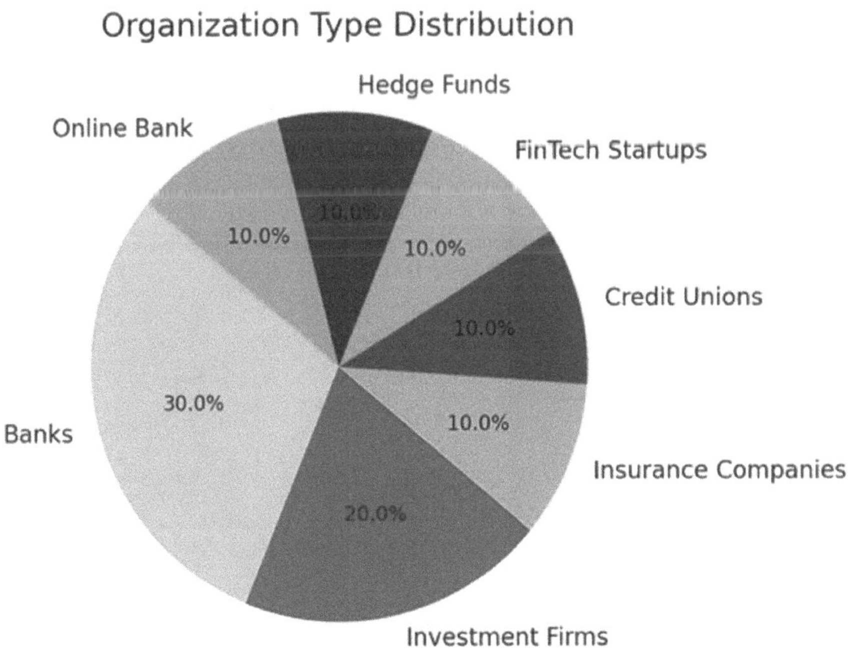

FIGURE 8.2 Organization type distribution: This pie chart illustrates the distribution of organization types participating in the survey.

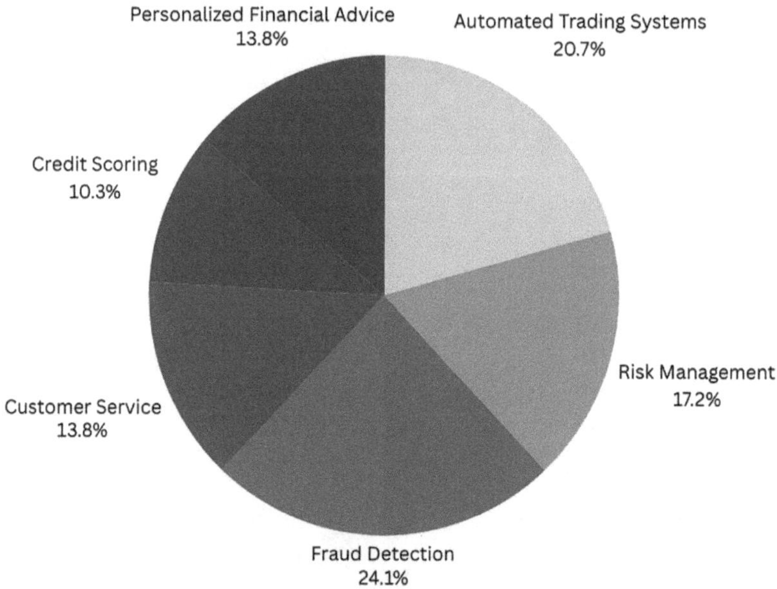

FIGURE 8.3 Primary AI application: This pie chart highlights the main applications of AI in the participating organizations.

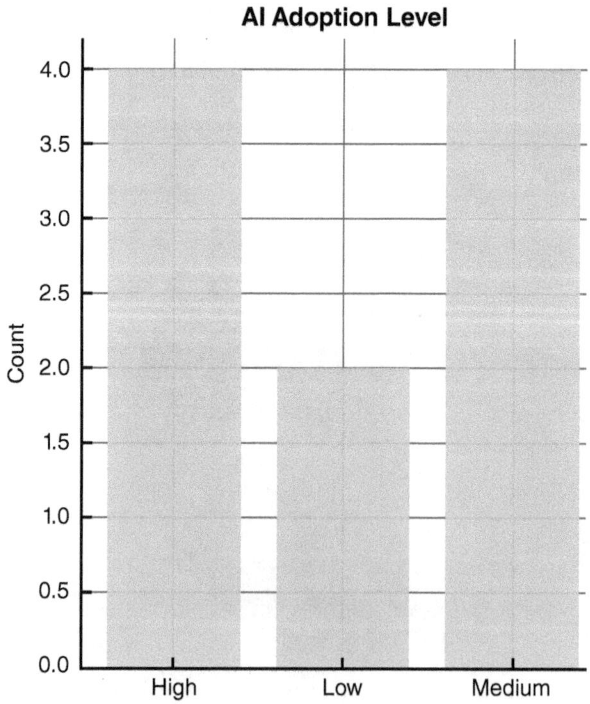

FIGURE 8.4 AI adoption level: This bar chart displays the levels of AI adoption among the surveyed organizations.

This bar chart presents the extent of AI adoption among the surveyed organizations. The majority of organizations have a **Medium AI adoption level (55)**, followed by those with **High AI adoption (50)**. A smaller portion of organizations report a **Low AI adoption level (40)**. The chart provides insight into the varying degrees of AI implementation across different financial sectors (Figure 8.5).

This bar chart illustrates the overall satisfaction levels of participants regarding AI implementations in their organizations. The majority of respondents are **Satisfied (60)**, followed by those who are **Very Satisfied (45)**. A smaller group remains **Neutral (20)**, while an equal number of participants are **Dissatisfied (20)**. The chart provides insights into user perceptions and acceptance of AI technologies in financial and business operations.

8.9.2 Conclusion

AI is revolutionizing the financial sector by introducing efficiencies, enhancing decision-making, and improving customer experiences. While the benefits are substantial, addressing challenges such as data privacy, regulatory compliance, and bias is crucial for sustainable and ethical AI integration. As technology evolves, the financial industry will continue to leverage AI to drive innovation and growth. The mixed-methods approach adopted in this research ensures a robust and holistic understanding of AI's impact on the financial sector. By integrating quantitative and

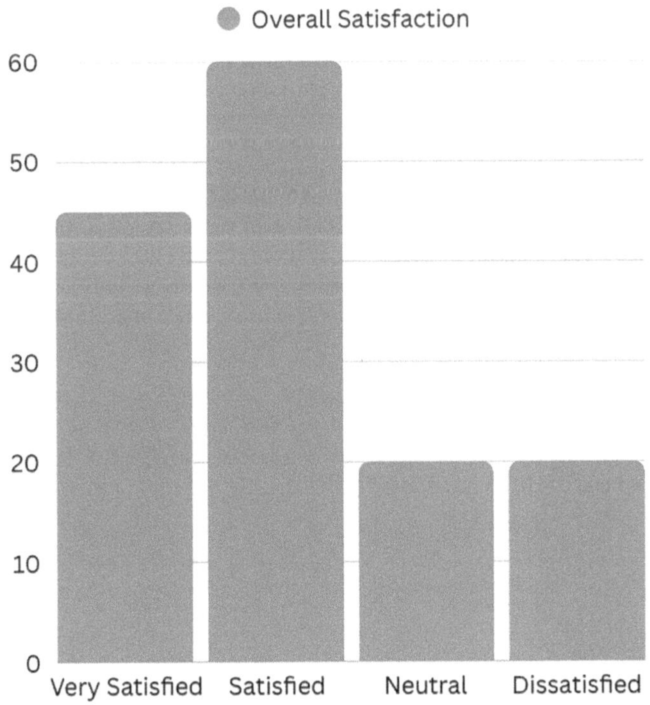

FIGURE 8.5 Overall satisfaction: This bar chart depicts the overall satisfaction levels of participants with AI implementations.

qualitative data, the study provides a detailed examination of how AI is transforming finance, highlighting both the opportunities and challenges that lie ahead. This methodology not only captures the current state of AI in finance but also sets the foundation for future research in this dynamic field.

BIBLIOGRAPHY

Ansari, M. A. A., Sajid, M., Nawaz Khan, S., Antohi, V. M., Fortea, C., Laura Zlati, M. (2024). Unveiling the effect of renewable energy and financial inclusion towards sustainable environment: Does interaction of digital finance and institutional quality matter? *Sustainable Futures, 7*, 100196. https://doi.org/10.1016/j.sftr.2024.100196

Cheng, K., Jin, Z., & Wu, G. (2024a). Unveiling the role of artificial intelligence in influencing enterprise environmental performance: Evidence from China. *Journal of Cleaner Production*, 440, 140934.

Cheng, Y.H., Zhang, C.Y., et al. (2024b). Exploring large language model based intelligent agents: Definitions, methods, and prospects. *arXiv*:2401.03428. https://doi.org/10.48550/arXiv.2401.03428

Cubric, M. (2020). Drivers, barriers, and social considerations for AI adoption in business and management: A tertiary study. *Technology in Society*, 62, Article 101257.

Jimeno-Morenilla, A., Azariadis, P., Molina-Carmona, R., Kyratzi, S., & Moulianitis, V. (2021). Technology enablers for the implementation of industry 4.0 to traditional manufacturing sectors: A review. *Computers in Industry*, 125, 103390–103403. https://doi.org/10.1016/j.compind.2020.103390

Kehayov, M., Holder, L., & Koch, V. (2022). Application of artificial intelligence technology in the manufacturing process and purchasing and supply management. *Procedia Computer Science*, 200, 1209–1217. https://doi.org/10.1016/j.procs.2022.01.321

Kumar, N., Antoniraj, S., Jayanthi, S., Mirdula, S., Selvaraj, S., Rajkumar, N., & Senthilkumar, K. R. (2024). Educational Technology and Libraries Supporting Online Learning. In K. Senthilkumar (Ed.), *AI-Assisted Library Reconstruction* (pp. 209–237). IGI Global. https://doi.org/10.4018/979-8-3693-2782-1.ch012

Rajkumar, N., Viji, C., Mohanraj, A., Senthilkumar, K. R., Jagajeevan, R., &Kovilpillai, J. A. (2024). Ethical Considerations of AI Implementation in the Library Era. In K. Senthilkumar & R. Jagajeevan (Eds.), *Improving Library Systems with AI: Applications, Approaches, and Bibliometric Insights* (pp. 85–106). IGI Global.

Liang, X. L., He, J., & Liu, P. P. (2020). The influence of cognitive ability on academic achievement of junior middle school students: A mediated moderation model. Psychological Development and Education, 36, 449–461. https://doi.org/10.16187/j.cnki.issn1001-4918.2020.04.08

Virvou, M., Tsihrintzis, G. A., and Tsichrintzi, E. -A. "VIRTSI: A novel trust dynamics model enhancing artificial intelligence collaboration with human users – insights from a ChatGPT evaluation study," *Information Sciences*, vol. 675, Art. 120759, May 2024. https://doi.org/10.1016/j.ins.2024.120759

9 AI and Fintech
Revolutionizing the Financial Landscape

Nakka Venkatarathnam, Mahabub Basha Shaik, Dilshod Kamilov, Karthik Reddy, and Gurramkonda Reddeppa Naidu

9.1 INTRODUCTION

9.1.1 AI's Role in Conventional Banking

The use of artificial intelligence (AI) has transformed the conventional financial industry, from the inner workings of banks to the management of individual investors' portfolios. This in-depth analysis delves into various ways AI is being used in conventional finance. It explains how AI is changing areas such as compliance, risk management, algorithmic trading, customer service, credit scoring, compliance, NLP, predictive analytics, blockchain, and cryptocurrency (Krishna et al. 2022). Because of the high degree of uncertainty in the market and the potential for huge losses, risk management is a top priority for banks and other financial organizations. The use of sophisticated algorithms by AI to sift through mountains of data in search of abnormalities, trends, and correlations is crucial in reducing these dangers. AI technologies help financial professionals make better choices to protect assets and reduce risks by analyzing market patterns, historical data, and other pertinent aspects. AI also shows its strength in conventional banking in the field of fraud detection. The fight against fraud, including money laundering, identity theft, and unapproved transactions, is a constant one for financial institutions. As watchful guardians, fraud detection systems powered by AI keep a constant eye on all transactions in real time, looking for any signs of unusual behavior. In order to safeguard financial institutions and their clients from possible losses, these systems use complex algorithms that can detect fraudulent patterns and behaviors. This allows for quick action to avoid financial crimes. The development of AI has accelerated the rise of algorithmic trading, which is revolutionizing the financial markets. The use of sophisticated algorithms allows these AI-powered trading systems to swiftly analyze market data, spot trading opportunities, and execute buy and sell orders with pinpoint timing. Algorithmic trading utilizes AI's computing capacity and prediction ability to help investors take advantage of market swings and maximize profits via trading techniques. In the age of AI-driven solutions, there has been a dramatic change in customer service and customization. Chatbots and virtual assistants driven by AI

DOI: 10.1201/9781003645849-9

help financial institutions provide 24/7 customer care, answering questions, fixing problems, and giving customers tailored financial advice. Financial institutions may streamline their processes with the use of AI-driven interactions that improve the client experience, leading to higher satisfaction and loyalty (Altan & Milson, 2024).

Also, AI has changed the game when it comes to credit scoring and underwriting by providing a faster, more accurate way to determine a person's creditworthiness. Credit risk assessment techniques that have been around for a while tend to be inaccurate and inefficient since they use subjective criteria and little data. In contrast, AI algorithms draw from a wide variety of data sources, such as financial records, income levels, spending patterns, and even unconventional data like social media engagement. Faster, data-driven lending choices and more accurate credit ratings are both possible, thanks to AI algorithms that sift through this mountain of data. Another area where AI is having a significant influence is portfolio management. This field provides investors with advanced tools to optimize their investment strategies and control risk. Portfolio management tools driven by AI analyze market patterns, evaluate risk variables, and distribute assets across diverse portfolios using complex algorithms. To improve investment performance and reach long-term financial goals, these systems dynamically alter portfolio allocations and investment methods in response to changing market circumstances, taking advantage of opportunities while minimizing risks. Given the complexity and constant evolution of regulatory standards, financial institutions face substantial hurdles when it comes to compliance and regulatory reporting. AI systems automate transaction monitoring, identify suspicious activity, and guarantee compliance with regulatory requirements, all of which simplify compliance operations. To ensure regulatory compliance and limit legal liability, AI systems sift through mountains of data in search of any compliance concerns, highlighting outliers and producing detailed reports (Rathore, 2016).

With the use of predictive analytics, financial experts may more confidently foresee market patterns, economic situations, and data-driven judgments. Machine learning algorithms sift through mountains of data, economic indicators, and market patterns to create models that may foretell how the market and economy will behave in the future. Financial institutions and investors may improve performance and outcomes by using this information to make proactive strategy adjustments, take advantage of new possibilities, and reduce risks. Through its ability to analyze news stories, social media postings, and analyst reports—all of which include unstructured data—natural language processing (NLP) has become a game-changer in conventional finance. NLP algorithms driven by AI sift through mountains of text for patterns, attitudes, and other pertinent information that may affect market dynamics. Financial experts may improve their decision-making and risk management tactics by combining conventional sources with unstructured data to get a full picture of market mood, new trends, and investor sentiment (Abbas, 2023).

There are new possibilities for efficiency, security, and transparency at the cutting edge of conventional banking at the junction of AI, blockchain technology, and cryptocurrencies. By analyzing blockchain data, AI algorithms may improve security protocols, identify fraudulent transactions, and optimize bitcoin ecosystem activities. The ever-changing world of digital assets may be daunting for investors, but with the aid of AI-driven predictive analytics, they can anticipate market patterns in cryptocurrencies and make more educated investment choices. When it comes to analyzing and predicting market trends, AI is crucial because of its capacity to analyze massive volumes of market data. Financial experts and investors may benefit from AI algorithms' analysis of past price movements, trade volumes, and macroeconomic factors when deciding how to allocate assets and mitigate risk. With the use of AI, quantitative researchers and strategists may create and refine trading strategies with the use of mathematical algorithms and statistical models. Improving the efficacy and efficiency of quantitative research, these AI-driven tools allow researchers to sift through massive datasets, put theories to the test, and discover lucrative trading opportunities in a variety of financial markets (Mossavar-Rahmani & Zohuri, 2024).

When it comes to managing one's own money and investments, robo-advisors are a big deal. These AI-powered investment advising systems analyze users' risk appetite, financial objectives, and personal preferences to provide tailored investment portfolio recommendations. The use of AI by robo-advisors, which provides personalized investment advice and portfolio management services, has made wealth management more accessible and affordable for people. AI-powered systems also shine in sentiment research, which involves keeping tabs on news stories, online forums, and social media in order to predict how investors will act in the market. These technologies provide insights into public opinion, patterns in market sentiment, and future events that might move markets by analyzing textual data and extracting sentiment signals. With the use of sentiment research, investors may better foresee how the market will move, allowing them to better respond to new possibilities and reduce the impact of potential threats. To take advantage of minute price differences in the market, high-frequency traders use AI algorithms to execute several deals very quickly. In order to find arbitrage opportunities and execute transactions with minimum delay, these complex AI-driven algorithms examine market data in real time. AI is having a revolutionary effect on the trading and investing industries, as high-frequency trading (HFT) businesses use it to take advantage of temporary market inefficiencies and make money. Better understanding of market patterns, customer behavior, and economic activity may be gleaned via the use of alternative data sources that AI makes possible, including satellite images, consumer buy transactions, and geolocation data. Financial experts may improve their investing and trading choices by gaining a holistic view of market dynamics via the use of many datasets in their study (Naqvi et al., 2024).

Financial goods and services may benefit from dynamic pricing models that use AI algorithms to improve pricing strategies in response to market demand, rival pricing, and consumer behavior. To further optimize profitability while minimizing credit risk, risk adjustment algorithms driven by AI evaluate each customer's risk profile and adapt terms and prices accordingly. In addition, companies can keep updated on the ever-changing regulatory environment and make sure they are meeting compliance requirements with the aid of AI-driven regulatory compliance solutions. These solutions automate the monitoring of regulatory changes, compliance risks, and create regulatory reports. Reducing human burdens and the danger of non-compliance fines and reputational harm, these technologies expedite compliance activities. These uses highlight the many ways AI is changing the face of conventional banking and boosting innovation, efficiency, and competition throughout the world's financial system.

Market research, quantitative analysis, sentiment analysis, robo-advisory services, HFT, alternative data analysis, dynamic pricing, risk adjustment, and regulatory compliance automation are all areas where AI is already making waves in the financial sector. In conventional finance, AI has several potential uses, including but not limited to: algorithmic trading, compliance, risk management, fraud detection, customer service, credit scoring, portfolio management, NLP, blockchain, and predictive analytics. As the world of conventional finance is constantly changing, financial institutions and investors may benefit from AI by making better decisions, running their operations more efficiently, reducing risks, and opening up new avenues for development and innovation (Arslanian & Fischer, 2019; Padmanaban, 2024).

9.1.2 Impact of Banking, Investments, and Insurance

Recent years have seen revolutionary changes in the financial services industry, particularly in banking, investing, and insurance, driven mostly by new technologies and shifting customer preferences. Concepts like digital banking, robo-advisors, decentralized finance (DeFi), and InsurTech have emerged as a result of this transformation, marking the beginning of a new age in financial services. Within this vast panorama, these sectors have an effect that goes far beyond the ease of transactions; they have a significant bearing on economic landscapes, company strategy, and personal financial habits. With the rise of online banking, customers' and companies' relationships with banks have been transformed. People no longer have to deal with tedious paperwork and lengthy lines; instead, they can manage their money easily using user-friendly websites and mobile apps. Digital banks have completely transformed the way customers interact with their money. They allow for instantaneous transactions, real-time access to account information, tailored financial advice, and loan applications. In addition, financial organizations are now more likely to work together and share data thanks to open banking initiatives and APIs. Through these interdependent platforms, consumers have easier and more convenient access to a wider variety of financial goods and services offered by various suppliers. At the same time, blockchain technology is causing a stir in the banking industry, thanks to the improvements it brings to transaction security, transparency, and efficiency. Solutions enabled by blockchain technology enable speedier cross-border payments, lower transaction costs, and decrease fraud risks by using decentralized ledger technology. Another alternative to centralized financial institutions that has been gaining traction is decentralized finance or DeFi. Decentralized financial platforms eliminate middlemen by using smart contracts and blockchain technology to provide automated market-making protocols, decentralized exchanges, and peer-to-peer lending. A more inclusive and innovative financial system is the result of this democratization of finance, which gives consumers more agency over their assets and makes it possible for them to engage in financial activities on their own. Turning our attention to the investing world, robo-advisors and algorithmic trading are two examples of digital technologies that have revolutionized the investment management environment. Robo-advisors are online financial advisory firms that use AI algorithms to automate the process of managing client portfolios according to their individual needs and comfort levels with risk. Affordable and easily accessible investing solutions are offered by these platforms, which dynamically optimize asset allocations, rebalance portfolios, and evaluate market trends. Institutional investors have also taken an interest in algorithmic trading, which uses AI-driven methods to make trades very quickly and take advantage of market inefficiencies. Institutions may better manage risks in today's fast-paced markets and optimize profits with the help of these advanced trading algorithms (Aggarwal et al., 2024; Khan, 2024).

For those looking to diversify their portfolios and increase their potential returns, alternative investments have become an attractive alternative to more conventional asset types. Alternative investment methods including venture capital, real estate crowdfunding, and cryptocurrencies have grown in popularity in the last several years. By providing fractional ownership, liquidity, and transparency in hitherto illiquid markets, blockchain technology has been essential in democratizing access to these alternative assets. Digital assets are attracting a growing amount of capital from companies and institutional investors who see them as a way to protect themselves against inflation and geopolitical instability. Furthermore, there has been a rise in environmental, social, and governance (ESG) investing, which reflects the increasing desire from investors for opportunities to invest in a sustainable and socially responsible way. Companies' efforts in areas like corporate governance, social responsibility, and environmental sustainability are evaluated using ESG criteria, which are included in investment decision-making processes. To help investors achieve their financial goals while also making a beneficial impact on society and the environment, ESG-focused products and indexes are available.

Now let's shift gears to the insurance industry, where new technologies have sparked a digital revolution and given birth to the rapidly expanding InsurTech sector. The goal of InsurTech firms is to improve client experiences, reduce risks, and simplify insurance operations via the use of technology. Traditional insurance practices are being transformed by InsurTech businesses, who are offering solutions such as parametric insurance, usage-based insurance, digital underwriting, and claims processing. When it comes to insurance, AI and ML algorithms are game-changers for things like risk assessment, fraud detection, and customized pricing. By sifting through mountains of data, such as client demographics, behavioral patterns, and claims history, these AI-powered prediction algorithms precisely identify risk factors and set appropriate insurance rates. In addition, chatbots and virtual assistants powered by AI improve customer service by offering immediate assistance, swiftly processing claims, and increasing consumer satisfaction overall. Insurance transactions are becoming more secure, transparent, and efficient thanks to blockchain technology, which is also shaking up the business. Secure data exchange, faster claims settlement, and immutable records are all made possible by blockchain-powered systems, which also reduce administrative expenses and eliminate fraud concerns. With the use of smart contracts, policyholders may enjoy speedier and more transparent coverage, as well as parametric insurance products that pay out according to predetermined criteria (Kumar & Megha, 2022; Kasowaki & Deniz, 2024).

A digital revolution is altering the future of finance, and the banking, investments, and insurance industries are leading the way. The delivery and consumption of financial services are undergoing extraordinary changes due to technological advances. These developments include digital banking, blockchain-powered solutions, robo-advisors, decentralized finance, and InsurTech. These innovations bring new problems and regulatory concerns, but they also provide chances for financial services to be more efficient, accessible, and inclusive. In order to succeed in the ever-changing digital economy, banks, investment firms, and insurance companies must welcome innovation and adjust to new circumstances swiftly (Rajendran et al. 2023).

9.1.3 Trends and Market Dynamics

The banking, investing, and insurance industries are quite susceptible to market trends and dynamics. For financial institutions, investors, and insurers to successfully navigate the developing environment, it is necessary to understand these trends and dynamics. What follows is an examination of key market factors and trends influencing these industries.

1. One of the most notable developments in the financial services, investment, and insurance industries is the continuous digital transformation. The banking industry is capitalizing on digital technologies to improve client experiences, simplify processes, and spur innovation in response to the ever-increasing speed of technological advancement. Many developments are part of this trend, such as the proliferation of online banking, the use of automated financial advisers (robo-advisors), and the birth of new companies that provide digital insurance (InsurTech). Traditional business models are being transformed by digital transformation, which is also transforming the delivery and consumption of financial services.
2. The widespread use of remote and contactless services in the financial sector was hastened by the COVID-19 epidemic. Consumers' reliance on digital channels for banking, investing, and insurance grew in response to social distancing measures. The banking industry was quick to respond, allowing customers to create accounts online, get financial advice virtually, and file claims electronically. Customers will likely keep this pattern going even after the epidemic ends, as they value accessibility, safety, and convenience when it comes to their money.
3. Thirdly, ESG investing has been on the rise, which is a reflection of the increasing demand from investors for environmentally and socially responsible investment possibilities. ESG stands for environmental, social, and governance. To make sure their investments are in line with their beliefs and have a good impact on society and the environment, more and more investors are looking at environmental, social, and governance (ESG) concerns. Financial institutions have responded to this trend by providing investment products that prioritize environmental, social, and governance (ESG) factors and by incorporating ESG criteria into their overall investing strategy.
4. The traditional investment landscape has grown to a great extent. Cryptocurrencies, Real Estate Crowdfunding, and Venture Capital are just a few examples of alternative investments that have grown in recent years. Thanks to blockchain technology, these alternative assets are now accessible

to a wider audience, and marketplaces that were previously unliquid now have fractional ownership, liquidity, and transparency. Digital assets are attracting a growing amount of capital from companies and institutional investors who see them as a way to protect themselves against inflation and geopolitical instability. As a result of this shift, diversified portfolios and conventional investing methods now include a wider variety of assets.

5. InsurTech businesses are using technology to revolutionize old insurance procedures, causing a surge of innovation in the sector. Insurance technology startups are using AI to simplify claims processing, provide digital underwriting, and provide customized pricing. The use of blockchain technology is also improving the efficiency, transparency, and security of insurance transactions. To adapt to the changing insurance industry, established players are teaming up with newcomers in the industry, or "InsurTech," to take advantage of digital change and remain competitive.
6. The environment in which financial institutions, investors, and insurers operate is constantly being shaped by regulatory changes. All across the financial sector, market dynamics, compliance needs, and company strategy are affected by regulatory changes. In order to reduce regulatory risks and maintain stakeholders' confidence and credibility, financial institutions must monitor regulatory changes and comply with changing regulatory norms.
7. The banking, investing, and insurance industries are making more use of data analytics and AI to improve decision-making, automate operations, and acquire actionable insights. Robo-advisors in asset management, better risk evaluation and fraud detection in insurance, and individualized banking experiences are all made possible by AI-driven algorithms. This trend highlights how the financial sector may enhance efficiency, innovation, and competitiveness by adopting data-driven tactics and using AI.
8. Insurers, investors, and financial institutions continue to prioritize cybersecurity and data privacy as digitalization progresses. Financial systems and consumer data are particularly vulnerable to cyberattacks, data breaches, and privacy abuses. To preserve sensitive information and keep customers' confidence, financial institutions must comply with legal regulations, establish data protection policies, and invest in strong cybersecurity measures.
9. The financial sector is seeing a surge in efforts to personalize client experiences and improve data analytics in response to the advent of digitalization. Banks and other financial organizations are starting to personalize their offerings to each client by mining their data for insights powered by AI. Personalization efforts strive to increase client involvement, loyalty, and company development via individualized investment suggestions, insurance coverage alternatives, banking solutions, and focused marketing campaigns.
10. In the financial industry, institutions are increasingly seeking partnerships and collaborations to foster innovation and increase market reach by using complementary strengths and skills. For instance, in a partnership between Fintech startups and more established banks, the former may get access to innovative technology, while the latter can tap into the knowledge of

regulators and clientele of the former. Similarly, novel InsurTech solutions like health insurance wearable tech and insurance products based on telematics are made possible by collaborations between insurers and IT businesses.

11. The rise of digital payments and Fintech innovation is changing the way money is transferred and is putting pressure on established banking structures. The ease, speed, and security offered by mobile payment solutions, digital wallets, and peer-to-peer payment systems are driving their rising appeal among consumers. In the financial technology sector, new entrants are shaking things up and changing the rules in areas like payment processing, remittances, and financial inclusion. Additionally, stablecoins and central bank digital currencies (CBDCs) are on the rise, which will open up new possibilities for monetary policy, financial inclusion, and cross-border transactions, further disrupting the payments environment.
12. There is a rising focus on green finance and sustainable investing methods, which contribute to the industry-wide trend of sustainability and environmental responsibility. More and more, when making investment choices, investors are looking for projects and businesses with good sustainability credentials based on environmental, social, and governance (ESG) factors. In response to this trend, financial institutions are providing green bonds, sustainability-linked loans, and ESG-focused investment products to satisfy investor demand and aid in the shift to a more sustainable economy. Additionally, sustainability is becoming more and more included in regulatory frameworks, which is promoting openness and responsibility in sustainable financing projects.
13. To better handle regulatory compliance obligations, financial institutions are increasingly turning to RegTech solutions. Automation of compliance procedures, monitoring of regulatory changes, and assurance of conformity with regulatory requirements are all goals of RegTech solutions, which use cutting-edge technologies like blockchain, AI, and machine learning. Financial institutions may increase operational efficiency, reduce compliance risks, and streamline compliance operations with the use of RegTech solutions, which also reduce human labor.
14. The finance sector has seen a rapid uptake of remote work and digital transformation projects due to the COVID-19 pandemic. Many banks and other financial organizations have made investments in cybersecurity measures, collaboration tools, and digital infrastructure to facilitate remote operations and guarantee company continuity as remote work becomes the standard. Financial institutions are accelerating digital transformation efforts and improving their online products to suit growing client expectations, as the epidemic has highlighted the significance of digital channels and contactless services. These supplementary trends and market dynamics emphasize how the banking, investing, and insurance industries are dynamic and ever-changing as a result of technical advancements, shifting consumer habits, new regulations, and worldwide macroeconomic patterns. Investors, insurers, and financial institutions may position themselves for success in an

increasingly dynamic and competitive world by keeping informed of these developments and embracing new possibilities (Irfan et al., 2023; Lee, 2023; Dabaghia et al., 2024; Siddiqui, 2023; Noor et al., 2023; Bodemer, 2024).

9.2 REVOLUTIONIZING TRADITIONAL PRACTICES

9.2.1 Strategies for Investing and Algorithmic Trading

Adopting fresh perspectives on investing and trading tactics is essential to shaking up the financial industry's established norms. Algorithmic trading is one method that is rapidly becoming popular. Using computer algorithms to automatically execute transactions based on established criteria is known as algorithmic trading, algo trading, or automated trading. Using this strategy, automated systems that can quickly and accurately assess market data, spot trading opportunities, and execute orders take the role of human traders. The advent of algorithmic trading has been a game-changer for investors' approach to risk management, trade execution accuracy, and taking advantage of market inefficiencies. Trading signals and investment choices are made by algorithmic trading using complicated mathematical models and statistical analysis. These programs can sift through mountains of market data—price changes, trade volumes, and everything else that matters—to find trends and patterns that human traders would miss. Algorithmic trading systems are able to respond instantly to shifting market circumstances by constantly learning from data and use AI and machine learning methods (Janani et al. 2023). Algorithmic traders are able to anticipate market shifts and seize new chances because of their adaptable nature. Fast and efficient trade execution is a major advantage of algorithmic trading. Unlike human traders, algorithmic trading algorithms can process orders in milliseconds. In lightning-fast markets, where microsecond-long judgments may dictate the fate of whole trades, this advantage in speed becomes even more important. Algorithmic trading makes trading more disciplined and consistent by automating the process, which removes human emotions and mistakes. Algorithmic traders may keep their trading discipline and control their emotions with this methodical technique. Trading algorithms also allow for the implementation of complicated trading strategies that would be very difficult, if not impossible, to carry out manually. These methods might be as basic as algorithms that track trends or as complex as market-making and arbitrage techniques. Statistical arbitrage tactics, for instance, seek for assets that are underpriced and then capitalize on price differences across similar assets. Strategies that use HFT attempt to capitalize on minute price changes by rapidly executing several deals. An array of trading methods may be made available to traders via the use of algorithmic trading techniques, allowing them to maximize their performance in various market situations. The elimination of entry restrictions for private traders and investors has democratized access to the financial markets, and algorithmic trading has also made trading techniques more efficient. Only large, well-funded institutions with access to advanced trading tools and resources employed algorithmic trading in the past. But now even ordinary traders may take advantage of algorithmic trading thanks to the rise of internet trading platforms and other technological developments. These days, even casual traders may find algorithmic trading platforms and software that provide them with pre-made trading strategies, algorithms that they can tweak to their liking, and tools for backtesting their systems. Traders should be aware that algorithmic trading, despite its many advantages, has certain difficulties and hazards.

Potentially large financial losses due to technical issues or system breakdowns are one of the main dangers of algorithmic trading. Erroneous trades or order executions caused by a software flaw or network difficulty, for instance, might result in significant losses quickly. The use of strong risk management controls and safeguards, including position limits, circuit breakers, and failover methods, may help traders reduce these risks and protect themselves from market disruptions and unforeseen occurrences. Algorithmic trading also has the risk of being too dependent on past data and outcomes from backtests. Although algorithmic trading algorithms may sift through mountains of market data in search of trends that might recur, it's important to remember that the past is no guarantee of the future. Because of how quickly markets may shift, it's not always possible to rely on past trends. In order to stay ahead of the curve and prevent their algorithmic trading systems from underperforming or overfitting, traders need to keep a close eye on the market and make adjustments as needed. There are worries about the honesty, openness, and fairness of the market because of algorithmic trading. certain worry that the use of co-location services and very rapid execution rates in HFT tactics can offer certain traders an unfair edge and make the market more unstable and unpredictable. Concerned about the potential systemic dangers posed by algorithmic trading, regulators have reacted by enacting rules and supervision mechanisms to increase market fairness. To curb manipulative trading, authorities may implement restrictions on certain types of trades, install circuit breakers, and keep tabs on market activities. By facilitating the rapid and efficient implementation of complex trading strategies via the automation of trade execution, algorithmic trading has radically altered conventional investing practices. Trading results may be more disciplined and consistent when algorithmic traders use computer algorithms and cutting-edge technology to analyze market data, find trading opportunities, and execute orders precisely. Technical issues, model overfitting, and regulatory worries are just a few of the hazards and obstacles that traders face while using algorithmic trading. Notwithstanding these obstacles, algorithmic trading is broadening participation in financial markets and changing the face of finance (Sharma & Manhas, 2024; Gupta & Sharma, 2024; Kaakandikar & Dighe; Ahmadi et al., 2023).

9.2.1.1 The Function of Robo-Advisors in Financial Planning

Individuals' approaches to money management and asset investment have been radically transformed by the rise of robo-advisors, a major player in the wealth management business. Without the need for human participation, these automated investment platforms may provide investment management and financial guidance via the use of algorithms and technology. In financial management, robo-advisors play an important yet multi-faceted role that has changed the game. To begin, robo-advisors make investing possible for a wider range of people by making their services more accessible and affordable. Hiring a financial adviser and getting their individualized recommendations on investments and managing a client's portfolio used to be prohibitively expensive and reserved for the very wealthy. However, robo-advisors have leveled the playing field when it comes to wealth management by making low-cost, automated investing options available to individuals of all wealth levels. This accessibility has created chances for those who may not have had access to conventional wealth management services before. Second, robo-advisors make investing easier and lower the bar to entry for first-time investors. A lot of individuals do not invest at all or make ill-informed choices because they find investing complicated or scary. By providing automated portfolio management, user-friendly interfaces, and guided investment methods, robo-advisors streamline the investing process. With little to no expertise or understanding of finance required, investors may build diverse portfolios that fit their risk tolerance, objectives, and time horizon with a few clicks. Those who are unfamiliar with the financial markets will find investing easier and more accessible because of this (Azaan & Elsa, 2024).

In addition, robo-advisors use algorithms and quantitative models to provide investing advice that is both objective and data-driven. While human advisers are susceptible to biases, emotions, and conflicts of interest, robo-advisors base their investing judgments on objective criteria and mathematical algorithms. In order to suggest appropriate investment plans and asset allocations, these algorithms examine a number of elements, such as risk preferences, investment objectives, and market circumstances. Robotic investment advisers (robo-advisors) assist clients achieve their financial goals by providing advice that is more consistent and unbiased since they eliminate human prejudices. Also, robo-advisors make money management more open and accountable. Through user-friendly reports and dashboards, investors can see their whole portfolio, including assets, performance, and fees. Because investors can see exactly where their money is going and how it's being handled, they have more faith in the robo-advisor platform. Additionally, robo-advisers provide a cost-effective alternative to conventional wealth management organizations for investors looking for professional investment management services. Typically, their fees are cheaper than those of traditional financial advisors. Also, robo-advisors use tech to make investing more scalable and tailored to each client's needs. Automated investment advisers (robo-advisors) use complex algorithms and machine learning to create unique portfolios for each client based on their unique needs and objectives. Investors' risk tolerance, investment horizon, and financial goals inform the personalized suggestions they get. Investors of all sizes may benefit from the constant and individualized guidance offered by robo-advisors because of how effectively their services can grow to handle a large number of customers. Robo-advisors provide investors with the advantage of managing risk and diversifying their portfolios. Robotic investment advisers build diversified portfolios that disperse risk across various investment types and asset classes by using current theories of portfolio management and asset allocation. The effect of market volatility may be lessened and the chance of suffering substantial losses due to particular securities or market downturns can be reduced via this diversification. To further guarantee that investments are in line with clients' risk choices and long-term goals, robo-advisors rebalance portfolios on a regular basis to maintain target asset proportions. Achieving a balanced risk-return profile and optimizing investment results over time may be achieved via this rigorous approach to portfolio management (Kayode, 2023).

Investors may have exposure to several asset classes and investment opportunities via robo-advisors, such as equities, bonds, ETFs, and more. The investment products offered by these platforms are usually hand-picked after they have passed quality, liquidity, and cost-effectiveness checks. Investors have the option to personalize their portfolios according to their preferences and investment goals, or they may choose from pre-built portfolios that are tailored to various risk profiles and investing objectives. Because of this leeway, investors may improve their chances of reaching their long-term financial objectives by constructing diverse portfolios that are specific to their situation and investing style. Investors may reduce their tax burden and increase their after-tax returns with the aid of robo-advisors, who provide automated tax optimization solutions. One of these methods is known as tax-loss harvesting, and it entails selling assets at a loss to lower taxable income by offsetting capital gains. While still achieving their financial goals and diversifying their portfolios, robo-advisors may help individuals save money on taxes by methodically taking losses from their investments. To further maximize after-tax returns and improve overall portfolio performance, robo-advisors may also include tax-efficient asset placement methods. These strategies involve moving tax-efficient assets to taxable accounts and tax-inefficient investments to tax-advantaged accounts. Robo-advisors are always in the process of improving the investing experience and the results for their clients by adding new features and capabilities. Some robo-advisors, for instance, provide goal-based investing features that let users plan for the future and monitor their progress towards objectives like saving for retirement, paying for college, or purchasing a house. Investors may remain focused on their goals with the support of these tools, which bring clarity and direction to their financial planning efforts (Paris, 1924).

In addition, to address the rising demand for SRI choices, robo-advisors are integrating ESG (environmental, social, and governance) factors into their investment strategies. Investors may tailor their investment portfolios to their own beliefs and priorities in terms of social responsibility, environmental sustainability, and corporate governance standards with the help of robo-advisors that include ESG factors into the process of building and selecting investments. This development highlights the importance of robo-advisors in assisting clients in making ethical and environmentally conscious investment choices, and it is indicative of a larger trend towards more sustainable investment methods. With their user-friendly interfaces, low fees, transparency, and tailored investing strategies, robo-advisors are revolutionizing the wealth management industry. Automated platforms like this use data-driven algorithms and technology to simplify investing, provide investors advice that is based on facts and not opinion, and ultimately help them reach their financial objectives. The wealth management business is going to be changed by robo-advisors for the better. These tools allow investors to build diverse portfolios, optimize taxes, set investing goals, and include environmental, social, and governance (ESG) factors.

9.2.1.2 AI in Credit Assessment and Risk Management

With the help of AI, financial institutions now have strong new tools for assessing creditworthiness, managing risk, and making better lending choices. This has completely changed the way the sector does credit assessments and risk management. By using AI algorithms and machine learning approaches, conventional credit assessment procedures have been revolutionized (Kalyan et al. 2023). This has allowed financial institutions to evaluate credit risk in a more precise, streamlined, and impartial manner than in the past. The use of predictive analytics models to determine a borrower's creditworthiness is a key use of AI in the credit evaluation process. In order to determine the probability of default or delinquency, these models examine large volumes of data, such as financial records, income, job status, debt-to-income ratios, and other pertinent variables. More accurate risk assessments and lending choices are made possible by AI algorithms that use historical data and patterns to find correlations and predicted signs that conventional credit scoring systems may miss. As time goes on, credit evaluation models driven by AI may learn from fresh data and improve their predicting powers. When applied to massive datasets, machine learning algorithms may spot patterns, outliers, and trends that might indicate a shift in credit risk ratings. AI models may improve their accuracy and prediction capacity in evaluating credit risk by staying up-to-date with changing market circumstances and borrower behaviors via this adaptive learning process. Financial organizations may save time and costs by automating and streamlining the credit evaluation process with the help of AI. AI algorithms may streamline operations and shorten the time it takes to approve credit by automating mundane but necessary processes like data collecting, verification, and analysis. This not only speeds up the loan application process but also frees up staff to concentrate on higher-level, more strategic work (Agrawal et al., 2024).

In addition, AI improves risk management by detecting possible credit risks and portfolio weaknesses via early warning systems and real-time monitoring. Borrowers' financial troubles or worsening credit quality may be detected by AI algorithms that examine transaction data, market patterns, and macroeconomic factors. Financial institutions may reduce their exposure to risk by reevaluating their lending practices, establishing risk mitigation techniques, or reorganizing their loan portfolios in response to newly identified hazards. Risk management relies heavily on fraud detection systems enabled by AI to spot suspicious activity and fraudulent behaviors as they happen. These systems examine transaction patterns, look for irregularities, and flag possibly fraudulent transactions for further investigation using sophisticated analytics and machine learning algorithms. In order to safeguard their assets and the interests of their clients, financial institutions may enhance their defenses against fraud and financial crimes by using AI technology. Using AI, banks may create unique plans for managing risk and reducing it based on the specifics of each borrower's profile and situation. AI algorithms may use consumer data and patterns of behavior to classify clients into various risk groups, allowing for more targeted risk management strategies. By delivering customized solutions that address each client's specific needs, this method boosts customer happiness and loyalty while simultaneously making risk management tactics more effective. In addition, AI makes it easier to run stress tests and scenario s, which are great tools for gauging how well loan portfolios can withstand unfavorable events and how much credit risk exposures might be affected by economic downturns. Financial institutions may benefit from AI algorithms' ability to model numerous scenarios and evaluate possible outcomes under diverse situations. This allows them to better detect weaknesses, quantify losses, and create backup plans to reduce risks. By taking a preventative stance towards risk management, financial institutions may fortify their ability to withstand risk and thrive in volatile markets. Better creditworthiness assessments, automated and streamlined lending procedures, fraud detection and prevention, and personalized risk management methods are just a few ways in which AI has revolutionized the financial industry's approach to credit evaluation and risk management. Financial institutions may improve their credit risk evaluation, lending decision-making, and asset protection capabilities with the use of modern analytics and machine learning algorithms. The expansion of AI's function in credit evaluation and risk management is anticipated to propel innovation and efficiency in the financial industry as the technology evolves further (Sharma et al., 2021).

9.2.1.3 AI for Financial Technology (Fintech) Applications

When it comes to financial technology (Fintech), machine learning and deep learning have been game-changers in a number of areas, such as risk assessment, investment management, lending, payments, and banking. Improvements in efficiency, accuracy, and innovation in financial services are made possible by Fintech businesses' use of these cutting-edge technologies, which allow them to analyze massive volumes of data, derive valuable insights, and automate decision-making processes. Among the many uses of ML and DL in the financial technology sector, fraud prevention and detection stands out. In order to evaluate transactional data, find trends, and spot abnormalities that might indicate fraudulent actions, Fintech businesses use complex algorithms. Fintech organizations may safeguard their clients' money and maintain their reputation by using machine learning models. These models continually learn from new data and adapt to developing fraud strategies, resulting in improved detection rates and reduced false positives. Also, credit scoring and risk assessment for loans are two areas where machine learning algorithms are vital. Machine learning algorithms may assess borrowers' creditworthiness more effectively and efficiently than conventional credit scoring techniques by examining a variety of data sources, such as financial records, income, work status, and patterns of behavior. Because of this, Fintech lenders may reduce credit risk, increase access to credit for disadvantaged groups, and make data-driven lending choices.

Algorithmic trading and investment management also make heavy use of machine learning algorithms for analyzing market data, finding trading opportunities, and optimizing investment strategies. Financial technology companies use models of predictive analytics to do things like automatically execute transactions, evaluate risk-return profiles, and anticipate market patterns. Fintech investors may boost portfolio diversity, generate better investment performance, and capitalize on market inefficiencies more efficiently by utilizing the power of machine intelligence. To glean insights from news stories, social media feeds, and consumer reviews—all examples of unstructured data—NLP and sentiment analysis use machine learning and deep learning approaches. To improve client interaction, provide tailored financial products, and make better investment choices, Fintech businesses use NLP algorithms to sift through textual data, extract pertinent information, and measure market sentiment (Yalamati, 2023).

Additionally, customized marketing and customer segmentation both make use of machine learning algorithms to target certain consumer categories with specialized product offers and advertising campaigns. Fintech businesses can increase customer happiness and loyalty by studying consumer data, purchase histories, and browsing habits to find trends and preferences, forecast future buying behaviors, and provide personalized promotions and suggestions to each customer. Automated underwriting and risk assessment may be achieved via the use of machine learning algorithms in insurance and InsurTech applications. A more accurate assessment of insurance risk, competitive policy pricing, and a streamlined underwriting process are all outcomes of using machine learning models to analyze a variety of risk factors, such as demographic data, health metrics, and claims histories. This leads to faster approvals and better customer experiences. Chatbots and virtual assistants, which use machine learning and deep learning, are being used in Fintech applications to improve customer assistance and service. In order to save operating expenses and increase customer satisfaction, chatbots may use their natural language comprehension and generation skills to engage with consumers in real time. They can answer queries, provide tailored suggestions, and even enable self-service transactions. In order to detect suspicious behaviors, identify high-risk consumers, and maintain regulatory compliance, machine learning algorithms are used in know your customer (KYC) and anti-money laundering (AML) compliance procedures. By analyzing transactional patterns, monitoring client habits, and flagging potentially fraudulent or illegal activity, Fintech businesses may successfully comply with regulatory requirements and limit the dangers of financial crime. Finally, cybersecurity apps use ML and DL to identify and stop cyber dangers including malware, phishing, and data breaches. To protect their systems and sensitive financial data from hackers, Fintech businesses utilize algorithms that detect anomalies, behavioral analytics, and predictive modelling to find signs of cyber assaults, fortify their defences, and prevent unauthorized access. A wide range of financial technology applications have been revolutionized by machine learning and deep learning. These include cybersecurity, customer service, fraud detection, credit scoring, algorithmic trading, consumer segmentation, insurance underwriting, and regulatory compliance. Fintech firms may drive value for clients, investors, and stakeholders by improving efficiency, accuracy, and innovation in financial services via the power of sophisticated analytics and automation. Machine learning's impact on Fintech is only going to grow as the technology develops, leading to more innovations and changes in the financial sector (Yalamati, 2023; Zakaria et al., 2023).

9.3 INNOVATIVE SOLUTIONS IN FINTECH

9.3.1 Identifying and Preventing Fraud

The security of financial transactions and the protection of institutions and customers from fraudulent activity have become critical, making innovative Fintech solutions for fraud detection and prevention crucial. With the use of state-of-the-art technology like big data analytics, AI, and machine learning (ML), Fintech businesses are creating advanced fraud detection systems that can identify and stop fraudulent transactions as they happen. The use of AI and machine learning algorithms to sift through mountains of transaction data in search of patterns suggestive of fraudulent activity is a game-changer in the fight against fraud. It is possible for Fintech businesses to identify possibly fraudulent transactions for further investigation using these algorithms, which may spot abnormalities, strange behavior, and suspect patterns in real time. Detection rates and false positives may be improved and fraud protection measures can be strengthened with the use of AI-powered fraud detection systems that learn from fresh data and adapt to changing fraud techniques. On top of that, financial technology firms are using sophisticated behavioral analytics methods to identify fraudulent activity based on specific user actions and patterns of transactions. The financial technology industry is able to detect suspicious activity by constructing profiles of typical user behavior based on their interactions, surfing habits, and transaction histories. Even for complex or previously unseen fraud schemes, behavioral analytics allow Fintech businesses to identify attacks in real time. In an effort to beef up security and forestall illegal access to customer accounts, Fintech firms are incorporating biometric authentication technologies like voice recognition, fingerprint identification, and face recognition into their fraud detection systems. To further prevent fraudsters from impersonating genuine users or gaining unauthorized access to accounts, biometric authentication adds an extra layer of protection by authenticating the user's identity using distinct biological traits. In addition, Fintech businesses are using blockchain technology to make financial transactions more secure, transparent, and less susceptible to fraud. It is practically hard for fraudsters to influence the financial system or tamper with transaction records due to blockchain technology's decentralized and immutable record-keeping. Fintech firms may boost consumer trust and confidence, decrease the likelihood of fraud, and ensure the security of financial transactions by using blockchain-based solutions (Sharma & Manhas, 2024; Gupta & Sharma, 2024).

Financial technology firms are also investigating new avenues for fraud prevention via predictive modeling and sophisticated data analytics. Fintech firms may create predictive models to reduce the likelihood of fraud by studying past data, current market patterns, and other pertinent aspects. To lessen the chances of monetary losses and reputational harm, Fintech organizations should use predictive modeling to proactively detect and handle new fraud risks. Financial technology firms are working together with government agencies to better fight fraud and financial crime. Together with regulators and law enforcement, Fintech firms can investigate and punish fraudsters, disrupt criminal networks, and prevent future fraudulent acts by exchanging information and intelligence about existing and new dangers. For the sake of everyone involved, it is critical that regulators, law enforcement, and Fintech businesses work together to make the financial ecosystem safer. Safeguarding financial transactions and protecting institutions and customers from fraudulent activity requires creative solutions in Fintech for fraud detection and prevention. Fintech companies can build more secure and transparent financial transactions, reduce the risk of financial losses and reputational damage, and detect and prevent fraud in real time by utilizing advanced technologies like AI, ML, big data analytics, behavioral analytics, blockchain, and predictive modelling. The significance of Fintech in detecting and preventing fraud is projected to grow as the sector adapts to new technology, which will cause more innovation and disruption (Kaakandikar & Dighe; Ahmadi et al., 2023).

9.3.2 Improving the Customer Experience with the Help of AI

Financial institutions are among the many that have made improving the customer experience with AI a top priority. By enabling streamlined and customized interactions across all consumer touchpoints, AI-powered technologies are transforming the way financial institutions engage with their clients. Through customized suggestions and services, AI greatly improves the consumer experience. Algorithms powered by AI can sift through mountains of consumer data, including purchase histories, tastes, and habits, to provide tailored product suggestions and deals. Financial institutions may use AI to provide individualized investment advice, targeted promotions, and product recommendations that connect with consumers and promote engagement. In addition, chatbots and virtual assistants driven by AI are revolutionizing customer service in the banking sector. With great precision and in real time, these intelligent systems can handle a variety of consumer requests, including account inquiries, transaction help, product information, and support inquiries. AI chatbots may improve customer satisfaction and loyalty by understanding and responding to consumer inquiries efficiently using NLP and machine learning skills. They can provide quick support and resolve problems rapidly. All aspects of the client experience may be personalized with the help of AI, not only product suggestions. To better understand consumer preferences and habits, AI algorithms may sift through consumer interactions across many channels, like as websites, mobile applications, and social media platforms. By doing so, banks and other financial institutions may improve client engagement and build stronger relationships via the use of tailored experiences across all touchpoints, including targeted marketing campaigns, user interface customization, and interactive technologies (Gupta & Sharma, 2024; Ahmadi et al., 2023).

Through proactive interaction and predictive analytics, AI also improves the customer experience. Financial institutions may proactively reach out to clients with relevant offers, help, or support before they even know they need it by evaluating historical data and predictive modeling approaches using AI algorithms. This allows for a better understanding of customer requirements and preferences. Proactively engaging with consumers in this way shows that you understand their wants and preferences, which increases satisfaction and boosts loyalty and retention. In order to get useful insights into client sentiment and perception, financial institutions may utilize sentiment analysis tools powered by AI to monitor and analyze customer comments, reviews, and social media discussions in real time. Financial institutions can increase customer satisfaction and loyalty by learning how their customers feel about their brand, products, and services. This knowledge allows them to proactively address customer concerns, improve their offerings, and create experiences that connect with customers emotionally. Consumers are given more agency and knowledge over their financial situation with the use of AI-powered personal financial management (PFM) solutions. In order to provide individualized insights and suggestions for improved financial management, these smart tools examine clients' financial data, which includes income, expenditures, and savings objectives. With the use of AI-powered personal financial management (PFM) solutions, consumers are able to better manage their money, establish and reach savings goals, and create tailored budgets, all of which contribute to higher levels of customer satisfaction and loyalty. Through the development of intelligent chatbots, proactive engagement, sentiment analysis, and tools for personal financial management, AI is radically altering the way customers interact with the financial sector. The use of AI-driven solutions allows financial institutions to provide consumers with consistent, tailored experiences across all touchpoints, increasing happiness, loyalty, and revenue. With the continuous advancement of AI technology, the role of this technology in improving customer experience in the financial sector is projected to become even more crucial. This, in turn, will drive greater innovation and change in the delivery and consumption of financial services (Kaakandikar & Dighe; Ahmadi et al., 2023).

9.3.3 The Possible Effects on Financial Regulations from AI

Everyone from regulatory bodies to financial institutions has to give serious thought to the many regulatory concerns that have resulted from the introduction of AI into the financial industry. Regulators are confronted with the issue of keeping up with the rapid advancement of AI technologies and their growing impact on the financial sector. They must ensure that AI applications comply with current regulatory frameworks while simultaneously tackling any unforeseen regulatory hurdles. The need for openness and explicability in AI-driven decision-making procedures is a vital regulatory consequence of AI in the financial sector. Especially in domains like algorithmic trading, credit scoring, and risk assessment, it might be difficult to comprehend how AI algorithms reach certain choices due to their increasing complexity and autonomy. Financial institutions are expected to ensure that the reasoning behind AI-driven choices is clear and understandable. This will help regulators build accountability and confidence among stakeholders. The use of AI algorithms raises ethical questions about their potential prejudice and lack of impartiality, which authorities in charge of these industries have to address. There is a risk that AI algorithms may unintentionally reinforce preexisting biases in data sets, which might result in discriminatory or unjust treatment of certain demographics. To make sure that AI in finance promotes equality, justice, and inclusion, regulators are looking at methods to reduce bias in AI algorithms. Some examples of these efforts include data governance, algorithmic transparency, and fairness testing. Financial system stability and safety must be prioritized alongside AI-driven innovation, a task that regulators are attempting to master. The lack of adequate regulation and supervision of AI applications like robo-advisors and algorithmic trading might lead to the introduction of new elements of systemic risk. To ensure the safety of the financial system and the integrity of the market, regulators are attempting to design suitable supervisory procedures and risk management frameworks to keep an eye on and hopefully lessen the dangers of AI-driven innovation. The potential effects of AI on financial service users' privacy and security are also being investigated by authorities. Some worry that weak customers might be manipulated or exploited by AI-driven customization and data analytics, and that client data would not be appropriately secured. In order to guarantee that financial AI apps adhere to relevant legislation and safeguard customers' rights and interests, regulators are formulating rules and regulations for data security, privacy, and cybersecurity. Given the worldwide nature of financial markets and the cross-border movement of data and services, authorities must tackle the international component of AI regulation in finance. In order to provide regulatory certainty, uniformity, and interoperability for financial institutions that operate in more than one country, it is crucial to harmonize regulatory approaches and standards across countries. The development of common principles and norms for regulating AI in finance is being spearheaded by international regulators, who are working together to encourage collaboration and coordination across borders. AI has several potential effects on financial market integrity and investor protection, which the authorities are now investigating. Some worry that market surveillance technologies and AI-driven trading algorithms might lead to insider trading, market manipulation, or other types of wrongdoing. To protect investors' trust and the integrity of the market, regulators are taking steps to improve their ability to monitor the market and to identify and prohibit abusive activities in AI-driven trading. Financial developments powered by AI, such as blockchain-based financial products and decentralized finance (DeFi), present difficulties that regulatory bodies are working to resolve. Increased openness, responsibility, and safeguarding of investors are three areas where these advances provide novel regulatory hurdles. In order to make sure that AI-driven financial breakthroughs follow all the rules while encouraging innovation and competition, regulators are working on frameworks to handle these issues (Dabaghia et al., 2024).

Not only that, but authorities are looking at how AI may affect financial oversight and compliance. Financial institutions may benefit from regulatory compliance tools and surveillance systems driven by AI in terms of their ability to comply with rules and identify possible infractions more efficiently. To prevent these instruments from jeopardizing the financial system's integrity or undermining the efficacy of regulatory monitoring, regulators are scrambling to guarantee their accuracy, reliability, and transparency. Concerns about algorithmic bias, the influence on marginalized groups, and the loss of jobs are among the ethical and social concerns that authorities are attempting to resolve in relation to AI in the financial sector. To prevent discrimination and damage to people or groups, regulators are attempting to guarantee that AI applications in the financial sector are fair, transparent, and accountable. Additionally, in order to produce ethical standards and best practices for the prudent use of AI in the financial sector, regulators are collaborating with stakeholders from the academic, business, and nonprofit sectors. Officials in charge of overseeing the financial industry are investigating how AI can affect innovation centers and regulatory sandboxes. Financial regulators are thinking about ways to incorporate AI-driven technologies into regulatory sandboxes to test and validate new AI-powered financial products and services, with the right protections in place to keep consumers and the system safe (Bodemer, 2024).

On top of that, authorities are dealing with the difficulties of overseeing non-bank financial institutions and Fintech businesses driven by AI. Financial security, market honesty, and consumer protection are all areas where these companies often operate outside of conventional regulatory systems. To properly oversee these businesses, authorities are looking into new avenues, such as collaborating with other regulators and international organizations and using supervisory tools powered by technology. For their part, financial authorities are thinking about how AI will change regulatory reporting and data management. The use of AI in regulatory reporting may increase data quality and accuracy, as well as the control and supervision of regulatory bodies. In an effort to improve regulatory reporting systems and guarantee that financial institutions report accurately and on time, regulators are looking at methods to use AI technology. The regulatory consequences of AI in the financial sector are intricate and diverse, necessitating thorough analysis and cooperation among authorities, legislators, and representatives from the industry. In order to address issues of openness, equity, stability, privacy, consumer protection, and market integrity, regulators must find a way to encourage innovation while also encouraging compliance with regulatory standards. Regulatory authorities may encourage the ethical and responsible use of AI in financial services by creating suitable frameworks, standards, and supervisory procedures. This will allow for the full realization of AI's advantages while minimizing its drawbacks (Noor et al., 2023; Olubusola et al., 2024.

REFERENCES

Abbas, F. "Deciphering the Future of Finance: Anticipating Emerging Trends and Disruptive Technologies Shaping the Financial Landscape," *Accounting & Management Research Review*, vol. 2, no. 1, pp. 15–21, 2023.

Aggarwal, K. K., A. Sharma, R. Kaur, and G. Lakhera, "Algorithmic FinTech Pioneering the Financial Landscape of Tomorrow," In *Algorithmic Approaches to Financial Technology: Forecasting, Trading, and Optimization*, Amandeep Singh, Sanjay Taneja, Pawan Kumar (eds.), IGI Global, 2024, pp. 27–45.

Agrawal, S. S., N. Rose, and K. PrabhuSahai, "The Fintech Revolution: AI's Role in Disrupting Traditional Banking and Financial Services," *Decision Making: Applications in Management and Engineering*, vol. 8, no. 1, pp. 243–256, 2024.

Ahmad, A. Y. A. B., S. S. Kumari, S. MahabubBasha, S. K. Guha, A. Gehlot, and B. Pant, "Blockchain Implementation in Financial Sector and Cyber Security System," In *2023 International Conference on Artificial Intelligence and Smart Communication (AISC)*, IEEE, Greater Noida, India, 2023, January, pp. 586–590.

Altan, B., and S. Milson, "AI-Powered Data Revolution: Navigating the Big Data Landscape," *EasyChair*, no. 11898, 2024.

Arslanian, H., and F. Fischer, *The Future of Finance: The Impact of FinTech, AI, and Crypto on Financial Services*. Springer, 2019.

Azaan, S., & Elsa, J. (2024). The Rise of Automated Accounting: Navigating the Digital Landscape.

Dabaghia, M. N., A. Alhorani, T. M. R. Al-Qaruty, R. N. Darwazeh, and A. Y. Areiqat, "Revolutionizing Finance: How FinTech, RegTech, and AI are Redefining the Financial Landscape," *Kurdish Studies*, vol. 12, no. 2, pp. 540–546, 2024.

Gupta, R., and N. Sharma, "The Art and Science of Learning Machines: Navigating the Landscape of AI," *Eastern European Journal for Multidisciplinary Research*, vol. 1, no. 1, pp. 11–13, 2024.

Irfan, M., M. Elmogy, and S. El-Sappagh, (Eds.), *The Impact of AI Innovation on Financial Sectors in the Era of Industry 5.0*. IGI Global, 2023.

Janani, S., M. Sivarathinabala, R. Anand, S. Ahamad, M. A. Usmani, and S. M. Basha, "Machine Learning Analysis on Predicting Credit Card Forgery," In *International Conference on Innovative Computing and Communication*, Singapore: Springer Nature Singapore, 2023, February, pp. 137–148.

Kalyan, N. B., K. Ahmad, F. Rahi, C. Shelke, and S. M. Basha, "Application of Internet of Things and Machine Learning in Improving Supply Chain Financial Risk Management System," In *2023 IEEE 2nd International Conference on Industrial Electronics: Developments & Applications (ICIDeA)*, IEEE, Imphal, India, 2023, September, pp. 211–216.

Kasowaki, L., and B. Deniz, "Revolutionizing Big Data: AI Algorithms and Predictive Analytics," *EasyChair*, no. 11685, 2024.
Khan, K., "AI in Finance Disruptive Technologies and Emerging Opportunities," *Journal of Artificial Intelligence General Science (JAIGS)*, vol. 3, no. 1, pp. 155–170, 2024.
Krishna, S. H., N. Vijayanand, A. Suneetha, S. M. Basha, S. C. Sekhar, and A. Saranya, "Artificial Intelligence Application for Effective Customer Relationship Management," In *2022 5th International Conference on Contemporary Computing and Informatics (IC3I)*, IEEE, Uttar Pradesh, India, 2022, December, pp. 2019–2023.
Kumar, K., and K. Megha, "Transforming the Landscape of Indian Banking and Financial Industry Through Artificial Intelligence," *EPRA International Journal of Economics, Business and Management Studies (EBMS)*, vol. 9, no. 11, pp. 161–165, 2022.
Mossavar-Rahmani, F., and B. Zohuri, "Artificial Intelligence at Work: Transforming Industries and Redefining the Workforce Landscape," *Journal of Economics & Management Research*, vol. 5, no. 2, pp. 2–4, 2024.
Naqvi, G., M. Afzaal, and M. Shafeeq, "Navigating Tomorrow's Banking Landscape: Exploring the Role of AI, Unraveling Issues and Confronting Challenges," *Journal of Management Practices, Humanities and Social Sciences*, vol. 8, no. 2, pp. 1–11, 2024.
Noor et al., "Revolutionizing Indonesia's Financial Landscape: The Impact of Information Technology on the Growth of Financial Technology Start-Ups," *Multidisciplinary Reviews*, vol. 6, no. 4, pp. 2023031–2023031, 2023.
Padmanaban, H., "Revolutionizing Regulatory Reporting through AI/ML: Approaches for Enhanced Compliance and Efficiency," *Journal of Artificial Intelligence General Science (JAIGS)*, vol. 2, no. 1, pp. 57–69, 2024.
Rajendran, P., R. Thomas, K. N. Marimuthu, and N. Jamal, "Financial Technology (Fintech) Revolution: Reshaping the Landscape of Financial Services," *European Economic Letters (EEL)*, vol. 13, no. 4, pp. 636–644, 2023.
Rathore, B. "Revolutionizing the Digital Landscape: Exploring the Integration of Artificial Intelligence in Modern Marketing Strategies," *Eduzone: International Peer Reviewed/Refereed Multidisciplinary Journal*, vol. 5, no. 2, pp. 8–13, 2016.
Sharma, P., and S. Manhas, "The Future of Finance: Revolutionizing the Industry with Artificial Intelligence," In *Leveraging AI and Emotional Intelligence in Contemporary Business Organizations*, Dipanker Sharma, Bhawana Bhardwaj, Mohinder Chand Dhiman (eds.), IGI Global, 2024, pp. 187–210.
Sharma, Y., B. Balamurugan, N. Snegar, and A. Ilavendhan, "How IOT, AI, and Blockchain Will Revolutionize Business," In *Blockchain, Internet of Things, and Artificial Intelligence*, Naveen Chilamkurti, T. Poongodi, Balamurugan Balusamy (eds.), Chapman and Hall/CRC, 2021, pp. 235–255.
Yalamati, S., "Enhance Banking Systems to Digitalize Using Advanced Artificial Intelligence Techniques in Emerging Markets," *International Scientific Journal for Research*, vol. 5, no. 5, pp. 1–24, 2023.
Zakaria, S., S. M. A. Manaf, M. T. Amron, and M. T. M. Suffian, "Has the World of Finance Changed? A Review of the Influence of Artificial Intelligence on Financial Management Studies," *Information Management and Business Review*, vol. 15, no. 4 (SI), pp. 420–432, 2023.

10 AI-Driven Mobile Banking Applications and Financial Literacy Programs

Empowering Self-Help Group Women

Sangeetha Rangasamy, Shampa I. Dev, and Thomas Mangara

10.1 INTRODUCTION

Financial inclusion will improve access to banking linkage among the self-help group (SHG) members and support to overcome social exclusion [1]. Presently, AI-driven mobile banking applications significantly facilitate socio-economic development; they also address the acute challenges of the SHG women and facilitate better financial services, leading to socio-economic development [2]. Technology tools help to overcome the barriers to financial inclusion by providing financial knowledge and skills. AI-driven financial literacy focuses on the serious issues of SHG women and helps them access financial services for socio-economic development [3]. To meet different unique demographic requirements of society, it provides tailor-made educational content and financial services. This knowledge will help the SHG women to improve their financial literacy, and mobile banking services will help them make financial decisions without compromising the family's needs and priorities [4]. Entrepreneurial ventures have given opportunities to generate income for SHG women and make strategic decisions to optimize their financial resources and facilitate socio-economic empowerment. Financial literacy programs with AI applications helped SHG women develop self-confidence and leadership skills and made them change agents in society [5]. With the help of Chatbot AI support, SHG women can access many multi-regional languages without any barriers to using financial services. Machine learning algorithms can support in providing tailor-made services to underserved communities. Advanced analytics are incorporated to develop innovative financial products such as micro-loans, microcredits, and micro-insurance based on the creditworthiness and risk appetite of the SHG women members. This will bring the SHGs behavior of being responsive with respect to

DOI: 10.1201/9781003645849-10

financial matters. AI-driven mobile banking financial services and literacy programs have a far-reaching socio-economic impact on SHG women by generating additional income-generating streams, poverty alleviation, household welfare, and community development [6].

Financial inclusion is an effective way of achieving a stable economy through financial literacy. Women constitute nearly half of the world's population, and their involvement in the system is appreciated. In developing countries with large populations and the least literacy, it is a big task to involve financial inclusion. However, with the efforts of government involvement and AI support, the trend is changing. SHG is one of the pioneer programs which can involve more marginalized women and make them involved for socio and economic benefit. Access to financial services and making informed financial decisions are important to achieve empowerment and eradicate poverty. In this context, artificial intelligence (AI) will be a helping hand in supporting mobile banking applications and financial literacy programs for women in an SHG.

Traditional financial institutions, like banks, were not able to involve more rural people in a financial system due to its fewer branches and illiterate people; they were not ready to be involved in the banking process for lending and buying money, and people were not so aware of the policies involved and accessibility to the internet. Additionally, in the traditional way, the extensive paperwork and strict documentation requirements imposed by banks often discourage individuals, especially those with limited education.

Traditional banking presents additional hurdles for women, characterized by gender bias and discrimination, curtailing financial autonomy. Cultural norms and the necessity of collateral for loans further disadvantage women. Consequently, numerous women unjustly face barriers to critical credit access, impeding their economic empowerment and financial independence, particularly in entrepreneurial endeavors. It also highlighted how AI-enabled services would facilitate sex-disaggregated data and gender-intelligent regulatory frameworks to support inclusive digital banking solutions for women [7].

AI and machine learning are catalyzing agents for the banking sector and the SHG. Banks can track the records of individuals' spending and investment patterns and assist customers in maintaining financial disciplines accordingly. SHG members can easily afford AI through mobile and internet facilities and can access bank and government facilities. Both banks and SHG work to ensure the sustainable progress of society and families.

10.1.1 Status of Financial Inclusion and Financial Literacy

FinTech firms play a major role in bridging the gap in financial inclusion and gender disparities in India. They support the financial system by facilitating more accessible, cost-effective, and user-friendly financial services for all segments of society, including underserved demographics. It is interesting to note the improvement in the Financial Inclusion Index by the Reserve Bank of India from 43.4 in 2017 to 56.4 in 2022 to 60.1 in March 2023 [8]. This is possible with the evolution of FinTech firms with digital wallets, mobile money, peer-to-peer lending and inventive micro-insurance products.

It is noteworthy that the Government of India initiated the Digital India mission. It enabled the JAM trinity – comprising Jan Dhan, Aadhar and Mobile internet connectivity, which empowered individuals, marginalized businesses and especially women to access financial services seamlessly through smartphones [9]. Yet another notable digital facility is UPI (Unified Payment Services), which enables bank account linkage with mobile numbers [10].

Despite government and other government representatives like NABARD soliciting the promotion of financial inclusion and literacy, significant gaps persist in underserved populations such as SHG women [11]. For example, Pradhan Mantri Jan DhanYojana (PMJDY) has improved banking accessibility. However, rural areas remain vulnerable.

As an initiative, a survey was conducted in 2019 to understand the improvement in financial inclusion and literacy levels compared to 2013. The survey evaluated financial literacy based on criteria comprising financial knowledge, financial behavior, and financial attitude among individuals. Interestingly, only 21% of women met the threshold criteria in the three parameters assessed, showcasing an improvement from the 16% recorded in 2013. These challenges and gaps can be better addressed by leveraging technology to improve financial inclusion and literacy among SHG women.

In India, FinTech works toward filling the gap between financial inclusion and reducing gender disparity. FinTech supports facilitating more accessible, cost-effective, and user-friendly financial services for all segments of society, including underserved demographics. The financial inclusion index shows significant growth from 43.4 in 2017 to 60.1 in March 2023 from the RBI report. This is possible with the help of FinTech firms by applying mobile money digital wallets, peer-to-peer lending and inventive micro-insurance products [8].

The government of India initiated the Digital India Mission on July 1, 2015, and it enabled the JAM trinity- comprising Jan DhanYojana, Aadhar and mobile connectivity, which empowered individuals, marginalized businesses and especially women to access financial facilities without any hurdle through the smartphones [9]. Another notable financial service for the transaction of money is UPI- Unified Payment Services, which links the bank account to the mobile [10].

Government and other government representative organizations like NABARD are working for financial inclusion and financial literacy for the group, which has significant gaps in deprived populations such as SHG women. For example, Pradhan Mantri Jan DhanYojana (PMJDY) has improved banking accessibility. However, rural areas remain vulnerable [11].

The survey was conducted in 2019 to ensure financial inclusion and financial literacy in 2013. Financial literacy consists of financial knowledge, behavior, and attitude among individuals. Interestingly, only 21% of women met the threshold criteria in the three parameters assessed, showcasing an improvement from the 16% recorded in 2013. Technology is a supporting factor in improving financial inclusion and financial literacy and can bridge the gap and challenges SHG women face.

10.1.2 Need for Technology Solution

One of the objectives of the National Strategy for Financial Education 2020–2025 is to improve the usage of digital financial services safely and effectively among vulnerable populations, especially SHG members. It is possible through technology interventions, especially AI-driven mobile banking applications, which will support improving financial inclusion and literacy through accessible banking services [12]. Even the underserved populations and SHG members will access financial services remotely through their smartphones.

10.1.3 Empowerment for Economic Decision-Making

Empowerment of SHG women through their involvement in economic decision-making in households and communities is possible with their improved access to financial services. It is also important to provide them with tools and resources for financial management and technology interventions to monitor their finances and invest in economic activities to contribute to household savings and investment. This will result in women's empowerment, well-being, gender equality and better social inclusion, leading to the attainment of the 2030 agenda for sustainable development [13].

10.1.4 Personalized Mobile Banking Solutions at a Glance

New-generation banks, namely ICICI, HDFC Bank, Kotak Mahindra, Axis Bank, and SBI, are pioneers in offering personalized mobile banking services. It includes customized debit cards, budget management, savings and spending tracker, spending patterns and personalized recommendations (loan and investment) according to an individual's preferences. The same can be extended to SHG members through mobile banking services; the present level of underserved status can improve [14].

It was observed through earlier studies that men perceive mobile banking solu tions as more useful than their women counterparts. This may be due to their social beliefs that men take more financial responsibility [15,16]. However, more and more women can be brought into the financial system through financial literacy initiatives and training on mobile banking solutions. The advent of branchless banking models will facilitate unique AI-driven banking applications, namely multilingual support and educational resources on financial management, making banking services more accessible and inclusive. The financial resilience of SHG women can be improved by spreading the same services available to all demographic segments.

10.1.5 AI-Driven ML Model for Better Banking Solutions

In the banking sector, machine learning has the potential to deal with huge volumes of databases. It helps to work on the pattern of the individual transactions, chat interaction with the bank personnel or corporate records. It will help to work on the customer's requirements and internal operations with machine learning support. Integrating machine learning into banking helps to detect fraud and refine the credit assessment procedures, ensure regulatory adherence, and enhance customer interactions.

Mobile banking and its applications encourage customers to make financial decisions effectively where machine learning is integrated into mobile banking. Machine learning is the tool by the bank that can analyze the customer spending pattern and give personalized suggestions for better management. For instance, TransUnion Bank has collaborated with the Mint app with the ML application to provide a credit score for a customer to evaluate and retain the customer for a lifetime [17].

The development of strategies and processes and customer satisfaction with the bank are maintained by AI. Research indicates that AI has potential applications and acceptance from the organizational standpoint [18]. AI tools enhanced the greater business opportunities than the traditional strategy decision and risk model creation approach. Integration of AI and ML in the banking sector will enhance the operational workflows. Neural network approach is used for the defaults and early repayment prediction in the banks. AI-driven data mining is used to demonstrate the credit score than the conventional approach.

Machine Learning- driven is used to know the customer credit risk. Using AI technology such as Machine Learning and data mining to be used to enhance the credit score, analyzing and approval procedures. For instance, a customer credit scoring model is developed by the data mining neutral techniques. AI-supportive financial models will help to develop the prediction, trends, risk, analyze the expenditure patterns and can be used for the SHG members for taking financial decisions.

In total, AI-mobile-driven banking with the pre-financial literacy to SHG women members work for the betterment of life, and mobiles are user friendly and all banking apps are available in the regional Multi-languages also and need not to visit banks every time. AI-financial literacy programs can improve financial knowledge, skills and promote financial decision-making. Technology and tailored intervention will work as a reducing literacy gap, improving financial literacy and fastening toward the sustainable economic empowerment of SHG.

10.2 GLOBAL INITIATIVES ON TECHNOLOGY SOLUTIONS FOR IMPROVED FINANCIAL INCLUSION

Mobile banking has given tremendous opportunities for the banking sector and customers, whether a person is from the organized sector or an unorganized one. Mobile-driven AI has increased the number of customers. One can open a bank account without physical presence with a multi-regional language, which has increased the number of account holders. India has created enormous opportunities for the financial sector by creating a 92% internet density. It also facilitated governments and NGOs in establishing mobile-based financial literacy programs to make informed decisions about their savings and investments in alignment with their goals. It brings the need for caution that access to loans through the AI system provides an accessibility advantage. However, excess borrowing and unsustainable debts must be handled with improved financial education through mobile applications.

Policymakers across the globe pay much attention to financial inclusion since it is considered a strong pillar of human development. At the same time, one must acknowledge the shortcomings of the traditional financial system in attracting all segments of society. Penetration of the internet and its impact on mobile banking services, along with AI, might provide a better reach and inclusion of the unbanked population with better financial literacy [19]. It explores another avenue to get the attention of government and policymakers on the spending and investment in Technology Infrastructure, especially on AI in the Asia Pacific region, which is expected to reach US$4.29 Bn by 2024 [20]. In this context, various initiatives of advanced and emerging nations are explored and presented below to capture the support system prevailing in other nations to support marginalized populations.

10.2.1 Advanced Countries

Country-level financial literacy ranges between 71% and 13% [21]. These nations, namely Australia, Canada, Finland, Germany, Israel, The Netherlands, Sweden, and the United Kingdom, are considered as financially literate advanced nations. The best practices of these economies' financial literacy initiatives and their success, outcome, and impact can be explored. It is also alarming to note that there is lower financial literacy among women and the poor. Another dimension to look at is the level of financial literacy among the adult population that availed of loans with a low understanding of interest risk in mind. It indicates that financial knowledge needs to be converted into a financial skill to equip them better to apply while processing financial services for their financial requirements.

10.2.2 Developing Countries

It is interesting to note the contribution of AI to Vietnam's financial services industry. Algorithmic Credit Scoring is widely used in Vietnam to evaluate customers' creditworthiness while sanctioning a credit. It was highlighted that traditional credit scores are outdated. Hence, CredoLab used three-dimensional data, namely traditional, transactional and behavioral data, to develop credit scoring. Traditional data from a bureau depicts transaction history, transactional data from banks about telecommunication and utility bills exhibits the ability to pay, and behavioral data from mobile devices reflects their intention or willingness to pay [22]. Accordingly, a credit score is being assigned. Hence, combining technology and financial services transforms the financial services industry. At the same time, the percentage of people involved in the FinTech process to enhance financial inclusion and financial literacy to attain better socio-economic development is negligible. As per the World Bank report, roughly one-third of adults, around 1.7 billion people [23,24] and 200 million businesses [25] remain unbanked. Here are some well-known AI-based FinTech firms in developing nations. Ant Group's AI-based Customer Service Chatbot manages nearly 2–3 million daily queries using a deep learning model to trace fraudulent activities. Another company, UBA in Nigeria, uses a chatbot to help customers transfer money, pay utility bills, buy air tickets, and check and monitor account balances. In Kenya, SafaricomChatbot assistant Zuri facilitates customers with subscription management, reversal of money transferred to the wrong account, cancellation of SMS services, top-up during airtime and checks M-PESA.

In the same way in South Africa, TymeBank interacts with customers online through kiosks. One interesting fact is that there are only 250 employees who serve customers at a low cost compared to about 50,000 employees in South African Bank. In all four examples, the outcome was very effective and positive [24].

10.3 MOBILE BANKING APPLICATIONS TRANSFORM TRADITIONAL BARRIERS

10.3.1 Loan Disbursement

The partnership between banks and digital solutions providers, driven by the integration of AI, ML, and other technologies, has extended into the lending sector. This collaboration encompasses every stage of the loan process, from customer application to onboarding, approval, credit disbursement, and management to collection and recovery. Banks are leveraging AI to overcome traditional obstacles in lending. They collaborate with digital solution providers facilitated by AI technology. By harnessing AI algorithms, banks can analyze vast amounts of data, including non-traditional sources, to assess creditworthiness more accurately. This approach allows banks to reach underserved population segments, such as self-help groups, small businesses, and individuals with limited credit histories.

Additionally, AI-driven solutions streamline the loan approval process, reduce the risk of defaults, and enhance customer experience. It is very interesting to refer to the impact created by a challenger bank by leveraging technology to reach the excluded population segment with more affordable and useful products and services. Since its inception in 2018, it has on-boarded more than 2 million customers, 50% of whom are women [26].

10.3.2 Entrepreneurship and Income Generation Activities

Digital banking solutions and AI strongly influence the financial inclusion of marginalized segments of society, especially the women members of SHG globally. It is not just the inclusion; it is to support them with risk detection, measurement, and management, address the information asymmetry problem, and provide customer support through chatbots, fraud detection, and cybersecurity. This will result in prudent decisions on entrepreneurial activity, leading to better income generation [27]. It is also important to focus on how these SHG members organize and manage their debt sources for their entrepreneurial activities. In most cases, over-indebtedness also affects their entrepreneurial and income-generating activities. It was explored how AI and ML can help overcome poverty by better managing their indebtedness [28]. The same AI and ML model can be employed by the SHG members to support their entrepreneurial venture by profiling and describing their indebtedness to reduce the vulnerability and adverse effect on the performance of SHG members and the group.

10.3.3 Access to Relevant Information

The internet penetration resulted in wide access to data and information. Recently, the non-conscious algorithm Google searches source information from millions of possible entries and makes recommendations to the users [29]. Considering the development in information technology, there is huge potential in mobile banking with AI to support the self-help group in achieving better penetration and success.

10.3.4 Scalability

AI and ML come with the great advantage of handling volume and variety of data to extract meaningful information to achieve data-driven decisions.

10.4 AI-DRIVEN FINANCIAL LITERACY PROGRAMS

Financial literacy is crucial for individuals to make informed decisions about their finances. However, traditional financial literacy programs often need help reaching and engaging diverse populations effectively. Innovative solutions can be sought through AI-driven financial literacy programs to provide personalized learning experiences and interactive learning tools. It will also help in overcoming the biases in AI algorithms. The main intention of an AI-driven financial literacy program is to improve the impact and effectiveness of financial decision-making. Machine learning algorithms in the AI-driven Financial literacy program will gather information on the participants' learning experiences, which can help improve the quality of content and delivery mechanism. The data on the participants' financial habits and preferences can be collected before or during the program to provide personalized recommendations and relevant engagement. For example, an AI-driven financial literacy mobile application can collect data on a user's spending habits during the program. Real-time personalized solutions on budgeting and personal financing can be provided.

10.4.1 Tailored Learning Experiences

The one-size-fits-all approach is mostly seen in traditional literacy programs, making the program less reachable to masses with diverse backgrounds, learning aptitudes, financial backgrounds and goals. On the other hand, AI-driven programs will design content and adapt delivery methods to meet the individual needs of each participant. For example, a financial literacy app may use machine learning algorithms to understand participants' financial knowledge and customize the content to an appropriate difficulty level.

10.4.2 Interactive Learning Tools

Interactive learning tools can be embedded into AI-driven financial literacy programs to encourage and engage participants better. The most popular tools to explain financial concepts in real-world scenarios are quizzes, simulations and games. The power of these tools is better experienced through the retention level experienced among the participants with the interactive learning tools. For example, gamification techniques used as rewards and recognition plans embedded in the financial literacy app to solve the scenario-based questions orient the participant on the financial challenges.

10.4.3 Addressing Biases in AI Algorithms

AI-driven financial literacy programs will have challenges in terms of biases in algorithms. It will lead to improper and inequitable recommendations, especially to the individuals of marginalized and underrepresented segments. Careful designing, training and testing of the algorithms with diverse datasets will ensure the fairness and accuracy of the AI-driven programs. It will also help in enforcing protection to mitigate bias in decision-making.

10.4.4 Ethical Considerations in AI Adoption within the Financial Sector

AI-driven financial literacy programs will be scrutinized to incorporate the ethical aspects of AI technology in the Indian financial sector. AI-algorithms-based recommendations have the potential to influence the financial decisions of individuals; it is important to use them ethically and responsibly. It can be achieved by ensuring data privacy, transparency and accountability in algorithm-based decision-making. Potential discrimination in algorithms will be carefully monitored to overcome bias risks. This will build trust and confidence among the users, facilitating informed financial decisions.

Leveraging AI technology will help enhance the outcomes of financial literacy programs by empowering individuals to make better financial decisions. However, it is important to address ethical considerations for the responsible use of AI technology.

10.5 AI-BASED COMMUNITY ENGAGEMENT AND PEER LEARNING IN SHG

The use of AIs in SHG will ensure and enhance faster peer learning and community engagement, which include chat boats for customer services, pattern and payment behavior of members, use of algorithms to understand credit histories, prediction of default risks, risk minimization by informed credit support, accessibility to remote areas at any time, easy detection and information of fraudulent activities and sharing of investment opportunities etc.

AI-based community engagement and peer learning among SHG members can easily be made possible by including Gen Zs, millennials, and boomers. A mix of like-minded and disciplined groups of boomers, millennials, and Gen Zs will foster the digital skills of the SHG members and reduce the gulf of the digital divide.

10.6 LONG-TERM IMPACT AND SUSTAINABILITY OF SHG THROUGH AI

India has started incorporating financial inclusion by integrating financial technology with the digital ecosystem for more accessibility to a large population. Efficient allocation of resources through AI-enabled services to the SHG, Joint Liability Groups and Farmer Liability Groups is provided to attain economic growth, social inclusion, and the protection of the environment to facilitate sustainable development. Sustainable goals are to focus on zero hunger, no poverty, good health, decent work, quality education and gender equality, faster innovation and the well-being of mankind and the environment. Digital Financial Inclusion has helped to reduce the gender gap between males and females by increasing economic growth through the SHG, which the women create. Financial inclusion will lead to the growth of the economy as well as the well-being of humans. Appropriate handling and strong decision-making, guidance, risk-taking, and acceptance of changes in modern trends, like the use of science and technology for ease and accuracy, need to be incorporated for the sustainable existence of SHGs. In the long term, SHG will bring gender equality into society, and assert their rights within households and communities. This group not only brings financial assistance at a small scale but also helps to assist skill development and initiate entrepreneurship among women. It also brings collective action for the cause, pooling resources and standing each other in various social issues. In the process of inclusive and sustainable development, the women are not only the beneficiaries but also active agents of changing their communities through resilience, determination and collective action, which will positively impact socio-economic life. Women empowerment will occur when she questions society's existing norms and culture to uplift their lives. Women's empowerment is a multi-faceted issue, not only measured in finance. Many programs related to women's empowerment are involved with microfinance, and they certainly help improve women's lives. Empowering women is related to the financial and behavioral aspects, a training and awareness program she has been exposed to. Microfinance will have a minimalist effect and need to look for a greater impact on the empowerment of women; for a greater impact, there is a need for education and awareness among men and women is necessary. Many programs like the National Rural Livelihood Mission (NRLM) and Deendayal Anthyodaya Yojana (DAY-NRLM) aim to strengthen the SHG and work towards sustainable livelihoods. At the same time, the effectiveness, reach and outcome of government initiatives can be better managed through the use of AI technology.

10.7 IMPACT OF AI-DRIVEN SOLUTIONS ON THE SOCIO-ECONOMIC DEVELOPMENT OF SHG WOMEN

Social and economic well-being represents individuals' welfare state and well-being, which measure development. Social well-being is achieved through social relationships, stability, and peace, which can be measured with social capital and empowerment. Economic well-being is measured through basic needs like food, clothing, shelter, education, transportation and financial security for the present and future. Information and communication technology has given new opportunities for developing poor communities. More than 11 billion SHGs exist in India, providing services to more than 138 million households. The scale of opportunity is remarkable (National Bank for Agricultural and Rural Development, 2021).

In the world of technology and finance, AI has created a footprint and demonstrated its accuracy with faster and cheaper transactions. Systematic qualitative service from financial and non-financial agencies is necessary for inclusive growth, sustainable development, and women's empowerment. With artificial intelligence, banks need not go into each one. It has a cost advantage in providing the service to its customers. AI helps predict the customer's loan repayment pattern, attitude and integrity. India is the fastest growing FinTech market, and a recent study shows that 52% of the population utilizes the FinTech service. FinTech believes that customer service satisfaction is the priority. To increase the efficiency and accuracy of the work, many SHGs started to opt for digital tools and platforms to access financial services and government programs and facilities. There is a positive relationship between smartphone ownership and structural social capital and empowerment in terms of freedom of movement and entrepreneurial intention. Structural social capital is civic participation, political participation and social networks. Information technology intervention in the SHG can positively impact tribal culture and economic development. SHG has the potential to bring tribal cultures and their artisan works, such as bamboo works and crafts, to the mainstream of society, and they can be financially independent. During 2015–2016, NABARD decided to incorporate mobile apps in SHG through the E-SHAKTI project to bring transparency and credibility to bookkeeping. It will help to trace the history of the individual financial and nonfinancial records to all stakeholders. The stakeholder may be a banker, and he will have a clear picture of the SHG of that group and performance. Accordingly, he can provide financial assistance and suggestions. All the SHG members know about cashless transactions and banking procedures. Still, individually, they need business correspondence to complete the transactions due to fear of making a mistake SHG members need proper practical training in mobile applications to operate the mobile on behalf of the SHG group.

10.8 STRENGTHS, WEAKNESS, OPPORTUNITIES AND CHALLENGES IN AI-DRIVEN MOBILE BANKING SOLUTIONS FOR SHG

AI-driven mobile banking solutions greatly help women in the SHG. These banking solutions use AI technologies to make personalized banking services available on mobile devices to promote financial inclusion. Their accessibility and convenience of use empower the underserved populations, mostly women. AI-driven banking solutions offer tremendous benefits and numerous opportunities; however, weaknesses and challenges must be addressed (Figure 10.1).

10.8.1 Strengths

Listed here are some of the strengths:

1. **Accessibility:** AI-driven mobile banking technologies make banking accessible at the tip of the fingers. Banks are located at a considerable distance, and the time, effort and money expended to reach the bank for transactions cause considerable hurdles. AI-based digital banking enables SHG women to access banking services anytime, anywhere, on their mobile devices. This empowers women to manage their finances and banking needs effectively.

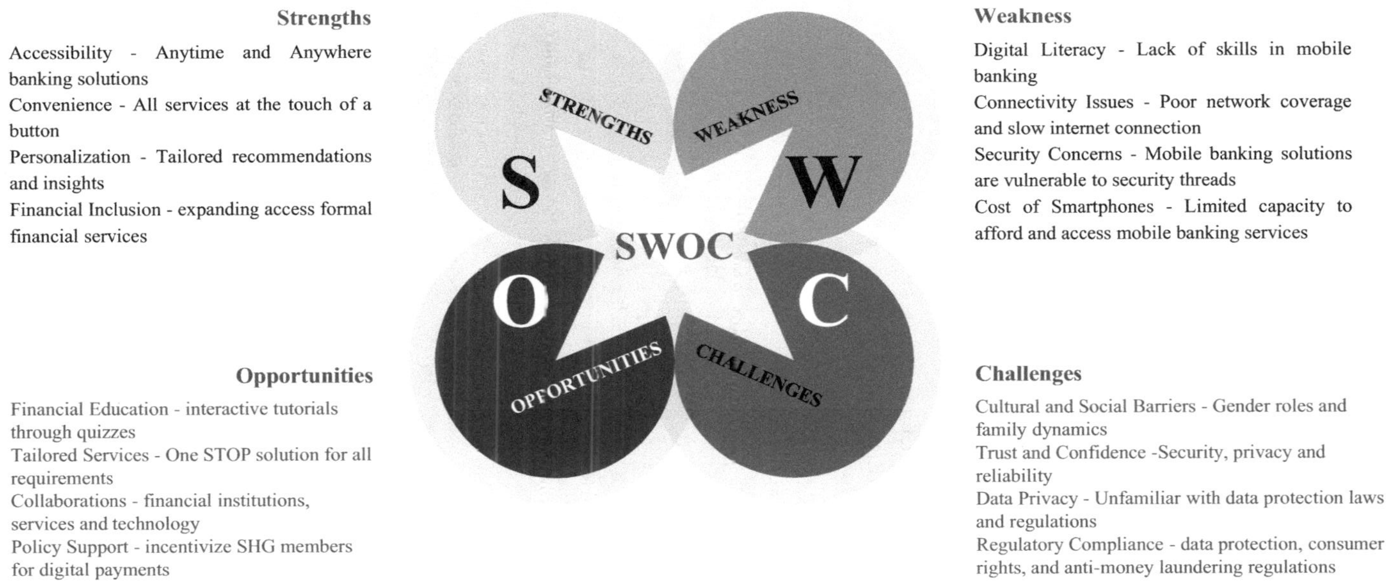

FIGURE 10.1 SWOC analysis. (*Source*: Authors own creation.)

2. **Conveniences:** AI-driven mobile banking offers a wide range of services like bill payments, fund transfers, and account management at the touch of a button. SHG women can perform transactions and access financial information without the need to visit a physical bank branch, saving time and effort.
3. **Personalization:** AI algorithms analyze user data to provide personalized banking experiences for SHG women. AI algorithms will provide tailor-made recommendations according to the users' financial habits and other patterns, helping SHG women make informed decisions to achieve their financial goals.
4. **Financial inclusion:** AI-driven mobile banking solutions contribute to broader financial inclusion efforts by reaching underserved populations across India where banking infrastructure and penetration are very limited.

10.8.2 Weaknesses

1. **Digital literacy:** Digital literacy is poor among SHG women. They must gain the necessary skills and the confidence to engage in mobile banking. With the skills required, their ability to benefit from these mobile banking technologies is much higher.
2. **Connectivity issues:** To fulfill the vision of Digital India, the BharatNet project has been launched to provide last-mile internet connectivity to Gram Panchayats through Wifi or Fiber to the Home. (Digital India Programme.) However, the connectivity problem still needs to be solved in rural areas. Poor connectivity and slow internet speeds hinder access to mobile banking technologies, which disadvantages SHG women.
3. **Security concerns:** Mobile banking technologies, like any other, are susceptible to phishing attacks, malware and data breaches. Lack of digital literacy and security breaches bring distrust and reluctance to use mobile banking technologies.
4. **Cost of smartphones:** SHG women need more resources to buy smartphones. Cultural background also does not support either. SHG women may not own smartphones or may have old devices, and all the features of mobile banking technologies may need to be fixed.

10.8.3 Opportunities

1. **Financial education:** Given the background of the problem, the government has a vision for digital India, under which many programs have been launched. AI-driven mobile banking technologies present immense opportunities for financial inclusion and improving the financial and digital literacy of SHG women. If this huge population is tapped for financial literacy, financial transactions will increase, eventually leading to financial growth.
2. **Tailored services:** AI-driven mobile technologies can offer tailor-made services considering the population's specific needs and geography. Thus

micro loans, saving accounts, and insurance policies can be offered based on the specific requirements of the SHG women.

3. **Partnerships and collaborations:** Partnerships between financial institutions, technology companies and Non-profit organizations can facilitate the development and deployment of AI-driven mobile banking solutions for SHG women. These partnerships combine resources like technology expertise and networks can help enhance the impact of financial inclusion initiatives.
4. **Policy support:** Government policy interventions like smartphone subsidies, digital payment incentives, and data protection regulatory frameworks can create a conducive environment for innovation in the mobile banking industry, thus leading to the development and adoption of AI-driven solutions.

10.8.4 Challenges

1. **Cultural and social barriers:** Social norms and cultural beliefs surrounding mobile banking and the use of the technology might negatively influence the adoption rate of such technology. The adoption of mobile banking applications may face obstacles due to women's access to and usage of these apps being shaped by gender roles, family dynamics, and community expectations.
2. **Trust and confidence:** Another challenge is to earn the trust and confidence of SHG women as users of mobile banking technologies. Fears of money security, data privacy, and reliability often act as a huge deterrent. So, the foremost challenge is to build trust and confidence in the product and the services provided.
3. **Data privacy:** SHG women need to be more familiar with data protection measures and regulations adopted by the State. They generally express concern over the adoption of AI-driven banking solutions. AI-driven mobile banking technologies rely on vast amounts of user data for effectiveness. The success of personalized recommendations depends upon the vast amount of user data being effectively analyzed to produce such recommendations.
4. **Regulatory compliance:** Financial institutions and technology providers must adhere to regulatory criteria and norms when creating and implementing AI-driven mobile banking solutions to reduce legal and reputational concerns, compliance with consumer rights, anti-money laundering laws, and data protection rules is crucial.

By providing accessible, convenient, and personalized banking services, AI-driven Mobile banking solutions offer significant potential for SHG Women. Addressing the challenges mentioned above is essential to utilize the full potential of these technologies. Establishing partnerships, policy support, customized services, financial inclusion, and increased financial literacy, with a constant nudge to embrace AI-driven mobile banking solutions etc. would provide a conducive environment for overall growth and economic development.

10.9 WAY FORWARD

Customized products through service unbundling: Conventional banking systems offer bundled products. Credit or debit cards, overdraft facilities, checking accounts with theft alerts, transaction alerts, credit score reports, etc., are bundled with the savings account. The customer may not require these bundled products. FinTech companies have started reshaping this landscape by offering personalized services. Disintegrating the bundled products allows customers to choose the ones they require. This gives the customer a greater sense of autonomy and control. This benefits women seeking financial solutions as it gives them increased flexibility. For instance, Dvara Smart Gold provides micro savings and investment options for rural women, enabling them to invest in gold and build savings with contributions as small as ₹10 per day (Figure 10.2).

Improving financial literacy through technology: FinTech companies leverage digital platforms to improve financial inclusion and literacy. They cater to the requirements of the underserved populations. They provide them with educational resources, videos and infographics aimed at ease of using these platforms. They also generate confidence in the user. Additionally, personalized financial counseling is available to the user. For example, Saksham is a platform developed by the National Bank for Rural and Urban Development (NABARD). This platform adds elements of gamification, to make financial education engaging. It caters effectively to SHG women as it is available in multiple Indian languages.

Expanding financial access: Small-scale entrepreneurs, like SHG women who cannot provide collateral for loans, rely on microloans from Grameen Financial Services. These banks ascertain their creditworthiness in a non-traditional way, like assessing their mobile phone usage and transactions. Similarly, platforms like Kisan Network and Jai Kisan cater specifically to farmers, offering mobile-based solutions for accessing agricultural inputs, credit, and market information. Phonepe and Gpay are the digital platforms that enable cashless transactions. This empowers individuals, to conveniently manage their payments, receive remittances, and access other services securely.

Lowering financial service costs: Indian FinTech firms have helped in greatly reducing overall costs by shifting away from brick-and-mortar banks and their operational expenses. They leveraged technology to reduce the cost of financial services. Platforms such as Paytm and Google Pay offer affordable or free transactions, bypassing traditional processors. Robo-advisors introduced in most platforms, provide cost-effective portfolio management, making professional investment advice accessible to a wider audience. Peer-to-peer lending platforms drive down interest rates, benefiting both borrowers and lenders. By establishing partnerships with micro-entrepreneurs, innovators like Paynearby extend affordable financial services to rural customers like SHG women.

Enhancing customer experience with hyper-personalization: As discussed in the preceding section Indian FinTech companies have embraced personalization, by tailoring financial products and services to individual requirements. This is made possible with the use of advanced data analytics and artificial intelligence, to study

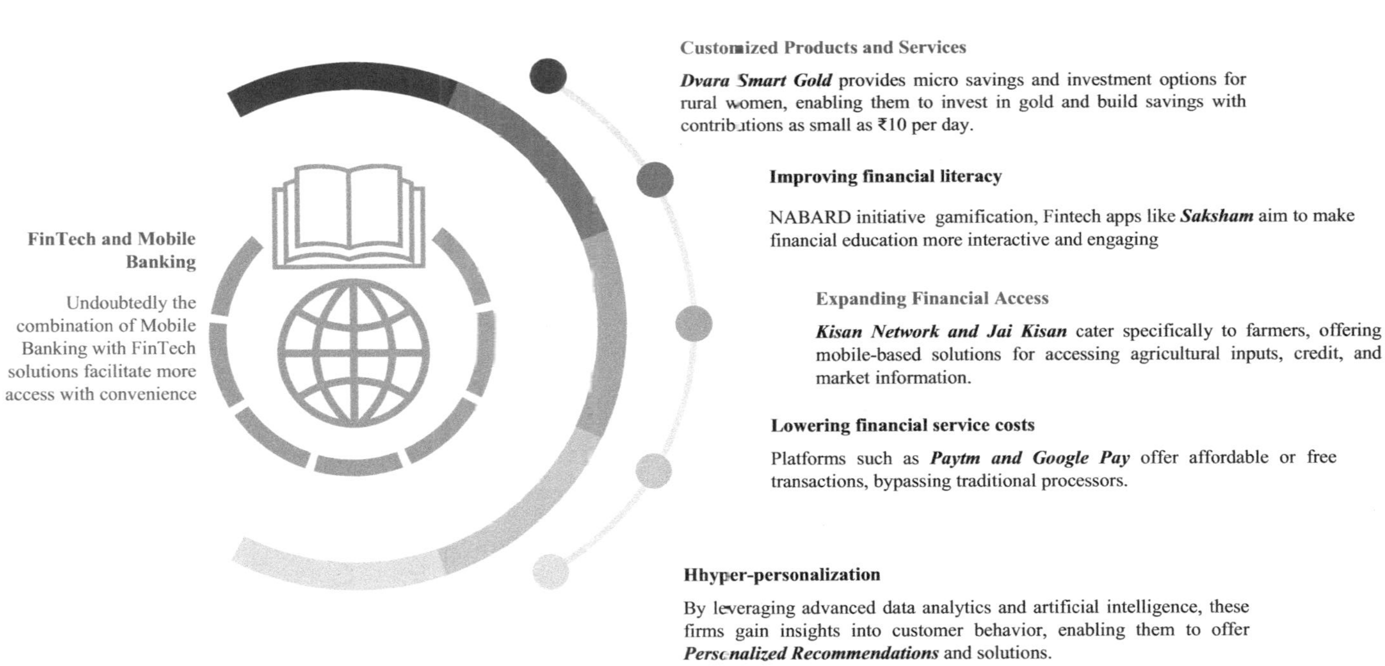

FIGURE 10.2 Way forward. (*Source*: Author's creation.)

customer usage patterns and their behavior. For example, they may provide shorter repayment terms to women with seasonal businesses or lower interest rates to those with a strong repayment history. Similarly, they use alternative data sources for credit assessment. Bot-advisors are installed to suggest investment insights and suggestions based on investors' risk profiles and goals. This hyper-personalized approach empowers customers to make informed decisions and enhances customer satisfaction and promotes greater financial literacy.

10.10 CONCLUSION

In the modern era, AI has omnipresence; without AI, a day would not be completed. India stands 2nd largest population to use the internet with 1.2 billion in 2023; in this, 1.03 billion population use the internet through mobile only. The Digital India program (July 1st, 2015) is one of the supporting programs to transform society into a digitally empowered and knowledge economy. AI can improve the quality of life by providing accurate predictions, solutions to problems, financial guidance, etc. Women in India use only 31% of the internet, and there is an effective gap between male and female mobile internet users, which is about 40%. Mobile phones are easy and comfortable devices for everyone, including those in rural areas [30]. Mobile phones help people connect and get global information, which may improve socio-economic aspects. It also helps to build social connections through WhatsApp groups, Facebook, Instagram, etc. It will help to uplift the social life of marginalized segments of the economy. Socializing with other group members of SHG, financial institutions, and other segments of the economy will result in identifying various income-generating opportunities. Here is the added advantage of digital economy and mobile banking applications with AI to support SHG women members. Based on the browsing behavior and pattern, AI will recommend banking and other allied services, leading to income generation and entrepreneurial activities. However, to achieve this state with equitable access to banking services, infrastructure to be built in, awareness programs on digital mobile applications, financial literacy, and income-generating entrepreneurial activities to be organized for SHG members. The program's effectiveness can be measured through the socio-economic development of participants, especially the SHG women.

ACKNOWLEDGEMENTS

This chapter is an outcome of our externally funded research Project. We thank Indian Council of Social Science Research (ICSSR) for the funding opportunity. Literature survey helped us to contribute to this chapter.

REFERENCES

1. S. Maity, "Self help groups, microfinance, financial inclusion and social exclusion: Insight from Assam," *Heliyon*, vol. 9, no. 6, p. e16477, Jun. 2023, https://doi.org/10.1016/j.heliyon.2023.e16477
2. M. H. Fujo, S. Katwale, and M. A. Dida, "Forecasting financial resilience: An analysis of practices and limitations in predicting trends – A case study of micro-credit in Tanzania", In *AOBMER-V9*, María-Dolores Guillamón (ed.), BP International, pp. 152–173, Feb. 2024.

3. Z. Zhang, J. Song, T. Shu, and T. Zhao, "Changes in rural financial exclusion's supply and demand factors from the perspective of digital inclusive financial policies," *Cogent Economics & Finance*, vol. 12, no. 1, Jan. 2024, https://doi.org/10.1080/23322039.2024.2305480
4. M. Pal and H. Gupta, "Sustainable women empowerment at the bottom of the pyramid through credit access," *Equality, Diversity and Inclusion*, vol. 42, no. 1, pp. 157–171, Sep. 2022, https://doi.org/10.1108/EDI-02-2022-0028
5. N. Alrefaei, P. G. Aquinas, and O. A. Al-Maamari, "Self help group (SHG) in India: A path toward empowerment and poverty reduction," *Social Work with Groups*, vol. 46, no. 3, pp. 249–263, Dec. 2022, https://doi.org/10.1080/01609513.2022.2159612
6. R. B. Swain and M. Floro, "Microfinance, vulnerability and risk in low income households," *International Review of Applied Economics*, vol. 28, no. 5, pp. 539–561, Jun. 2014, https://doi.org/10.1080/02692171.2014.918937
7. S. Appaya and S. B. Abbas, "Empowering women through digital financial inclusion," *World Bank Blogs*, Mar. 16, 2024. https://blogs.worldbank.org/en/psd/empowering-women-through-digital-financial-inclusion
8. By BL Mumbai Bureau, "Financial inclusion index improved to 60.1 in March 2023 against 56.4 in March 2022," *BusinessLine*, Sep. 15, 2023. https://www.thehindubusinessline.com/money-and-banking/financial-inclusion-index-improved-to-601-in-march-2023-against-564-in-march-2022/article67312470.ece
9. S. Sinha, "Gender Digital divide in India: Impacting women's participation in the labour market," in *Reflecting on India's Development*, 1) National Institute of Labour Economics Research and Development (NILERD) (ed.), Springer eBooks, 2018, pp. 293–310. https://doi.org/10.4236/ajibm.2017.710084
10. R. Gochhwal, "Unified Payment Interface—An advancement in payment systems," *American Journal of Industrial and Business Management*, vol. 07, no. 10, pp. 1174–1191, Jan. 2017, https://doi.org/10.4236/ajibm.2017.710084
11. I. Bajaj and M. Kaur, "Validating multi-dimensional model of financial literacy using confirmatory factor analysis," *Managerial Finance*, vol. 48, no. 9/10, pp. 1488–1512, Jun. 2022, https://doi.org/10.1108/mf-06-2021-0285
12. Z. Yanting and M. Ali, "Artificial intelligence, digital finance, and financial inclusion: A conceptual framework," in *Financial Inclusion Across Asia: Bringing Opportunities for Businesses*, Choi Meng Leong, Muhammad Ali, Syed Ali Raza, Chin-Hong Puah, Ibrahim Halil Eksi (eds.), Emerald Publishing Limited eBooks, 2023, pp. 77–85. https://doi.org/10.1108/978-1-83753-304-620231006
13. "Woman's Role in Economic Development by Ester Boserup, Su Fei Tan, Camilla Toulmin – books on Google Play," Jul. 01, 2013. https://play.google.com/store/books/details?id=nv7ingskXC4C
14. N. Singh and N. Sinha, "A study on mobile banking and its impact on customer's banking transactions: A comparative analysis of public and private sector banks in India," *FIIB Business Review*, vol. 5, no. 2, pp. 57–70, Apr. 2016, https://doi.org/10.1177/2455265820160207
15. H. Nysveen, P. E. Pedersen, and H. Thorbjørnsen, "Explaining intention to use mobile chat services: Moderating effects of gender," *Journal of Consumer Marketing*, vol. 22, no. 5, pp. 247–256, Jan. 2005, https://doi.org/10.1108/07363760510611671
16. P. Cruz, B. F. N. Lineu, P. Muñoz-Gallego, and T. Laukkanen, "Mobile banking rollout in emerging markets: Evidence from Brazil," *International Journal of Bank Marketing*, vol. 28, no. 5, pp. 342–371, Jan. 2010, https://doi.org/10.1108/02652321011064881
17. Henry Stewart Publications, "The role of bank–FinTech partnerships in creating a more in...: Ingenta Connect." https://www.ingentaconnect.com/content/hsp/jdb001/2024/00000008/00000004/art00006

18. O. H. Fares, I. Butt, and S. H. M. Lee, "Utilization of artificial intelligence in the banking sector: A systematic literature review," *Journal of Financial Services Marketing*, vol. 28, no. 4, pp. 835–852, Aug. 2022, https://doi.org/10.1057/s41264-022-00176-7
19. A. Yasir, A. Ahmad, S. Abbas, M. Inairat, A. H. Al-Kassem, and A. Rasool, "How artificial intelligence is promoting financial inclusion? A study on barriers of financial inclusion." Accessed: Apr. 18, 2024. [Online]. Available: https://doi.org/10.1109/ICBATS54253.2022.9759038
20. J. K. Hentzen, A. Hoffmann, R. Dolan, and E. Pala, "Artificial intelligence in customer-facing financial services: A systematic literature review and agenda for future research," *International Journal of Bank Marketing*, vol. 40, no. 6, pp. 1299–1336, Nov. 2021, https://doi.org/10.1108/IJBM-09-2021-0417
21. *Financial Literacy around the World*, Google Books. https://books.google.com/books/about/Financial_Literacy_Around_the_World.html?hl=&id=jhw0jwEACAAJ
22. N. Lainez, Institute of Research for Development, and ISEAS – YusofIshak Institute, "The prospects and dangers of algorithmic credit scoring in Vietnam: Regulating a legal blindspot," Technical Report, Jan. 2021. [Online]. Available: https://www.researchgate.net/publication/348860356
23. "How financial inclusion can be improved by new technologies," *World Economic Forum*, Nov. 21, 2022. https://www.weforum.org/agenda/2022/05/new-technologies-improve-financial-inclusion/
24. N. Kshetri, "The role of artificial intelligence in promoting financial inclusion in developing countries," *Journal of Global Information Technology Management*, vol. 24, no. 1, pp. 1–6, Jan. 2021, https://doi.org/10.1080/1097198x.2021.1871273
25. "The Global FinDex Database 2017: Measuring Financial Inclusion and the Fintech Revolution By AsliDemirguc-Kunt, LeoraKlapper, Dorothe Singer, Saniya Ansar – books on Google Play," Apr. 01, 2018. https://play.google.com/store/books/details?id=lYxaDwAAQBAJ
26. I. Jeník, M. Flaming, A. Salman, and Consultative Group to Assist the Poor, *Inclusive Digital Banking: Emerging Markets Case Studies*. CGAP, 2020. [Online]. Available: https://documents.worldbank.org/curated/en/099420002142211027/pdf/P16768404eeaca0550a94c071433b7d8fea.pdf
27. D. Mhlanga, "Industry 4.0 in finance: The impact of artificial intelligence (AI) on digital financial inclusion," *International Journal of Financial Studies*, vol. 8, no. 3, p. 45, Jul. 2020, https://doi.org/10.3390/ijfs8030045
28. M. B. Ferreira et al., "Using artificial intelligence to overcome over-indebtedness and fight poverty," *Journal of Business Research*, vol. 131, pp. 411–425, Jul. 2021, https://doi.org/10.1016/j.jbusres.2020.10.035
29. S. Makridakis, "The forthcoming artificial intelligence (AI) revolution: Its impact on society and firms," *Futures*, vol. 90, pp. 46–60, Jun. 2017, https://doi.org/10.1016/j.futures.2017.03.006
30. A. T. Rashid, "Digital inclusion and social inequality: Gender differences in ICT access and use in five developing countries," *Gender, Technology and Development*, vol. 20, no. 3, pp. 306–332, Jan. 2016, https://doi.org/10.1177/0971852416660651

11 Chatbots in Marketing and Financial Sector

Impact on Customer Engagement Valence

R. Esther Hepziba, A. Millicent Serena, and Alamelu Mangai Raman

11.1 INTRODUCTION

Artificial Intelligence is rapidly finding its place in various fields and its increasing presence will be felt in the days to come as it is evident from reliable statistics. Chatbot is an artificial intelligence software designed to have conversations with customers like human agents. Chatbot usage by global marketers is going to increase by $994 million in 2023 and it is projected to grow even more and would attain $3 billion in another ten years. Maryia Fokina (2023). Marketing chatbots aid customers in resolving product inquiries, offering suggestions, and guiding them through the purchasing process (Tuten and Solomon 2017).

In 2017, Bank of America unveiled Erica, a chatbot designed to offer a range of services including notifications, account balance updates, savings advice, and assistance with bill payments and transactions (Bank of America 2017). Similarly, American Express introduced AmEx, a customer service chatbot that informs users about credit card benefits, provides real-time sales notifications, and offers personalized product or event recommendations based on contextual information (PYMNTS 2017).

This technology is being used by marketers to enhance customer engagement. If the interaction with the chatbots proceeds in a favorable manner, customers are satisfied and this results in positive engagement with the marketers, products, and the company eventually. If the customers are not satisfied with the interactions, this may lead to negative engagement. Folstad and Brandtzaeg (2017) stated when customers interact with chatbots, their pragmatic and hedonic attributes contribute to positive and negative engagement. With this in the background, this study aims to find out, chatbot awareness and customer usage experience using primary data. Chatbots have evolved progressively and have been used in areas such as finance, education, healthcare, customer relationship, company websites, politics and even in the kids segment.

Every company which has a website has their own online marketing platforms within the site. These platforms are the point of contact for customers. Several companies use chatbots to connect with customers even at odd hours, for prompt customer service when customer care executives may not be available. Moreover,

DOI: 10.1201/9781003645849-11

chatbots do not experience fatigue and they can work tirelessly and continuously. Chatbots engage with visitors on websites, assess leads by asking pertinent questions, and arrange appointments or demonstrations (Breazeal & Harris 2018).

When the service offered through chatbots is done in a satisfactory manner, customers are also happy and stay positively engaged with the marketers and the company. If the service offered through chatbots is not appealing to the customers, this may have a negative impact on their engagement with the company. Chatbots assess user preferences and actions to provide tailored product suggestions, leading to increased sales and customer satisfaction (Hannon & Koop 2017). Positive engagement is advantageous to both marketers and customers and the economy of our country. This favorable engagement leads to positive outcomes such as customer retention and loyalty (Hepziba & John 2020).

Financial institutions employ chatbots to aid customers with account queries, transaction histories, balance checks, and basic financial guidance (Kachhi et al. 2019). Chatbots also offer advice to customers on financial planning and provide personalized financial guidance, investment suggestions, budgeting assistance, and retirement planning based on user input and financial objectives (Konig et al. 2020). Financial institutions utilize chatbots to detect fraudulent acts and to take care of secure transactions as well. Chatbots equipped with machine learning algorithms scrutinize transactions in real time to identify anomalies and potential fraudulent activities, bolstering security measures. The computational intelligence of chatbots is utilised here.

11.2 THEORETICAL FRAMEWORK

11.2.1 Types of Chatbots

Chatbots can be classified under three broad categories, such as Rule-Based chatbot which is the basic type, the Independent chatbot and NLP chatbots.

Rule-based chatbots elicit information from the users and analyze and present options in button forms. These bots are used in the place of frequently asked questions.

Independent chatbots use machine learning and keywords to digest user queries and respond appropriately.

NLP chatbots are advanced bots so much so that they comprehend the context and understand the intention of the customers and manage multiple queries comfortably.

11.2.2 Chatbots in Financial Sector

Basic agent chat addresses a wide range of customer inquiries by frontline staff. Basic routing is based on frontline staff availability.

Proactive chat engages customers proactively based on their browsing behaviour.

Blended chat provides enhanced customer experience with 24/7 availability of chatbots for greeting customers.

Chatbots address low-level transactional inquiries (e.g., password resets, address changes, claim statuses) Integration with backend systems to retrieve customer details and personalize services.

Chatbots with automation automatically trigger complex workflows (e.g., making policy changes, processing bill payments). Automated processing of simple or small claims from acceptance to payment, all initiated via chat.

11.2.3 Evolution of Chatbots in Marketing and Financial Institutions

In marketing, the evolution of chatbots in marketing has been a fascinating journey. Chatbots were primarily used for basic functions such as answering frequently asked questions (FAQs) and providing simple customer support on websites (Murray 2016, Statista 2017). With advancements in artificial intelligence (AI) and natural language processing (NLP), chatbots have become more sophisticated and capable of understanding and responding to complex user queries in real time (Rometty 2016). Marketers began leveraging chatbots for personalized marketing initiatives, delivering tailored product recommendations, content suggestions, and targeted messaging based on individual preferences and behaviour (Hoeffler & Ariely D. 1999, Hubspot 2018). Chatbots in marketing started leveraging advanced analytics and predictive insights to deliver more targeted and relevant marketing messages, optimize campaign performance, and measure ROI effectively (Li & Bernoff 2011, Forrester 2018).

The evolution of chatbots within the financial sector has been a dynamic journey characterized by technological advancements, evolving customer expectations, and industry-specific challenges.

Financial institutions initially explored chatbots for rudimentary functions such as responding to frequently asked questions (FAQs) and offering basic account information (KPMG 2017). Advancements in artificial intelligence (AI) and natural language processing (NLP) enabled chatbots to evolve, enabling them to comprehend and address complex queries in real-time (Deloitte 2018, PwC 2017). Financial institutions shifted focus towards personalization, utilizing chatbots to deliver customized recommendations, financial advice, and targeted product offerings based on individual customer preferences (McKinsey & Company 2017, Accenture 2018). It started to expand beyond text-based interfaces to support omni-channel experiences, integrating with various platforms including websites, mobile apps, social media, and voice assistants like Amazon Alexa and Google Assistant (EY 2018, Capgemini 2019) Chatbots in the financial sector began leveraging advanced analytics and predictive insights to offer proactive recommendations, detect fraudulent activities, and anticipate potential customer needs. Such has been the transformative journey of chatbots in the financial sector, highlighting the evolution from basic functionalities to sophisticated AI-driven solutions focused on enhancing customer experiences and operational efficiencies (IBM 2018, EY 2019).

Chatbots have emerged as a potent marketing channel due to their effectiveness in lead generation and driving sales conversions. Upon visiting a website, a chatbot can extend a personalized greeting and effectively steer visitors towards relevant products and services, guiding them through the sales funnel and generating valuable sales leads. For existing customers, chatbots excel at cross-selling or upselling by delivering tailored recommendations. Leveraging the familiarity and trust already established with your brand, it becomes easier to entice existing customers into additional purchases (aivo.co 2019). Moreover, chatbots serve as a dynamic platform for presenting offers and discounts to both existing and potential customers, incentivizing purchases and fostering customer engagement. This helps in increasing sales conversions. As stated by Hu et al. (2018) a chatbot was developed with the capability to discern tone and generate responses akin to those of human agents in response to user inquiries. Consequently, it is determined that this technology enhances the consumer experience by imbuing empathy and enthusiasm, integrating data to formulate coherent responses, tailored to user queries.

11.2.4 Chatbots Used Indian Companies (Dilmegani 2021)

The advanced type of chatbot is used by several marketers to engage customers and promote their companies. As a result, they have been able to increase their revenue considerably.

Leo Coffee has incorporated a chatbot **"Yello.ai"** which handles all customer queries and offers customized blends of coffee. This chatbot updates on new stock of products since it has been integrated with shopify. This has improved customer engagement.

Jio Mart, Jio Health hub and Tally are companies using the chatbot **"Haptik"** to provide personalized and prompt services to their customers and have been able to expand their customer base and revenue.

Mahindra & Mahindra uses the chatbot, "**Zoho SalesIQ**" to know their customer preferences and to respond to the customer queries, through which they are able to generate positive customer engagement.

Similarly, the company **"No-Broker" uses** the chatbot called "**Gupshup**" to aid customers to upload their property pictures and to get connected with prospective seekers.

Kaarva uses **verloop.io** as a one-point contact for their customers.

"Ask Disha" is a popular chatbot that is used in Indian railway ticket booking sites.

HDFC Bank has introduced **EVA**, an AI-powered chatbot, to aid customers with a variety of banking services including account balance inquiries, fund transfers, bill payments, and more. EVA is accessible through HDFC Bank's website and mobile app, offering customers quick and convenient support.

ICICI Bank offers iPal, an AI-driven chatbot, to assist customers with banking inquiries, credit card services, loan applications, and other financial services. iPal is available on ICICI Bank's website and mobile app, providing users with comprehensive support (www.icicibank.com)

Axis Bank provides AXAA, an AI-powered virtual assistant, to deliver personalized banking services such as account information, transaction assistance, product recommendations, and addressing customer queries. AXAA is accessible through Axis Bank's website and mobile app

Kotak Mahindra Bank offers Keya, an AI-driven chatbot, to assist customers with account inquiries, fund transfers, bill payments, and other banking activities. Keya is accessible through Kotak Mahindra Bank's website and mobile app, enhancing customer service and convenience (https://www.kotak.com/en/digital-banking/ways-to-bank/keya.html)

Yes Bank has introduced YES ROBOT, an AI-powered chatbot, to provide banking assistance to customers including account inquiries, fund transfers, card-related services, and other financial transactions. YES ROBOT is available on Yes Bank's website and mobile app, offering users efficient support (https://www.yesbank.in/digital-banking/yes-robot)

11.2.5 Chatbot Implementation and Outcomes in Financial Sector

The significance of chatbots in banking cannot be overstated. Forbes emphasizes their capacity to handle up to 80% of routine customer inquiries. This capability not only enhances the customer experience but also yields substantial cost benefits. According to Fenergo, banks spend approximately $1.07 billion annually on customer on-boarding processes, a cost that chatbots can significantly reduce through automation. They provide a level of personalization that has emerged as a crucial differentiating factor in the financial services sector. A survey conducted by Deloitte as part of their "Global Banking Outlook" reveals that 73% of customers prefer engaging with banks offering personalized experiences, a demand effectively met by chatbots (Webuters 2024).

The case studies of Bank of America's Erica and American Express's AmEx exemplify successful implementations of chatbots in the financial sector. Erica, introduced by Bank of America in 2017, is an AI-powered virtual assistant embedded within the bank's mobile banking app. It offers customers a wide array of financial services, from account management to bill payments, leveraging natural language processing (NLP) for user interactions. The initiative has garnered widespread adoption among Bank of America's customer base, with millions regularly engaging with the chatbot. Erica's integration has notably streamlined customer service processes, reducing wait times and enhancing overall satisfaction levels (Bank of America 2017).

On the other hand, American Express introduced AmEx, a chatbot integrated into its customer service platform. By employing machine learning algorithms, AmEx analyzes user data to provide personalized assistance and recommendations to cardholders. This implementation has significantly elevated the customer experience by delivering timely and relevant information, consequently boosting engagement and satisfaction levels. Moreover, the chatbot has played a pivotal role in optimizing customer service operations and alleviating the burden on human agents (American Express, n.d.). These case studies underscore how Erica and AmEx have effectively enhanced customer service, operational efficiency, and customer engagement within the financial sector.

HDFC Bank, a leading private sector bank in India, introduced Eva, an AI-powered chatbot, aimed at enhancing customer service and providing banking assistance.

Eva is seamlessly integrated into HDFC Bank's website and mobile banking app, offering customers the convenience of interacting with the chatbot through text or voice commands. It offers a comprehensive range of services, including account balance inquiries, fund transfers, bill payments, and assistance with various banking products and services.

The implementation of Eva has seen widespread adoption among HDFC Bank customers, serving as a convenient and efficient channel for accessing banking services.

Notably, the chatbot has contributed to reducing wait times for customer inquiries, improving response rates, and elevating overall customer satisfaction levels (HDFC Bank, n.d.).

ICICI Bank, one of India's largest private sector banks, introduced iPal, another AI-powered chatbot, to provide customer support and assistance with banking transactions. iPal is available on ICICI Bank's website and mobile app, offering customers the convenience of interacting with the chatbot in multiple languages. It provides a wide array of services, including account inquiries, fund transfers, bill payments, and product information. The implementation of iPal has been pivotal in enhancing customer service efficiency at ICICI Bank, handling a significant volume of customer inquiries and transactions. The chatbot has effectively reduced the workload on human agents, increased service availability, and significantly improved the overall customer experience (ICICI Bank, n.d.).

HDFC Bank and ICICI Bank have successfully leveraged chatbot technology to enhance customer service delivery, streamline banking operations, and elevate customer satisfaction levels in the Indian financial sector (Figure 11.1).

Chatbots address customer problems through messages maintaining a casual conversation, understand their problems by zeroing down to the specific issues, refine and optimize the conversation, and respond appropriately in a pleasant manner (Figure 11.2).

The above image illustrates how a chatbot conversation happens. The bot asks leading questions, gets cues from the answers and poses customized questions, based on customer's responses.

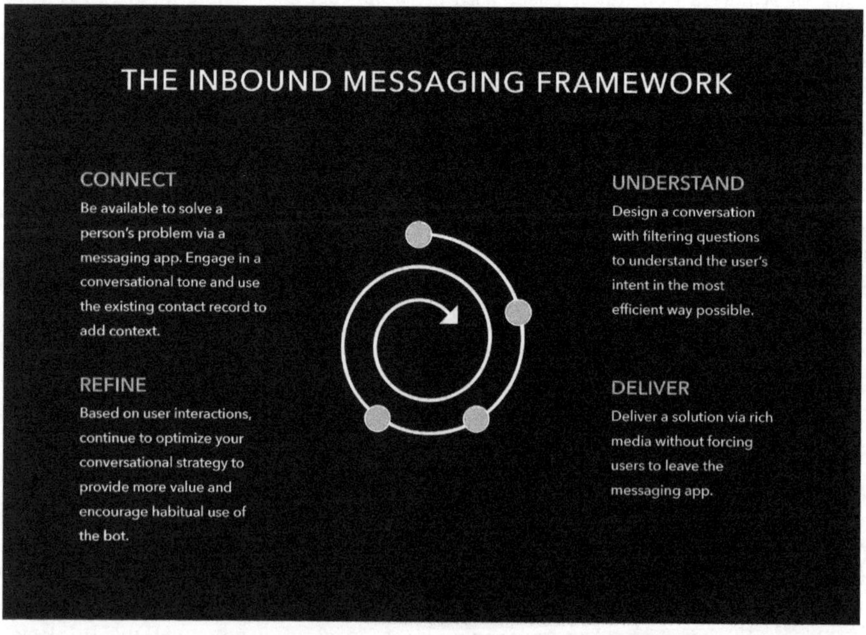

FIGURE 11.1 Chatbot engagement process. (*Source*: Hubspot.com.)

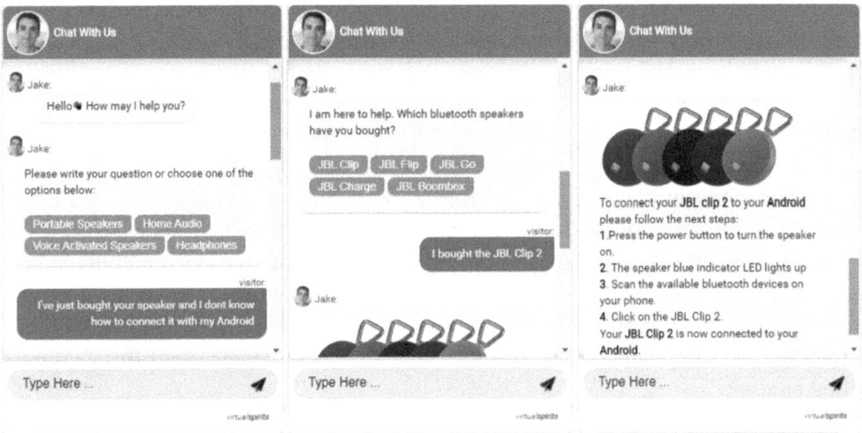

FIGURE 11.2 Chatbot conversation. (*Source*: virtualspirits.com.)

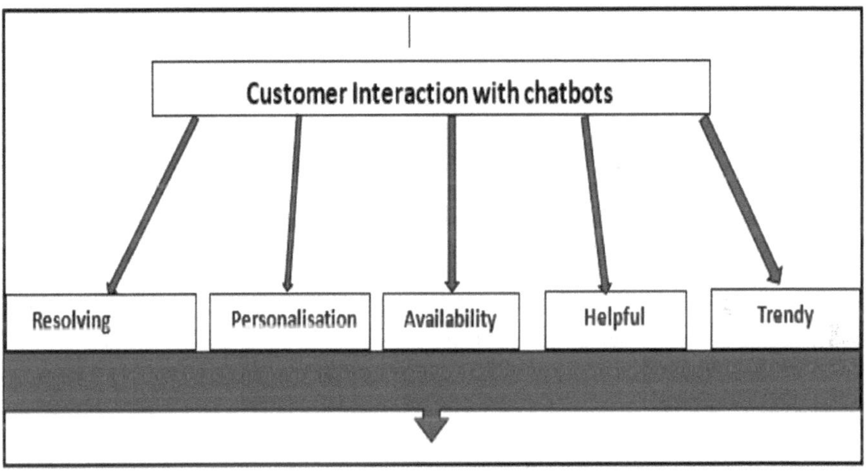

FIGURE 11.3 Conceptual model and engagement of chatbots.

11.2.6 Factors Influencing Customer Engagement during Chatbot Usage

Based on the earlier study carried out by Esther Hepziba and Florence John (2020) few factors have been used in this study to collect primary data.

Factors such as Resolving Problems, Personalization, Availability, Helpful and Trendy have been used to find out customer experience, during their interaction with chatbots in online marketing (Figure 11.3).

11.3 RESEARCH QUESTION

This research aims to answer the question,

Whether the users/customers are satisfied with the chatbot assistance in online marketing sites, financial institutions/banking sites, based on factors such as chatbots being helpful, making customers feel **trendy**, making **personalised** chats, **resolving problems** promptly and being **available 24x7,** which leads to customer engagement which would be positive or negative based on the level of satisfaction.

11.3.1 Customer Engagement with Chatbots

In order to find out the nature of customer experience and engagement with chatbots, a properly structured questionnaire was framed and responses were collected from 100 chatbot users. In order to provide clarity to the users on chatbots, a brief introduction was given in the questionnaire that in online marketing sites (clothing, grocery, electronic gadgets, ticket booking, banking and all categories of goods) a message icon pops up, a chat starts with a welcome message and this feature is called chatbot.

11.3.2 Demographics

Respondents were both male and female with 67.4% of them being female respondents and the age of the users was in the range 18–25 years. Majority of the respondents were college students and the remaining were job holders (Table 11.1).

11.3.3 Literature Review and Customer Response

TABLE 11.1
Literature and Customer Opinion

Literature	Factors	Parameters and Percentage	Interpretation
Bayan Abu Shawar and Eric Atwell (2007) have found that chatbots can be helpful in e-commerce, retrieving information, and business apart from having normal conversations.	**Helpful**	**Chatbot Assistance** • Ticket booking sites (30.4%) • Online Shopping sites (65.2%) • Educational institution sites (54.3%) • Hospital/healthcare sites (21.7%) • Banking sites (30.4%) • Food Delivery apps (52.2%)	Majority of the respondents have mentioned that they are assisted by chatbots in online shopping sites.
Cheng and Jiang (2020) state that chatbots are more efficient in handling customer queries when compared to human agents.	**Resolving Problems**	• Satisfied with the solutions offered by chatbots (50% agree, 43% Neutral) • Understand queries and provide appropriate answers (50% agree and 37% Neutral) • Quick response to queries and complaints (48% are neutral, 37% have agreed)	Most of them are satisfied with the answers and solutions provided by chatbots and few have been neutral in their opinion.

(*Continued*)

TABLE 11.1 (*Continued*)
Literature and Customer Opinion

Literature	Factors	Parameters and Percentage	Interpretation
Chiara Valentina Misischiaa et al. (2022) mention that in general people like to maintain a trendy lifestyle and prefer customised services. According to their study, customers like to stay updated on the latest products and services.	**Trendy**	• Chatbot usage makes customers trendy (30% have agreed and 37% are neutral) • Chatbots update on new products and latest information (50% have agreed to this)	Customer have mentioned that chatbots provide information on latest products and services that helps them to maintain a trendy lifestyle
Chatbots conversation leads to a favourable user engagement. Chatbots are available for customers which reduces their anxiety through optimised chats.	**Personalisation**	• Chatbots provide suggestions relevant to me (50% have agreed, 17% strongly agreed) • Provide information based on past search (50% have agreed)	Majority of the customers have responded that the chatbots conversations are personalised.
Eleni Adamopoulou and Lefteris Moussiades (2020) claim through their research that Chatbots are available at all times for customer service which has helped in cost reduction in companies.	**Availability**	• Chatbots are available anytime they want their queries answered (41.3% have agreed). • Prefer talking to bots rather than making a call to human agents (30% of them have agreed and 28% of them have disagreed) • Prefer using websites where chatbot assistance is available (40% have agreed and an equal number have remained neutral) • Prefer using the same site again since chatbot assistance is convenient (40% have agreed 13% have strongly agreed and few neutral)	On availability, the majority of them have agreed and though few have mentioned they prefer talking to bots rather than making calls, still an equal number of them prefer calling human agents. For website revisit where bots are available most of them have agreed.

11.4 STATISTICAL ANALYSIS

Correlation results show that there exists a significant relationship between the perception that Chatbots help to provide recent product related information and customers feeling trendy about usage of Chatbot facility. Also, a significant relationship is found to exist between customers repeating their visit to websites which offer

Chatbot assistance and their perception about the ability to respond to their queries in an appropriate way (Tables 11.2 and 11.3).

The perception of the customer in getting an immediate response has a moderate but significant relationship with their satisfaction level achieved based on solutions offered by Chatbots (Tables 11.4–11.6).

Criterion variable: User Satisfaction in using Chatbots services. From regression output, it is seen that, since Chatbots are able to provide relevant suggestions, it increases the satisfaction level of users in availing the Chatbot services at a statistically significant level.

TABLE 11.2
Correlation Results Showing the Relationship Among Variables on Usage of Chatbots

Parameter	Chatbots - Understand Queries and Provide Appropriate Answers	I Feel Trendy When I Use Chatbots
Chatbots provide new product information and latest updates	−0.30	0.46
I prefer using the services of websites in which Chatbots assistance is available	0.35	0.48
I will use the same site again since Chatbots assistance is convenient for me	0.36	0.17

TABLE 11.3
Correlation Output Showing the Relationship Between Level of Satisfaction with the Solutions Offered by Chatbots and Corresponding Customer's Perception

Parameters	Chatbots Help in Getting Immediate Response	I Am Satisfied with the Solutions Given by Chatbot for My Queries
Chatbots help in getting immediate response	1	0.41
I am satisfied with the solutions given by chatbot for my queries	0.41	1

TABLE 11.4
Regression Statistics Considering the Level of User Satisfaction with Respect to the Solutions Offered by Chatbots as the Criterion Variable

Regression Statistics	
Multiple *R*	0.35
R Square	0.13
Adjusted *R* Square	0.08
Standard Error	0.60
Observations	46

TABLE 11.5
ANOVA for the Level of User Satisfaction with Respect to the Solutions Offered by Chatbots as the Criterion Variable

ANOVA	*df*	*SS*	*MS*	*F*	Significance F
Regression	2	2.195913261	1.097956631	3.08	0.05
Residual	43	15.30408674	0.355908994		

TABLE 11.6
Regression Analysis Considering the Level of User Satisfaction with Respect to the Solutions Offered by Chatbots as the Criterion Variable

Regression Output	Coefficients	Standard Error	*t* Stat	*P*-Value
Intercept	2.11	0.61	3.48	0.00
Queries and complaints are solved quickly by Chatbots	0.09	0.12	0.75	0.46
Chatbots are able to give suggestions relevant to me	0.30	0.13	2.27	0.03

11.5 DISCUSSION & SUGGESTIONS

- Respondents have mentioned that chatbots are helpful and most of them have mentioned that they are assisted by chatbots in online shopping sites. Educational institution websites and food delivery applications are also platforms where most of them have assistance from chatbots.
- When it comes to resolving queries and complaints most of them are satisfied. Whereas there are customers with neutral opinions who are potential customers who are not able to decide. These respondents can be brought to the positive side of the continuum by the marketers by optimizing the chatbots to provide them with suitable and accurate answers for their queries. Resolution of problem by chatbots is a key factor that determines customer satisfaction (Kvale et al. 2020).

- Most of them have responded that chatbots provide relevant suggestions and answers which has made them happy and there is considerable success for marketers in this aspect.
- In the availability aspect, users are satisfied but quite a number of them have remained neutral and few have disagreed. This is attributed to the reason that though chatbots are available they prefer explaining to a human agent who will understand their queries better. However, a greater percentage of them have mentioned that they would visit the website again if chatbots are available since it is convenient for them when human agents are not accessible.
- From the inferential analyses carried out, it has been found that chatbots are able to provide a pleasant experience to customers during their online purchases by providing them solutions to their queries and by offering instant responses. It is also observed that when chatbots offer relevant suggestions the level of satisfaction improves significantly.
- It is found that chatbots provide detailed and updated information on products which makes the customers feel trendy and customers repeatedly visit the websites where chatbots are integrated, which reveals customer loyalty. Usage of chatbots is a strategy that can be implemented to improve loyalty of customers. In the research carried out by Liss Jenneboer et al. (2022), it has been stated that utilizing a chatbot for handling grievances, emerges as a prevalent occurrence. Ultimately, when a chatbot exceeds the expectations of a user lodging a complaint, it results in a positive customer experience, subsequently leading to customer satisfaction and it has been asserted that there exists a correlation between customer experience and satisfaction when engaging with a chatbot, consequently fostering customer loyalty. In light of this, it is highly probable that there exists a favourable relationship between the use of chatbots and customer loyalty.
- Earlier research confirms the importance of emotional experiences in determining customer satisfaction. Both the quality of information provided by chatbots and the emotional engagement they offer, play crucial roles in enhancing customer satisfaction and strengthening brand relationships. Consumers value both the quality of information received and the emotional connections they form with chatbots, indicating a trend towards humanizing technology (Magno and Dossena 2020)
- Kim and Chang (2020), in their research, stated that reusing a service is driven by the user's intention to continue using it regularly, often influenced by past experiences and perceived benefits. This intention is crucial for maintaining a lasting relationship between the user and the service provider. Factors such as user satisfaction play a significant role in determining this intention.
- For instance, when users have low expectations and experience high performance, it tends to increase satisfaction and subsequently, their likelihood to continue using the service. Conversely, dissatisfaction negatively affects the intention to continue use. Studies have shown that factors like service quality, brand image, and reliability contribute to user satisfaction, ultimately

impacting their intention to reuse the service. Therefore, it is imperative to identify variables that affect user satisfaction and consequently, their intention to reuse the service. Hence in the current study, it has been identified that a quick relevant response to queries by chatbots and trendy feeling by customers increase repetitive visits to the site.

The above results and discussion show that,

- Customers still hesitate to use chatbots or chat with bots, the transition from traditional modes to a new mode is happening gradually.
- Many online marketing platforms have not exploited the full potential of chatbots and they are yet to implement it. So awareness has to be created among marketers and customers on the advantages and various latest features of bots.
- Many of the customers have a neutral opinion with respect to preference towards using chatbots, which shows that chatbots are convenient, but for crucial situations, they prefer customer care executives. A hybrid mode should be facilitated by marketers, which provides the option to switch over to human agents when the problem is beyond the handling capacity of bots.
- Marketers have to build trust among customers by ensuring that there would be no breach of privacy or security when they are engaging with chatbots. Before implementing chatbots in banking sites, the same should be tested to ensure that there will not be any potential data leakage and the bot is secure for transactions and conversations.
- When chatbots falter in consumer financial markets, they not only betray customer trust but also pose significant risks of widespread harm. Errors in this domain carry grave consequences, particularly when they jeopardize an individual's financial well-being. Recognizing and effectively managing customer disputes is crucial; often, dispute resolution is the primary means to swiftly rectify errors before they escalate (Consumer Financial Protection Bureau 2023).
- According to Galitsky and Ilvovsky (2019), chatbots are also operational within the realm of personal finance, delivering content through online communication. Its responses are predetermined with shared outcomes and automatically generated questions, indicating that the suggested technology innovatively facilitates interaction between system and user. However, there is a scarcity of information for meaningful dialogue, and authenticity remains a concern.
- Dispensing inaccurate information regarding consumer financial products or services, for instance, could have dire repercussions. It might trigger inappropriate fees, potentially leading to more severe outcomes like defaults, forcing customers into selecting subpar options or causing other detrimental effects.
- Marketers should also explore sites of international companies that have incorporated chatbots in their websites and have been successful and efficient in chatbot usage. Several companies have established favorable engagement with customers through the efficient usage of chatbots.

- From such success stories, Indian marketers can also try to adopt this new technology for hassle-free customer engagement and also to retain customers by providing them quick responses, which can be done by chatbots in an efficient manner.
- Marketers should also create awareness among customers on safe usage of chatbots, by not revealing sensitive personal data.
- The waiting time of customers is reduced when they try to call a customer care executive when bots are used for customer complaints and queries. This can be realized only when chatbots are used extensively in online marketing platforms and create awareness among customers on the ease of use.
- The respondents are not frequent users, since chatbot features are very less in Indian online marketing platforms. From the neutral responses for a few questions, it is evident that their chatbot usage is low. Though the usage is less, customers have expressed that their experience and interactions with the chatbot were good. Users are satisfied with the chatbots but they do not overlook the fact that anytime human engagement is better. This shows that marketers have to fine-tune the chatbots to be almost humane in their interactions.
- If customers undergo unpleasant experiences with their chatbot interactions, this would result in dissatisfied customers leading to negative customer engagement. Hence marketers have to strategically design the chatbots to simulate human beings to provide a pleasant experience to the customers to maintain positive engagement.

Earlier research states that employing a social-oriented communication style for chatbots, as opposed to a task-oriented approach, fosters customers' perception of warmth towards chatbots, consequently leading to enhanced customer satisfaction Ying Zu et al. (2022).

11.5.1 Limitations and Future Research

This study has been carried out only for the age group ranging from 18 to 25 years living in Chennai. This study can be extended for other age groups and other locations. The sample size can also be increased to get more accurate results. Research can be carried out by selecting a specific segment or a specific type of chatbot to reveal in-depth information.

11.5.2 Business Implications

This research establishes that good customer experience with chatbot leads to customer satisfaction through primary data analysis and literature review. This is extremely beneficial to the marketers since it reduces cost and establishes good connectivity with the customer base. Since it is evident that this technology leads to customer satisfaction, investing in this infrastructure is a wise choice (Lubbe and Ngoma 2021). The cost of customer service provision can be brought down by automating numerous tasks that currently rely on manual intervention. Additionally, its high level of customization will enable tailored interactions to suit diverse contexts, fostering more personalized engagements with users (Shaji George et al. 2023).

In 2019, Lowell, a prominent credit management services provider in Europe, faced challenges with managing consumer inquiries, fulfilling routine requests, and retrieving payment records efficiently. Partnering with Crayon, a Microsoft Partner renowned for its expertise in emerging technologies, Lowell embarked on developing an advanced call centre automation solution. The Lowell bot was designed to offer consumers an efficient means of obtaining advice, setting up payment plans, accessing answers to common queries, and managing their credit accounts seamlessly. Azure, Azure Bot Service (AI), Azure Cognitive Services (AI) were the key services utilised. Introducing this brought a notable 20% increase in first-call resolution rates, elevating them from 50% to 70% (Valorem 2021).

Abbie, a chatbot implemented by Allstate insurance company in 2016, proved to be significantly swifter and more effective compared to contacting a human customer service representative via phone. This effectiveness is evidenced by the fact that, 3 years post-release, Abbie was fielding over 100,000 inquiries monthly from thousands of AllState agents and employees across the nation (Kaur 2019).

As Patil and Kulkarni (2019) have mentioned in their research, the integration of AI, particularly in the form of Chatbots, within financial services is crucial not only for financial institutions but also for front-end financial customers and back-end technology companies. This technology-driven human conversation within financial services holds the promise of enhancing the customer interface with financial products and services. Chatbot advisors in financial services hold significance primarily due to their utility, user-friendliness, influence in social media, efficiency, and cost-effectiveness. Despite the absence of human interaction, Chatbot advisors are poised to play a pivotal role in customer engagement. They provide round-the-clock customer service, addressing issues such as password or PIN resets, incorrect debit/credit transactions, and other technical support needs. Chatbots can be used to improve small businesses also. In small businesses, chatbots can be used to alleviate workload pressures by streamlining tasks rather than adding to them. An efficient chatbot can manage common inquiries, thereby enabling the sales team to tackle more complex interactions. Given the resource constraints faced by small businesses, leveraging data, automation, and digital interactions becomes increasingly vital. Tools like chatbots have the potential to liberate small business owners and their teams, allowing them to concentrate on core business activities (Fuscaldo 2023).

Thus chatbots are more efficient than human beings, reducing cost and enhancing customer engagement and improving businesses. Marketers have to adopt this technology and use the opportunity to improve their businesses through which trade and commerce can flourish, which in turn will raise the standard of living in the country.

11.6 CONCLUSION

By leveraging chatbots, banks can enhance customer satisfaction by improving their product and service performance, bolstering their reputation and trust in technology utilization, and enhancing overall credibility. Chatbots emerge as vital service delivery channels, ensuring personalized assistance while minimizing individual communication and maximizing technology utilization. Although the initial investment in chatbot technology may be relatively high, they ultimately contribute to reducing transaction costs and personnel expenses while increasing profitability and operational capacity through enhanced customer experiences (Eren 2021). Chatbots have the potential to enhance service delivery and reduce operational costs, serving as incentives for banking and other financial institutions. Therefore, as AI technologies continue to evolve, it is crucial to acknowledge that chatbots will increasingly adopt a conversational approach to humanize their interactions and service delivery. It is essential for banking and financial institutions to bolster their adoption of chatbots, as they possess the inherent capability to proactively market and sell financial services and products while addressing both current and emerging challenges (Nair et al. 2021). Widespread usage of chatbot technology is necessary for customers to get more awareness on the benefits of chatbots.

Customer engagement definitely improves on chatbot usage and implementing the strategies and results discussed in this study will leverage positive customer engagement and relationship. As evident from the literature review it enhances customer loyalty also. This makes customers revisit the websites or portals where they find it convenient and comfortable to use, because of chatbot assistance. A significant portion of individuals seeking customer support expect prompt responses to their inquiries and effective solutions to their issues. Therefore, it can be inferred that the introduction of chatbots in the country will not have a negative impact on customer satisfaction, as these essential elements are present in chatbot services. It is also observed that societal acceptance of chatbots is limited. This can be attributed to several factors, primarily the language barrier. Hence it becomes imperative that marketers use this emerging technology to provide satisfaction to ensure positive customer engagement during shopping and banking. This enables an economic boost that is essential for the business houses and to the society.

REFERENCES

Accenture. (2018). Banking Technology Vision 2018. https://acnmedia.accenture.com/PDF/Accenture%2BTechnology%2BVision%2B2018%2BExecutive%2BSummary%2BFINAL.PDF.pdf

Adamopoulou, E., & Moussiades, L. (2020). Chatbots: History, Technology, and Applications. *Machine Learning with Applications*, 2, 100006.

aivo. co. (2019). How Chatbots Are Helping the Finance Industry. https://www.aivo.co/blog/chatbots-in-finance-industry

American Express. (n.d.). Introducing the Amex Bot for Messenger. https://about.americanexpress.com/press-release/american-express-introducing-amex-bot-messenger

Bank of America. (2017). Bank of America Introduces New AI-Driven Virtual Financial Assistant. https://www.businesswire.com/news/home/20180518005038/en/Bank-of-America-Delivers-First-Widely-Available-AI%E2%80%93Driven-Virtual-Financial-Assistant

Breazeal, C. L., & Harris, P. L. (2018). Beyond Advertising: Exploring the Potential and Challenges of Programming Robots to Enhance Children's Cognitive and Socioemotional Skills. *Cognitive Development*, 48, 57–71.

Capgemini. (2019). Conversational Commerce: Why Consumers Are Embracing Voice Assistants in Their Lives. https://www.capgemini.com/news/press-releases/smart-talk-how-organizations-and-consumers-are-embracing-voice-and-chat-assistants/

Cheng, Y., & Jiang, H. (2020). How Do AI-Driven Chatbots Impact User Experience? Examining Gratifications, Perceived Privacy Risk, Satisfaction, Loyalty, and Continued Use. *Journal of Broadcasting & Electronic Media*, 64,592–614.

Consumer Financial Protection Bureau. (2023). Chatbots in Consumer Finance. https://www.consumerfinance.gov/data-research/research-reports/chatbots-in-consumer-finance/chatbots-in-consumer-finance/

Deloitte. (2018). Reimagining the Digital Bank. https://www2.deloitte.com/content/dam/Deloitte/us/Documents/financial-services/us-fsi-dcfs-2018-banking-outlook.pdf

Dilmegani, C. (2021). Chatbot Companies in India. *AI Multiple Research*. https://research.aimultiple.com/chatbot-companies-in-india/

Eren, B. A. (2021). Determinants of Customer Satisfaction in Chatbot Use: Evidence from a Banking Application in Turkey. *International Journal of Bank Marketing*, 39(2), 94–311.

Fuscaldo, D. (2023). How Chatbots Can Help Grow Your Small Business. *Business News Daily*. https://www.businessnewsdaily.com/16018-chatbots-for-growth.html

EY. (2018). How Can Banks Take Advantage of Intelligent Virtual Assistants? https://www.ey.com/en_us/insights/financial-services/is-financial-services-ready-for-generative

EY. (2019). How Artificial Intelligence Is Transforming the Banking Industry. https://www.ey.com/en_gr/insights/financial-services/how-artificial-intelligence-is-reshaping-the-financial-services-industry

Fokina, M. (2023). Chatbot Statistics. https://www.tidio.com/blog/chatbot-statistics/

Følstad, A., & Brandtzaeg, P. B. (2017). Users' Experiences with Chatbots: Findings from a Questionnaire Study. *Quality and User Experience*, 5, 3. https://doi.org/10.1007/s41233-020-00033-2

Forrester. (2018). Predictions 2019: B2C Marketing.

Galitsky, B., & Ilvovsky, D. (2019). On a Chatbot Conducting Virtual Dialogues. *Proceedings of the 28th ACM International Conference on Information and Knowledge Management*, Beijing, China, November 3–7, 2019, 2925–2928.

Hannon, C., & Koop, G. (2017). Evaluating the Impacts of Nonlinear Storytelling on Engagement and Recall in Informative Digital Narratives for Children. *Journal of Communication*, 67(4), 593–616.

HDFC Bank. (n.d.). Eva – Your Virtual Assistant. https://www.hdfcbank.com/personal/ways vto-bank/eva

Hepziba, E., & John, F. (2020). Role of Chatbots in Customer Engagement Valence. *Psychology and Education*, 57(9), 2181–2186.

Hoeffler, S., & Ariely, D. (1999). Constructing Stable Preferences: A Look into Dimensions of Experience and Their Impact on Preference Stability. *Journal of Consumer Psychology*, 8(2), 113–139.

Hu, T., Xu, A., Liu, Z., You, Q., Guo, Y., Sinha, V., Luo, J., & Akkiraju, R. (2018). Touch Your Heart: A Tone-aware Chatbot for Customer Care on Social Media. *Proceedings of the 2018 CHI Conference on Human Factors in Computing Systems*, Montreal QC, Canada, April 21–26, 2018, 1–12.

IBM. (2018). The Cognitive Bank: AI-Powered Analytics Reinventing Financial Services. https://www.ibm.com/investor/att/pdf/IBM_Annual_Report_2018.pdf

ICICI Bank. (n.d.). iPal – The Chatbot. https://www.icicibank.com/personal-banking/ipalchatbot

Jenneboer, L., Herrando, C., & Constantinides, E. (2022). The Impact of Chatbots on Customer Loyalty: A Systematic Literature Review. *Journal of Theoretical and Applied Electronic Commerce Research*, 7(1), 212–229.

Kachhi, H., Fakirani, H., & Desai, T. (2019). Detecting Fraud Using Machine Learning Techniques: A Case Study of Fraudulent e-Transaction Detection. *International Journal of Information Management*, 49, 484–493.

Kaur, K. (2019). The Business Impact of Chatbots: Two Case Studies. *Chatbot Journal*.

Kim, M., & Chang, B. (2020). The Effect of Service Quality on the Reuse Intention of a Chatbot: Focusing on User Satisfaction, Reliability, and Immersion. *International Journal of Communication*, 16(4), 1–15.

König, L. M., Ziegler, A., Jäger-Biela, D. J., & Händel, M. (2020). Benefits and Challenges of Learning Analytics Dashboards: Insights from Seven Higher Education Institutions. *International Journal of Learning Analytics and Artificial Intelligence for Education*, 2(1), 130–151.

KPMG. (2017). The Changing World of Customer Experience in Banking. https://assets.kpmg.com/content/dam/kpmg/dk/pdf/DK-2018/06/shaping-the-future-of-customer-experience-0207.pdf

Kvale, K., Freddi, E., Hodnebrog, S., Sell, O. A., & Følstad, A. (2020). Understanding the User Experience of Customer Service Chatbots: What Can We Learn from Customer Satisfaction Surveys?. *Chatbot Research and Design: 4th International Workshop, CONVERSATIONS 2020*, Virtual Event, November 23–24, 2020, Revised Selected Papers.

Li, C., & Bernoff, J. (2011). *Groundswell: Winning in a World Transformed by Social Technologies*. Harvard Business Press.

Lubbe, I., & Ngoma, N. (2021). Useful Chatbot Experience Provides Technological Satisfaction: An Emerging Market Perspective. *South African Journal of Information Management*, 23(1), 1–8.

Magno, F., & Dossena, G. (2020). The Effects of Chatbots' Attributes on Customer Relationships with Brands: PLS-SEM and Importance–Performance Map Analysis. *The TQM Journal*, 35(5), 1156–1169. https://doi.org/10.1108/TQM-02-2022-0080

McKinse & Company. (2017). The Future of Bank Risk Management. https://www.mckinsey.com/industries/financial-services/our-insights/the-future-of-bank-risk-management

Misischiaa, C. V., Poeczeb, F., & Straussa, C. (2022). Chatbots in Customer Service: Their Relevance and Impact on Service Quality. *Procedia Computer Science*, 201, 421–428.

Murray, S. (2016). Chatbots: The Future of Conversational Commerce and Marketing. *Business Horizons*, 59(2), 135–145.

Nair, K., Anagreh, S., Sunil, A., & Gupta, R. (2021). AI-Enabled Chat Bot to Drive Marketing Automation for Financial Services. *Journal of Management Information and Decision Sciences*, 24(1), 1–18.

Patil, K., & Kulkarni, M. S. (2019). Artificial Intelligence in Financial Services: Customer Chatbot Advisor Adoption. *International Journal of Innovative Technology and Exploring Engineering (IJITEE)*, 9(1), 4296.

PYMNTS. (2017). American Express Unveils New Amex Bot at Facebook's F8. https://www.pymnts.com/chatbot-tracker/2017/american-express-unveils-new-amex-bot-at-facebooks-f8-messenger-chatbot/

PwC. (2017). Chatbots in Financial Services: A Powerful Tool. https://www.pwc.com/gx/en/industries/financial-services/assets/pwc-global-fintech-report-2017.pdf

Rometty, G. (2016). IBM's Ginny Rometty on the Promise of Watson and AI.

Shaji George, A., Hovan George, A. S., & Gabrio Martin, A. S. (2023). A Review of ChatGPT AI's Impact on Several Business Sectors. *Partners Universal International Innovation Journal (PUIIJ)*, 1(1), 9–23. https://puiij.com/index.php/research/article/view/11

Shawar, B. A., & Atwell, E. (2007). Chatbots: Are they Really Useful?. *Journal for Language Technology and Computational Linguistics*, 22(1), 29–49.

Statista. (2017). Share of Chatbots by Function.

Tuten, T. L., & Solomon, M. R. (2017). *Social Media Marketing*. Sage Publications.
Valorem. (2021). Chatbots in Banking and Financial Services Industry Case Studies. https://go.valorem.com/rs/689-NXX-809/images/Chatbots-in-FinServ-Industry-Analysis.pdf
Webuters. (2024). How Chatbots Are Transforming the Banking Industry? https://www.webuters.com/how-chatbots-are-transforming-the-banking-industry
Zu, Y., Zhang, J., & Deng, G. (2022). Enhancing Customer Satisfaction with Chatbots: The Influence of Communication Styles and Consumer Attachment Anxiety. *Frontiers in Psychology*, 13, 902782. https://doi.org/10.3389/fpsyg.2022.902782

12 Assessing the Role of Artificial Intelligence in Regulatory Compliance for Indian Fintech Startups

Sonali Srivastava, Manisha Singh, Ahmed A. Elamer, and Amit Verma

12.1 INTRODUCTION

Regulatory compliance programs are often thought of as designed to cope with the requirements of an audit or to deal with a specific problem as it arises. However, the intentions of such solutions are fundamentally centered on establishing how an organization can operate. Compliance with ethical standards and regulatory norms is a principal yardstick of legitimacy for an organization or a social group. Achieving a high level of adherence and fulfilling the mandates of operational norms not only confers a certain air of credibility and respect in the eyes of the rest of society but also provides a level of protection from intrusions of civil authority (Hadi et al., 2023). For large compliance programs, a compliance infrastructure can be very significant. This includes all the purpose-built or dedicated hardware, software, electronic data, data storage, data networking, and data transport facilities used for compliance. These means are intended to ensure that data is secured from unauthorized access.

Regulatory compliance is an organized manner for ensuring that an organization's operations comply with applicable laws and regulations. Regulatory compliance strives to ensure that an organization meets all its compliance obligations and operates in a well-managed, risk-averse environment. (Alaassar et al., 2021) The key to keeping operational activities in line with these functions of a compliance program is to ensure that everyone involved in the operations is scrutinized by a regulatory compliance effort (Rakha, 2023). Regulatory compliance risk is a crucial challenge for the business world, and the ever-evolving landscapes of the Fintech, banking, and financial industries amplify the significance of this challenge (Lemma, 2020; Hassan et al., 2023; Power, 2022). Despite the varied solutions to compliance that some businesses can adopt, regulatory compliance consumes nearly half of financial firms' work. It consumes significant resources which could be better used, increasing productivity in other sectors of the economy.

DOI: 10.1201/9781003645849-12

Fintech companies have been rapidly evolving, especially in India. As one of the world's fastest-growing economies, India has a vast potential for Fintech in digital payments, peer-to-peer lending, and many more. Nowadays, people are more likely to start their companies through limited liability partnerships or private limited companies. Such business entities are considered separate legal personalities and must comply with substantial legal and regulatory requirements (Bueno & Bright, 2020). Also, company operations involve a wide range of regulatory and contractual requirements. Failing to meet these requirements may lead to different consequences. For instance, the company itself may be sued for breach of the relevant regulations, which can lead to a criminal conviction if the breach is serious (Coffee Jr, 2021; Lund & Sarin, 2021; Chambers & Berger-Walliser, 2021). On the other hand, if the management is found to be in breach of their duties, they may face disqualification orders, fines, and even imprisonment. Failure to adhere to the rules and regulations laid down by the regulatory authorities in India can result in financial penalties, bad reputation, and, in some severe cases, even imprisonment of the startup's management (Noah et al., 2020) Regular non-compliance can potentially destroy a business by losing customer trust and litigation costs. These startups especially need to understand and appreciate the importance of regulatory compliance because most of them started their businesses to solve some problems with the help of technology. Many are focused on growth and innovation and regulatory compliance can be seen as a burden. However, in the long run, non-compliance or a breach of the law can be costly financially and in terms of the company's reputation (AllahRakha, 2023).

12.2 OVERVIEW OF REGULATORY COMPLIANCE IN INDIAN FINTECH STARTUPS

Also, compliance with anti money laundering laws and knowing your customer regulations are prerequisites for Fintech businesses that offer digital payments, remittance, or foreign exchange services. These startups must conduct real-time customer due diligence and monitor the transactions to ensure that the transactions are not related to money laundering or terrorism financing activities. (Baporikar, 2021) However, the manual nature of traditional compliance and reporting procedures poses a barrier to effectively enforcing regulations. This is where artificial intelligence (AI) comes into play. By leveraging the power of AI, Fintech companies can streamline their compliance processes and develop more effective risk management strategies (Guo & Polak, 2021) How AI can contribute to resolving the regulatory compliance obstacles encountered by Fintech startups in India.

Moreover, in a fast-paced and constantly evolving business and regulatory environment, startups often need help to satisfy the ever-increasing regulatory requirements while meeting their customers' demands (Baporikar, 2021).

Nonetheless, regulatory compliance is crucial for the growth of Fintech startups as it helps build and maintain the goodwill and trust of investors, customers, and the public. Fintech businesses usually handle a large amount of sensitive financial data, and a minor breach of law or regulation can result in significant financial loss and reputational damage (Allen et al., 2021; Sampat et al., 2024; Kaur & Lakshari, 2022)

In this respect, investors and customers are more likely to engage with and choose the services of the startups that can prove their internal management and operations comply with regulatory standards.

Regulatory compliance refers to the adherence to laws, rules, and regulations relevant to a particular industry. In India, Fintech startups are regulated by the Reserve Bank of India (RBI), the Securities and Exchange Board of India (SEBI), and other statutory bodies (Painoli et al., 2021). These regulators have laid down stringent data protection and privacy requirements, cybersecurity, anti-money laundering, foreign exchange, and outbound investments. Compliance with these regulations is a time-consuming, costly, and significant challenge for Indian Fintech startups (Rajeswari & Vijai, 2021). This is because startups often lack the necessary resources to establish a robust regulatory compliance mechanism and may not have the expertise to interpret and keep up with the complexity of the regulations (Figure 12.1).

The changing scene of the Indian Fintech industry brings a novel, cross-disciplinary arrangement of challenges, which may require regulators' perception of affiliations and intervention (Omarova, 2020). At the turn of the occasion, regulatory compliance in the Indian Fintech startups customarily fuses essential guidelines and standards agreed upon by regulators to ensure that the market works suitably. Startups in the Indian Fintech scene must concede to various government regulatory obligations, ensuring the protection of buyer data and exhibiting consistency with 'know your customer' and adversarial tax avoidance rules (Painoli et al., 2021). As such, managing regulatory compliance can require genuine effort and money, as powerfully affirming the changing regulatory plans and ensuring that writers and heads handle the huge manual interpretations for consistency can be problematic and slippery. This is the spot artificial knowledge, which in this setting portrays machines designed to and will surely think and learn and can assume an inexorably evident activity in aiding the successful course of complex regulatory periods that oversee new Indian Fintech organizations. Showing certain undertakings with new

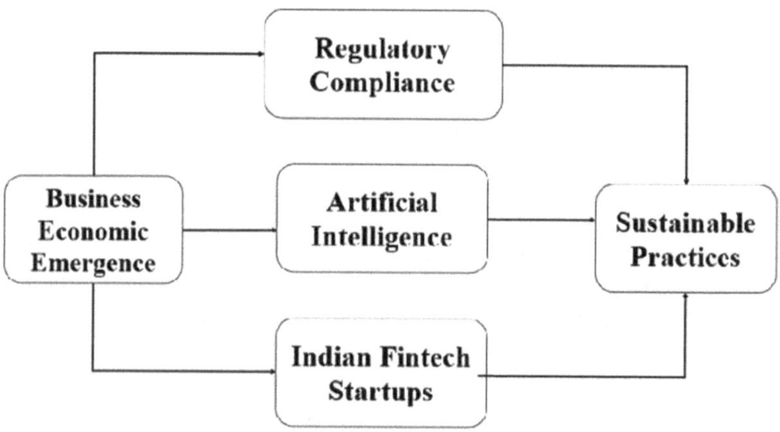

FIGURE 12.1 Regulatory compliance mechanism for Indian Fintech startups.

data, undertakings, and systems can empower them to self-mastermind the data and out and out relocate any mistakes or excess. This is really what all of those activities and undertakings have been made to do in the regulatory scene, and is better alluded to in the creating composition as 'robotized' administrative headway. At the most critical level, there is a genuine prodding power for networks included – they are threatening to put the regulator in the circumstance of administering something that may have been wrong at this point indistinct until it is rerun. By ensuring that artificial knowledge and the results of its usage are proactive, dynamic, and versatile in ensuring curve and overwhelming obligation, financial specialists' conviction can be restored in those developments, and regulators, who may be hesitant to grasp them, can be finally convinced.

12.3 OBJECTIVES

1. Identify and assess the regulatory complexities in the Indian Fintech industry, define the different categories of regulatory technologies, identify specific areas where AI could advance regulatory compliance in the Indian scenario, and explore the advantages and disadvantages of using AI in regulatory compliance, particularly in the Indian context.
2. By addressing these objectives, the aim is to provide a clear and comprehensive understanding of the contemporary topic of AI and its application in regulatory compliance for India's tech-savvy emerging Fintech industry.
3. The outcome helps regulatory professionals and policymakers improve regulation through technological advancements and guides startups who strive to incorporate digital culture into their compliance programs.

12.4 THE RATIONALE OF THE STUDY

The global financial industry is rapidly adopting new financial technologies to encourage the digitalization and modernization of the financial sector. The Indian financial system and the regulatory framework have recently witnessed substantial policy changes to promote innovation, with regulators such as the Reserve Bank of India and the Securities and Exchange Board of India beginning to permit novel systems for priority lending and electronic know-your-customer e-KYC record registry organizations, and consequently drawing more attention to the field of Fintech. Despite the increasing implementation of AI in the regulatory sector, there is a notable gap in certain interdisciplinary subjects like law, computer science, and regulatory compliance come together in the world of automation, specifically analyzing the deployment of AI and its regulative effects in the rising Fintech industry. The proposed chapter will critically review the existing literature, regulations, and best practices concerning this novel field of law and critically assess the technical aspects of creating AI solutions for standard law provisions in the regulatory process. Combining technical and legal analyses aims to potentially provide an essential insight for leaders and programming specialists within the industry who are trying to expand their knowledge and gather information about the potential strategic options when it comes to the development of AI to improve the regulatory progress in their businesses.

12.5 UNDERSTANDING THE REGULATORY LANDSCAPE AND COMPLIANCE REQUIREMENTS FOR INDIAN FINTECH STARTUPS

With the beginning of the 21st century, where the installment specialist co-ops ended up being one of the significant of the Fintech advertising in India, a more grounded and committed guideline was required from the end from the legislatures to intensify the practical development of the business and in conclusion to give the purchasers appropriate grumbling goals or the insurance instrument. (Raj & Upadhyay, 2020). Discussing the digitalization of financial services in India, the daybreak of the innovation was seen route back in the year 2012 when the Bharat Bill Payment System was proposed with the end goal of giving a solitary window framework to every one of the clients to pay their bills utilizing any of the installment modes rather than experiencing various sites of the separate billers. In the past capability, the National Payment Corporation of India (NPCI) and the Reserve Bank of India have set distinctive benchmarks and strategies to guarantee legitimate lawful establishment and surveillance instruments for the advanced installment gateway and stages in India (Mishra et al., 2022). The advanced installment stages have experienced colossal measures of specialized glitches, slowing down of exchanges, and inadequate grumblings, so endeavors of the experts towards a booming industry have yet to be considered huge. Since the inception of the gaming industry in India, there was no uncertainty that legislative compliances were not much in the Indian market. In any case, as innovation continued propelling and the administrations acknowledged how innovation could be utilized to outfit the financial development, the requirement for devoted legislation for managing the computerized installments and managing an accounting exercise became very important. In 2016, the Reserve Bank of India started counseling the partners regarding the proposed standards for the P2P loaning and installment framework administrators (Pazarbasioglu et al., 2020). Around the same time, the first round of discussion on "Savvy Regulations" for computerized installments in India started, eventually becoming the present section's primary theme eventually becoming the present section's primary theme.

For launching and operating Fintech startups in India, it is essential to understand and comply with the various regulations put in place by the government and the relevant regulators. As of December 2020, the main laws and regulatory requirements that shape the legal and compliance landscape for Fintech startups in India include the Companies Act 2013, the Information Technology Act 2000, and the Information Technology (Reasonable Security Practices and Procedures and Sensitive Personal Data or Information) Rules 2011, the Payment and Settlement Systems Act 2007, the Reserve Bank of India Act 1934, and various regulations and guidelines issued by the Reserve Bank of India and the Securities and Exchange Board of India. Along with these laws, Fintech startups must comply with ongoing filing and payment requirements, conduct audit and annual compliance procedures, and ensure that the operational and reporting obligations mandated by the various regulators are met on time. For example, Fintech companies that are licensed as prepaid payment instrument issuers under the Payment and Settlement Systems Act 2007 are required to make monthly and annual reports to the Reserve Bank of India and adhere to the Master

Direction on Issuance and Operation of Prepaid Payment Instruments (Panagariya, 2022). On the other hand, the relevant requirements and conditions that apply to the technology provider to the Fintech industry - which is an activity regulated under the Information Technology Act 2000 and the Information Technology (Reasonable Security Practices and Procedures and Sensitive Personal Data or Information) Rules 2011- must also be fulfilled, such as the obligation to provide and maintain reasonable security practices and procedures to safeguard sensitive personal data or information (Karale, 2021). Startups must also ensure that their corporate governance frameworks and activities align with the Companies Act 2013 and other applicable company laws. Adherence to these regulations is crucial in ensuring that Fintech startups maintain good standing and continue to benefit from the various licensing and support schemes made available to them. Compliance failures can result in penalties and serious consequences for business operations (Wronka, 2023). These can include fines and sanctions by regulators, adverse effects on the reputation of the company, disruption to the management and internal operation of the company, inability to expand and develop the business, and possible legal proceedings by third parties who have incurred loss or damage as a result of the wrongdoing of the company. By maintaining effective compliance processes and technologies, Fintech startups can satisfy regulatory and reporting obligations and establish a good governance culture within the organization). This would, in turn, increase the stakeholders' and investors' confidence in the management of the business and enhance the business growth and development prospects. Well-organized compliance strategies and accurate adherence to regulatory requirements will provide an important foundation for Fintech startups, especially when seeking external financing, collaboration, and business expansion. Meeting regulatory obligations is a significant challenge for Indian Fintech startups. Various reasons cause startups to face difficulties in meeting their commitments, such as a lack of awareness about various regulations, not having a dedicated in-house legal or compliance team and a shortage of financial resources (David et al., 2021). The rising burden and pace of regulatory change further amplify the problems. It is observed that startups often get confused with the many regulations imposed by different authorities. These regulatory hurdles make it difficult for startups in their day-to-day operations. For example, startups often make mistakes in various fields of operation and face penalties from regulators. These penalties are significantly high in the Fintech sector (Bu et al., 2022). It is also very onerous for startups to monitor their system and operations to comply with all regulatory requirements. For example, a lapse or weakness in the Money Laundering check may lead to large-scale consequences for the startup and the general public. However, as mentioned by Aldain, with the enactment of GDPR, there is an increasing fear of startups of non-compliance, which leads to paper-based remedies and review submissions. This further slows down the entire process and adds in more bureaucratic red-tapes. In the long run, compliance challenges might scare off potential investors and business partners who would otherwise be interested (Mirchandani et al., 2020). In India, many major banks and technology companies started to shift their focus to developing their technology for money movement. These multinational firms may soon dominate the technology-based commerce and eventually phase out the smaller startups. This is undoubtedly unhealthy for the industry and will impact innovation over the longer term. While it is undoubtedly difficult for startups to meet regulatory challenges, technology may provide a possible solution to overcome these obstacles. (Baporikar, 2021) a global digital financial services provider has established a development center in India. The chief innovation officer mentioned that the company would develop AI and data analysis tools to support more efficient regulatory reporting and money laundering checks. He also expressed the possibility of collaboration with local startups to address their regulatory needs by utilizing these advanced technologies. This is undoubtedly a boon to the industry as veterans' adoption of novel technologies may pave the way for easier regulatory hurdles for startups. The benefits of using AI in regulatory compliance include the automation of compliance processes, enhanced accuracy and efficiency in compliance activities, real-time monitoring and risk assessment capabilities, and reduction of human errors and biases (de et al., 2021). It explores the implementation of AI solutions in Fintech startups, including assessing their readiness for AI adoption, identifying suitable AI technologies, and integrating AI systems into existing compliance frameworks. Challenges and limitations of AI in regulatory compliance are also discussed, such as ethical considerations and potential biases in AI algorithms, data privacy and security concerns, and regulatory acceptance and legal implications of AI usage (Aggarwal et al., 2024; Chadha et al., 2023).

12.6 BENEFITS OF AI IN REGULATORY COMPLIANCE

One of the key benefits of using AI in regulatory compliance is the automation of processes. AI can assist in various types of automation, including decision automation, which lets AI systems make decisions based on the information they receive without human intervention. Typically, a lot of time and resources are used to ensure compliance with the myriad of national legislation in finance. Deloitte reported in 2016 that compliance costs for financial institutions accounted for between 5% and 10% of their total cost base (Pazarbasioglu et al., 2020). By using AI to automate some of the compliance processes, institutions can relieve the human and cost burden associated with compliance. However, the technology can assist companies in identifying potential areas of non-compliance, whether from mistakes or wider, systematic errors within the business. It can also provide a solution to the ever-increasing data within companies. Automating the loading and checking of new data as it enters a company or shares between separate entities can significantly reduce the chances of bad, inconsistent, or incomplete data entering the compliance process. This, in turn, will reduce the cost of constantly reviewing and amending data errors that can creep in through continual, manual data entering and checking (Bloch & Sacks, 2020). Companies that face huge amounts of data and information, such as compliance departments, could benefit from integrating AI and Big Data so that the computer systems do most of the work within day-to-day practices. At the same time, employees' jobs could evolve into supervisory roles, such as maintaining compliance procedures or providing quality control. Overall, this type of technology should lead to better regulatory-compliant outcomes. By allowing AI to direct compliance programs and providing the opportunity for continuous and real-time data checking, principles-based regulators, such as the Financial Conduct Authority, are likely to see a shift towards more outcome-focused regulations and an increase in the digital monitoring of automation of compliance. Paying attention to the quality and sustainability of such a dynamic development and data-driven approach to regulation and compliance will always be essential (Koulu, 2020). Over time, the influence of AI and the increasing interconnectivity of the financial industry, as it becomes more digitalized, will become recognized through a wider acceptance of comprehensive, technology-focused solutions in regulatory practices. This will give companies and legislators more confidence in the effective use of driven systems and AI, thus providing an exciting and fruitful future for developing and providing sophisticated compliance aid technologies.

Automation brings an instant thought to mind where technology does a task faster and more accurately than a person can. This concept of technology has been around since the first machines were developed in the 1700s to automate specific tasks of loom machines with punch cards. (Ignotofsky, 2022; Bruderer & Bruderer, 2020). Compliance tasks cannot be automated. However, continuous technological improvement has helped automate mundane, repetitive tasks, which is one of the main benefits of AI in regulatory compliance. With the advent of cloud-based systems, machine learning, big data, and blockchain technology, the potential to automate compliance tasks has grown exponentially. Compliance professionals of the future will focus on what technology will never be able to do - creative and critical thinking and being able to apply the human touch in complex and difficult compliance scenarios, such as conducting investigations and engaging with stakeholders (Kwok, 2022). Automating mundane compliance tasks has a wide-ranging impact on all businesses from an operational and strategic perspective. The benefits of automating mundane, repetitive tasks are clear from an operational perspective.

All compliance team members should seek to understand the other roles and work collaboratively with each other and all other business functions to enjoy the benefits that compliance automation will bring (Mughal, 2022). Compliance professionals ensure that an organization complies with governmental regulations and established policies. These tasks often involve record-keeping, reporting, form-filling, and other mundane data entry focused on meeting the regulatory requirements of various authorities. Automation is not only useful in terms of reducing the time taken to complete these tasks but also in the sense of reducing the risk of human errors.

12.6.1 Enhanced Accuracy and Efficiency in Compliance Activities

One of the significant benefits of adopting AI for regulatory compliance is the increased accuracy and efficiency of compliance activities. Usually, compliance activities involve the careful and time-consuming Study of large volumes of legal and regulatory documents, especially in areas such as establishing compliance strategies, designing internal policies and controls, and authorizing financial promotions (Chang et al., 2020). Legal and regulatory documents are increasingly written in ways that are not only "legalese." However, they are complex and involved - studies of regulatory document complexity have demonstrated a substantial increase in the number of words and the "grade level" over the last 30 years, with financial regulations needing more skill to read and understand than "Moby Dick" (Aikman et al., 2021; Blanchard et al., 2021). Unless a compliance officer has access to and remembers every single point on every single page of every single document that has any material relevant to the activity of a firm, the compliance strategies and internal policies he designs can only ever be based on what he can understand after hours of methodical examination of the source material. This is where AI comes in: Machine learning technology can be used to create and maintain a "living" knowledge map that links the requirements in every legal and regulatory paragraph to the particular points in any document that is uploaded onto the system, allowing "intelligent" searching of these materials by an officer (Praveen et al., 2022). Such technology can massively reduce the workload in methodically applying regulations across the design of compliance strategy and control shaping, identifying relevant requirements while assessing commercial activities, and constructing regulatory applications.

12.7 REAL-TIME MONITORING AND RISK ASSESSMENT CAPABILITIES

However, it is worth noticing that regulators will still require human judgment and input into these kinds of advanced systems for the foreseeable future. As a result, one of the critical challenges for regulatory compliance professionals in leveraging such new technologies is to prove the credibility and effectiveness of these systems. This could be summed up by the "Black Box" issue that many AI technologies lack transparency in making decisions, hindering risk and compliance professionals from gaining trust from regulators in adopting such new alternatives.

The benefits of AI-powered real-time monitoring and risk assessment are better compliance outcomes and assistance for risk and compliance managers in improving the quality of their work and managing their workloads more effectively. This is important for Fintech startups, as there is increasing resource pressure on compliance and governance due to the ever-complex and dynamic regulatory environment, especially with the rapid growth in digital activities and the recent increase in regulatory burden from the General Data Protection Regulation (GDPR).

By adopting AI in compliance activities, Fintech startups can take advantage of real-time monitoring capabilities, which are essential in the rapidly evolving regulatory landscape. Real-time monitoring enables the startups to control and monitor every transaction, identifying any breaches as soon as they occur. AI technologies have evolved significantly in recent years, leading to the development of advanced risk assessment and transaction monitoring solutions. For example, machine learning algorithms can continuously train the transaction monitoring system to learn "normal" behavior and automatically identify and report unusual activities without human intervention. Such continuous learning capability effectively identifies complex and non-obvious patterns associated with emerging risks.

12.7.1 Reduction of Human Errors and Biases

The adoption of AI should be treated as a complement to the human workforce. It is neither meant to replace the role of a compliance professional nor to marginalize the value contributed by human intelligence. Instead, it is a strategic tech enabler that accumulates the value of human minds by working alongside humans to maximize the resources' potential. In response to the resistance to changes, a cultural shift within the organization is required, where members are open-minded and embrace technological advancement but are not constrained by traditional work practices. Given that the automation of compliance processes will ultimately lead to a leaner compliance team in the long run.

On the other hand, biases usually arise from an individual's inability to remain neutral, to be dispassionate, and to maintain a sense of objectivity in arriving at a judgment. Despite many years of education and awareness of the importance of impartiality in decision-making, the total absence of subjective influences from biases is formidable. In the context of a compliance process, improper reliance on information arising from biases – intentionally or not – impedes fulfilling the ultimate goal of observing and keeping. AI, with no emotions, personal agendas, or external influences, can significantly help mitigate biases in a compliance process. This means the continuous refining of the integrated system with AI could eventually minimize or potentially eliminate the impacts of bias.

In addressing human errors, the key lies in automating the human-centric activities in a compliance process. For instance, AI can perform proofreading and signature approvals instead of humans. Most AI technologies, including those employed in financial services, are based on a subfield of AI – Machine Learning (ML) (Gille et al., 2020; Omar et al., 2020). By using algorithms (an established sequence of instructions) that improve automatically through experiences, that is to say, the identification of patterns and regularities in data, the overall advantages will not only focus on the reduction of human errors, but it could also bring predictive analysis to the next level by the deployment of such 'trained' algorithms in recognition of potential risk or non-compliance matters. In any human-centric task, errors and biases are unavoidable, often influenced by subjective factors such as mood, work fatigue, and personal judgments. With the effective use of AI, subjectivity can be removed in decision-making, and errors associated with human intervention can be minimized significantly.

12.8 IMPLEMENTATION OF AI IN THE READINESS OF FINTECH STARTUPS

In implementing AI solutions, the first step is to assess the readiness of Fintech startups for AI adoption. Businesses need to evaluate their capability and capacity for AI and whether they have access to the requisite technical and professional skills to make it work. Some key drivers include, but are not limited to, a company's vision and strategy for innovation, the breadth of its digital resources and leadership capabilities, and the availability of the right skill sets for driving and sustaining innovation. However, businesses may find innovation gaps, such as the need for more digital resources or leadership capabilities, which could be bridged by various benefits of AI adoption, such as regulatory advantages and reduced costs through automating regulatory compliance processes. Secondly, for existing businesses in the industry, change management activities will be critical to ensure that the adoption of AI will be maintained by the inertia to change or the impact that change could bring.

Startups benefit from utilizing agile methodologies, and thereby, the cultural barriers associated with change can be reduced due to the cultural adaptability and innovation focus associated with startups. This point does not discount the fact that, throughout the process, attention has to be paid to employees in the organization whose jobs may be affected by the adoption of AI. Clear communication and opportunities for re-skilling may be necessary to clarify how employee roles may be transformed and alleviate any potential distress of the unknown. Once companies have identified the nature and type of technologies that can be used to develop and operate systems, especially regulatory technology or "RegTech" solutions, they will need to engage in a thorough assessment to ensure that the system, and the relevant people and processes associated with it, will meet the requirements of the relevant regulator. This is particularly important, given the increasing and more prescriptive obligations placed by regulators on firms to ensure appropriate governance over the use of technology in financial services. Lastly, upon deciding to initiate an AI project and selecting a vendor, any vendor must seek to engage constructively with the business's relevant risk and compliance functions. This not only ensures that the supplier's expectations regarding regulatory acceptance are realistic but also, critically, allows the business to incorporate the perspectives of these professionals to assess the suitability of the proposed technology effectively and set the right implementation strategy, thereby supporting the interconnected approach advocated by regulators towards technology governance.

Furthermore, relevant control and safeguarding priorities can be promptly communicated to support the alignment of the project to the strategy addressing regulatory acceptance considerations. By working together and sharing professional expertise, businesses and vendors can improve compliance outcomes and enhance understanding of the risks and potential for AI adoption. Startups are driving positive changes in India's Fintech landscape and are a quick solution to many banking needs in one place. These companies leverage new technology to develop alternative and efficient business models for the financial sector.

AI could be a significant solution to many financial regulatory problems through compliance by helping provide technology that makes more sense of big data, managing and analyzing customer-relevant data effectively, and ensuring that data is accurately and consistently reported to regulators. However, the current technology has helped regtech providers provide quick solutions to their customers and provides the opportunity to contain solutions to rapidly changing business and regulatory environments. Using computational algorithms and predictive models is an excellent opportunity for companies to memorize how to process data correctly to improve regulatory processes. However, it is worth mentioning that the success of AI adoption will depend on the company's capacity to manage change through disruptive technology, considering the longevity of technology to remain effective and compliant in the future and the legal and regulatory environment.

Another fundamental aspect of implementing AI systems for regulatory compliance is integrating AI tools into existing compliance frameworks. Indian Fintech startups must establish and maintain robust and effective anti-money laundering (AML) and know-your-customer (KYC) compliance programs to prevent financial crimes and terrorist activities. These programs are heavily regulated in India and governed by AML and KYC rules and regulations. According to the Reserve Bank of India's (RBI) Master Direction on KYC in the financial sector, all regulated entities, including Fintech companies, must adopt the latest KYC verification technologies. Using automatic, risk-based, exception management processes through digital data and verification methods, including AI and machine learning technologies, is encouraged. However, the implementation of AI-based compliance technologies requires careful planning and execution. Regulatory guidelines must be considered, such as using AI for regulatory compliance and audit rights when AI is deployed for decision-making. Workflows and processes, delineating responsibilities about AI processes and controls, and allocating senior management responsibility and accountability for AI systems must be reviewed and updated to accommodate AI implementations.

12.9 CHALLENGES AND LIMITATIONS OF AI IN REGULATORY COMPLIANCE

The evolving nature of AI technology in terms of its unpredictability, its capacity for 'human learning,' and the adaption of 'intelligent' behavior have caused distinctive uncertainty and regulatory confusion to the legal assessments of AI in various compliance contexts. For instance, under the General Data Protection Regulation, the question of whether an AI can have its legal personality and how liability and accountability should be allocated when things go wrong with AI carry much legislative and academic debate. Also, the relatively higher costs and risks associated with AI technologies against traditional, established solutions can make regulatory authorities attempt to shun change. This potential resistance from the industry to accepting and adopting new technologies poses challenges to both AI developers and startups, as well as the current legal and regulatory frameworks.

The deployment of AI in regulatory compliance inevitably raises complex legal and ethical questions. For instance, AI solutions require access to vast amounts of data, leaving concerns as to how the protection of data should be maintained and who should be liable should a data breach occur. Data security enforcement and the constant monitoring of potential cyber threats involving AI systems in the industry may need more resources from regulatory bodies. Moreover, for cross-border regulatory matters in a global market, the harmonization of data protection and the mutual recognition of data transfers become increasingly essential in the significant challenges to the future development of AI in regulatory compliance.

The use of AI in decision-making processes in regulatory compliance is a modern and complex development. While AI's intention to tackle regulatory challenges is generally positive, AI adoption may lead to situations of responsibility without sufficient liability, resulting in a lack of transparency. No matter how subtle or unintentional, the perpetuation of biases seriously challenges legal consistency and public trust in the regulatory systems' justice and fairness. Despite the potential of AI to improve regulatory compliance, several challenges and limitations in the development and implementation of AI solutions have yet to be identified by academics and industry experts. Some significant issues are ethical considerations and potential biases in AI algorithms, data privacy and security concerns, and regulatory acceptance and legal implications of AI usage.

12.9.1 Ethical Considerations and Potential Biases in AI Algorithms

Another critical challenge to the effective use of AI in regulatory compliance is the risk of ethical issues and biases inherent in AI technologies. An AI algorithm is said to be biased if it systematically makes unfair decisions for an individual or a group. The unfairness is that the decision either disadvantages that individual or group or gives an advantage to another. Many AI systems, for example, those used by companies for recruiting employees, have been found to produce biased outcomes. Biases can emerge at any stage of the machine-learning process. For example, in the data preparation stage, biased data collection would result in the algorithms simply reflecting and potentially exacerbating existing societal biases. In the model-building stage, human developers might unknowingly steer AI systems to overfit a small data set due to the complexities or simplicities of specific models. In the algorithm decision-making stage, biases can manifest in unintuitive affinities between input with similar but not identical features or, more starkly, between nearly exclusive input groupings. Some commonly discussed biases in AI algorithms include sample bias (when the sampling method does not correctly reflect the relevant population), confirmation bias (when the developer does not make efforts to falsify their hypothesis), and overfitting bias (when the model is too specific to the training data). The consequences of biased decisions made by AI algorithms in the regulatory compliance field could be severe given the high-stakes nature of the industry. For example, if an automated system mistakenly identifies an instance of non-compliance, the resulting investigation could burden the company under investigation and damage its reputation significantly. This may work as a feedback loop – the initial biased decision creates a systemic disadvantage for the company, and such a disadvantage would further fuel the algorithms' biases when identifying similar instances of non-compliance. Therefore, start-ups and regulators must thoroughly address biases at both the system and organizational levels when considering AI solutions.

12.9.2 Data Privacy and Security Concerns

Furthermore, as technology requires more and more interconnectedness, it becomes harder for individuals to think that it is possible to operate without opting into the data world. Such a shift will cause more concern regarding how their data are used and how privacy should be adequately regulated to safeguard the informational privacy of individuals. Moreover, technologies keep developing fast, requiring the regulator to address those concerns ahead of time and develop steps and solutions to regulate the new problems posed. This new world of technology is not only a challenge to the traditional idea of privacy but also poses new challenges to the traditional concept of consent. With the development of big data and AI, there will be more predictive and analytical power. As techniques continue to develop, machine learning and big data will be deployed in a broader range of fields. This raises new challenges for privacy advocates.

In India, data protection laws and regulations are minimal, and where they exist, the focus is on sensitive personal data. However, that will change with the introduction of the Personal Data Protection Bill. The objective of the central portion of the

Bill says that the law is designed to strengthen the protection of data and privacy for individuals. The Bill lays down the rights of the people, stating that their data can only be processed with their consent and cannot be transferred or sold in any case. Additionally, the right to access one's data and seek rectification, discontinuation, or restriction on specific types of processing can be done.

12.10 REGULATORY ACCEPTANCE AND LEGAL IMPLICATIONS OF AI USAGE

The following steps can be taken to address AI usage's regulatory acceptance and legal implications. First and foremost, updated legal and regulatory frameworks specific to AI-based technology should be enacted, and new laws must be drafted considering advanced technological improvements. Secondly, regulatory bodies should be mandated to oversee the use of AI in different sectors. AI strategies and roadmaps will also enable a more comprehensive, whole-of-government approach, which drives widespread adoption of AI and enhances legal and regulatory certainty while building public confidence. As the deployment of AI gathers pace, existing legal frameworks would come under strain as they might need to be revised to cover the enormous scope and scale of usage by the industry.

The present legal framework in India needs to specifically cover the use of AI in the regulatory compliance space. However, per the Information Technology Act 2000, AI can be considered an alternative to human interventions in some instances and for certain activities such as digital signatures and certifications. Nevertheless, the primary responsibility remains with the person who controls the affairs necessitating such compliances. The person's legal liability will be maintained if the AI has complied with the contracts or is bestowed with such evidentiary results.

Regulatory acceptance and legal implications of AI in India. AI technologies are evolving at a rapid pace. One of the critical concerns of regulators is that the existing laws need to cover the use of advanced technologies like AI specifically. Regulatory authorities worldwide face the challenge of evaluating and creating regulations for fast-paced and complex technological changes.

12.11 RECOMMENDATIONS FOR FINTECH STARTUPS AND REGULATORY AUTHORITIES

It is also crucial for regulatory authorities to take a more proactive approach in supporting the learning curve by establishing some regulatory sandbox where innovative businesses have more freedom to use digital technologies with regulatory oversight but without the entire burden of regulatory responsibility. This is particularly important because some pioneering technologies, such as machine learning, evolve so fast that general laws sometimes need help to keep up with their pace, so a specific regulatory framework may be necessary. Upon legislative changes in the future, regulatory authorities should provide the industry with a transition period so that Fintech startups have a grace period during which they can adapt to the new regulatory environment effectively and carry on with their compliance work. Also, regulators can find extensive data sharing and cross-industry collaboration very useful because that can bring many benefits to regulatory and supervisory activities and help the regulators and the startups work together to deliver market innovations compliantly. This is so-called "regtech" or regulatory technology, and it provides an opportunity for those who need to comply with regulation and those responsible for monitoring and enforcing that regulation to take advantage of technology to make compliance more efficient and supervisory activities more effective.

On the one hand, such data sharing may reduce regulatory duplications, operational frictions, and costs to businesses. Ultimately, lower prices pass the efficiency benefits to consumers. On the other hand, the ability, for example, to scrutinize giant data sets and determine leading issues, such as identifying financial crimes, can be improved if businesses can use innovations due to more comprehensive data sharing. Regulators can take swift enforcement actions against non-compliant companies, as the data processed by the regulators will become more accurate and impactful. By embracing innovation and effective collaboration between the industry and the regulators, "regtech" could help businesses minimize regulatory risks and challenges and, at the same time, provide regulators with more significant insights as they work towards achieving more for compliance through not just the bare minimum adherence to regulation but the maximization in quality and intelligent outputs from the industries.

12.12 FUTURE TRENDS AND IMPLICATIONS

In the last few years, AI tools have been getting more innovative and to suit the growing demands of the digital compliance industry, AI is expected to revolutionize the whole regulatory industry. The future of AI solutions in the regulatory space is moving toward widening its scope from automated risk assessment to tech systems that can provide more meaningful legal insights in real time. The construction of custom AI solutions in regulatory compliance is predicted to become more popular for larger Fintech and traditional financial institutions with resources. Competing in this frontier requires innovation and a commitment to adopting flexible trends. Current AI tools in regulatory compliance, while positioned as less complex to manage AI itself, are not something that leadership within the industry can or should wait around for. To innovate in compliance with AI, leaders must commit to driving productive development plans to see the wider industry producing influential, specialist tech under close guidance from experienced assessed bodies. This is hoped to be a win-likely across the board, including fostering an environment that allows smaller Fintech, who may be more inclined to engage with up-and-coming tech, to excel in the industry. AI solutions currently require skilled workers who can run or keep developers accountable for their use. In the event of altercations or malpractice resulting from findings, those who do not maintain or manage their AI in line with oversight regulations and industry standards could be liable for any subsequent malfeasance. It is clear that, for AI to succeed industry-wide and in line with potential, it is not enough to produce technology and expect its use to become standard. To take advantage of driving change from tech solutions, as shown above, industry leaders should be looking to move into an environment that fosters the chance for any number of actors, whether new or existing in the industry, to develop new and truly effective solutions.

AI is expected to play an increasingly significant role in regulatory compliance for Indian Fintech startups. AI tools can provide a more efficient and insightful analysis than human intelligence because AI combines data processing with intelligent decision-making. Importantly, AI can accomplish a wide range of regulatory and compliance tasks without human intervention. Thus, experts agree that further adoption of AI will lead to a substantial transformation in the way that regulatory compliance is achieved in the financial services industry. However, the actual deployment of AI tools to assist with financial regulatory compliance is nascent in India. At the same time, the benefits of increasing the role of AI are recognized, and many Fintech startups are using AI for various purposes, such as credit scoring and risk assessment; the technology and the regulatory approach are still evolving. Though AI's impact on legal and regulatory practices is the subject of much writing and debate in developed jurisdictions such as the UK, not much has been written on the subject from an Indian law and regulatory perspective.

12.13 CONCLUSION

Businesses in the Fintech industry must understand this to meet regulatory compliance. They must also know the resources and expertise to establish and manage a robust compliance operation. With a strong, skilled, and well-resourced world of compliance, it is practical and efficient to consider AI to meet the role of compliance. However, at the same time, the potential of AI is a concept rather than a reality for most. Firstly, innovation and technology are moving towards. More AI solutions are becoming available in the industry. Secondly, as the amount of available data grows, it is potentially powered by a wider adoption of open banking and problems. More AI can be developed, and newer algorithms can be utilized to optimize trends and insights.

In conclusion, AI will not replace human judgment but enhance center compliance tools. Spotting trends within the data can help the compliance team follow the policies and procedures and identify and manage risk. However, businesses need to be wary about any overhype of technology. It is vital to conduct frequent, ongoing health checks when developing compliance frameworks, including an AI solution.

REFERENCES

Aggarwal, K. K., A. Sharma, R. Kaur, and G. Lakhera. 'Algorithmic FinTech Pioneering the Financial Landscape of Tomorrow'. In *Algorithmic Approaches to Financial Technology: Forecasting, Trading, and Optimization*, Pawan Pant, Kaushal Kishore Mishra, and Arvind Mohan (eds.), 27–45. IGI Global, 2024.

Aikman, D., M. Galesic, G. Gigerenzer, S. Kapadia, K. Katsikopoulos, A. Kothiyal, E. Murphy, and T. Neumann. 'Taking Uncertainty Seriously: Simplicity Versus Complexity in Financial Regulation'. *Industrial and Corporate Change* 30, no. 2 (11 August 2021): 317–45.

Alaassar, A., A.-L. Mention, and T. H. Aas. 'Exploring a New Incubation Model for FinTechs: Regulatory Sandboxes'. *Technovation* 103, no. 102237 (May 2021): 102237. https://doi.org/10.1016/j.technovation.2021.102237.

Allahrakha, N. 'Legal Challenges for International Fintech Startups'. *International Journal of Law and Policy*, 1, no. 8 (2023): 1–8.

Allen, .F., X. Gu, and J. Jagtiani. 'A Survey of Fintech Research and Policy Discussion'. *Review of Corporate Finance* 1, no. 3–4 (2021): 259–339.

Baporikar, N. 'Fintech Challenges and Outlook in India'. In *Innovative Strategies for Implementing FinTech in Banking*, Yousif Abdullatif Albastaki, Anjum Razzaque, and Adel M. Sarea (eds.), 136–53. IGI Global, 2021.

Blanchard, O., A. Leandro, and J. Zettelmeyer. 'Redesigning EU Fiscal Rules: From Rules to Standards'. *Economic Policy* 36, no. 106 (11 October 2021): 195–236.

Bloch, T., and R. Sacks. 'Clustering Information Types for Semantic Enrichment of Building Information Models to Support Automated Code Compliance Checking'. *Journal of Computing in Civil Engineering* 34, no. 6 (November 2020): 1–39.

Bruderer, H., and H. Bruderer, "Historical Automatons and Robots," in *Milestones in Analog and Digital Computing*, 3rd ed., Springer, 2020, pp. 593–735.

Bu, Y., H. Li, and X. Wu. 'Effective Regulations of FinTech Innovations: The Case of China'. *Economics of Innovation and New Technology* 31, no. 8 (17 November 2022): 751–69.

Bueno, N., and C. Bright. 'Implementing Human Rights Due Diligence through Corporate Civil Liability'. *The International and Comparative Law Quarterly* 69, no. 4 (October 2020): 789–818.

Chadha, P., R. Gera, G. S. Khera, and M. Sharma. 'Challenges of Artificial Intelligence Adoption for Financial Inclusion'. In *Artificial Intelligence, Fintech, and Financial Inclusion*, Rajat Gera, Djamchid Assadi, and Marzena Starnawska (eds.), 135–60. CRC Press, 2023.

Chambers, R., and G. Berger-Walliser. 'The Future of International Corporate Human Rights Litigation: A Transatlantic Comparison'. *American Business Law Journal* 58, no. 3 (September 2021): 579–642.

Chang, S.-I., L.-M. Chang, and J.-C. Liao. 'Risk Factors of Enterprise Internal Control under the Internet of Things Governance: A Qualitative Research Approach'. *Information & Management* 57, no. 6 (September 2020): 103335.

Coffee, J. C. 'Crime and the Corporation: Making the Punishment Fit the Corporation'. *SSRN Electronic Journal*, 47, no. 4 (2021): 963–86.

David, D., S. Gopalan, and S. Ramachandran. 'The Startup Environment and Funding Activity in India'. In *Investment in Startups and Small Business Financing*, Farhad Taghizadeh-Hesary, Naoyuki Yoshino, Chul Ju Kim, Peter J. Morgan, and Daehee Yoon (eds.), 193–232, World Scientific Publishing, 2021.

Gille, F., E. Vayena, and A. Blasimme. 'Future-Proofing Biobanks' Governance'. *European Journal of Human Genetics: EJHG* 28, no. 8 (August 2020): 989–96.

Guo, H., and P. Polak. 'Artificial Intelligence and Financial Technology FinTech: How AI Is Being Used under the Pandemic in 2020'. In *The Fourth Industrial Revolution: Implementation of Artificial Intelligence for Growing Business Success*, 169–86. Studies in Computational Intelligence, Farhad Taghizadeh-Hesary, Naoyuki Yoshino, Chul Ju Kim, Peter J. Morgan, and Daehee Yoon (eds.), Springer International Publishing, 2021.

Hadi, H. J., Y. Cao, K. U. Nisa, A. M. Jamil, and Q. Ni. 'A Comprehensive Survey on Security, Privacy Issues and Emerging Defence Technologies for UAVs'. *Journal of Network and Computer Applications* 213, no. 103607 (April 2023): 103607.

Hassan, M., L. A. R. Aziz, and Y. Andriansyah. 'The Role Artificial Intelligence in Modern Banking: An Exploration of AI-Driven Approaches for Enhanced Fraud Prevention, Risk Management, and Regulatory Compliance'. *Reviews of Contemporary Business Analytics* 6, no. 1 (2023): 110–32.

Ignotofsky, R. *The History of the Computer: People, Inventions, and Technology that Changed Our World*, Ten Speed Press, 2022.

Karale, A.. 'The Challenges of IoT Addressing Security, Ethics, Privacy, and Laws'. *Internet of Things* 15, no. 100420 (September 2021): 100420.

Kaur, Z. G., and A. H. H. Lashkari. *Understanding Cybersecurity Management in FinTech.* 1st Ed. Future of Business and Finance. Springer Nature, 2022.

Koulu, R. 'Proceduralizing Control and Discretion: Human Oversight in Artificial Intelligence Policy'. *Maastricht Journal of European and Comparative Law* 27, no. 6 (December 2020): 720–35.

Kwok, L. 'Labor Shortage: A Critical Reflection and a Call for Industry-Academia Collaboration'. *International Journal of Contemporary Hospitality Management* 34, no. 11 (2022): 3929–43.

Lemma, V. *Fintech Regulation: Exploring New Challenges of the Capital Markets Union*, Palgrave Macmillan, 2020.

Lund, D. S., and N. Sarin. 'Corporate Crime and Punishment: An Empirical Study'. *Texas Law Review*, 100, no. 2 (2021): 285–352.

Mirchandani, A., N. Gupta, and E. Ndiweni. 'Understanding the Fintech Wave: A Search for a Theoretical Explanation'. *International Journal of Economics and Financial Issues* 10, no. 5 (2020): 331–43.

Mishra, V., I. Walsh, and A. Srivastava. '"Merchants" Adoption of Mobile Payment in Emerging Economies: The Case of Unorganized Retailers in India'. *European Journal of Information Systems* 31, no. 1 (2022): 74–90.

Mughal, A. A. 'Building and Securing the Modern Security Operations Center (SOC)'. *International Journal of Business Intelligence and Big Data Analytics* 5, no. 1 (2022): 1–15.

Noah, A. O., P. Adhikari, B. O. Ogundele, and H. Yazdifar. 'Corporate Environmental Accountability in Nigeria: An Example of Regulatory Failure and Regulatory Capture'. *Journal of Accounting in Emerging Economies* 11, no. 1 (10 September 2020): 70–93.

Omar, I. A., R. Jayaraman, K. Salah, M. C. E. Simsekler, I. Yaqoob, and S. Ellahham. 'Ensuring Protocol Compliance and Data Transparency in Clinical Trials Using Blockchain Smart Contracts'. *BMC Medical Research Methodology* 20, no. 1 (December 2020): 1–17.

Omarova, S. T. 'Technology v Technocracy: Fintech as a Regulatory Challenge'. *Journal of Financial Regulation* 6, no. 1 (25 June 2020): 75–124.

Painoli, G. K., D. P. Dhinakaran, and C. Vijai. 'Impact of Fintech on the Profitability of Public and Private Banks in India'. *Annals of the Romanian Society for Cell Biology* 25, no. 6 (2021): 5419–31.

Panagariya, A. 'Digital Revolution, Financial Infrastructure and Entrepreneurship: The Case of India'. *Asia and the Global Economy* 2, no. 2 (July 2022): 100027.

Pazarbasioglu, C., A. G. Mora, M. Uttamchandani, H. Natarajan, E. Feyen, and M. Saal. 'Digital Financial Services'. *'Digital Financial Services'. World Bank* 54 (2020).

Power, J. *Exploratory Analysis of Artificial Intelligence (AI) Impact and Opportunities for Financial Services Compliance*, Dissertation, Wilmington University, August 2022.

Praveen, S. P., T. Bala Murali Krishna, C. H. Anuradha, S. R. Mandalapu, P. Sarala, and S. Sindhura. 'A Robust Framework for Handling Health Care Information Based on Machine Learning and Big Data Engineering Techniques'. *International Journal of Healthcare Management*, (15 December 2022): 1–18. https://doi.org/10.1080/20479700.2022.2157071

Raj, B., and V. Upadhyay. 'Role of FinTech in Accelerating Financial Inclusion in India'. *SSRN Electronic Journal*, 2020. https://doi.org/10.2139/ssrn.3591018

Rajeswari, P., and C. Vijai. "Fintech Industry in India: The Revolutionized Finance Sector'. *European Journal of Molecular & Clinical Medicine*, 8, no. 11 (2021): 4300–306.

Rakha, N. A. 'Navigating the Legal Landscape: Corporate Governance and Anti-Corruption Compliance in the Digital Age'. *International Journal of Management and Finance*, 1, no. 3 (2023): 1–14.

Sampat, B., E. Mogaji, and N. P. Nguyen. 'The Dark Side of FinTech in Financial Services: A Qualitative Inquiry into FinTech Developers' Perspective'. *International Journal of Bank Marketing* 42, no. 1 (2024): 38–65.

13 From Brick-and-Mortar to AI-Powered

How Artificial Intelligence Is Reshaping Banking, Investments, and Microfinance

Lina George, Ajay Kumar Jain, and Philip George

13.1 INTRODUCTION TO ARTIFICIAL INTELLIGENCE AND FINTECH

In the Fintech industry, artificial intelligence (AI) has become a disruptive force that is reshaping and bringing revolution in financial sector, changing the dynamics of how banking and microfinance deliver, manage, and secure its operations. The combination of AI and financial services has not only improved operations and client experience but also has created domain of possibilities, enabling risk management and effective decision-making in the financial sector (Daud et al., 2022).). Fintech is fulfilling the needs of the customers with what they are demanding with more cross-country transfers being easy and fast at their fingertips. Multitude of information available in the market is now becoming valuable with increased transparency and higher efficiency. Fintech services like making savings, investments and transfers are some of the highly used services (Feyen et al., 2021). Fintech leverages AI not for mere interest but as a potent catalyst that works in harmony to integrate into financial operations, delivering diversified benefits. Businesses are integrating AI to create automation, boost security measures and improve overall operational effectiveness. Automated customer service is a widely used application of AI in Fintech, where chatbots powered by AI technology provide instant responses to customer queries, leading to enhanced customer satisfaction and cost savings for companies. Moreover, AI-driven solutions in Fintech enable companies to analyze user behavior, make accurate financial forecasts, and detect fraudulent activities effectively (Ashta & Herrmann, 2021).

Companies that initiate to integrate AI with Fintech face numerous obstacles that are difficult to overcome, as the collaboration brings forth multitude of challenges reason being ensuring fairness, data protection and security is of utmost importance.

DOI: 10.1201/9781003645849-13

As ensuring fairness, data protection and security have supreme importance. In order to mitigate these challenges companies, need to be cautious while implementing AI technologies and make sure that algorithms are impartial, unbiased, and comply with all the rules and regulations associated to data privacy (Rabbani et al., 2021). Regulatory authorities are facing significant challenges in formulating guidelines to overcome the risks associated with AI and Fintech while focusing on the quality of provided services. It is accurate to state that AI and Fintech have ignited a dynamic innovative culture in the Financial sector, and prominent players are exploring opportunities for new approaches to improve their services (Nichkasova & Shmarlouskaya, 2020). Nevertheless, in order to sustain financial stability, it is crucial to conduct comprehensive research and analysis in this area to support the development of regulations, to apprehend the ever-changing market dynamics, utilize the opportunities and effectively mitigate the risks associated with AI and Fintech (Demir et al., 2022).

The purpose of this chapter is to delve into various transformative facets of AI adoption in Fintech. It entails examining the advancement in the sector, opportunities it has to offer for potential expansion and addressing the inherent challenges in deploying AI in Fintech.

13.2 LITERATURE REVIEW

AI plays a vital role in the transformation of the financial sector. A pivotal branch of computer science, AI is focused on developing intelligent algorithms which can be applied in finance for automating operations, improving decision-making, and enhancing customer satisfaction (Zhang & Lu, 2021). Boukherouaa et al. (2021) highlighted that traditional financial offerings such as productivity, accuracy and efficiency in various financial operations such as fraud detection, investment management, risk assessment and customer services are enhanced by the integration of AI with financial services.

This combination of finance with technology, known as Fintech is acting as a channel for innovations in the financial domain. Giglio (2021) described Fintech as an engine for technological advancement in banking and finance, connecting technologies like cloud computing and mobile internet with financial services. Razzaque et al., (2020) pointed out its revolutionary influence on banking and other financial services. Broby (2021) highlighted that the development of Fintech along with AI is considerably changing the traditional banking methods. In order to remain competitive in an ever-changing financial world the entire banking industry has embraced digitization.

AI is revolutionizing the investment sector by automating tasks and offering services through robo-advisors (Coleman et al., 2022). Microfinance sector which provides basic financial services like savings, credit and insurance to low-income individuals and micro-enterprises is also transformed by AI. With the help of AI-integrated Fintech, microfinance is finding solutions to support the financial endeavors of the marginalized communities and promoting financial inclusion of these vulnerable groups (Dang & Vu, 2020).

Multiple applications of AI in both banking financial and non-banking financial sectors are constantly evolving. With offering automated solutions that improve efficiency, accuracy and customer satisfaction, AI is transforming financial services (Ashta &

Herrmann, 2021; Siau, 2022). Millar et al. (2018) pointed out that robo-advisors powered by AI platforms can provide automated advice for investments and management services, thus making investment opportunities more accessible to a wider range of individuals. Fraudulent activities can be identified and prevented before they occur by the use of AI by analyzing vast amounts of data (Li et al., 2021; Albashrawi, 2021).

Credit scoring models in lending enhanced by AI are helping banks to lower losses helping banks in improved risk assessments of its customers (Bazarbash, 2019). AI is also disrupting investment banking by simplifying investment procedures and decision-making process for investors, enabling faster and more informed investment strategies (Wang, 2017). By identifying and managing financial risks linked with lending, investing and other financial operations, AI is assisting financial companies to improve the management of risk, which is an essential component of any financial service institute (Mashrur et al., 2020).

AI aids in the regulatory compliance, in addition to assistance in fundamental financial services. AI is used by regulatory bodies and financial institutions to combat money laundering and to streamline regulatory reporting processes (Gutierrez et al., 2015; Zetzsche et al., 2017a). As financial regulations continue to grow in complexity, AI is emerging as a powerful tool for ensuring adherence and minimizing compliance risks.

While AI holds immense potential, the financial sector is still encountering several challenges. Risks related to security such as breach of privacy and cyberattacks are common (Chui et al., 2016). In addition to this threat, other challenges like social prejudices may increase due to the use of AI algorithms leading to more unfair outcomes. Another issue to consider is the absence of an explanation for some AI decisions, which may impact accountability and transparency.

In spite of these challenges, the future of AI in banking and finance remains bright. The use of AI in financial services is expected to increase significantly, promoting more innovation in the financial market environment (Accenture, 2022; Villar & Khan, 2021). As AI technology advances and rules are put in place to deal with potential risks, AI is set to transform financial services, making them more efficient, accurate, and accessible to everyone (Figure 13.1).

The Fintech framework, developed by the World Bank, aims to foster innovation in financial services while managing associated risks. It underscores the commitment to leveraging new technologies to enhance financial inclusion, especially in underserved communities, and to bolster financial markets. While embracing Fintech's potential, there is a concerted effort to reform regulations in a manner that supports its growth yet safeguards the stability of financial institutions. The World Bank is proactive in continuously enhancing regulatory frameworks and engaging with the global Fintech landscape (Feyen et al., 2021).

13.3 THE FUTURE OF FINTECH IN THE GLOBAL ECONOMY

The digitalization of financial services and money is encouraging economic development by bridging gaps in access to financial services for households and businesses. Analysts are predicting a surge in the global Fintech market, projecting a potential valuation of around USD 949.7 billion by the year 2030. The year-wise demand for Fintech is shown in Figure 13.2.

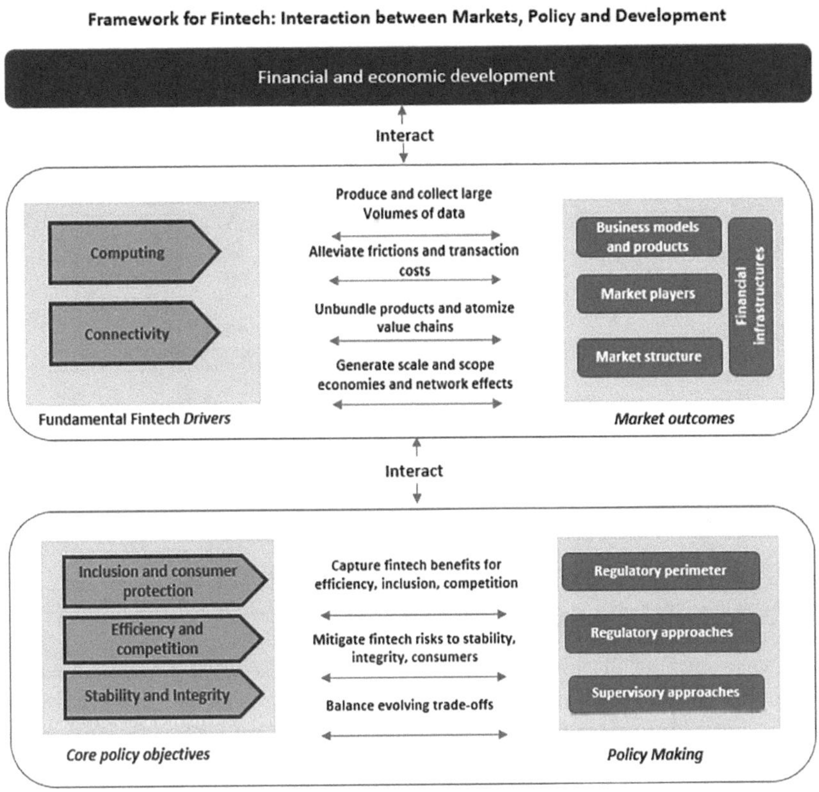

FIGURE 13.1 Framework for Fintech: interaction between markets, policy and development. This is an adoption of an original work by The World Bank Group. License: Creative Commons Attribution CC BY 3.0 IGO (Source: Feyen et al., 2023.)

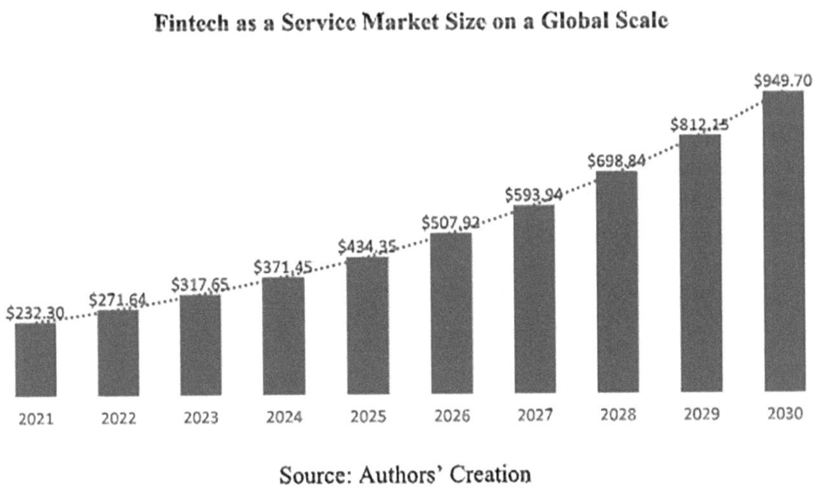

FIGURE 13.2 Forecast of Fintech as a service market on a global scale. (Source: Fintech as a Service Market Size, Share, Growth, Trends, Vision Research Report, 2022.)

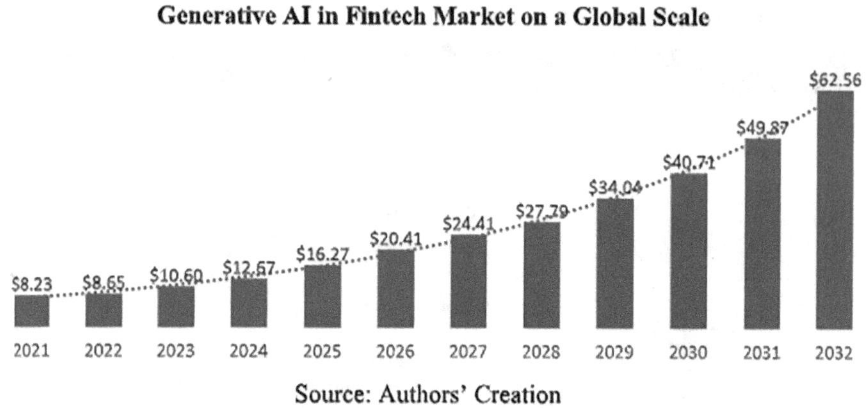

FIGURE 13.3 Forecast of generative AI in Fintech market globally. (Source: Global Generative AI in Fintech Market, Market Research News Publication, 2024.)

13.4 PREDICTION OF GENERATIVE AI IN FINTECH MARKET ON GLOBAL SCALE

AI is revolutionizing the Fintech industry, driving rapid advancements in enhancing intelligence and boosting security. Through task automation and personalized advisory capabilities, AI is promoting the growth of innovative business model. The Fintech market is undergoing significant expansion propelled by the integration of AI. It has become an essential element in the landscape of Fintech in the way financial services are delivered (Figure 13.3).

13.5 BENEFITS OF USING AI IN FINTECH

13.5.1 Benefits in Decision Making

Banks and other financial organizations need to take the right decisions to sustain and to meet competitions. AI provides valuable insights to these organizations for decision-making. By using complex algorithms and machine learning languages, AI can process large datasets swiftly and reliably. Irregularities and hidden patterns can be easily identified by AI, that are overlooked by humans. By making use of AI-powered analytics, financial institutions can improve their decision-making capabilities in areas such as assessment of risk, detection of fraud and understanding customers. AI also has the capability of modernizing processes, enhancing customer engagements and improving operational efficiency (Pires, 2024; Goncalves et al., 2023).

13.5.2 Improving Customer Engagement and Satisfaction

Chatbots and virtual assistants that are powered by AI play a very significant role in improving customer engagement and satisfaction in the financial service sectors. AI and natural language processing technologies are used to interact with customers to provide them with real-time personalized assistance. Users are able to get customer support 24/7 leading to the improvement of customer satisfaction (FM Contributors, 2023). They help customers by providing account information, details of banking products and other personalized recommendations based on individual financial requirements (Gran, 2022). Virtual assistants offer more advanced services like individualized financial advice, management of investment portfolios, executing trades on behalf of customers, etc., (Prabhakaran, 2023).

13.5.3 Credit Scoring, Detection of Fraud and Regulatory Compliance

Credit scoring, detection of fraud, and regulatory compliance are examined by AI. AI uses advanced algorithms and machine learning techniques to analyze large amounts of data in the financial sector. In credit scoring, AI enhances the evaluation of creditworthiness by analyzing traditional credit data alongside alternative sources like payment history and social media activity, leading to more accurate risk assessments and lower default rates (Zagha, 2024; Johnson, 2023). For fraud detection, AI scrutinizes transaction data to identify anomalies and suspicious activities, enabling swift detection of fraudulent activities and minimizing false declines, thus enhancing security and customer experience (Dunlea, 2023). AI automates compliance checks, simplifies regulatory reporting, and also predicts potential non-compliance scenarios leading to improved operational efficiency and prevent violations by enabling proactive measures (Dunlea, 2023; Bevz, 2024).

Trading algorithms on investment strategies, portfolio management and market efficiency: Customers can make use of AI for understanding trading algorithms for making strategies for investments, managing and improving the portfolio performance. Traders are able to diversify their portfolio more effectively, optimize the portfolio performance and manage risk with advanced tools like dynamic stop loss mechanisms with the help of AI (Intrinio, 2023; Addy et al., 2024). AI algorithms predict market volatility in real time, adjust trading strategies promptly, and provide actionable insights based on historical data and market trends, leading to minimized losses and improved profitability (Addy et al., 2024). AI-driven algorithms also execute high-frequency trades with split-second precision, capitalizing on market inefficiencies and enhancing market efficiency (Dabaghia et al., 2024).

13.5.4 Advancing Financial Inclusion

Marginalized and underserved communities can have access to credit and banking services with the use of AI technologies. Through the use of credit scoring models, AI can enhance financial inclusion for individuals with limited credit histories to access loans by making use of social media and other alternative sources (Mhlanga, 2020). Using AI-powered digital identity verification technologies like biometric authentication, individuals are able to have access to financial services without the traditional identification documents. Individuals can make informed financial decisions through the assistance of AI-driven chatbots and virtual assistants, which provide them with personalized financial guidance and education, thereby empowering them to make informed financial decisions and improve their financial literacy (Fazal et al., 2022).

13.5.5 Risks Associated with AI in Fintech

The swift adoption of AI in Fintech has highlighted the need to balance the opportunities and risks associated with these innovations. Though AI can streamline operations, refine decision-making processes, and provide personalized services, it presents challenges like data privacy, algorithmic biases, and regulatory compliance adherence. Even though AI has significant impact, the adoption of AI is often met with doubt due to financial, legal, security, and operational barriers. Ryu (2018) identified these barriers as potential barriers to embracing Fintech. The risks associated with AI in Fintech are explained below.

Data security and privacy: With the advancement of AI, new threats such as audio and video impersonation, personalized phishing, interfering AI-controlled systems, extensive blackmail, and data manipulation have emerged. Personalized phishing can exploit data from social media data to enhance disruption success rates. Hackers could also disrupt banks' AI-powered security measures, increasing vulnerability to blackmail (Akinbowale et al., 2020; Kaloudi & Li, 2020).

AI is vulnerable to cybercriminals who can manipulate systems or introduce fraudulent information into data sets, leading to more sophisticated and complex attacks. Ethical hacking poses significant risks to the banking and financial industries, as individuals may be persuaded to reveal sensitive information and access credentials. The development of AI has been marred by unethical behavior, including privacy infringements, biased outcomes, and decision-making that cannot be challenged (Ranjan et al., 2020; Almutairi & Nobanee, 2020; Soni, 2020).

Algorithmic bias: AI in the finance industry can perpetuate discrimination by creating bias in pricing and service quality standards due to pre-existing prejudices embedded in data. Data biases, including inaccurate and incomplete information, can exacerbate financial exclusion and reduce confidence in the technology, especially among disadvantaged groups or minority groups. Customers' digital footprints, which serve as indicators for income, personal character, and social reputation, can be influenced by algorithmic bias, which arises from inadequately trained data or improperly designed models. This can result in protected groups receiving disparate impacts due to the prediction system copying structural bias embedded in the data (Li et al., 2021; Nunn, 2020; Selbst, 2017; Brevini & Pasquale, 2020).

Over-reliance on AI: AI has the potential to significantly impact human welfare, as it can replicate, exceed, or augment human abilities with high autonomy and efficiency. However, it may lack understanding of human ethics, morality, and common sense, potentially causing harm and distress. AI is often trained on data from human conduct, potentially perpetuating biased behavior. It can shape perceptions and priorities in decision-making but can also be misleading. The opacity of AI algorithms can lead to users making wrong decisions. AI's dual nature brings insidious risks, such as enhancing capability but introducing risk, stress, or administrative workload. AI tools may benefit people but may also exhibit bias, worsen disparities, disrupt employment, and deskill workers (Han et al., 2022; Araujo et al., 2020; Okamura & Yamada, 2020; Ghassemi et al., 2021; Ernst et al., 2019).

Regulatory compliance challenges: The integration of big data and advanced algorithms in Fintech has exposed informational voids and regulatory oversights. Research by Jagtiani and Lemieux (2019) and Yadav and Brummer (2019) suggest various regulatory approaches to mitigate risks, including informal advisories, exemption letters, experimental regulatory environments, and exploratory programs. However, the ambiguous use of alternative data in credit risk assessment is a significant concern for the Fintech sector. Zetzsche et al. (2017b) advocated for a dynamic regulatory framework that progresses through stages, starting with a testing environment, advancing to a regulatory sandbox, conditional licensing, and full license, aiming to foster innovation while ensuring consumer protection and market integrity.

Operational risks: Potential failures also called as operational risks may arise due to inadequate internal processes, personnel, or systems. Operational risks can be of seven types, namely risks arising due to fraud, employment practices, client satisfaction, product issues, physical asset damage, and business process disruptions. These risks can deter customer adoption of Fintech services. These risks can be reduced with the help of the auditors. Prioritizing and organizing risks based on impact and urgency ensures timely response. Risk management teams must be proficient in financial data analysis and use both qualitative and quantitative methodologies to evaluate risks.

13.6 CONCLUSION

This chapter explores the transformative potential of AI and Fintech, exploring how they reshape the financial landscape. By providing valuable insights, improved customer experiences, and modernized operations, AI and Fintech pave the way for a more inclusive financial system, empowering deprived communities and boosting economic growth. However, moving ahead with this transformative journey necessitates meticulous risk mitigation strategies. Data security vulnerabilities, algorithmic bias, regulatory hurdles, and operational setbacks require careful consideration.

This chapter suggests a few recommendations for financial institutions to address the various challenges.

1. **Prioritizing algorithmic transparency and accountability:** Financial institutions should explain how algorithms arrive at decisions to build trust in AI-powered judgments. Customers must be allowed to challenge these decisions for fairness and accuracy.
2. **Strengthening cybersecurity defenses:** Sensitive financial data should be protected from breaches and cyberattacks, by adequate investment in cutting-edge cybersecurity measures.
3. **Embracing regulatory collaboration:** Financial institutions should collaborate with regulatory bodies, to develop and adhere to robust regulations governing AI adoption in finance.
4. **Promoting financial inclusion with AI:** Financial products should be designed using AI to cater to the needs of underserved communities, ensuring equitable access to credit and other financial services.
5. **Upskilling the workforce:** Staff should be continuously trained with the necessary skills so as to work effectively with AI technologies promoting a human-AI partnership that optimizes operational efficiency and decision-making.
6. **Driving innovation through R&D:** Resources should be allocated for continuous research and development in AI ensuring financial services remain efficient, customer-centric, and adaptable within the dynamic digital landscape.

Financial institutions should leverage the innovative possibilities of AI and Fintech to establish a more secure, equitable, and prosperous financial environment for all by implementing these ideas into practice and cultivating a culture of responsible AI adoption. This chapter primarily focuses on the positive contribution of AI in Fintech, overlooking the potential downsides and societal impacts. It offers general solutions without probing into the complexities of algorithmic bias and regulatory changes. A balanced analysis with real-world examples, ethical considerations and targeted solutions could provide a more insightful understanding. Future research should investigate deeper into the ethical considerations surrounding AI in Fintech, particularly regarding the transparency of algorithmic decision-making and potential biases within algorithms and their influence on loan approvals, investment strategies, and insurance premiums can be explored in detail.

REFERENCES

Accenture. Top 10 trends for 2022, setting course beyond the watershed, 2022. https://www.accenture.com/content/dam/accenture/final/industry/banking/document/Accenture-Banking-Top-10-Trends-2022.pdf

Addy, W. A., Ajayi-Nifiṣe, A. O., Bello, B. G., Tula, S. T., Odeyemi, O., &Falaiye, T. Algorithmic Trading and AI: A Review of Strategies and Market Impact. *World Journal of Advanced Engineering Technology and Sciences*, 11(01), 258–267, 2024. https://doi.org/10.30574/wjaets.2024.11.1.0054

Akinbowale, O. E., Klingelhöfer, H. E., & Zerihun, M. F. Analysis of cyber-crime effects on the banking sector using the balanced score card: A survey of literature, *Journal of Financial Crime*, 27(3), 945–958, 2020. https://doi.org/10.1108/JFC-03-2020-0037

Albashrawi, M. Detecting financial fraud using data mining techniques: A decade review from 2004 to 2015. *Journal of Data Science*, 14, 553–570, 2021. https://doi.org/10.6339/JDS.201607_14(3).0010

Almutairi, M., & Nobanee, H. Artificial intelligence in financial industry, 2020. https://papers.ssrn.com/sol3/papers.cfm?abstract_id=3578238

Araujo, T., Helberger, N., Kruikemeier, S., & De Vreese, C. H. In AI we trust? Perceptions about automated decision-making by artificial intelligence. *AI & Society*, 35(3), 611–623, 2020.https://doi.org/10.1007/s00146-019-00931-w

Ashta, A., & Herrmann, H. Artificial intelligence and fintech: An overview of opportunities and risks for banking, investments, and microfinance. *Strategic Change*, 30, 211–222, 2021. https://doi.org/10.1002/jsc.2404

Bazarbash, M. *Fintech in financial inclusion: machine learning applications in assessing credit risk.* International Monetary Fund, 2019. https://www.imf.org/en/Publications/WP/Issues/2019/05/17/FinTech-in-Financial-Inclusion-Machine-Learning-Applications-in-Assessing-Credit-Risk-46883

Bevz, R. The role of AI and ML in transforming credit risk management in banking. *Avenga Magazine*, 2024. https://rauva.com/blog/role-ai-data-driven-decision-making

Boukherouaa, E. B., AlAjmi, K., Deodoro, J., Farias, A., & Ravikumar, R. Powering the digital economy: Opportunities and risks of artificial intelligence in finance. (IMF Departmental Paper No. 2021/024). International Monetary Fund, 2021. https://www.imf.org/en/Publications/Departmental-Papers-Policy-Papers/Issues/2021/10/21/Powering-the-Digital-Economy-Opportunities-and-Risks-of-Artificial-Intelligence-in-Finance-494717

Brevini, B., & Pasquale, F. Revisiting the Black Box Society by rethinking the political economy of big data. *Big Data & Society*, 7(2), 2020. https://doi.org/10.1177/2053951720935146

Broby, D. Financial technology and the future of banking. *Financial Innovation*, 7(1), 47, 2021. https://jfin-swufe.springeropen.com/articles/10.1186/s40854-021-00264-y

Chui, M., Manyika, J., &Miremadi, M. Where machines could replace humans-and where they can't (yet). *The McKinsey Quarterly*, 1–12, 2016. https://www.mckinsey.com/capabilities/mckinsey-digital/our-insights/where-machines-could-replace-humans-and-where-they-cant-yet

Coleman, B., Merkley, K., & Pacelli, J. Human versus machine: A comparison of robo-analyst and traditional research analyst investment recommendations. *The Accounting Review*, 97(5), 221–244, 2022. https://papers.ssrn.com/sol3/papers.cfm?abstract_id=3514879

Dabaghia, M. N., Alhorani, A., Al-Qaruty, T. M. R., Darwazeh, R. N., & Areiqat, A. Y. Revolutionizing finance: How FinTech, RegTech, and AI are redefining the financial landscape. *Kurdish Studies*, 12(2), 540–546, 2024. https://doi.org/10.58262/ks.v12i2.042

Dang, T. T., & Vu, H. Q. Fintech in microfinance: A new direction for microfinance institutions in Vietnam. *Asian Journal of Business Environment*, 10(3), 13–22, 2020. https://db.koreascholar.com/Article/Detail/396801

Daud, S. N. M., Khalid, A., & Azman-Saini, W. N. W. FinTech and financial stability: Threat or opportunity? *Finance Research Letters*, 47, 102667, 2022. https://doi.org/10.1016/j.frl.2021.102667

Demir, A., Pesqué-Cela, V., Altunbas, Y., &Murinde, V. Fintech, financial inclusion and income inequality: A quantile regression approach. *The European Journal of Finance*, 28(1), 86–107, 2022. https://doi.org/10.1080/1351847X.2020.1772335

Dunlea, J. AI & machine learning for regulatory compliance. *Akkio*, 2023. https://www.akkio.com/post/compliance-artificial-intelligence

Ernst, E., Merola, R., & Samaan, D. Economics of artificial intelligence: Implications for the future of work. *IZA Journal of Labor Policy*, 9(1), 2019. https://doi.org/10.2478/izajolp-2019-0004

Fazal, A., Ahmed, A., Abbas, S., &Inairat, M. How artificial intelligence is promoting financial inclusion? A study on barriers of financial inclusion. *Paper presented at the 2022 International Conference on Business Analytics for Technology and Security (ICBATS)*, Dubai, UAE, 2022. https://doi.org/10.1109/ICBATS54253.2022.9759038

Feyen, E., Frost, J., Gambacorta, L., Natarajan, H., & Saal, M. Fintech and the digital transformation of financial services: Implications for market structure and public policy, *BIS Papers*, Monetary and Economic Department, 2021. https://www.bis.org/publ/bppdf/bispap117.pdf

Feyen, E., Harish, N., & Matthew, S. *Fintech and the Future of Finance: Market and Policy Implications*. Washington, DC: World Bank, 2023. https://doi.org/10.1596/978-1-4648-1914-8. License: Creative Commons Attribution CC BY 3.0 IGO.

Fintech as a Service Market, Vision Research Report 2022. https://www.visionresearchreports.com/fintech-as-a-service-market/39655

FM Contributors. The Use of Chatbots and Virtual Assistants in Financial Services. Finance Magnates, 2023. https://www.financemagnates.com/institutional-forex/technology/the-use-of-chatbots-and-virtual-assistants-in-financial-services/

Ghassemi, M., Oakden-Rayner, L., & Beam, A. L. The false hope of current approaches to explainable artificial intelligence in health care. *The Lancet Digital Health*, 3(11), e745–e750, 2021. https://doi.org/10.1016/S2589-7500(21)00208-9

Giglio, F. Fintech: A literature review. *European Research Studies Journal*, 24(2B), 600–627, 2021. https://doi.org/10.5539/ibr.v15n1p80

Global Generative AI in Fintech Market, Market Research News Publication. 2024. https://www.linkedin.com/pulse/generative-ai-fintech-market-size-share-6ok5f/

Goncalves, A. R., Meira, A. B., Shuqair, S., & Pinto, D. C. Artificial intelligence (AI) in fintech decisions: The role of congruity and rejection sensitivity. *International Journal of Bank Marketing*, 2023. https://doi.org/10.1108/IJBM-07-2022-0295

Gran, B. How banking virtual assistants can improve your banking experience. *ForbesAdvisor*, 2022. https://www.forbes.com/advisor/banking/banking-virtual-assistants/

Gutierrez, F. H., Levin, S. C., Chambers, M. A., et al. FinCEN proposes AML requirements for registered investment advisers. *Banking and Financial Services Policy Report*, 34, 15–18, 2015. https://www.fincen.gov/news/news-releases/fincen-proposes-aml-regulations-investment-advisers

Han, S., Kelly, E., Nikou, S., & Svee, E.-O. Aligning artificial intelligence with human values: Reflections from a phenomenological perspective. *AI & Society*, 37(4), 1383–1395, 2022. https://doi.org/10.1007/s00146-021-01247-4

Intrinio. AI in the stock market: Uses, trends, and impact, 2023. https://intrinio.com/blog/ai-in-the-stock-market-uses-trends-and-impact

Jagtiani, J., & Lemieux, C. The roles of alternative data and machine learning in fintech lending: Evidence from the Lending Club consumer platform. *Financial Management*, 48(4), 1009–1029, 2019. https://doi.org/10.1111/fima.12295

Johnson, B. AI in credit risk management for large enterprises: What it is, how it works, challenges, and solutions. *High Radius Magazine*, 2023. https://www.highradius.com/resources/Blog/ai-in-credit-risk-management/

Kaloudi, N., & Li, J. The AI-based cyber threat landscape: A survey. *ACM Computing Surveys (CSUR)*, 53(1), 1–34, 2020. https://doi.org/10.1145/3372823

Li, Y., Yi, J., Chen, H., & Peng, D. Theory and application of artificial intelligence in financial industry. *Data Science in Finance and Economics*, 1(2), 96–116, 2021. https://doi.org/10.3934/DSFE.2021006

Mashrur, A., Luo, W., Zaidi, N. A., & Kelly, A. R. Machine learning for financial risk management: A survey. *IEEE Access*, 8, 203203–203223, 2020. https://ieeexplore.ieee.org/stamp/stamp.jsp?arnumber=9249416

Mhlanga, D. Industry 4.0 in finance: The impact of artificial intelligence (AI) on digital financial inclusion. *International Journal of Financial Studies*, 8(3), 45, 2020. https://doi.org/10.3390/ijfs8030045

Millar, C. C. J. M., Groth, O., & Mahon, J. F. Management innovation in a VUCA world: Challenges and recommendations. *California Management Review*, 61(1), 5–14, 2018. https://research.utwente.nl/en/publications/management-innovation-in-a-vuca-world-challenges-and-recommendati

Nichkasova, Y., & Shmarlouskaya, H. Financial technologies as a driving force for business model transformation in the banking sector. *International Journal of Business and Globalisation*, 25(4), 419–447, 2020. https://www.inderscienceonline.com/doi/abs/10.1504/IJBG.2020.109120

Nunn, R. Discrimination in the age of algorithms. In W. Barfield (Ed.), *The Cambridge Handbook of the Law of Algorithms*, pp. 182, 2020. https://assets.cambridge.org/97811084/81960/frontmatter/9781108481960_frontmatter.pdf

Okamura, K., & Yamada, S. Adaptive trust calibration for human-AI collaboration. *PLOS One*, 15(2), e0229132, 2020. https://doi.org/10.1371/journal.pone.0229132

Pires, J. The role of AI in data-driven decision making. Rauva, 2024. https://rauva.com/blog/role-ai-data-driven-decision-making

Prabhakaran, V. Chatbots and virtual assistants in banking, 2023. https://www.linkedin.com/pulse/chatbots-virtual-assistants-banking-prabakaran-v/

Rabbani, M. R., Bashar, A., Atif, M., Jreisat, A., Zulfikar, Z., & Naseem, Y. Text mining and visual analytics in research: Exploring the innovative tools. In *2021 International Conference on Decision Aid Sciences and Application (DASA)* (pp. 1087–1091). IEEE, Sakheer, Kingdom of Bahrain, 2021. https://doi.org/10.1109/DASA53625.2021.9682360

Ranjan, S., Gupta, D. R., & Gupta, D. A. Artificial intelligence in financial acumen: Challenges and opportunities. *Cosmos Journal of Engineering & Technology*, 10(1), 1–5, 2020. https://www.cosmosjournal.in/wp-content/uploads/2020/08/CET-JJ206-Shiv-Ranjan.pdf

Razzaque, A., Cummings, R. T., Karolak, M., & Hamdan, A. The propensity to use FinTech: Input from bankers in the Kingdom of Bahrain. *Journal of Information and Knowledge Management*, 19(1), 2040025, 2020. https://doi.org/10.1142/S0219649220400250

Ryu, H.-S. What makes users willing or hesitant to use Fintech?-The moderating effect of user type. *Industrial Management and Data Systems*, 118(3), 541–569, 2018. https://www.emerald.com/insight/content/doi/10.1108/IMDS-07-2017-0325/full/html

Selbst, A. D. Disparate impact in big data policing. *Georgia Law Review*, 52, 109, 2017. https://papers.ssrn.com/sol3/papers.cfm?abstract_id=2819182

Siau, K. L., Nah F. F. H., Qian, Y., & Eschenbrenner, B., & Chen, L. Artificial intelligence in financial technology, 2022. https://scholars.cityu.edu.hk/en/publications/artificial-intelligence-in-financial-technology(ba357101-3e8b-4312-9d39-7571177e4231).html

Soni, V. D. Role of artificial intelligence in combating cyber threats in banking. *International Engineering Journal for Research & Development*, 4(1), 7, 2020. https://doi.org/10.17605/OSF.IO/JYPGX

Villar, A. S., & Khan, N. Robotic process automation in banking industry: A case study on Deutsche Bank. *Journal of Banking and Financial Technology*, 5(1), 71–86, 2021. https://doi.org/10.1007/s42786-021-00030-9

Wang D. Traditional financial institutions are ready to move. Is it more advantageous to set foot in intelligent investment advisory. *China's Strategic Emerging Industries*, 70–72, 2017. http://www.pbc.gov.cn/english/130739/3661511/3662543/3682281/2018121016480125835.pdf

Yadav, Y., & Brummer, C. Fintech and the innovation trilemma, 2019. https://scholarship.law.vanderbilt.edu/faculty-publications/1084/

Zagha, N. S. Artificial intelligence real use cases for credit scoring in banks and fintech firms, 2024. https://www.linkedin.com/pulse/artificial-intelligence-real-use-cases-credit-scoring-nasser-sami-ee6be/

Zhang, Y., & Lu, Y. Study on artificial intelligence: The state of the art and future prospects. *Journal of Industrial Information Integration*, 23, 100224, 2021. https://doi.org/10.1016/j.jii.2021.100224

Zetzsche, D. A., Buckley, R. P., Arner, D. W., & Barberis, J. N. From FinTech to TechFin: The regulatory challenges of data-driven finance. *NYU Journal of Law & Business*, 14, 393–446, 2017. https://papers.ssrn.com/sol3/papers.cfm?abstract_id=2959925

Zetzsche, D. A., Buckley, R. P., Barberis, J. N., & Arner, D. W. Regulating a revolution: From regulatory sandboxes to smart regulation. *Fordham Journal of Corporate & Financial Law*, 23, 31, 2017b. https://papers.ssrn.com/sol3/papers.cfm?abstract_id=3018534

14 Multifaceted Role of Artificial Intelligence and Its Applications in Redefining the Landscape of Financial Services

Aashka Thakkar

14.1 OVERVIEW OF ARTIFICIAL INTELLIGENCE

It would be hard to visualise existence without mobile phones or internet access. They are now essential components of our way of life and have additionally significantly disrupted almost all sectors. The revolution in technology is changing how clients access financial services and products, and the financial services (FS) business is certainly not an exemption. While there has been some contemporary shift in the industry, what is significant is the ongoing influx of driven-by-technology applications into almost every financial segment. Fintech is a catchphrase for a trend that has emerged at the nexus of tech and finance that is drastically altering the existing status quo in the sector and speeding up development. Nowadays, the term "AI" refers to an extensive array of technological innovations which reinforce countless of the products and offerings we use on a daily basis, ranging from virtual assistants which provide real-time assistance to customers. The use of artificial intelligence (AI) involves the concept as well as practice of setting up AI-powered machines that can carry out operations like speech recognition and identification of patterns that hitherto are essential to the expertise of humans. Processing of natural languages, predictive modelling, advanced machine learning (ML), and other innovations are all included under the broader concept of AI. AI is quickly becoming an enormous phenomenon that is changing organisations, industries, and our standard of life. Businesses will end up in a more advantageous position to innovate, stand out, and reach higher productivity standards if they establish excellent data and AI underpinning. Businesses understand that data and AI are the engines for business innovation, but they also understand that more work has to be done to |||realise the entire potential of these technologies. Since the year 2024 has approached, the tech sector stands ready for breakthroughs as the amount we depend on technology-enabled

 DOI: 10.1201/9781003645849-14

machines to complete everyday operations grows. Approximately 13 AI companies have been absorbed by behemoths comprised of Apple, Google, Amazon, and other tech giants Microsoft, and Meta. Within the software advancement of the business world, it represents a significant movement in the realm of technology. It highlights the wide-ranging effects of cutting-edge technology, thus the possible impact of AI when combined with current digital methods is expected to cause a major upheaval in the world's economy.

The proposed CompTIA IT Industry Outlook 2024 survey states:

- The implementation of AI into an extensive spectrum of technological innovations and commercial operations is being actively pursued by 22% of companies.
- Thirty-three percent of businesses are employing AI in only a handful of instances.
- Forty-five percent of organisations are nevertheless within the planning phase stage.

Despite the various hyperbole waves surrounding the field of AI, especially detractors appear to agree that ChatGPT's emergence represents a sea change. When the introduction of generative AI became crucial, advances in imaging algorithms led the way; this time around, the use of NLP is leading the way. In addition to language used by humans, AI has the ability to comprehend and amalgamate numerous information kinds such as pictures, recordings, software programmes, and even complex structure information from molecules. The uses of AI are expanding daily. However, as the excitement surrounding the application of AI technologies for business purposes grows, discussions about accountable AI and AI morals become vitally relevant. The ability for organisations to regulate their operations effectively, communicate with their clients in real time and safeguard uninterrupted operations continues to expand with the development of the power of AI. Businesses are continually coming up with innovative concepts and approaches for expanding as developments in technology occur. The worldwide intelligence (AI) industry is expected to develop with an average CAGR of 37.3% between 2023 and the year 2030, according to Grand Review Research. By 2030, it is anticipated to have surpassed $1,811.8 billion. As per the PwC, sizing the price of AI has immense opportunities for boosting worldwide economies. By the year 2030, AI has been estimated to have a more significant global economic impact in comparison to both China and India together. Around 2030, AI will have the potential to contribute $15.7 trillion to the entire global economy—more double the total gross domestic product (GDP) of both India and China today.

The Forbes Advisor poll indicates that companies are utilising AI solutions for a variety of purposes:

- Fifty-six percent of businesses are utilising AI to boost productivity and optimise their day-to-day operations.
- Fifty-one percent are resorting to AI for assistance in combating fraud and cybercrime.
- Virtual personal advisors are used by 47% of organisations as AI tools.

- Regarding managing client relationships, 46% of businesses use ML.
- In order to handle inventory, 40% of business enterprises make use of AI.
- Thirty-five percent of companies have employed AI while creating the content.
- Concerning recommendations regarding products, 33% leverage AI.
- Thirty percent of companies utilise artificial intelligent technology in conjunction improve managing their supply chains and finance.
- Twenty-six percent embrace algorithmic intelligence in order to identify skilled labour and fill positions of power.
- AI is being employed by 24% to differentiate between target markets.

14.2 AI AND FINTECH

AI in the Financial Services Industry or Fintech is an acronym used to denote the implementation of AI algorithms in the finance industry. Fintech's use of AI has revolutionised the industry by bringing cutting-edge technologies that improve making choices, expedite procedures, and offer customers individualised solutions. There are many different applications in the financial sector that arise from the combination of Fintech and AI. Understandings regarding predictive analytics, evaluation of efficiency, budgeting, real-time computing tasks, customer support, automated information discovery, and numerous other domains have been driven by the use of AI in financial services. Financial institutions can use the aforementioned set of innovations to gather information from virtual excursions, analyse markets and clients more accurately, and connect with clients in an interface which replicates human cognitive abilities and interactions on an extensive basis. AI is an emerging innovation having applications across numerous sectors, including financial services. Financial Services is able to benefit through employing computational intelligence more substantially than its counterpart economies since the innovation's primary advantage is its versatility to handle an enormous quantity of information gathered. Several companies involved in financial planning, financial services, and coverage are currently using AI. The broad spectrum of software that uses AI in multiple activities related to finance. Virtual assistants powered by AI, for instance, can help banks and other financial institutions interact with the people they serve. Trading using algorithms has been made feasible by algorithmic methods for ML, which are also useful for customer relationship management, identification of fraudulent activity, and managing risks. The total size of the globe's sector devoted to the use of AI was approximately $136.55 billion for the year 2022, and this number is projected to grow swiftly in the times ahead owing to increasing interest in AI innovations, technological disruption, plus enhanced competitiveness amid the rapidly expanding world's economy. AI-driven innovations are being used by businesses today to help them stay up with the rapid pace of development. A study conducted in 2021 by Savanta and Oracle titled "Money and Machines" found that 85% of corporate executives desire the use of AI to assist them.

These are three typical applications of computational intelligence that businesses are using. Firstly, businesses have simplified repetitive tasks, like those for payment procedures, by leveraging AI's ability to provide intelligent segmentation and authentication. In order to prevent fraudulent activities, consolidate the accounts, and effectively speed up permissions, enterprise resource planning (ERP) platforms featuring embedded AI capabilities are now able to proactively identify tangible receipts, recognise the essential data (such as supplier name, as well as items acquired, and the corresponding cost), and upload it into their ERP platforms. Banking interactions are further secured by AI-enhanced biometric identification and authorisation. Technologies for automatic speech recognition, fingerprint scanning, as well as identification of faces are becoming more and more widely used for the verification of identity. Risk Mitigation driven by AI customised suggestions for policies, and the handling of claims are just a few of the advances that are transforming the insurance sector. Faster reimbursements for claims and better risk management are the results of this. One factor contributing to the rise of decentralised finance is AI. Conventional banking services are being reinvented by decentralised financial services like borrowing, lending, and trading made possible by intelligent agreements and fuelled by AI algorithms.

14.3 THE ROLE OF AI IN DISRUPTING THE FINANCIAL SERVICES LANDSCAPE

Throughout the middle of the 1990s, the banking and finance sector endured a significant transformation. The financial services industry has been substantially impacted by technological developments, and owing to e-commerce banks and mobile phone banking, it is now more digital than ever. These days, the primary points of differentiation in any business are speed and ease of use. The majority of employees hail from the millennial generation including Gen Z, who has grown accustomed to getting all the details they need as well as making decisions with only one swipe on the displays of their handheld gadgets. Experts estimate that by 2030, AI will have saved financial institutions roughly $1 trillion. The investigation found that over 35% of banks are already utilising AI to improve recommendation engines, reduce response times, and carry out predictive analytics and speech recognition. Organisations are always learning how to employ AI for their unique needs, and new application areas are always emerging.

Using AI to enhance the customer experience is one of the most important innovation trends. Certain customer-focused solutions, like as chatbots, are becoming commonplace. Simultaneously, algorithmic analytics, task mechanisation, and process automation are becoming increasingly common in the banking industry as companies recognise the advantages these technologies provide. Numerous uses of algorithmic learning are currently demonstrating its immense potential and the world of finance is not an exception. The ability to collect, interpret, and organize massive volumes of data is one of the primary benefits of algorithmic learning in the financial sector. ML-based technologies demand minimal or no assistance from individuals. They have the ability to interact with information pertaining to the prospective by using numerous adoption rates, acquire knowledge through historical data, and identify correlations in it. The aforementioned models are also used in certain instances to forecast outcomes.

The terms ML and robotics have the greatest prevalence while discussing the topic of AI. The AI segments are really helpful and may yield incredible outcomes rapidly, allowing visitors to assess the benefits of the latest innovations and its potential for return on investment. The AI's incredible processing power for processing enormous data streams as well as producing insightful analysis via identification of patterns has been extensively demonstrated in the BFSI area. The payment processing and financial service industry, which has been rife with fraudulent transactions and faux pas schemes, has benefited immensely from AI. The payment industry has advanced significantly from trade to paper currency to plastic currency finally towards contactless payment The widespread modern point-of-sale of now will seem antiquated as AI marks the beginning in the next phase of seamless and transparent interactions. Fantastic instances are Amazon's initiatives to eliminate the retail point of checkout backlog. The financial services industry will be undergoing a transformation owing to blockchain technology and digital currency, as well as the years to come, we might expect to see additional advancements in this area. This could involve the emergence of fresh blockchain applications, the production of creative digital assets, and the expansion of existing digital currencies platforms.AI and neural network systems are additionally implemented by Fintech organisations, and they have a possibility to increase the precision as well as effectiveness of the banking industry. More advancements in this field are anticipated, such as the application of AI to streamline procedures and improve the precision of forecasts. Along with bringing emerging rivals, financial technology has improved the standard of financial products and services and lowered costs in the financial industry as a whole. Customers have benefited the most from this since they now possess more choices and alternatives where they pertain concerning handling their finances. A greater number of individuals can now access financial products and services thanks to Fintech, especially in under banked individuals or underprivileged places. Customers now find it simpler to handle their personal finances and make significant financial choices as a result of this.

The BFSI sector has benefited enormously using AI as follows:

- Keeping running expenses to the lowest possible level
- Strengthening customer service
- Boosting risk mitigation
- The automation of routine tasks
- Accelerating your pace of operation
- Increasing the precision and effectiveness of processing data

According to one report by Business Insider, AI could potentially save the financial services industry almost $1 trillion by 2030 and $447 billion by 2023.

14.4 AI AND ITS IMPLEMENTATION IN INDIA

Given that AI solely helps with automated processes, error minimisation, and the management of repetitive operations, the requirement for based on AI instruments and platforms is growing throughout India due to the swift digital transformation of nearly every major economic sector, including finances and banking, medicine, automobiles, and wireless technology. Let's begin by examining a few significant forecasts that indicate India will lead the world in AI in the next years. AI boasts the power for boosting India's GDP by $957 billion by 2035 as well as increase the nation's rate of growth by around 1.3%. Additionally, this revolutionary innovation is ideally positioned to tackle issues like accessibility and cost of high-quality healthcare, education, and transport solutions. However, there are a number of major bumps in the road that have the potential to impede the widespread acceptance of AI products in India, so the sailing is not exactly pleasant. Certain of these significant concerns have been brought to light by the Data Privacy and Security Council of India (DSCI) via a recently published document. A synopsis of the obstacles that are preventing the broad acceptance of solutions fuelled by AI in India may be found online.

The NASSCOM and the software giant Microsoft collaborated to set up the AI incorporation Index for India, which was decided that is designed to assist organisations in understanding and taking advantage of AI's maximum potential and propel enormous scale technological advancement and digital evolution. The measure was created in response to the growing adoption of AI in organisations due to their rapid digital transformation. Additionally, the index will aid businesses in assessing where they stand on the AI competency curve, which is identifying any deficiencies, and developing stronger competencies and remedies. The index, which was created with assistance from the EXL team and Capgemini, evaluates the adoption of AI throughout the nation across the following four key industries: banking and financial services, CPG and Retail, Health Services, and Manufacturing and Automobile. According to the Index results, there are currently four levels in the advancement of AI development: explorer, enthusiastic, specialist, and propagator. The maturity rating is awarded for every industry in accordance with accomplishments in six areas: ability monetary investments, AI a plan of action data and technological preparedness, innovation, ethical behaviour and corporate governance.

Of all four sectors, manufacturing and automobile received the highest ranking (2.52) out of the four industry categories, next to CPG and Retail (2.52), the banking and financial services (2.42), and Medicine (2.35). At this point, the government and business organisations across the nation aspire to integrate AI into nearly every aspect of life including private businesses, government agencies and operations, and retail settings. It is astounding how computational intelligence has permeated practically every aspect of life; no one might have imagined that AI would be employed in particular areas of arrangement. At the moment, both the governmental and entrepreneurs across the nation aspire to integrate AI into nearly all spheres of life including the private sector's operations, public sector workflows, and retail settings. Despite the fact that the bulk of Indian start-ups in finance technology are barely a decade old, their expansion and advancement over the last several years have been phenomenal. There were over 2,100 financial technology firms operating in India as of December 2021. By the year 2025, the Indian financial technologies market is projected to be valued at USD 150 billion. In 2021, Fintech start-ups in India raised a total of USD 10.6 billion. India created 100 unicorn start-up companies in various industries as of 2022, with an overall value of more than USD 333 billion, 21 of those being Fintech start-ups. It is astounding how AI has permeated practically every aspect of life; no one might have imagined that AI would be employed in some particular arrangement. With a total market capitalisation of $31 billion, the Indian finance technology sector is one of the third biggest worldwide. An enormous shift is taking place; that is, holdings in mutual fund investments are expected to quadruple by 2025, while investments in banks are expected to exceed USD 28.5 trillion. To continue, India takes the lead in the world for promoting the use of financial technology. Paying attention to the increase in digitisation as the nation projects that online payments would account for USD 10 trillion, or approximately 65% of all financial operations, by 2026. The NPCI conceptualised the UPI gateway, a game-changing innovation that has completely revolutionised electronic payments. Over 6.58 billion monetary transactions have been made possible with UPI, which is responsible for 40% of all online transactions. Looking into it the banking and financial services investments in projects options in India for taking part in this banking revolution.

As per the survey of PwC regulators as well as government officials are the main drivers of financial technology expansion throughout India. They encompass the Jan Dhan, Aadhar, and Mobile devices. The JAM trio has promoted along with strengthened the inclusion of finances. The banking and finance industry in India was traditionally underrepresented due to its huge and youthful inhabitants.

14.5 AI SOLUTIONS TO THE BFSI SECTOR

According to the acronym signifies, Fintech is the amalgamation of financial technology and innovation. Undoubtedly, technological developments have consistently had an impact on the banking industry, thereby altering how it functions. Fintech kicked off with peer-to-peer financing, crowd financing, mobile payments, and transfer of funds, eventually expanded to include the application of blockchain technology, digital currency, and Robo-Financial planning. Leveraging new technologies, emerging companies are seeking to close the gaps throughout consumer engagement that established businesses have abandoned in most of these areas.

14.5.1 Financial Planning and Management

Creating an approach of integrating AI within investment strategies has grown increasingly significant for shareholders and portfolio managers because the technology emerges increasingly prevalent in the realm of finance. Investment professionals can create predictive models, analyse analytical and fundamental databases, and construct proposals for investments quicker and more efficiently in immediate form with AI. It transforms investing into an unsupervised procedure which demands less oversight, lowering expenses and increasing revenue at the same time. AI is additionally transforming investing in securities markets and handling investments. Algorithms equipped with AI are capable of analysing enormous amounts of data pertaining to markets, identifying patterns, as well as and making knowledge-driven financial conclusions. This makes it possible for dealers and asset managers to carry out transactions more successfully and accurately seize possibilities for investments. Additionally, instantaneous learning using market data allows AI systems to continuously improve along with adjusting their strategies.

AI is additionally transforming investing in securities markets and handling investments. Algorithms equipped with AI are capable of analysing enormous amounts of data pertaining to markets, identifying patterns, as well as and making knowledge-driven financial conclusions. This makes it possible for dealers as well as portfolio managers to carry out transactions more successfully and accurately seize possibilities for investments. Additionally, instantaneous learning using financial information allows AI systems to continuously improve their strategies.

14.5.2 Evaluation of Risk

The sheer amount of financial information that organisations handle mandates that the precision of the way that data gets handled also rises. Interestingly, the manipulative abilities and minds of humans cannot accomplish this matter. This creates a likelihood of the risk of fraud, as is currently destroying the majority of banking and insurance companies. According to a recent PwC investigation, approximately six fraudulent instances have been identified per organisation, and 47% of the businesses under investigation were victims of deception. A business needs to examine every transaction that occurs in massive data sets in order to identify every little risk. AI can help with this. Banking organisations have the ability to quickly sift across mounds of evidence and accurately identify irregularities with the use of AI audit tools.

14.5.3 Detection of Fraudulent Practices

Strong risk management and fraudulent detection techniques are critical for financial institutions due to the growing complexity of online criminal menaces they encounter. Strategies driven by AI are capable of analysing massive volumes of data, identifying trends, and spotting anomalies that can point to fraud. By automation of such procedures, AI reduces revenue losses and protects client data within banking organisations, enabling them to spot and avoid misconduct in real time. AI also strengthens algorithms for credit scoring and evaluating procedures, which enhances the handling of risks. Massive data sets are capable of being evaluated by algorithms that use ML, which can enable greater precision in financial standing determination. Banking organisations may now make better-informed lending choices swiftly, which reduces the likelihood of defaulting and improves their portfolio performance altogether.

Danske Bank, among the biggest financial services in Denmark, upgraded its fraudulent transaction detection capabilities by implementing an AI-powered system. The technique eliminated false alarms by 60% and improved identifying fraudulent activity effectiveness by 50%. One of the largest banking institutions in the entire world, J.P. Morgan Chase, has increased its fraudulent early detection rate by using in-house AI technologies that identify unauthorised operations. The business created a safety measure called "Early Attention," which uses AI to identify malicious software, computer viruses, and other sophisticated attacks that persist. The technology employs algorithms that utilise deep learning including big data in identifying harmful packages and fraudulent messages that target bank personnel in real time.

14.5.4 Credit Evaluation

Nevertheless, with AI risk scrutiny, these risks are neutralised. Numerous factors, such as credit card usage history, payment track record, amounts due, and duration of a borrower's credit history, are taken into account when evaluating creditworthiness. Even though AI makes it easier to swiftly sort through large amounts of data, it also has the power to greatly improve the procedure for assessing it. The creditworthiness of an individual can be assessed using AI credit evaluation using forecasted and historical data. In this manner, the historical-based credit barrier can be surmounted by new clients, attendees, and entrepreneurs who are starting businesses. Financial companies expect to gain from AI credit evaluation since it lowers risks and attracts more clients. Conversely, buyers grow better and have more impartial and superior exposure to financial services. In addition to lowering costs, the use of AI helps banks evaluate potential borrowers considerably more quickly and precisely. Solutions that use AI have the speed to evaluate a plethora of factors that could influence the financial institution's decision. AI employs more complex evaluation techniques than conventional methods to help banks determine if a potential applicant is extremely dangerous or just fails to possess a strong enough credit history. Technology driven by AI provides a greater level of neutrality. An important consideration, particularly in the development of financial apps, is that machines are not biased. Digital financial institutions and loan-issuing apps allow lenders to offer individualised options and include independent data—such as phone data—into the process of decision-making. The benefits of AI extend beyond banking to numerous other industries.

Metadata is a major tool used by banking and other organisations to determine a prospective client's trustworthiness. Statistics can provide information about revenue, financial standing, and other topics, but AI can identify clients with elevated risks and forecast which ones will default. For further assessment of the candidates' profiles of risk, this information might be subtracted. The following can result in less risk and possible financial losses while also greatly reducing the amount of time needed for the risk evaluation.

14.5.5 Minimise the Possibility of Mistakes

Financial institutions and other banking entities continue to interact through done by hand, individual-based, paperwork-intensive processes, even though they are primarily technological. These processes greatly raise operating costs and volatility because of the possibility of human error. These mistakes are frequently the main reasons for an invasion of security and the ensuing loss of income for the company. Improvements in AI can lower the potential for inaccuracy and the associated costs, from straightforward code violations to errors resulting from balancing an enormous amount of work.

14.5.6 Enhancing the Client Satisfaction

Embracing AI's capabilities in banking can be enjoyable, and once you start seeing how the innovation is revolutionising interpersonal relationships, you won't hesitate to make an investment in AI software applications. Strong and prompt interaction with clients is a requirement for any competitive organisation. Companies can accomplish a great deal with chatbots that operate as well as robots that are driven by AI. Chatbots, for instance, are capable of being configured to work around the clock, which enables them to handle client issues and questions from different regions of the world. They can additionally converse in a variety of languages and in human-looking forms, which proves advantageous when interacting with clients from different cultures. Finance professionals are able to leverage automated processes to a new degree with robotic assistants driven by AI. With the help of virtual assistants, users can streamline a variety of tasks, such as creating personalised notifications and utilising market data to guide the choices they make. Prominent powerful drivers along with participants in the AI breakthrough in the banking and financial services trend are chatbots powered by AI and robotic assistants. The aforementioned instruments have raised the bar for customised products and services, operations and promptly and appropriately responding to client inquiries.

Numerous solutions based on AI are being used by participants in the financial services sector today to improve the overall customer experience. Bank of America introduced Erica, an automated financial assistant, in 2018. After that, Erica has had over one billion conversations, a milestone that highlights the enormous future potential of chatbots that operate in financial services industries. Despite the effectiveness of chatbots which can have conversations with customers, interpersonal communication remains a valuable tool. When compared to AI-based chatbots to communicate some users or clients regard human interactions to be significantly more consistent and trustworthy. AI is an arbitrary term. Both the supporters and detractors of AI have reasonable points of view.

14.5.7 Prevention of Money Laundering

Prevention of money laundering, or AML, has gained importance in the battle towards growing financial crimes. AI has the power to completely transform AML by enhancing the capacity to identify and stop questionable activity. The term "real-data analysis, anomaly detection, and warning sign rising are all possible with AI tools. These algorithms may also continually acquire knowledge and assist in spotting risks that were previously undetected. Financial organisations can use AI to lower expenses and increase AML speed and accuracy while freeing up manpower for other vital tasks. J.P. Morgan Chase successfully upgraded its AML programme in 2021 by implementing an AI system. As a result, the company was able to increase the reliability of their AML operations and reduce errors in detection by 95%.

14.5.8 Algorithmic Trading

Over the past decade, there's seems to be a consistent increase in the prevalence towards products that are information-driven. A trillion dollars' worth of driven by data investments concluded two years ago. In what is known as "high-frequency signals trading," often referred to as statistical or algorithmic trading, the tools of ML as well as AI are used. The increasing popularity of this type of trade can be attributed to its many benefits. An enormous quantity of statistical information can be analysed far more quickly by AI-driven trading networks than by humans. They are compatible with organised and unstructured data. Because the processing of information happens quickly, choices and transactions happen quickly as well, giving investors more valuable information in the exact same amount of opportunity. The use of AI in banking goes much beyond its well-known uses in chatbots and other applications. A subtype of AI called algorithmic is essential in the trading industry. Large-scale datasets are processed by these algorithms to help with a range of financial tasks, such as risk management and finding profitable investment opportunities. Hedge portfolios, for example, use AI to obtain small advantages in quickly changing markets, demonstrating the technology's adaptability in deriving insightful information from intricate accounting records.

The art of algorithmic trading has also been transformed by AI algorithms, allowing for split-second choices in trading determined by feelings in media coverage and information from the markets. AI-powered solutions have enhanced the prevention of fraud and risk mitigation by assisting in the identification of odd trading trends and possible manipulations of the market. Also, AI has increased the accessibility of sophisticated investment methods for ordinary shareholders, creating greater chances for a broader spectrum of clients to profit from customised portfolios of investments. In addition to AI trading, investigation and information-driven choices are automated, freeing up investors' time to manage real-world transactions and provide client advice rather than conducting investigation. According to a poll, entrepreneurs who employed the use of algorithmic trading witnessed a 10% improvement in turnover. Furthermore, AI trading reduces the possibility of human error and increases the margin for efficiency by using prior financial information to guide judgements. An AI algorithm for trading could collect data from news sources and social media to identify market movements using sentiment modelling, a term that describes the process that involves gathering text and grammar and utilising language processing algorithms to discover patterns among subjectively content.

14.5.9 Moral Issues, Data Safety, and Privacy

The banking and finance sector is experiencing an upsurge in ML and AI, which brings with it numerous advantages as well as risks. It is important to exercise vigilance to avoid causing complications with enterprises, legislatures, or everybody when applying strategies to their financial advantage. Ensure that you comprehend the ideas of AI morality, data confidentiality, national security, and safeguarding individuals beforehand implementing artificial mental ability in finances or while implementing the use of ML applications for financial services. It is imperative that you make sure that all data security and protection regulations are met in order to adhere to the best practices of the AI-ML revolution in the BFSI sector. You don't want your financial company or organisation to be in a position where it is giving critical information or your clients to unreliable third parties or online hackers. In light of this, it's they will finish what follows by arguing that the AI-ML revolution in the BFSI sector has produced possibilities and made it possible to leverage contemporary technology in the banking industry for sustainable growth in a variety of ways.

14.5.10 Reduced Operating Cost

When it comes to multitasking, chatbots powered by AI are far more efficient than human operators. This efficiency improves the customer experience while reducing the operating expenses associated with managing a large number of operations and inquiries. Additionally, since increasingly client interactions are conducted online, the need for physical spaces like call centres or support centres are dwindling. Such tangible infrastructure reduction automatically results in lower property costs, usage, and operational expenses. Operations will be streamlined by enabling the automation of repetitive operations using RPA (Robotic Process Automation) and AI-driven programmes, which will enhance productivity and significantly reduce expenses.

14.5.11 Increased Accessibility in the Top Inclusion, as Well as a Global Reach

Chatbots using intelligence from computers are revolutionising the world of banking by removing obstacles related to languages and facilitating banking accessibility for all. The varied audience of clients is the rule rather than the case in today's increasingly globalised society. Chatbots powered by AI in banking and financial services address this obstacle by offering support in a variety of various dialects and languages. The capability to speak multiple languages represents more than simply a benefit; it makes accessible banking services possible. Such algorithms' capacity to adapt to various languages and make every customer feel valued and acknowledged, irrespective of language proficiency, is what's really amazing.

14.6 ADOPTION OF AI ON A GLOBAL LEVEL – THE FACTS

As per the report published by Statista Research Department in 2024 about Fintech worldwide, The American continent as a whole accounted for the greatest number of financial technology firms worldwide up to the start of 2024. In the Americas alone, there are over 13,100 financial technology companies—nearly over 1,500 in addition to the previous year. On the other hand, there were a total of 5,886 financial technology companies in the Asian Pacific continent and 10,969 in the European Middle East region. As it concerned a total of tech start-ups worldwide in 2023, the USA led the race with roughly five times the amount as the UK, who came second. At present, financial technology businesses' products and services are almost an integral component of daily life, because their number is growing every year. The majority of financial technology companies are based in China as well as the U.S., which together account for eight of the world's ten strongest Fintech businesses globally as of the beginning of the year 2024. The Irish payments processing gateway Stripe emerged and is the highest-valued financial unicorn globally in 2022, in spite of the dominant position of the US as well as China. Moreover, nearly 80% of financial organisations appreciate the probable advantages of AI, according to a recent Business Insider Information survey. According to the analysis, by 2023, applications involving AI could lead to reductions in expenses of up to $447 billion. In the field of banking solely for example, AI may decrease expenditures at the front desk through conversational financial services, the administrative office through effectively identifying fraudulent activity, and the operational desk through underwriting.

14.7 CONCLUSION

The banking sector is experiencing shifts as a result of the adoption of AI emerging more customer-centred, productive, and competitive. Numerous advantages are provided by driven by AI products, including increased productivity, better customer satisfaction, data-driven choice-making, and easier compliance with laws and regulations. Nevertheless, in order to guarantee that the implementation of AI is productive and beneficial for every party involved, the issues and worries concerning AI, which include security and confidentiality of data, moral implications, legislative and statutory implications, and workplace adaption, require being addressed. Because of its many potential uses, robotic intelligence is quickly becoming among the most significant advancements in the world of banking. AI is an excellent instrument for propelling BFSI organisations today, from enhancing protection to personalising the experience of clients. International AI use in the banking and financial services market is anticipated to grow at an average CAGR of 38% from 2019 and 2026, reaching around $2,47,367 million through the conclusion of the cycle, according to an analysis by Allied Market Researchers. A further investigation from Global Market Insights projects a 20% compound annual growth rate (CAGR) for AI in the banking and financial services global market between 2023 and 2032. It is expected to grow from $20 billion in 2022 to $100 billion by 2032.

BIBLIOGRAPHY

1. Akerkar, R., "Employing AI in business," in *Artificial Intelligence for Business*, R. Akerkar, Ed. Cham, Switzerland: Springer, 2019, pp. 63–74.
2. Anagnostopoulos, I. (2018). Fintech and regtech: Impact on regulators and banks. *Journal of Economics and Business*, *100*, 7–25.
3. Belanche, D., Casaló, L. V., & Flavián, C. (2019). Artificial intelligence in FinTech: Understanding robo-advisors adoption among customers. *Industrial Management & Data Systems*, *119*(7), 1411–1430.
4. Boot, A., Hoffmann, P., Laeven, L., & Ratnovski, L. (2021). Fintech: What's old, what's new? *Journal of Financial Stability*, *53*, 100836.
5. Caron, M. S. (2019). The transformative effect of AI on the banking industry. *Banking & Finance Law Review*, *34*(2), 169–214.
6. Daud, S. N. M., Khalid, A., & Azman-Saini, W. N. W. (2022). FinTech and financial stability: Threat or opportunity? *Finance Research Letters*, *47*, 102667.
7. Digalaki, E. (2022). The impact of artificial intelligence in the banking sector & how AI is being used in 2022. https://www.businessinsider.com/ai-in-banking-report?r=US&IR=T
8. Gomber, P., Kauffman, R. J., Parker, C., & Weber, B. W. (2018). On the fintech revolution: Interpreting the forces of innovation, disruption, and transformation in financial services. *Journal of Management Information Systems*, *35*(1), 220–265.
9. Jain, R. (2023). Role of artificial intelligence in banking and finance. *Journal of Management and Science*, *13*(3), 1–4. https://doi.org/10.26524/jms.13.27
10. Jindal, N. (2020). The impact of advertising and R&D on bankruptcy survival: A double-edged sword. *Journal of Marketing*, *84*(5), 22–40.

11. Kshetri, N. (2018). Blockchain's roles in meeting key supply chain management objectives. *International Journal of Production Economics, 193*, Blockchain and decentralized production management, Blockchain and decentralized production management, 75–85.
12. Li, Z., Li, X., & Xu, X. (2020). Artificial intelligence in the financial industry: A systematic literature review and future research directions. *Financial Innovation, 6*(1), 1–21. https://doi.org/10.1186/s40854-020-00183-4
13. Mishra, S., & Singh, A. K. (2020). Application of artificial intelligence in banking and finance: A review. *Journal of Applied Research in Finance and Economics*, 2(2), 87–100.
14. Narang, A., Vashisht, P. & Bhaskar, S. (2024). Artificial Intelligence in Banking and Finance. *International Journal of Innovative Research in Computer Science and Technology, 12,* 130–134. https://doi.org/10.55524/ijircst.2024.12.2.23
15. Natarajan, M., & Madhumitha, T. (2019). Impact of artificial intelligence on banking sector – An overview. *Journal of Applied Information Science and Technology, 12*(1), 45–51.
16. Prajapati, R., & Khatri, P. (2020). Role of artificial intelligence in banking sector: A systematic review. *Journal of Advanced Research in Dynamical and Control Systems, 12*(1), 109–120.
17. PricewaterhouseCoopers- Pw C. (2020). How mature is AI adoption in financial services? Retrieved May 15, 2021, from https://www.PwC.de/de/future-of-finance/how-mature-is-ai-adoption-in-financial-services.pdf.
18. Scholtus, M., Van Dijk, D., & Frijns, B. (2014). Speed, algorithmic trading, and market quality around macroeconomic news announcements. *Journal of Banking & Finance, 38*, 89–105.
19. Singh, A. (2018). Artificial intelligence in banking and finance. *Journal of Economics and Business, 1*(1), 13–18.
20. Tao, R., Su, C. W., Xiao, Y., Dai, K., & Khalid, F. (2021). Robo advisors, algorithmic trading and investment management: Wonders of fourth industrial revolution in financial markets. *Technological Forecasting and Social Change, 163*, 120421.
21. Wall, L. D. (2018). Some financial regulatory implications of artificial intelligence. *Journal of Economics and Business, 100*, 55–63.

15 Forecasting Financial Markets through AI

Exploring Machine Learning and Neural Network Models for Stock Price Prediction

Minakshi Rajput, Bharat Chaudhari, and Sharvari Tamane

15.1 INTRODUCTION

The stock market is an enormous cluster of markets and exchanges where the purchasing, auctioning, and delivery of shares of publicly held companies take place. It allows the companies to raise capital and investors to potentially earn a return on their investments by providing a trading platform. As the stock market is volatile in nature, people make investments based on future predictions. People find different methodologies and tools that maximize their profit by minimizing risks. One of the proven methods is multiple regression-based prediction of stock price [1]. The stock market helps in increasing the economic growth of a country. Profit in the stock market pushes an individual to spend more money on different products and services. This leads to an increase in manufacturing more products which helps in increased revenue [2]. Comparative analysis revealed a pool of 20 million investors in the Indian stock market of India, the world's third-biggest stock market [3]. Numerous researchers and data scientists are working on developing a model capable of accurately predicting stock market prices. If such a model could consistently provide precise predictions, its creator would become increasingly wealthy over time [3].

To address the problem of predicting a stock price due to the extremely volatile nature of the stock market, deep learning techniques such as long short term memory (LSTM) and pre-trained deep neural networks are implemented [4].

The ability of LSTM to store historical data over extended periods makes it ideal for predicting future stock prices, as stock prices are influenced by various historical factors [5].

Since stock prices are a time series attribute, predicting future prices requires considering past stock prices along with other relevant factors. Consequently, LSTM, a type of recurrent neural network (RNN), has proven successful in stock price prediction [6].

DOI: 10.1201/9781003645849-15

The RNN-based model was evaluated using data from the year 2018. To compare its performance, other linear regression algorithms, such as lasso regression, k-NN regression, and XGBoost, were also tested. The proposed algorithm demonstrated superior performance for stock price prediction, achieving a RMS error of 2.6% [7]. Support vector machines (SVMs) are more powerful as compared to Back Propagation for time series forecasting as it results in lower normalized mean square error (NMSE), MAE than BP [8].

The study employs an ensemble model comprising XGBoost, Random Forest, and LSTM for forecasting stock prices [9].

The LSTM neural network is utilized to predict Apple stock prices by using both single attribute and multiple input attributes, to assess the model's effectiveness in forecasting stock time series prediction [10]. This chapter examines the use of LSTM-based machine learning techniques and regression methods to predict stock values, considering factors such as close, high, open, volume, and low [11]. The study aims to determine the correlation between sentiments and stock values. It conducts a comparative analysis of three algorithms: multiple linear regression, SVM, and ANN. The stock price is estimated using sentiment analysis with the most effective prediction algorithm [12].

An integrated machine learning framework was proposed that combines information theory with ANN. This approach innovatively applies information entropy which enhances the ANN's time series modeling capability and is implemented for stock price forecast [13]. Various machine learning methods were compared for stock price prediction and evaluation was done based on MSE, RMSE, MAPE, and MAE [14]. ANNs, Neuro-Fuzzy Systems, TSLM, and RNN, along with their respective merits and demerits are studied for forecasting the stock market [15].

15.1.1 Performance Measure Used in Stock Price Prediction

Various evaluation metrics are used to evaluate the performance of stock price prediction frameworks. These are mean absolute error (MAE), mean square error (MSE), RMSE, F1 score, R-square, accuracy, recall, precision, AUC-ROC curves, Sharpe ratio, calibration curves, etc. [16].

15.2 RESEARCH METHODOLOGY

15.2.1 Data Collection

The main goal of this research is to predict upcoming stock prices by analyzing past data. To conduct the experiment, Nifty50 data for AXIS Bank spanning a decade from 2011 to 2021 is gathered from Kaggle. The dataset encompasses 15 features, including Turnover, Symbol, VWAP, Last, %Deliverable, Date, Open, Deliverable Volume, High, Volume, Prev.Close, Close, Series, Trades, Low. These features are explained below.

- **Date:** specifies trading date
- **Previous close:** The previous Close row refers to the close price of the previous day.

- **Open:** The Open row indicates the price at which a stock began trading when the market commenced on a given day.
- **High:** The High row represents the peak price at which a stock was traded during a specific timeframe.
- **Low:** The Low row shows the minimum price achieved during the same period.
- **Close:** The Close row denotes the closing price of a stock when the market closed.
- **Volume:** Volume is the total amount of trading activity during a period of time.
- **Trades:** The Close row refers to the number of trades executed during day.

Three distinct artificial intelligence approaches – machine learning, feedforward neural network, and RNNs (LSTM) – are chosen for experimentation. The stock price movement for AXIS BANK over the past 10 years is shown in Figure 15.1.

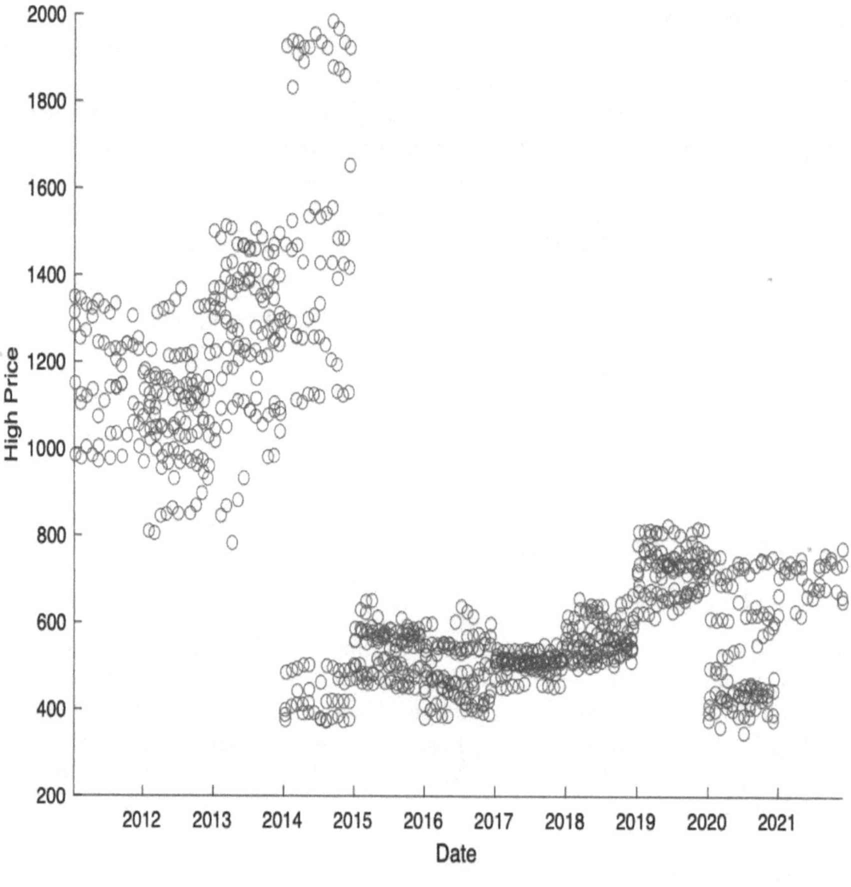

FIGURE 15.1 Stock price movement from year 2011 to 2021.

As observed in the graph, during the initial years of the period from 2011 to 2015, Axis Bank experienced notable growth as it expanded its operations and enhanced its market share. However, from 2016 to 2018, the bank faced increased volatility and encountered challenges. Factors such as concerns regarding asset quality, non-performing assets (NPAs), and regulatory changes may have influenced the stock price during this time. In the later period leading up to 2021, the bank displayed signs of recovery and stability (Figure 15.2).

All experimentations were carried out on the Mac Air Apple M2 8GB RAM Processor using R 4.3.3 programming and Matlab_R2020a.

15.2.2 Data Preprocessing and Data Visualization

The data is preprocessed for missing values. Axis Bank Dataset consists of approximately 2,456 with 400 records having missing values for attributes Trades, Deliverable Volume and %Deliverable. This missing data was imputed using the mean imputation method. The dataset contains no duplicate records. Insignificant attributes namely (Date, Symbol and Series) were excluded from the database, resulting in a final database size of 2,456 × 12. Following preprocessing, the data was divided into two sets: training and testing data sets using a 80:20 ratio. The objective was to predict the high price of the day's trading, with the High attribute serving as the response variable and the remaining 11 attributes as predictors. Six different regression models were trained on the training dataset, and the complete dataset could be visually explored to identify patterns, trends, and distributions, as observed in Figure 15.3.

Box plots provide an actual representation of the distribution of a continuous variable, making it easy to identify outliers based on their position relative to the rest of the data. Traditionally, points lying above the upper whisker are considered outliers, indicative of values significantly higher than expected, as illustrated in Figure 15.4. However, in this instance, these observations are not outliers but rather extreme values that hold validity within the context of the specific feature. Therefore, rather than excluding them, we have chosen to include these points in the dataset.

To visualize the correlation between any two completely different variables we plotted a scatter plot as shown in Figure 15.5. It shows there is a linear positive correlation between "High" and "previous close" as well as between the "Open" and "Previous Close" variables. There is no correlation between "Trades" and "High" as well as between "% deliverable" and "Deliverable volume".

As depicted in Table 15.1, the high price of the stock exhibits a positive correlation with attributes such as previous close, open, low, last, close, and VWAP. Conversely, there is an insignificant correlation between the high price and other attributes like volume, turnover, trades, deliverable volume, and % deliverable. As a result, we eliminated five insignificant variables that do not contribute to determining the stock's high price, namely volume, turnover, trades, deliverable volume, and % deliverable. Additionally, due to the multicollinearity of the dataset we removed the "Last" variable as both "last" and "close," one of them was discarded as both of them represent similar information. Thus, our final dataset comprises six variables, with "high" serving as the response variable and the remaining five as predictors.

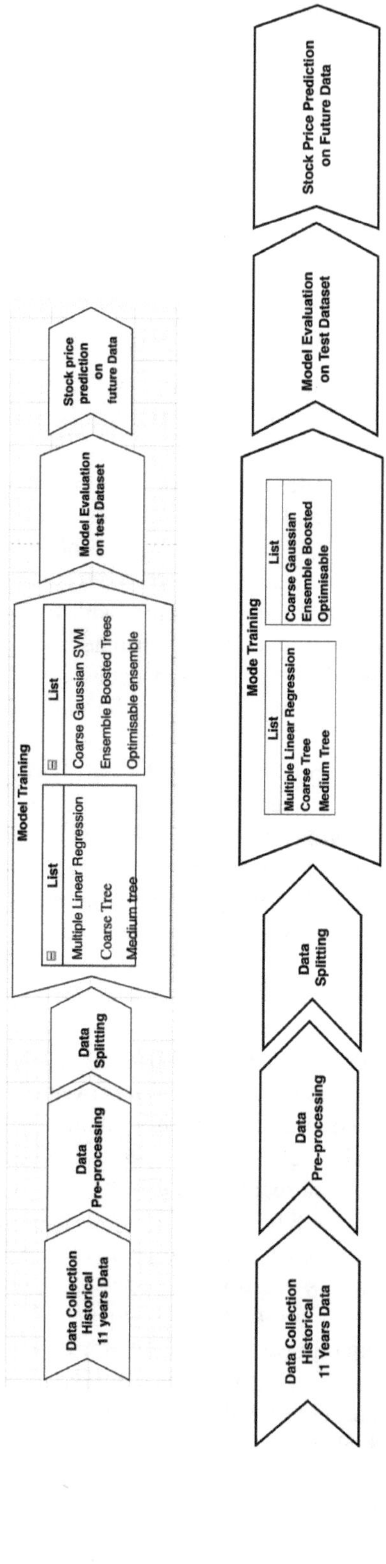

FIGURE 15.2 Machine learning approach for stock price prediction.

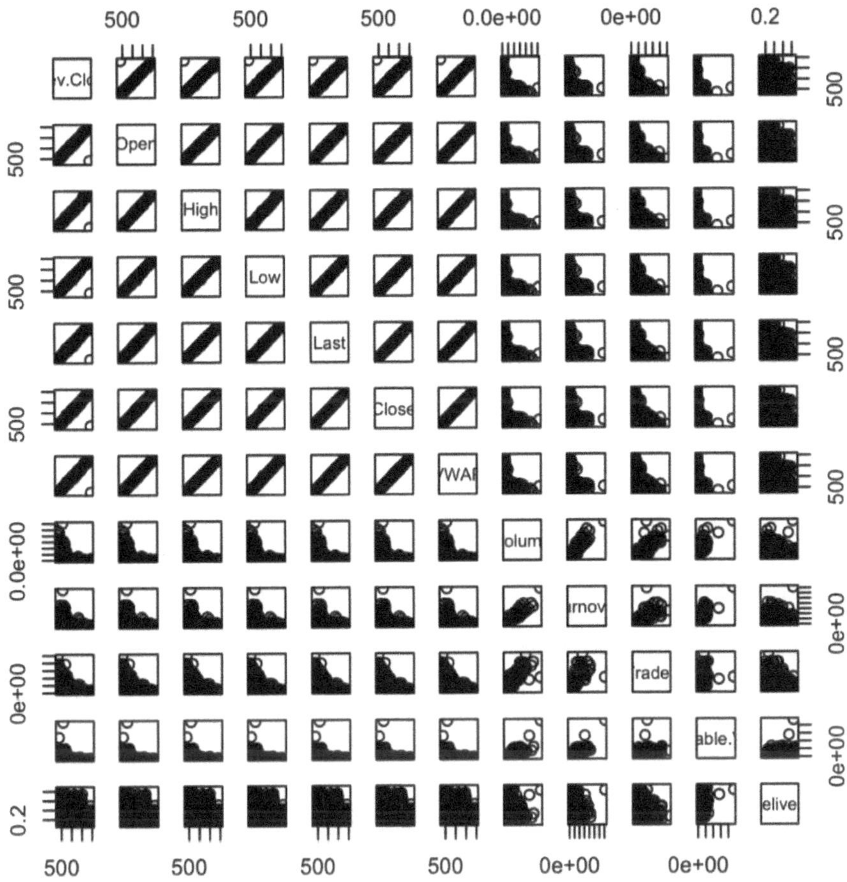

FIGURE 15.3 Data visualization in AXIS BANK dataset.

15.2.3 Approach 1: Machine Learning-based Stock Price Prediction

The dataset will be trained using six distinct machine learning regression techniques, such as SVMs, Gaussian regression models, regression trees and linear regression models, and ensembles of regression trees.

1. **Multi-linear regression model:** This model outlines how a response variable relates to predictor variables. In a linear regression model, linearity pertains to the linear nature of the coefficients for the predictors. The response variable that is a high value of the stock price is a linear combination of the remaining 11 predictor variables.
2. **Medium tree:** Medium Tree refers to a decision tree model of moderate size. A decision tree comprises nodes that symbolize the features, branches that signify the decisions, and leaf nodes that depict the outcome. The Minimum Leaf Size for this tree is set at 12.

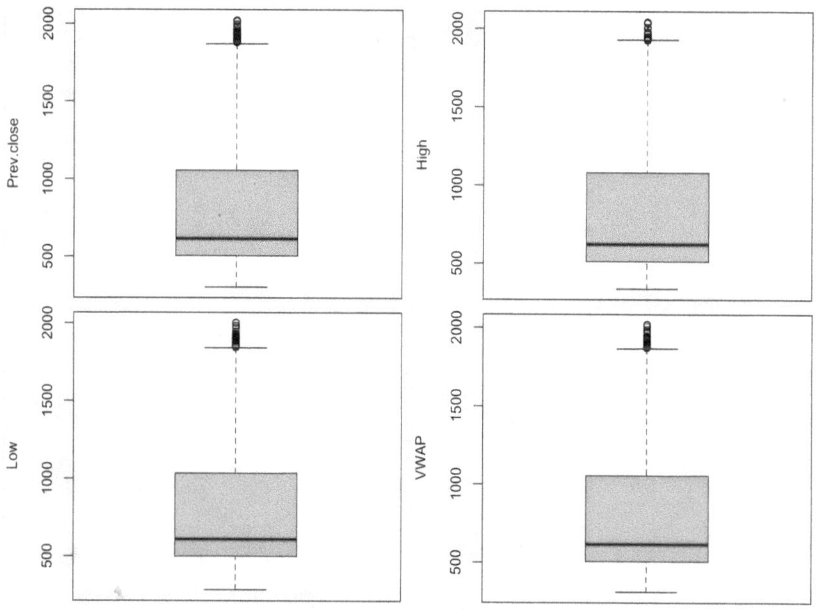

FIGURE 15.4 Box plots for outliers detection.

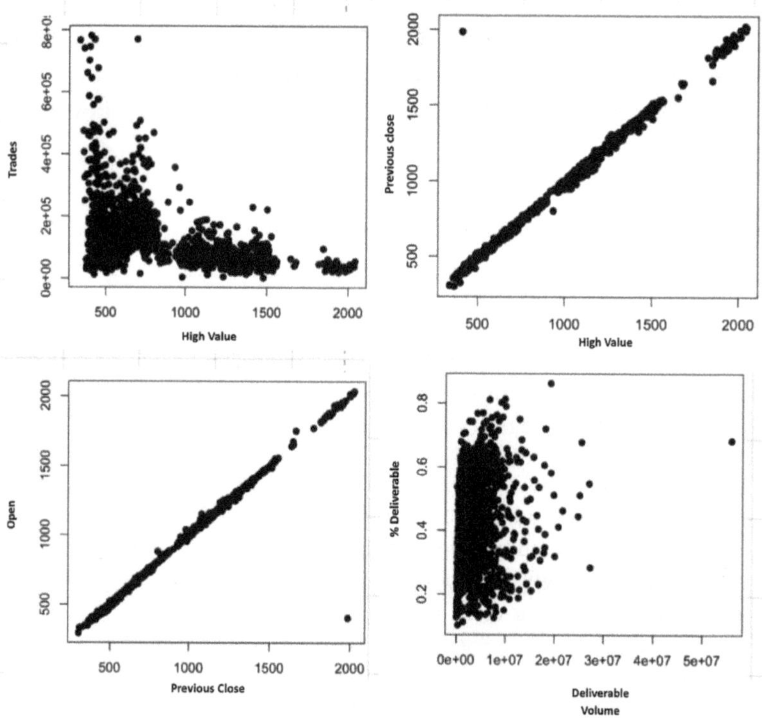

FIGURE 15.5 Scatter plots between different variables of AXIS dataset.

TABLE 15.1
Pearson's Correlation Values between Different Variables

	Prev.Close	Open	High	Low	Last	Close	VWAP	Volume	Turnover	Trades	Deliverable. Volume	X.Deliverble
Prev.Close	1.000	0.994	0.993	0.993	0.993	0.993	0.993	–0.442	–0.315	–0.36	–0.466	–0.15765
Open	0.994	1.000	0.999	0.999	0.998	0.998	0.999	–0.443	–0.314	–0.36	–0.467	–0.15794
High	0.993	0.999	1.000	0.999	0.999	0.999	0.999	–0.436	–0.306	–0.35	–0.462	–0.16310
Low	0.993	0.999	0.999	1.000	0.999	0.999	0.999	–0.447	–0.318	–0.36	–0.471	–0.15605
Last	0.993	0.998	0.999	0.999	1.000	0.999	0.999	–0.441	–0.311	–0.35	–0.466	–0.16089
Close	0.993	0.998	0.999	0.999	0.999	1.000	0.999	–0.441	–0.311	–0.36	–0.466	–0.16111
VWAP	0.993	0.999	0.999	0.999	0.999	0.999	1.000	–0.441	–0.312	–0.36	–0.466	–0.16062
Volume	–0.442	–0.443	–0.436	–0.447	–0.44	–0.441	–0.441	1.000	0.942	0.918	0.8438	–0.15345
Turnover	–0.315	–0.314	–0.306	–0.318	–0.311	–0.311	–0.312	0.942	1.000	0.906	0.8252	–0.13994
Trades	–0.362	–0.362	–0.353	–0.367	–0.35	–0.360	–0.360	0.918	0.906	1.000	0.7659	–0.12657
Deliverable. Volume	–0.466	–0.467	–0.462	–0.471	–0.46	–0.466	–0.466	0.843	0.825	0.765	1.0000	0.236951
X.Deliverble	–0.157	–0.157	–0.163	–0.156	–0.16	–0.161	–0.160	–0.153	–0.139	–0.12	0.2369	1.000000

3. **Coarse tree:** A Coarse Tree is a decision tree characterized by fewer branches and nodes, resulting in a simpler and less intricate structure compared to a more detailed or complex tree. Pruning, a technique employed to eliminate sections of the tree lacking substantial predictive power or generalization capability to unseen data, is utilized to create a coarser representation of the decision space. The Minimum Leaf Size for this tree is set at 36.
4. **Coarse Gaussian SVM:** SVR is a powerful technique for regression tasks, particularly when dealing with complex associations between features and target variables. It offers flexibility through the choice of kernel functions and robustness to outliers, making it suitable for a broad range of regression issues. Gaussian SVM implies the usage of a Gaussian kernel, commonly known as the radial basis function (RBF) kernel, is utilized in the SVM framework.
5. **Ensemble: (Boosted Trees):** Boosted Trees constructs a sequence of decision trees, where each subsequent tree aims to address and correct the mistakes made by the previous ones. Predictions from each tree are combined by weighted voting, where the impact of each tree on the final prediction is influenced by its learning rate and its performance on the training data. Hyperparameters setting: Minimum leaf size is set to 8, number of learners is 30, and learning rate is 0.1
6. **Optimizable ensemble:** Optimizable ensemble methods for regression problems are those that allow for efficient optimization of hyperparameters and parameters to achieve the best predictive performance. Hyperparameters such as learning rate, tree depth, number of trees, and regularization parameters can be optimized to improve performance. Ensemble methods used are Bag, LSBoost, Number of learners is set to 11, minimum leaf size is 18, Learning rate is 0.345, Number of predictors to sample are 4, Bayesian optimization method is used.

15.2.4 Approach 2: Two-Layer Feedforward Neural Network-based Prediction

A feed-forward network with two layers, incorporating sigmoid activation functions in the hidden layers and linear activation functions in the output layer (known as fitnet), is capable of approximating multi-dimensional mapping problems with high accuracy, provided it has sufficient neurons in the hidden layer and consistent data.

The network is trained with the backpropagation algorithm (Levenberg-Marquardt). Data is divided into training, validation, and testing sets. During the training phase, the network adjusts itself according to its error. In the validation phase, networks try to generalize. Once the network stops improving generalization, training automatically gets halted. After training the network, its effectiveness is measured by calculating the mean squared error (MSE). Further, the results are analyzed using visualization tools such as a regression fit or histogram of the errors. Out of total samples, 70% are used for training. The remaining 30% is divided 15% for validation and 15% for testing. Figure 15.6 shows the neural network architecture used for predicting future stock High price from six remaining attributes. Ten hidden neurons are set. Bayesian Regularization is used for training.

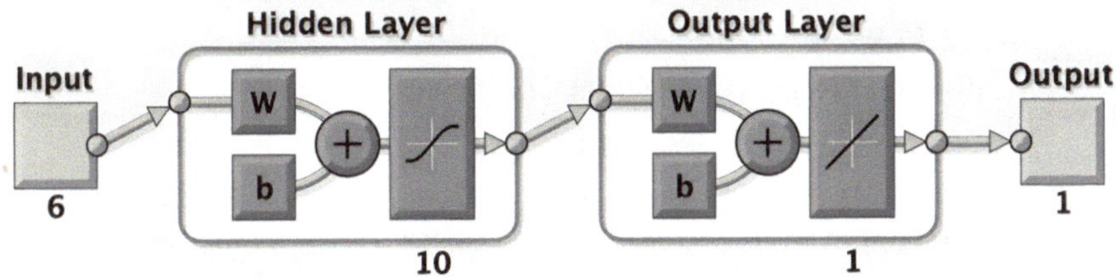

FIGURE 15.6 Feedforward neural network architecture for stock price prediction.

15.2.5 Approach 3: Time Series Neural Network-Based Prediction

Figure 15.7 shows the architecture for time series neural network. Stock price forecasting involves a type of dynamic analysis where historical data from one or more time series is utilized to estimate future values. We have predicted future Stock High Price y(t) by passing 'd=2' past value of high attribute series i.e. $(y-1)$, $(y-2)$¼$(y-d)$ and six remaining 'x' time series of attributes prev.close (x1), open (x2), low (x3), close (x4) and VWAP (x5). Volume (x6). Thus equation can be written as:

$$y(t) = f(y(t-1),\ldots, y(t-d), x(t-1),\ldots, (t-d) \qquad (15.1)$$

The total hidden layers are set to 10 and the number of delay 'd' as 2. The $d=2$ here specifies that the network will predict high stock prices for the next two days.

15.3 RESULTS AND EXPERIMENTAL ANALYSIS

We developed a Multi-Linear Regression model to forecast the Stock High Price based on six remaining significant variables. Model coefficients obtained are listed in Table 15.2.

In interpreting the results, the p-value of the F-statistic exceeds $2.2e^{-16}$, indicating high significance. This implies that at least one of the predictors is significantly associated with the stock's high Price. Notably, variables such as Low, Close, VWAP, and Volume exhibit significant correlations with Stock High Price. Conversely, the p-value for the t-statistics of Prev.close is less than $2.2e^{-16}$, indicating insignificance.

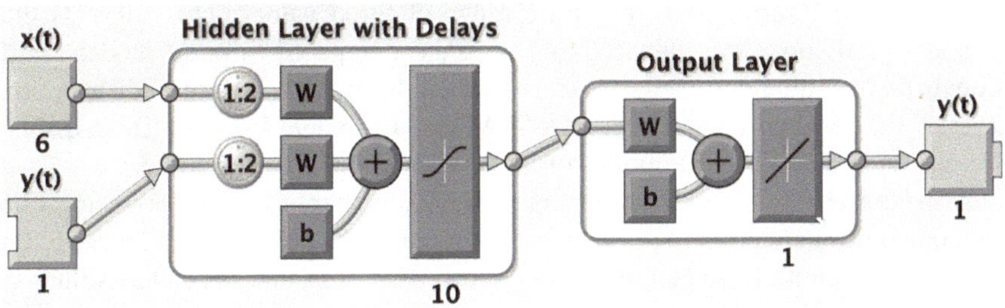

FIGURE 15.7 Neural network architecture used for stock price prediction.

TABLE 15.2
Multi-Linear Regression Model Coefficients

	Coefficients		
Intercept	**β0= −1. 193**	Low	**β3=−7.676E-01**
Prev. close (insignificant)	**5.283E-04**	Close	**β4=1.579E-01**
Open	**β1=3.506E-01**	VWAP	**β5=1.263**
Volume	**β2=6.622E-08**	***F* statistics:**	**2.605e+06**
Residual standard error:	**3.918**	***p*-value:**	**<2.2e-16**
***R*-squared adjusted:**	**0.9999**		

Thus, Prev.close is disregarded. The final multi-linear regression model equation is as follows:

$$\text{High} = -1.193 + 0.3506^{*}\ \text{Open} - 0.767^{*}\text{Low} + 0.157^{*}\text{Close} + 1.263^{*}\text{VWAP} + 6.62 \times 10 - 8^{*}\text{Volume}$$

In multi-linear regression, the R2 represents the correlation coefficient between the actual values and predicted values of the outcome variable (stock high price) Its value ranges from zero to one. We can say that with five predictor variables as listed in Eq. (15.1), the adjusted R2 = 0.99 which means that 99% of the variance in High Price can be predicted by all five predictor variables.

Figure shows the predicted vs. actual plot for all six machine learning models is shown in Figure 15.8. It is a graphical representation This involves evaluating the difference between the real values of the dependent variable and the values estimated by the regression model. The plot for linear regression is a perfect diagonal line where the actual High values match with the predicted High values exactly. It means that the model accurately captures the association between the predictors and response variables. For other plots the points slightly deviated from the diagonal line, indicating that the other model's predictions are not so perfect.

A residual plot in Figure 15.9 illustrates the residuals from a regression analysis, with the residuals plotted on the y-axis against the fitted values on the x-axis. In the residual plot for the multilinear regression model, the residuals exhibit random scattering around zero across the entire range of fitted values. This suggests that the model predictions are unbiased and accurate compared to other models, with residuals displaying a consistent variance and conforming to a normal distribution. However, the residual plots for Coarse SVM and Ensemble Boosted Trees display patterns that violate the assumptions of linear regression.

The response plots are shown in Figure 15.10. A response plot shows the estimated outcomes in relation to the sequence of records. As observed in Figure 15.10a, response plot for multi-linear regression shows that true and predicted values of response match maximum times, resulting in a better model.

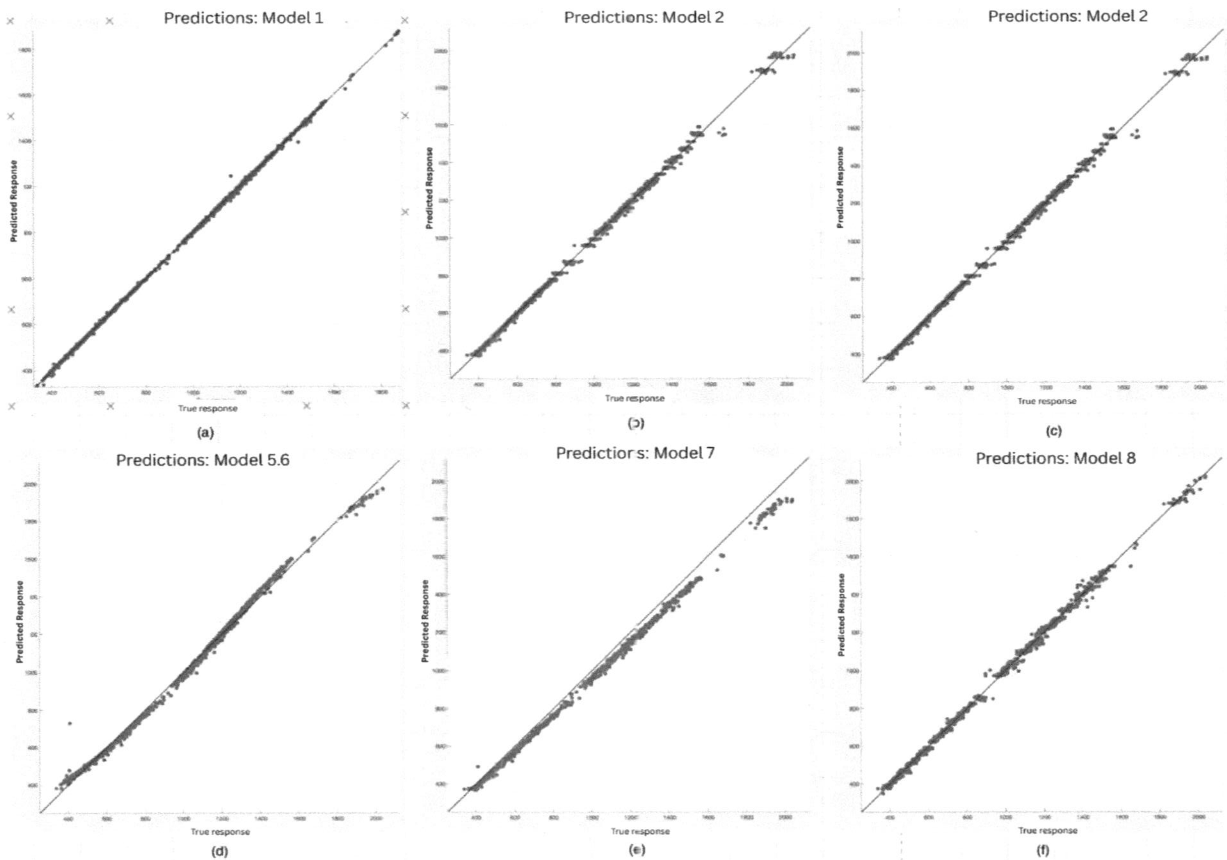

FIGURE 15.8 Predicted vs actual plot for regression models. (a) Multi-linear regression. (b) Medium tree. (c) Coarse tree. (d) Coarse Gaussian SVM. (e) Ensemble boosted trees. (f) Optimizable ensemble.

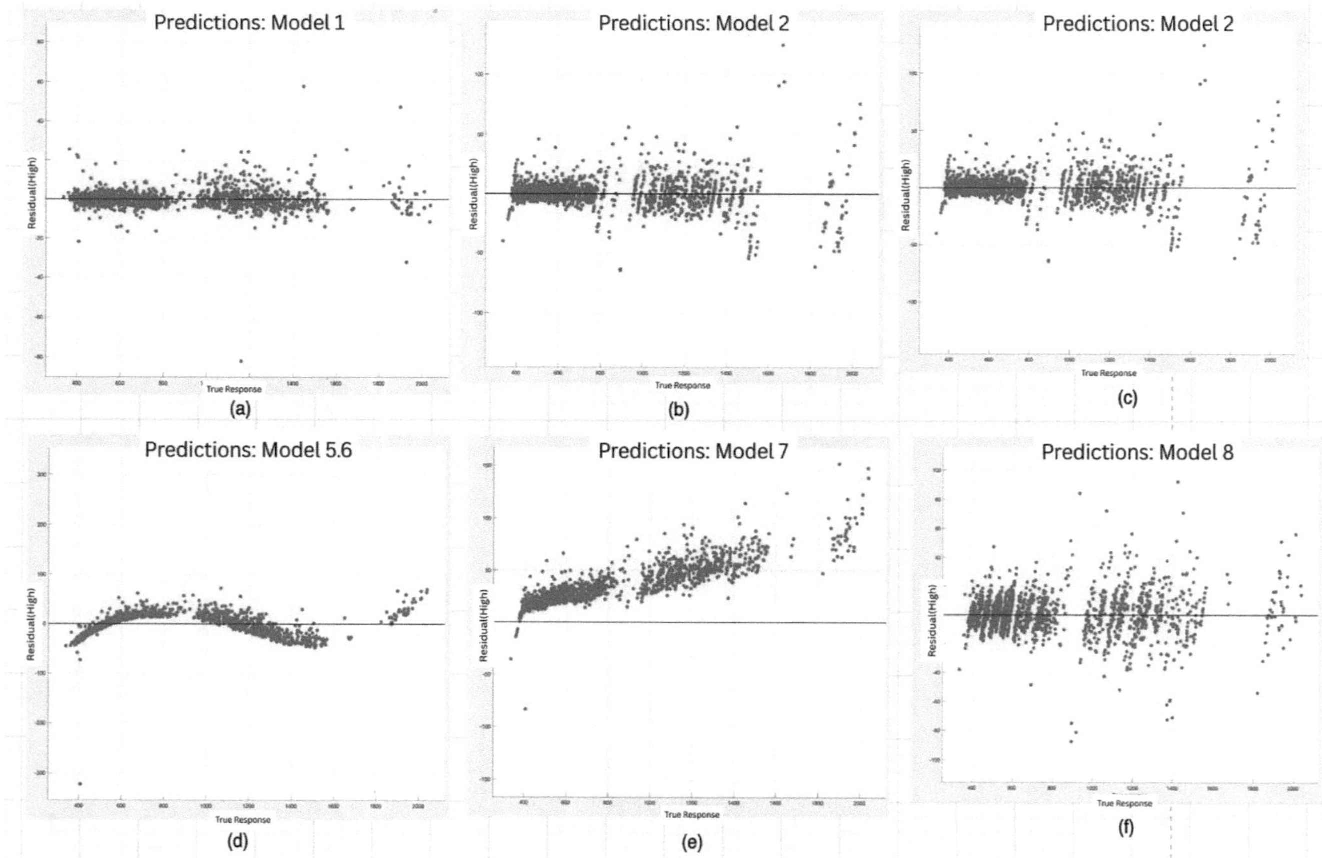

FIGURE 15.9 Residual plot. (a) Multi-linear regression. (b) Medium tree. (c) Coarse tree. (d) Coarse Gaussian SVM. (e) Ensemble boosted trees. (f) Optimizable ensemble.

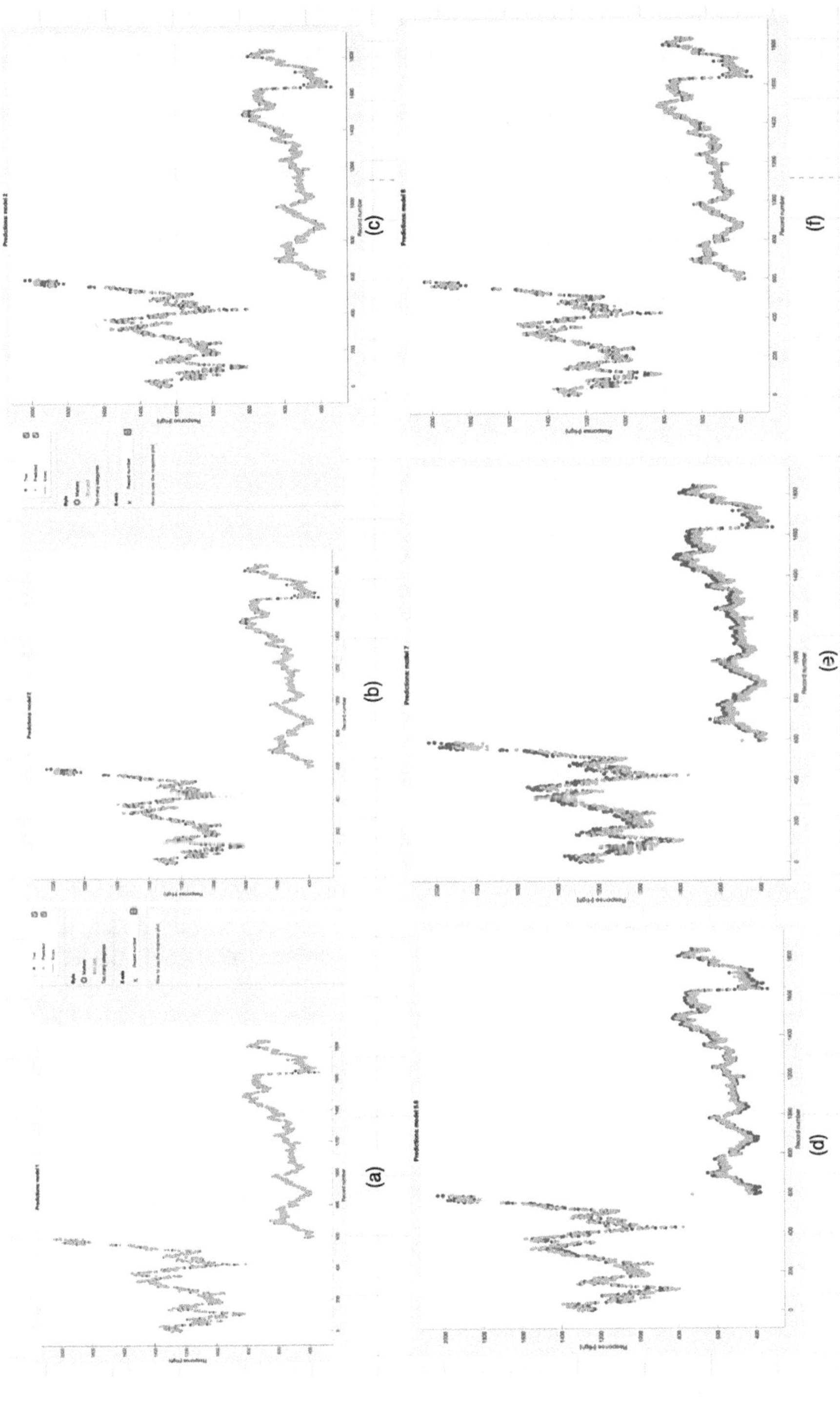

FIGURE 15.10 Response plot. (a) Multi-linear regression. (b) Medium tree. (c) Coarse tree. (d) Coarse Gaussian SVM. (e) Ensemble boosted trees. (f) Optimizable ensemble.

Table 15.3 lists the performance metrics of all implemented six regression models. One of the important metrics is MAE is a metric that measures the average absolute difference between the predicted values and the actual values of the dependent variable. MAE of 2.6 and 10 are obtained for training dataset and test dataset respectively for the multi-linear regression model. These values are comparatively better than MAE values obtained from the remaining five models.

Figure 15.11a shows the error histogram for trained feedforward neural networks. The x-axis typically represents the error values. The *y*-axis usually represents the frequency of each error value. The errors are centered around zero, which means that on an average neural network model is predicting the correct values. Figure 15.11b shows regression plots that display the neural network outputs with respect to targets for training, test sets and the whole dataset. In an ideal scenario, the data points should align along a 45-degree line, indicating that the network's predictions match the target values exactly. MSE quantifies the average of the squared deviations between predicted and actual values. Lower MSE values signify higher accuracy, while a value of zero denotes perfect accuracy with no errors. Regression R-values assess the strength of the correlation between the predicted and target values, where an R-value of 1 signifies a strong correlation and 0 indicates no correlation.

Figure 15.12 shows the performance of a time series neural network with the help of different plots. Figure 15.13a The plot illustrates the autocorrelation function of the errors, showing how prediction errors are correlated over time. As seen in the plot there is only one nonzero value of the autocorrelation function at zero lag, This value is the MSE. It means that The prediction errors were entirely independent of one another which is the feature of any perfect model. So we can say that the implemented time series neural net model has reached the requirements of a perfect model. Figure 15.13b shows input-error cross-correlation function which describes how the errors are related to the input sequences. For an ideal forecasting model, all of the correlations should be zero. In this case, the input is correlated with the error but the good thing is that all correlations are contained within the confidence interval centered around zero.

Figure 15.14a displays a histogram of the errors and illustrates how the differences between the target values and the predicted values are distributed after training a feedforward neural network. The bins on the chart align with the vertical bars, while the *y*-axis shows the quantity of samples from the dataset, which lies in a particular bin. From the plot, you can see that a bin represents the range of a particular error of 6.914 and for the training dataset, the height of that bin is approximately 1,280, while for the test dataset, it ranges between 1,300 and 1,500. It means that many samples have an error of approximately 6.914. Figure 15.14b shows the time series response. It shows the inputs, targets, and errors over time, highlighting which time points were chosen for training, testing, and validation.

Thus from experimental results, it is observed that multilinear regression and LSTM-based time series neural networks are the best suited models for the prediction of stock price.

Table 15.4 shows the results obtained for Neural Networks. Feedforward neural networks outperformed in predicting the highest price with MSE and MAE of 8.74 and 1.943 respectively.

TABLE 15.3
Performance Metrics for Machine Learning Approach

Model → Performance	LR		Coarse Gaussian SVM		Medium Tree		Coarse Tree		Ensemble Boosted Trees		Optimizable Ensemble	
Measures	Training	Test	Training	Test	Training	Test	Training	Test	Training	Test	Training	test
RMSE	4.7087	–	21.29	–	11.008	–	17.76	–	38.216	–	7.2522	–
R-Squared	1	–	1	–	1	–	1	–	1	–	1	–
MSE	22.855	1581.4	453.59	283.245	121.17	80.238	315.43	259.52	1,460	28.144	52.594	15.50
MAE	2.607	10.061	13.765	12.9261	6.17	4.99	10.137	9.4244	33.619	3.5079	4.2606	2.49
Training time	1 s 608 ms	–	84 ms	–	0.08776	–	0.073721	–	0.6744 s	–	54 s 310 ms	–

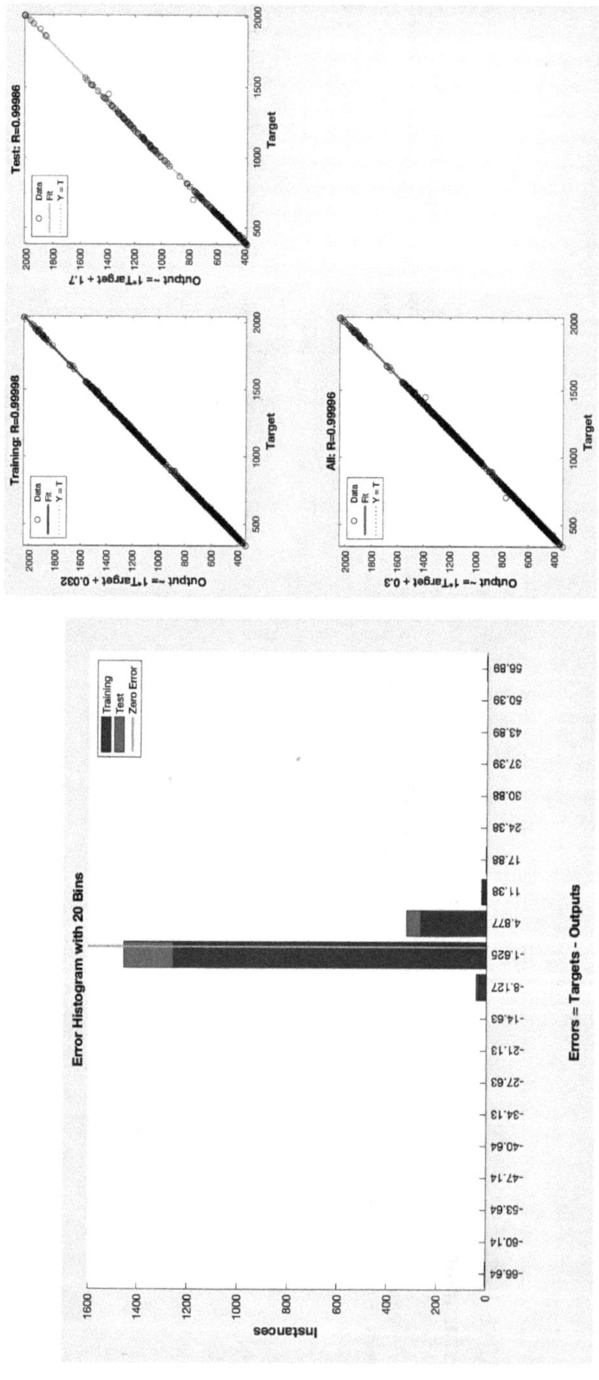

FIGURE 15.11 (a) Error histogram for trained neural network model. (b) Regression plot for feedforward two-layer network.

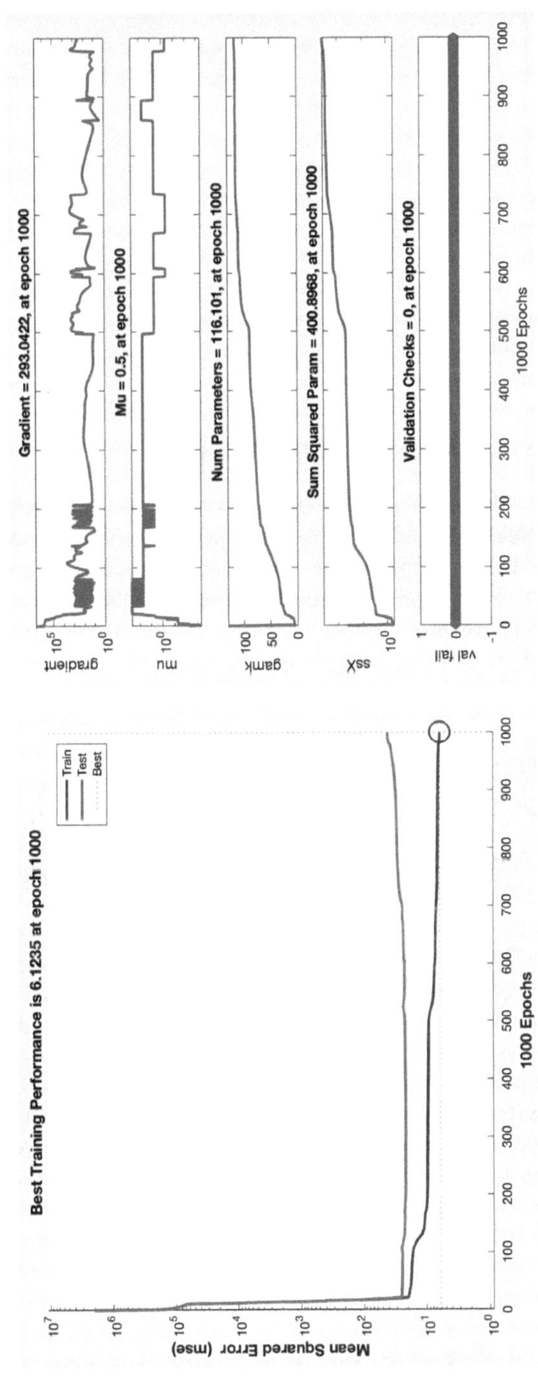

FIGURE 15.12 (a) Training performance of neural network. (b) Neural network training state at Epoch 1000.

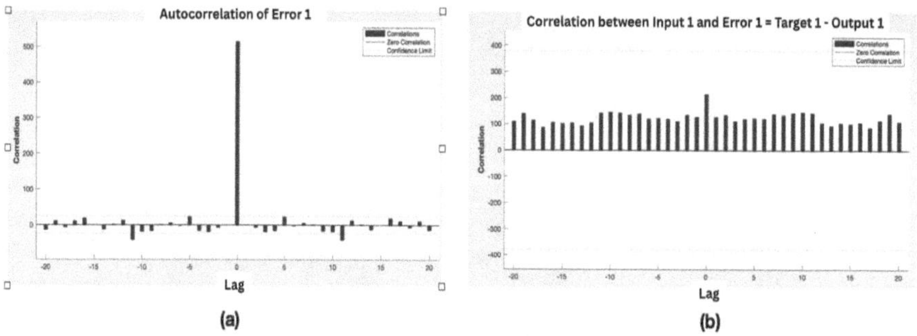

FIGURE 15.13 Error plots of time series neural network. (a) Error autocorrelation plot. (b) Input-error cross-correlation.

15.4 CONCLUSIONS AND FUTURE SCOPE

In conclusion, we can say that this study aimed to forecast future stock prices using historical data, specifically focusing on Axis Bank's Nifty50 data spanning from 2011 to 2021, collected from Kaggle. The dataset comprises 15 features, and three distinct artificial intelligence approaches: machine learning, feedforward neural network, and RNNs (LSTM) were employed for experimentation. Notably, the stock price movement for Axis Bank over the past decade displayed periods of significant growth, followed by volatility and challenges, and later signs of recovery and stability.

The experimentations were conducted using a Mac Air Apple M2 8GB RAM Processor with R 4.3.3 programming and Matlab_R2020a. Data preprocessing involved handling missing values and normalization, resulting in a final dataset of 2456x12 dimensions after excluding insignificant attributes. Six different regression models were trained on the dataset, and data visualization techniques provided insights into patterns and trends.

Furthermore, analyses revealed correlations between stock high prices and attributes such as previous close, open, low, last, close, and VWAP. Insignificant predictors were eliminated, and a multi-linear regression model was developed, showing high significance and accuracy in predicting stock high prices.

Among the implemented models, multi-linear regression and LSTM-based time series neural networks demonstrated superior performance in predicting stock prices. Overall, the findings underscore the effectiveness of these models in predicting stock prices using past data.

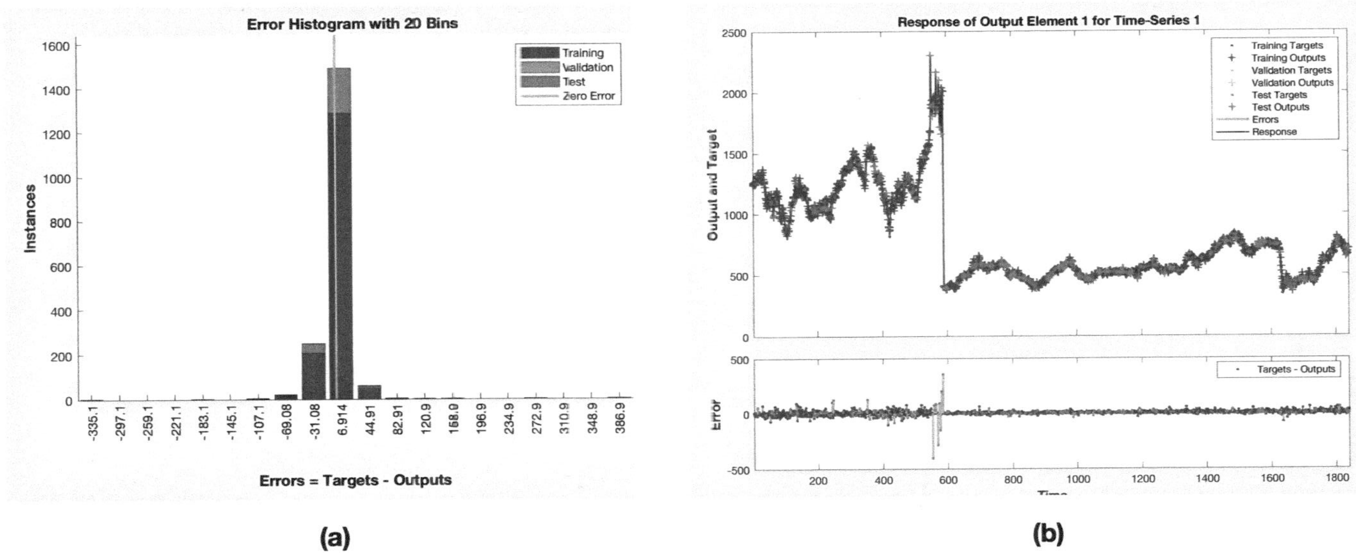

FIGURE 15.14 Training performance of time series neural network. (a) Error histogram. (b) Time series response.

TABLE 15.4
Results Obtained for Neural Networks

Evaluation Parameters	Feedforward Neural Network		Neural Network Time Series LSTM	
	Training	**Test**	**Training**	**Test**
R-Squared	0.9999	0.999	0.999	0.992
MSE	6.123	8.74	247.59	2027.33
MAE		1.943		11.8519

REFERENCES

1. A. Sharma, "Survey of Stock Market Prediction Using Machine Learning Approach," *International Conference on Electronics, Communication and Aerospace Technology ICECA 2017*, Coimbatore, India, 978-1-5090–5686-6/17.
2. https://www.investopedia.com/ask/answers/042215/how-does-performance-stock-market-affect-individual-businesses.asp#:~:text=The%20Stock%20Market%20and%20the%20Economy&text=Typically%2C%20the%20stock%20market%20and,gross%20domestic%20product%20(GDP)
3. R. Ray, P. Khandelwal and B. Baranidharan, "A Survey on Stock Market Prediction Using Artificial Intelligence Techniques," *2018 International Conference on Smart Systems and Inventive Technology (ICSSIT)*, Tirunelveli, India, 2018, pp. 594–598, https://doi.org/10.1109/ICSSIT.2018.8748680
4. Y. Guo, A thesis on "Stock Price Prediction Using Machine Learning," Södertörn University I School of Social Science Master, Economics Spring, 2022.
5. S. Hochreiter and J. Schmidhuber, "Long Short-Term Memory," *Neural Computation* 9(8): 1735–1780, 1997.
6. P. Raval, An article on "Stock Price Prediction Using Machine Learning with Source Code," 7 March 2024, https://www.projectpro.io/article/stock-price-prediction-using-machine-learning-project/571#mcetoc_1ftklmk3qe
7. A. K. Goel, R. Chakraborty, M. Agarwal, M. D. Ansari, S. K. Gupta and D. Garg, "Profit or Loss: A Long Short Term Memory Based Model for the Prediction of Share Price of DLF Group in India," *2019 IEEE 9th International Conference on Advanced Computing (IACC)*, Tiruchirappalli, India, 2019, pp. 120–124, https://doi.org/10.1109/IACC48062.2019.8971601
8. K.-j. Kim, "Financial Time Series Forecasting Using Support Vector Machines," *Neurocomputing* 55(1–2): 307–319, 2003, ISSN 0925–2312
9. G. Sonkavde, D. S. Dharrao, A. M. Bongale, S. T. Deokate, D. Doreswamy and S. K. Bhat, "Forecasting Stock Market Prices Using Machine Learning and Deep Learning Models: A Systematic Review, Performance Analysis and Discussion of Implications," *International Journal of Financial Studies*, 11(3): 1–22, 26 July 2023.
10. J. Du, Q. Liu, K. Chen and J. Wang, "Forecasting Stock Prices in Two Ways Based on LSTM Neural Network," *2019 IEEE 3rd Information Technology, Networking, Electronic and Automation Control Conference (ITNEC)*, Chengdu, China, 2019, pp. 1083–1086, https://doi.org/10.1109/ITNEC.2019.8729026.
11. I. Parmar et al., "Stock Market Prediction Using Machine Learning," *2018 First International Conference on Secure Cyber Computing and Communication (ICSCCC)*, Jalandhar, India, 2018, pp. 574–576, https://doi.org/10.1109/ICSCCC.2018.8703332.

12. R. Y. Nivetha and C. Dhaya, "Developing a Prediction Model for Stock Analysis," *2017 International Conference on Technical Advancements in Computers and Communication*, Melmaurvathur, India, 2017, 1–3.
13. Z. Yeze and W. Yiying, "Stock Price Prediction Based on Information Entropy and Artificial Neural Network," *2019 5th International Conference on Information Management (ICIM)*, Cambridge, UK, 2019, pp. 248–251, https://doi.org/10.1109/INFOMAN.2019.8714662.
14. P. Chinthan, R. Mishra, B. Prakash and B. Saleena, "Stock Market Prediction Using Machine Learning Techniques: A Comparative Study," In: Venkataraman, N., Wang, L., Fernando, X., Zobaa, A. F. (eds.), *Big Data and Cloud Computing. ICBCC 2022.* Lecture Notes in Electrical Engineering, vol 1021, 2023. Springer, https://doi.org/10.1007/978-981-99-1051-9_7.
15. M. Iyer and R. Mehra, "A Survey on Stock Market Prediction," *2018 Fifth International Conference on Parallel, Distributed and Grid Computing (PDGC)*, Solan, India, 2018, pp. 663–668, https://doi.org/10.1109/PDGC.2018.8745715.
16. G. Sekhon, An article on "Metrics for Evaluation of Algorithms for Stock Market Prediction" 3 February 2023, https://medium.com/@gianetan/metrics-for-evalution-of-alogrithms-for-stock-market-prediction-488a8980b35b#

16 AI-Powered Finance
Redefining the Financial Landscape

A. Sankaran, S. Vaidheeswaran, and A. B. Mohammed Yousuf

16.1 INTRODUCTION

In recent years, the intersection of artificial intelligence (AI) and financial technology (Fintech) has revolutionized the economy, marking an era characterized by unprecedented innovation and growth results. This symbiotic relationship between AI and Fintech changes traditional banking, investment and insurance models, redefining them through the use of standardized financial data and trading from manufacturing to detecting fraud and strengthening compliance with regulatory standards. AI is driving significant changes in all aspects of the financial services industry. This chapter delves into the dynamic interactions between AI and Fintech, highlighting the dramatic AI-enabled transformation of the financial ecosystem, AI-enabled finance, data applications, machine learning (ML) models, natural language processing (NLP), and individualized Through comprehensive analysis of key areas such as financial services, compliance, and collaborative efforts in traditional finance between institutions and Fintech startups, this study makes it clear that the AI-Fintech relationship is multifaceted.

Drawing insights from renowned publications, industry reports and discussions with industry professionals, this chapter brings together a wealth of knowledge to provide nuanced understandings of the evolving landscape of AI-powered Fintech solutions. As it analyzes real-time models, analyzes, designs and implements AI systems in finance alongside emerging trends, it seeks to provide valuable insights into how AI is reshaping the financial industry and generating innovation in unprecedented ways. As AI continues to conform and permeate each factor of economic services, it is vital for stakeholders to stay abreast of those developments and adapt their techniques as a result. Through collaborative efforts and an eager recognition of regulatory compliance, cybersecurity, and moral concerns, the financial industry can harness the transformative capacity of AI to create a more inclusive, green, and purchaser-centric economic surrounding. This chapter serves as a complete manual for navigating the complex interplay between AI and Fintech, offering treasured insights into the destiny of finance within the AI-driven era.

 DOI: 10.1201/9781003645849-16

16.2 METHODS

The insights offered in this chapter were synthesized from a combination of sources, including authoritative publications, industry reports, and discussions with industry experts. Information was gathered from diverse perspectives, ensuring a comprehensive understanding of the subject matter. Key components of the AI-Fintech relationship, such as AI-driven financial evolution, data utilization, ML models, NLP, algorithmic trading, personalized financial services, regulatory compliance, cybersecurity, ethical considerations, and collaborations between traditional financial institutions and Fintech companies, were analyzed and synthesized into coherent narratives. Additionally, real-time examples and case studies demonstrate the practical applications of AI within the financial industry.

16.2.1 AI-Driven Financial Evolution

The Fintech panorama is currently undergoing a seismic shift propelled by means of the transformative power of AI. Here's a sneak peek into the dynamic ways AI is reshaping financial services (Figure 16.1).

16.2.1.1 Tailored Financial Solutions

Imagine a world where financial services are as personalized as the individuals they serve. AI and personalized financial merchandise are not a dream but a truth. Robo-advisors and automated funding platforms stand as shining examples, guiding users closer to tailor-made economic decisions [1].

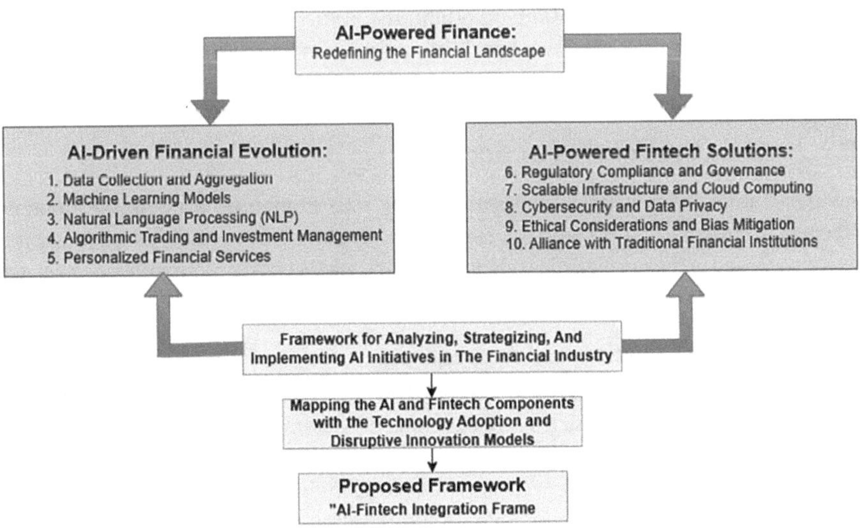

FIGURE 16.1 Architecture diagram.

16.2.1.1.1 Fortified Fraud Defense

In the relentless warfare against financial fraud, AI emerges as an impressive best friend. Its prowess in sifting via tremendous datasets in actual-time fortifies defenses, thwarting fraudulent sports before they even take root [1].

16.2.1.1.2 Streamlined Regulatory Adherence

Navigating the elaborate net of monetary policies is no longer a Herculean assignment, thanks to AI-powered RegTech answers. By automating compliance methods, companies can be aware of innovation without being slowed down via regulatory pink tape [1].

16.2.1.1.3 Financial Empowerment for All

AI is breaking down obstacles to monetary inclusion, empowering underserved communities with tailored financial merchandise designed to meet their particular needs [1].

16.2.1.1.4 Credit Assessment Redefined

Gone are the times of traditional credit scoring. AI-driven fashions faucet into opportunity facts sources like social media footprints, offering an extra holistic view of creditworthiness and beginning doorways for the ones previously overlooked [1].

16.2.1.1.5 Digital Wallets on the Move

Imagine a world wherein monetary offerings are just a tap away, even in the remotest corners. AI supercharges virtual wallets and mobile banking structures, making monetary services really handy to all [1].

The fusion of AI and Fintech isn't pretty much technological progress; it's about revolutionizing the economic panorama to be more inclusive, green, and customer-centric. As AI maintains to adapt, the ability for even extra groundbreaking modifications looms massive, heralding a future in which financial offerings are smarter, sleeker, and extra seamlessly incorporated into our lives.

16.2.2 Data Collection and Aggregation

The integration of synthetic intelligence (AI) into numerous aspects of financial offerings is indeed transforming the enterprise, revolutionizing how statistics is gathered, processed, and applied. Here's a summary of the key components concerned with this AI-pushed economic evolution:

16.2.2.1 Data Collection and Aggregation

AI permits financial institutions to accumulate and mix large quantities of records from diverse sources, consisting of economic statements, market records, and opportunity fact sets like social media content and geospatial imagery. This comprehensive statistics series empowers companies to gain deeper insights and make more informed choices, ultimately enhancing their aggressive gain.

16.2.2.1.1 Data Sources

Financial services corporations leverage a huge range of information sources to fuel their AI-driven initiatives. These sources embody conventional economic facts in addition to non-conventional assets such as social media, information, and satellite imagery. By incorporating diverse records units into their models, organizations can enhance the accuracy and robustness of their AI algorithms.

16.2.2.2 Data Integration and Connectivity

Seamless integration of statistics from various resources is critical for offering real-time insights and supporting informed decision-making in economic services. AI permits companies to integrate disparate information sets and create a unified view in their operations, main to higher fraud detection, compliance monitoring, and customer engagement strategies.

16.2.2.3 Data Refinement and Preparation

Before AI algorithms can efficiently examine economic facts, they ought to go through refinement and instruction tactics. This involves cleaning and structuring the data, ensuring its quality, and selecting relevant features for AI models to process. By refining the statistics, organizations can enhance the accuracy and reliability of their AI-driven insights and predictions.

These additives together make contributions to the modernization and optimization of the monetary industry, enabling businesses to harness the energy of AI for stepped forward decision-making, threat management, and customer service.

16.2.3 Machine Learning Models

ML models play a pivotal position in enhancing diverse economic offerings in the Fintech industry. Here's how they make a contribution to the regions you've cited:

ML algorithms analyze massive volumes of facts in actual time, detecting patterns and anomalies that can imply fraudulent hobbies. Over time, those models analyze new statistics and adapt to evolving fraud patterns, enhancing fraud detection capabilities [1].

ML fashions are used to expect marketplace risks and pick out future financial opportunities. They may be educated on information which includes economic interactions, mortgage repayments, and enterprise stocks to forecast lending, coverage, and stock market trends [2].

By studying client facts, ML models can segment customers into corporations based totally on behavior and preferences. This aids in personalizing offerings and targeting advertising and marketing efforts extra effectively [2].

Alternative credit score scoring fashions use ML to assess creditworthiness through the use of non-conventional facts assets, like social media activity. This affords opportunities for individuals with constrained credit score histories to access financial services [2].

Popular ML fashions used in those packages consist of decision bushes, random forests, and neural networks, that are recognized for their predictive accuracy and capability to handle complex, non-linear relationships inside data [3]. These improvements in ML are remodeling Fintech, making it more secure, customized, and inclusive.

16.2.4 Natural Language Processing

NLP stands as a cornerstone of AI innovation, wielding vast influence in revolutionizing the Fintech area. Here's a glimpse into its transformative packages:

16.2.4.1 Sentiment Analysis

NLP algorithms decode the sentiment concealed inside textual statistics, from consumer evaluations to social media chatter. Financial institutions leverage this insight to gauge public perception, shaping funding strategies and product development initiatives [1].

16.2.4.1.1 Real-Time News and Social Media Insights

Harnessing NLP, Fintech ventures reveal and dissect a deluge of real-time information emanating from information outlets and social structures. This analytical prowess unveils market developments and sentiment shifts, worthwhile for trading algorithms and threat management [2].

16.2.4.2 Deep Customer Feedback Analysis

Through NLP, Fintech entities delve into purchaser comments with surgical precision, unraveling insights to elevate provider requirements and product offerings [1].

The infusion of NLP into Fintech not only streamlines operations but also provides a competitive edge by fostering deeper insights and enhancing customer interactions. As NLP keeps its evolutionary journey, its packages in Fintech are poised to scale new heights, reshaping the industry's panorama with unheard of sophistication and efficacy [34].

16.2.5 Algorithmic Trading and Investment Management

Management represents the top of monetary sophistication, using advanced strategies to navigate the complexities of present day markets. Here's a concise overview of every issue:

16.2.5.1 Trading Strategies

At the coronary heart of algorithmic trading lies a meticulously crafted set of guidelines, known as trading techniques. These techniques leverage mathematical fashions to execute trades rapidly and successfully, based totally on predetermined criteria inclusive of price actions, timing, and buying and selling volume [14].

16.2.5.2 Portfolio Optimization

In the pursuit of top-rated returns while managing threat, portfolio optimization emerges as a crucial undertaking. It involves the artwork and science of constructing investment portfolios that strike an ideal balance between anticipated returns and danger tolerance. Employing mathematical fashions and metrics just like the Sharpe ratio, portfolio optimization pursues to maximize returns for a given stage of risk [5].

16.2.5.3 Market Analysis

A complete understanding of marketplace dynamics is integral for knowledgeable choice-making. Market analysis delves deep into factors like marketplace length, boom traits, and aggressive panorama, providing useful insights for traders and traders alike [9].

These components synergize to form the backbone of algorithmic buying and selling and funding control, empowering financial specialists with the equipment and insights needed to thrive in brand-new dynamic markets. Should you searching for deeper insights into any of those factors, feel unfastened to inquire similarly.

Personalized economic offerings offer tailor-made solutions to satisfy the particular wishes and options of individual customers. Here's a breakdown of the important thing factors highlighted:

- **Precision in financial recommendations:**
  Personalized economic services provide precise pointers based on elements such as a customer's financial desires, chance tolerance, and current lifestyles stage. This tailor-made method ensures that clients get hold of advice that is relevant and actionable for his or her precise circumstances.
- **Customized communication channels:**
  Customers have the flexibility to choose their preferred verbal exchange channels, allowing them to get hold of data and updates in the way that best suits their choices. Whether it is via e mail, cell apps, or in-character meetings, customized financial services adapt to the verbal exchange alternatives of every patron.
- **Enhanced customer experience:**
  By leveraging insights into patron conduct and options, economic institutions can create a more attractive and treasured banking revel. This more desirable client experience fosters more pride, loyalty, and consideration, in the end leading to stronger relationships between customers and their economic companies.
- **Data-driven insights:**
  Advanced analytics strategies, which include geospatial evaluation and NLP, permit economic institutions to derive customized insights from purchaser facts. These insights can inform decision-making methods, allowing establishments to provide targeted pointers and solutions that address particular consumer wishes and targets.

Overall, personalized economic offerings empower customers to manipulate their budget by way of presenting tailor-made guidance and guides that align with their specific economic occasions and desires. If you are interested in exploring personalized banking answers, reaching out to economic establishments that offer those services is an endorsed next step.

16.2.5.4 Robo-Advisors

Imagine you are a younger expert looking to make investments in your destiny but do not have the time or information to manage your portfolio actively. Enter robo-advisors like Wealthfront. By answering some easy questions about your economic desires, chance tolerance, and timeline, Wealthfront's algorithms construct a personalized investment portfolio tailor-made for your needs. As market situations exchange, the robo-guide constantly montiors video display units and adjusts your investments to keep you on track [1].

16.2.5.5 Chatbots for Customer Support

Picture this: You're a hectic entrepreneur trying to reconcile a discrepancy for your enterprise account past due at night. Instead of being ready until the subsequent enterprise day to speak with a customer service representative, you turn to the AI-powered chatbot of your bank, Chase. Within seconds, the chatbot assists you in resolving the difficulty, providing real-time help and saving you precious time and hassle [13].

16.2.5.5.1 Tailored Product Recommendations

Now, shall we embrace that you are an avid online consumer looking for the appropriate gift for a friend's birthday? As you browse through an e-commerce platform like Amazon, its AI-pushed advice engine analyzes your past purchases and browsing records in real time to indicate relevant present ideas, ensuring a personalized shopping revel in and growing the probability of locating an appropriate present [8].

These examples illustrate how personalized economic services leverage real-time statistics and AI generation to satisfy character wishes, decorate personal stories, and force better consequences in modern dynamic virtual panorama.

16.3 AI-POWERED FINTECH SOLUTIONS

They are catalyzing a profound transformation in the economic enterprise, harnessing advanced technology to raise offerings and streamline operations. Here's a better look at key regions in which AI is having big effect:

16.3.1 Financial Reporting

AI revolutionizes the procedure of economic reporting via expediting facts analysis, enabling institutions to rapidly generate comprehensive reports. For example, leveraging NLP, AI algorithms automate the extraction of pertinent information from financial files, ensuring speedy and unique reporting [1].

16.3.2 Fraud Detection

AI emerges as a stalwart in combatting financial fraud, leveraging its prowess to determine fraudulent activities via real-time evaluation of transaction patterns and anomaly detection. This proactive method is now not only effectively safeguards corporations toward economic crimes but also safeguards valuable property, potentially saving tens of millions of dollars [1].

16.3.3 Credit Scoring

AI algorithms redefine credit score scoring by delving into conventional credit histories along with alternative facts resources. This holistic technique complements accuracy and fosters financial inclusion via providing an extra complete evaluation of creditworthiness [2].

16.3.3.1 Personalized Financial Services

AI lends a non-public contact to economic services and products, tailoring services to match character person alternatives. By analyzing great datasets, AI crafts bespoke solutions that cater to precise wishes and alternatives, thereby improving the consumer experience [2].

16.3.4 Investment Strategies

AI-driven gear like TradeSmith's funding portfolio management platform exemplifies the electricity of algorithms in forecasting stock prices and optimizing exchange order execution timing. By empowering customers with insights derived from information evaluation, those gears facilitate informed investment decisions [3].

These illustrations underscore the pervasive impact of AI throughout diverse sides of Fintech, introducing innovative solutions that propel the industry forward. As AI continues to conform, its integration into Fintech is poised to deepen, with startups and hooked up entities alike embracing those technologies to stay aggressive and meet the dynamic needs of their customers.

16.4 REGULATORY COMPLIANCE AND GOVERNANCE

Regulatory compliance and governance function as pillars in upholding the integrity of the financial industry, ensuring adherence to legal and ethical standards. Here's a comprehensive exploration of three key components:

16.4.1 Know Your Customer Procedures

Know your customer (KYC) procedures are essential in verifying the identity of clients and assessing potential risks associated with their engagement. Financial institutions collect and verify basic personal information, such as names and addresses, and conduct screenings against various lists to ensure compliance with regulatory requirements.

16.4.2 Anti-Money Laundering Checks

To combat financial crime, anti-money laundering (AML) checks are crucial measures in customer due diligence. Ranging from basic identification verification to real-time transaction monitoring, these checks identify and mitigate the risks posed by individuals engaging in illicit activities. They are vital in safeguarding organizations from unwittingly facilitating money laundering and other criminal endeavors.

16.4.3 General Data Protection Regulation Compliance

GDPR stands as a cornerstone in data protection and privacy within the European Union and the European Economic Area. It empowers individuals with control over their personal data and mandates stringent rules for data processing, storage, and transfer. Compliance with GDPR not only ensures the protection of individual rights but also fosters trust and transparency in global business operations.

These components collectively reinforce the financial environment, demanding robust systems and processes to ensure ongoing compliance. By upholding regulatory standards and safeguarding data integrity, financial institutions maintain trust and accountability in their operations.

16.5 TOPICS WITH A CONCISE REVIEW

16.5.1 High-Performance Computing

High-Performance Computing (HPC) involves leveraging supercomputers and parallel processing techniques to tackle complex computational challenges. It finds applications in fields like scientific research, weather forecasting, and financial modeling, where vast computational power is essential for processing large datasets and running intricate simulations.

16.5.2 Cloud-Based Solutions

Cloud computing offers a versatile approach to delivering computing resources over the internet. Businesses leverage cloud services for storage, processing, and software applications, accessing resources on-demand without the need for physical infrastructure. Cloud solutions provide scalability, flexibility, and cost-efficiency, enabling companies to adapt swiftly to changing demands and optimize resource utilization.

16.5.3 Infrastructure as Code

Infrastructure as Code (IaC) is a methodology for managing and provisioning IT infrastructure through machine-readable definition files. It allows developers to automate the deployment and management of infrastructure components, ensuring consistency and repeatability across environments. By treating infrastructure as code, organizations can streamline operations, accelerate deployment, and enhance scalability.

16.6 OVERVIEW OF THE TOPICS NOTED

16.6.1 Encryption Techniques

Encryption serves as a cornerstone of cybersecurity, safeguarding sensitive data by converting it into an unreadable format known as ciphertext. Various encryption algorithms like advanced encryption standard (AES) and Rivest-Shamir-Adleman (RSA) ensure data confidentiality and integrity by requiring decryption keys to access the original plaintext.

16.6.2 Access Controls

Access controls are pivotal in regulating user access to resources within computing environments. They encompass different strategies such as discretionary access control (DAC), mandatory access control (MAC), and role-based access control (RBAC), each delineating rules and guidelines for managing permissions. These methods ensure that only authorized users can access specific data and resources.

16.6.3 Threat Detection and Response

Threat detection and response are integral components of cybersecurity aimed at identifying and mitigating cyber threats. Through continuous monitoring of networks and systems, potential threats are analyzed, and rapid responses are executed to minimize the impact of cyber attacks and uphold data security. This proactive approach is essential for maintaining the confidentiality, integrity, and availability of sensitive information.

These factors collectively shape a robust defense mechanism against cyber threats, ensuring the protection of data in today's digital landscape.

16.7 ETHICAL CONSIDERATIONS AND BIAS MITIGATION

16.7.1 Fairness and Transparency in AI Models

Fairness involves ensuring AI systems do not exhibit bias or discrimination against individuals or groups. Transparency involves making the AI decision-making process understandable and accountable to users. It's crucial to communicate how AI models were developed, the data they were trained on, and how they are monitored and updated to maintain fairness and transparency.

16.7.2 Ethical Use of Consumer Data

Ethical data management encompasses obtaining consent for data collection, ensuring data security, and using data in ways that respect individuals' privacy and rights. It's vital to handle consumer data responsibly to prevent harm or disadvantage. This includes adhering to privacy laws, protecting data from breaches, and using data only for intended and ethical purposes.

16.7.3 Bias Detection and Correction

Detecting and correcting bias in AI systems is essential to prevent unfair outcomes. This involves analyzing data and algorithms for biases and implementing strategies to mitigate them, such as ensuring diverse and representative data, adjusting algorithms during development, and correcting biases in the output. Continuous monitoring and updating are necessary to address any new biases that may emerge over time.

These principles guide the development and deployment of AI systems, ensuring they are ethical, equitable, and trustworthy. By prioritizing fairness, transparency, ethical data use, and bias mitigation, the AI community can build systems that benefit all users and society as a whole.

16.8 ALLIANCE WITH TRADITIONAL FINANCIAL INSTITUTIONS

Collaborations between traditional financial institutions and emerging Fintech organizations are reshaping the financial landscape, fostering innovation, and enhancing consumer experiences. Here's a succinct review of their impact across various sectors:

16.8.1 Banks and Credit Unions

Partnerships between banks and Fintechs are revolutionizing the banking sector, leading to enhanced digital services, improved operational efficiency, and greater access to financial products. Credit unions, with their focus on member benefits, are also leveraging Fintech collaborations to offer competitive rates and innovative solutions to their members.

16.8.2 Insurance Companies

While specific recent alliances may not be widely documented, insurance companies are increasingly leveraging Fintech solutions to transform risk assessment, claims processing, and customer engagement. These partnerships enable insurers to utilize advanced technologies to better serve their policyholders and adapt to evolving market demands.

16.8.3 Investment Firms

Collaborations between investment firms and Fintechs are driving innovation in the wealth management sector. By integrating Fintech solutions, investment firms can offer personalized investment strategies, expand distribution channels, and enhance client services. These partnerships empower investment companies to deliver more tailored investment solutions and improve overall customer experiences.

These collaborations represent a strategic shift in the financial industry toward embracing technology-driven solutions to meet the evolving needs of customers and businesses. By combining the stability and trust of traditional financial institutions with the agility and innovation of Fintech companies, these alliances are driving positive change and shaping the future of finance.

16.9 FRAMEWORK FOR ANALYZING, STRATEGIZING, AND IMPLEMENTING AI INITIATIVES IN THE FINANCIAL INDUSTRY

16.9.1 Models Elucidating Technology Adoption and Disruptive Innovation Dynamics

16.9.1.1 Need

Mapping the additives of AI-Fintech with the Technology Adoption Life Cycle and the Disruptive Innovation model is vital for navigating the complexities of era integration inside the financial area. It offers insights into the ranges of adoption, from early experimentation to large reputation, and highlights disruptive forces reshaping traditional practices. By aligning AI dimensions with those models, stakeholders can assume market dynamics, identify strategic opportunities, and mitigate dangers associated with innovation. This mapping enables informed selection-making, guiding the development and implementation of AI-driven solutions that force efficiency, competitiveness, and sustainable increase in the monetary panorama.

The Technology Adoption Life Cycle and the Disruptive Innovation model, each belong to the category of frameworks or theories used to understand and analyse the adoption and effect of new technology in various industries.

16.9.1.1.1 Technology Adoption Life Cycle

This version categorizes adopters of the latest technology into unique companies based totally on their willingness to strive for new improvements. It allows to expect and apprehend the tiers via which a generation passes as it is adopted through distinctive segments of the population or marketplace.

16.9.1.1.2 Disruptive Innovation Model

This model specializes in the disruptive outcomes of recent technology or innovations in current markets and industries. It explains how new entrants with progressive services or products can disrupt hooked up gamers and rework conventional markets.

Both models provide precious insights into how new technology is delivered, adopted, and ultimately impacts industries, albeit from slightly one-of-a-kind views.

16.9.1.2 Purpose of Aligning the Dimensions of AI-Fintech Landscape with the Models

Aligning AI and the dimensions of the financial panorama with fashions together with the Technology Adoption Life Cycle and the Disruptive Innovation model serves numerous vital functions:

- Understanding adoption dynamics
- Identifying target segments
- Assessing market readiness
- Strategic decision-making
- Mitigating risks and challenges

16.10 THE TECHNOLOGY ADOPTION LIFECYCLE MODEL

The Technology Adoption Lifecycle version, propagated by Everett Rogers, describes the adoption and diffusion of new technologies within a population or marketplace segment. In the context of AI and Fintech revolutionizing the financial landscape, this version can be implemented to understand how those technologies are being followed and integrated with the aid of numerous stakeholders in the monetary industry.

Here's how the Technology Adoption Lifecycle version will be associated with the title:

1. **Innovators and early adopters:** In the initial ranges of AI and Fintech adoption, innovators and early adopters in the economic enterprise embody these technologies. They are generally forward-thinking individuals or businesses willing to take risks and experiment with new answers to gain a competitive edge.
2. **Early majority and late majority:** As AI and Fintech solutions prove their price and reliability, the early majority and past due majority of financial establishments and specialists start to adopt those technologies extra broadly. This phase is characterized by way of increased funding in AI-powered equipment and systems to improve performance, decision-making, and client stories.
3. **Laggards:** Some stakeholders can be slower to adopt AI and Fintech answers because of diverse motives along with skepticism, resistance to alternate, or loss of assets. However, because the blessings of those technologies become more apparent and enterprise norms shift, even laggards may additionally sooner or later undertake AI and Fintech solutions to remain competitive within the evolving economic landscape.

By making use of the Technology Adoption Lifecycle model to the integration of AI and Fintech inside the economic enterprise, we will gain insights into the dynamics of adoption, diffusion, and transformation going on within the area. This model helps illustrate how AI and Fintech are revolutionizing the financial landscape by way of reshaping conventional practices, processes, and enterprise fashions.

16.10.1 Mapping of Technology Adoption Lifecycle Model with the Components of AI and Fintech

Let's map each of the ten additives cited to the kinds of the Technology Adoption Life Cycle:

1. **Innovators (technology enthusiasts):**
    - **Data collection and aggregation:** Innovators might also experiment with present-day statistics series strategies and aggregation strategies to collect insights for AI programs.
    - **Machine learning models**: Innovators expand and check novel machine-studying algorithms for fraud detection, risk control, and personalized financial pointers.
    - **Natural language processing:** Early adopters explore NLP technology for constructing superior chatbots and studying customer remarks in economic services.
    - **Algorithmic trading and investment management:** Innovators pioneer the usage of AI-powered algorithms for automatic trading and investment techniques.
2. **Early adopters (visionaries):**
    - **Personalized financial services:** Early adopters recognize the ability of AI in offering personalized monetary pointers and put money into enforcing AI-driven answers.

  - Collaboration with Traditional Financial Institutions: Visionaries forge partnerships among Fintech startups and traditional monetary institutions to leverage AI for modern services and products.
3. **Early majority (pragmatists):**
   - Scalable Infrastructure and Cloud Computing: Pragmatists adopt scalable cloud infrastructure to assist the growing demand for AI-powered economic offerings and records processing.
   - Cybersecurity and Data Privacy: Early majority adopters prioritize cybersecurity measures and data privacy rules to mitigate dangers related to AI-pushed financial offerings.
4. **Late majority (conservatives):**
   - **Regulatory compliance and governance:** Conservatives cognizance on making sure compliance with regulatory requirements and imposing governance frameworks for AI packages in financial offerings.
   - **Ethical considerations and bias mitigation:** Late majority adopters deal with moral issues and biases in AI algorithms to construct agreement with and transparency in financial services.
5. **Laggards (skeptics):**
   - These components might not be completely adopted by laggards; however, they will ultimately undertake them because the generation matures and becomes extra widespread.

By aligning the additives with the categories of the Technology Adoption Life Cycle, we can see how each aspect of AI in Fintech progresses from early experimentation and innovation to mainstream adoption, addressing exceptional wishes and concerns at each level of adoption.

16.10.1.1 Examples from Global Context

Some examples of companies/startups that align with each stage of the Technology Adoption Life Cycle in the Fintech industry:

1. **Innovators (technology enthusiasts):**
   - **Data collection and aggregation:** Plaid, Yodlee, Quovo
   - **Machine learning models:** Zest Finance, Ayasdi, Kensho (acquired by S&P Global)
   - **Natural language processing:** Kasisto, Clinc, EigenTechnologies
   - **Algorithmic trading and investment management:** Quantopian, AlphaSense, QuantConnect
2. **Early adopters (visionaries):**
   - **Personalized financial services:** Wealthfront, Acorns, Betterment
   - **Collaboration with traditional financial institutions:** Stripe, Square, TransferWise
3. **Early majority (pragmatists):**
   - **Scalable infrastructure and cloud computing**: Amazon Web Services (AWS), Microsoft Azure, Google Cloud Platform
   - **Cyber security and data privacy:** Fortinet, Palo Alto Networks, Crowd Strike

4. **Late majority (conservatives):**
   - **Ethical considerations and bias mitigation:** Fair Isaac Corporation (FICO), SAS, Experian
   - **Alliance with traditional financial institutions:** Plaid (partnering with banks for data connectivity), Stripe (collaborating with financial institutions for payment processing)
5. **Laggards (skeptics):**
   - (These companies may include traditional financial institutions or legacy technology providers that are slow to adopt new Fintech innovations.)

These examples illustrate how companies and startups in the Fintech industry align with the different stages of the Technology Adoption Life Cycle, from early experimentation and adoption to mainstream acceptance and eventual saturation within the market.

16.10.1.2 Examples from Indian Context

Here are some examples of companies/startups in the Indian Fintech industry that align with each stage of the Technology Adoption Life Cycle:

1. **Innovators (technology enthusiasts):**
   - **Data collection and aggregation:** Perfios, Cashfree, PayMate
   - **Machine learning models:** Credit Vidya, Signzy, Zest Money
   - **Natural language processing:** Vernacular.ai, Niki.ai, Active.ai
   - **Algorithmic trading and investment management:** Smallcase, Kuvera, Groww
2. **Early adopters (visionaries):**
   - **Personalized financial services:** Scripbox, Clear Tax, Bank Bazaar
   - **Collaboration with traditional financial institutions:** Razorpay, NiYO, MobiKwik
3. **Early majority (pragmatists):**
   - **Scalable infrastructure and cloud computing:** AWS India, Microsoft Azure India, Google Cloud India
   - **Cyber security and data privacy:** Quick Heal, Seqrite, Druva
4. **Late majority (conservatives):**
   - **Ethical considerations and bias mitigation:** CIBIL (Credit Information Bureau India Limited), CRIF High Mark, Equifax
   - **Alliance with traditional financial institutions:** BharatPe (partnering with banks for digital payments), Paytm Payments Bank, PhonePe (collaborating with financial institutions for digital payments)
5. **Laggards (skeptics):**
   - (These may include traditional banks or financial institutions that are slow to adopt new Fintech innovations, as well as legacy technology providers in the financial sector.)

These examples provide insights into how companies and startups in the Indian Fintech industry align with the different stages of the Technology Adoption Life Cycle, showcasing the diverse range of innovations and advancements occurring in the Indian financial technology landscape.

16.11 THE DISRUPTIVE INNOVATION MODEL

The Disruptive Innovation version describes how new technology or enterprise models can disrupt present markets and industries by way of providing less difficult, more handy, and frequently cheaper alternatives to incumbent services or products. In the context of AI and Fintech, this model can help explain how these technologies are essentially reworking the economic panorama by way of introducing progressive solutions that are undertaking conventional banking and economic practices.

Here's how the Disruptive Innovation model will be related to the identify:

1. **Disruptive technologies:** AI and Fintech are considered disruptive technology because they introduce new methods of turning in financial services that fundamentally exchange how customers engage with banks, funding companies, and different financial institutions. For example, AI-powered robo-advisors and cell payment apps disrupt traditional investment advisory and banking offerings by supplying automatic, user-pleasant options.
2. **New market entrants:** Fintech startups and technology corporations are regularly the first to introduce disruptive AI-based answers to the monetary industry. These new market entrants project hooked up gamers by imparting modern products and services that cope with unmet needs or pain factors among customers.
3. **Market segmentation:** Disruptive improvements to start with target niche marketplace segments which can be underserved or not noted by way of incumbent economic institutions. For instance, AI-driven lending platforms may additionally cater to individuals with limited credit history or small agencies that warfare to access conventional loans from banks.
4. **Incremental improvement:** Over time, disruptive innovations progressively improve in overall performance and reliability, making them more appealing to mainstream customers. As AI and Fintech answers mature, they'll begin to seize larger marketplace shares and compete at once with traditional financial offerings providers.
5. **Market transformation:** Ultimately, disruptive improvements can cause a metamorphosis of the economic landscape, with incumbent institutions adapting their techniques and business models to remain aggressive inside the face of technological disruption. This can also contain partnerships between traditional banks and Fintech startups, in addition to internal investments in AI and virtual capabilities.

By applying the Disruptive Innovation version to AI and Fintech inside the monetary enterprise, we are able to understand how these technology are reshaping traditional commercial enterprise models, consumer expectancies, and industry dynamics. This model helps illustrate the transformative effect of AI and Fintech on the monetary landscape and the possibilities and challenges they present to incumbent gamers and new marketplace entrants alike.

16.11.1 Mapping of Disruptive Innovation Model with the Components of AI and Fintech

Let's map every section of the Disruptive Innovation model with the provided components:

1. **Disruptive technologies:**
    - Robo-advisors, cellular charge apps, AI-driven lending structures, and other AI-powered solutions constitute the disruptive technology in the financial industry.
2. **New market entrants:**
    - 'Fintech startups and generation corporations' represent the brand new marketplace entrants, task mounted gamers by using offering progressive services and products, including 'personalized monetary services and algorithmic buying and selling platforms.'
3. **Market segmentation:**
    - 'AI-driven lending structures' focused on people with constrained credit score history and small corporations constitute market segmentation inside the economic enterprise.
4. **Incremental improvement:**
    - **As AI and Fintech answers mature, they grow to be more appealing to mainstream** clients, main to elevated adoption of 'robo-advisors, cell charge apps, and other AI-powered economic services.'
5. **Market transformation:**
    - Market transformation happens as disruptive improvements reshape the monetary panorama and force incumbent establishments to evolve.
    - 'Traditional banks and financial institutions accomplice with Fintech startups', put money into AI and virtual capabilities, and modify their strategies and enterprise fashions to remain competitive in the face of technological disruption.

This mapping illustrates how each phase of the Disruptive Innovation version corresponds to specific components of the furnished disruptive technologies in the monetary industry.

16.11.2 Examples from Global Context

Here are some examples of companies/startups that align with each phase of the Disruptive Innovation model in the Fintech industry:

1. **Disruptive technologies:**
    - **Robo-advisors:** Betterment, Wealthfront, Wealthsimple
    - **Mobile payment apps:** PayPal, Venmo, SquareCash
    - **AI-driven lending platforms:** LendingClub, SoFi, Kabbage
2. **New market entrants:**
    - **Fintech startups:** Robinhood, Revolut, Stripe
    - **Technology companies:** Google Pay, Apple Pay, Amazon Pay

3. **Market segmentation:**
   - **AI-driven lending platforms targeting individuals with limited credit history:** Upstart, Avant
   - **AI-based investment platforms catering to specific demographics:** Ellevest (targeting women investors), Acorns (targeting micro-investors)
4. **Incremental improvement:**
   - **Established Fintech companies expanding their offerings:** PayPal (adding Venmo for peer-to-peer payments), Square (expanding into business loans and payroll services)
   - **Traditional banks enhancing digital capabilities:** JP Morgan Chase (developing Chase Pay), Goldman Sachs (launching Marcus by Goldman Sachs for online banking and lending)
5. **Market transformation:**
   - **Partnerships between traditional banks and Fintech startups:** BBVA's acquisition of Simple, Capital One's partnership with Credit Karma
   - **Internal investments in AI and digital capabilities by traditional financial institutions:** Bank of America's Erica virtual assistant, Citigroup's Citi FinTech division

These examples demonstrate how companies and startups across the Fintech industry align with the different phases of the Disruptive Innovation model, from introducing disruptive technologies to reshaping the financial landscape through market transformation.

16.11.2.1 Examples from Indian Context:

Some examples of companies/startups in the Indian Fintech industry that align with each phase of the Disruptive Innovation model:

1. **Disruptive technologies:**
   - **Robo-advisors:** Scripbox, Groww, Kuvera
   - **Mobile payment apps:** Paytm, PhonePe, Google Pay
   - **AI-driven lending platforms:** MoneyTap, Lendingkart, Faircent
2. **New market entrants:**
   - **Fintech startups:** Razorpay, NiYO, BharatPe
   - **Technology companies:** Paytm, PhonePe, Zerodha
3. **Market segmentation:**
   - **AI-driven lending platforms targeting individuals with limited credit history:** Early Salary, Krazy Bee, Money View
   - **AI-based investment platforms catering to specific demographics:** IND Wealth (targeting high-net-worth individuals), Cube Wealth (targeting millennials)
4. **Incremental improvement:**
   - **Established Fintech companies expanding their offerings:** Paytm (adding financial services like Paytm Money and Paytm Payments Bank), PhonePe (expanding into insurance and mutual funds)

- **Traditional banks enhancing digital capabilities:** ICICI Bank (launching iMobile app for digital banking), HDFC Bank (offering digital loan processing and mobile banking)

5. **Market transformation:**
   - **Partnerships between traditional banks and Fintech startups:** HDFC Bank's partnership with Paytm, ICICI Bank's collaboration with PhonePe.
   - **Internal investments in AI and digital capabilities by traditional financial institutions:** Axis Bank's investment in AI-based chatbot AxisAha!, Kotak Mahindra Bank's digital banking initiatives.

These examples illustrate how companies and startups in the Indian Fintech industry align with the different phases of the Disruptive Innovation model, showcasing the diverse range of innovations and advancements occurring in the Indian financial technology landscape.

16.12 "AI-FINTECH INTEGRATION FRAMEWORK"–THE PROPOSED MODEL

The proposed model "AI-Fintech Integration Framework" for revolutionizing the Financial Landscape is described underneath:

1. **Discovery phase:**
   - **Identify opportunities:** Assess modern ache factors, inefficiencies, and client needs inside the economic enterprise in which AI and Fintech integration may want to provide fee.
   - **Market research:** Analyze rising traits, technological improvements, and competitor offerings in AI and Fintech to inform strategic decision-making.
2. **Design phase:**
   - **Solution development:** Design AI-powered Fintech answers tailored to address recognized possibilities, leveraging superior technology which include system learning, NLP, and predictive analytics.
   - **User-centric design:** Prioritize person experience and interface layout to ensure that AI-driven Fintech answers are intuitive, consumer-pleasant, and aligned with patron choices.
3. **Development phase:**
   - **Prototyping:** Build prototypes and minimum viable merchandise (MVPs) to test and iterate on AI-Fintech answers, amassing feedback from stakeholders and cease- customers.
   - **Agile development:** Adopt agile methodologies to facilitate speedy generation and non-stop development in the course of the development system.
4. **Deployment phase:**
   - **Implementation strategy:** Develop a phased rollout method for deploying AI-Fintech answers, thinking about elements inclusive of scalability, integration with current systems, and regulatory compliance.

- **Training and education:** Provide training and assistance to employees and users to make sure easy adoption and utilization of AI-pushed Fintech equipment and structures.

5. **Monitoring and optimization:**
   - **Performance monitoring:** Establish key performance indicators (KPIs) and metrics to song the effectiveness and impact of AI-Fintech answers on commercial enterprise results.
   - **Continuous improvement:** Use statistics analytics and comments mechanisms to pick out regions for optimization and enhancement, iterating on AI algorithms and capabilities to maximise price delivery.
6. **Governance and compliance:**
   - **Regulatory compliance:** Ensure that AI-Fintech answers observe applicable legal guidelines, policies, and industry standards governing data privacy, protection, and moral use of AI.
   - **Risk management:** Implement sturdy threat control practices to mitigate ability dangers related to AI-powered Fintech solutions, along with algorithmic bias, cybersecurity threats, and operational disruptions.
7. **Ecosystem engagement:**
   - **Collaboration and partnerships:** Foster collaboration and partnerships with different stakeholders in the AI and Fintech environment, which include era providers, enterprise institutions, educational institutions, and regulatory bodies.
   - **Innovation ecosystem:** Participate in industry forums, hackathons, and innovation initiatives to stay abreast of the present-day traits and possibilities in AI and Fintech, driving non-stop innovation and notion management.

The AI-Fintech Integration Framework provides a structured approach for growing, deploying, and optimizing AI-driven Fintech solutions inside the financial enterprise, facilitating the seamless integration of superior technology to revolutionize the financial landscape.

16.13 MAPPING OF THE PROPOSED MODEL "AI-FINTECH INTEGRATION FRAMEWORK" WITH THE COMPONENTS OF AI AND FINTECH

Let us map each of the components mentioned to the stages of the "AI-Fintech IntegrationFramework" proposed earlier:

1. **Discovery phase:**
   - **Data collection and aggregation:** Innovators discover advanced data series and aggregation strategies to discover possibilities for AI-Fintech integration.
   - **Machine learning models:** Early adopters expand and check ML models for fraud detection, chance control, and personalized monetary pointers all through the invention segment.

- **Natural language processing:** Innovators test with NLP technology for chatbots and patron feedback analysis as a part of coming across ability AI-Fintech packages.
- **Algorithmic trading and investment management:** Visionaries perceive possibilities to leverage AI-pushed algorithms for algorithmic buying and selling and funding control all through the invention phase.

2. **Design phase:**
   - **Personalized financial services:** Innovators layout AI-driven solutions for providing personalized monetary hints, catering to man or woman patron needs for the duration of the layout segment.
   - **Collaboration with traditional financial institutions:** Early adopters lay out collaboration techniques with conventional financial establishments to integrate AI-Fintech answers into existing systems and approaches.
3. **Development phase:**
   - **Scalable infrastructure and cloud computing:** Pragmatists expand scalable cloud infrastructure to assist the development and deployment of AI-Fintech answers for the duration of the improvement phase.
   - **Cybersecurity and data privacy:** Early majority adopters attention on imposing robust cybersecurity measures and information privacy protocols throughout the improvement section.
4. **Deployment phase:**
   - **Regulatory compliance and governance:** Conservatives make sure regulatory compliance and governance frameworks are in region for deploying AI-Fintech solutions to meet enterprise standards and guidelines.
   - **Ethical considerations and bias mitigation:** Late majority adopters address moral considerations and biases in AI algorithms to make certain equity and transparency in economic offerings.
5. **Monitoring and optimization:**
   - These components are ongoing tactics at some stage in the AI-Fintech integration lifecycle, with non-stop monitoring and optimization to ensure effectiveness and efficiency.

This mapping demonstrates how every component aligns with distinctive stages of the proposed AI-Fintech Integration Framework, from initial discovery and layout to improvement, deployment, and ongoing monitoring and optimization.

16.14 EFFECT OF SYNERGETIC COLLABORATION

This affiliation between AI enhancement and Fintech Revolution maintains to reform the monetary panorama, riding performance, accessibility, and competitiveness within the enterprise via the combined efforts and interactions between technological improvements, regulatory changes, and shifts in client behavior. The synergistic nature of those elements paintings together to drive efficiency, accessibility, and competitiveness inside the economic industry.

16.15 FUTURE DIRECTIONS

Here are some potential future directions for the topic "AI and Fintech: Revolutionizing the Financial Landscape":

1. **Enhanced personalization:** AI and Fintech can in addition evolve to offer even greater personalized financial answers tailor-made to individual preferences, behaviors, and life instances. This could involve deeper integration of AI algorithms to investigate substantial quantities of information and offer tremendously custom-designed suggestions for saving, making an investment, and economic making plans.
2. **Augmented intelligence:** As AI generation advances, there may be a shift closer to augmented intelligence, where AI tools and structures increase human selection-making instead of replacing it entirely. Fintech answers may want to leverage AI to empower monetary experts with information-driven insights, predictive analytics, and automation to beautify their talents and effectiveness.
3. **Ethical AI and responsible finance:** There will likely be extended emphasis on ethical AI practices and accountable finance ideas in the AI-Fintech ecosystem. This consists of addressing issues related to algorithmic bias, information privacy, transparency, and fairness in AI-powered monetary services to build acceptance as true with and confidence among customers and regulators.
4. **Blockchain and distributed ledger technology (DLT):** The integration of blockchain and DLT into AI-Fintech solutions should revolutionize regions consisting of payments, settlements, and clever contracts. By leveraging blockchain's transparency, immutability, and decentralized nature, Fintech agencies can enhance protection, reduce transaction expenses, and streamline processes throughout the financial industry.
5. **Regulatory sandboxes and innovation hubs:** Governments and regulatory bodies might also set up regulatory sandboxes and innovation hubs to facilitate experimentation and collaboration between AI startups, Fintech agencies, and traditional economic establishments. These tasks provide a controlled environment for checking out new AI-Fintech answers even as making sure compliance with regulatory requirements.
6. **Financial inclusion and access:** AI and Fintech have the capacity to pressure greater economic inclusion through increasing access to underserved populations, inclusive of the unbanked and underbanked. Future instructions should focus on growing revolutionary AI-powered answers to deal with boundaries to get entry to, which include credit score invisibility, loss of collateral, and geographic isolation.
7. **Cross-sector collaboration:** Collaboration between the financial quarter and other industries, which includes healthcare, schooling, and power, could liberate new possibilities for AI-Fintech innovation. For instance, AI-powered monetary services can be integrated into healthcare systems to facilitate affected person payments and coverage claims processing, or into instructional structures to provide personalized financial literacy training.

8. **Climate finance and sustainability:** With developing recognition of weather alternate and sustainability troubles, there may be multiplied demand for AI-Fintech answers that assist weather finance, inexperienced investments, and sustainable improvement dreams. Future directions could include developing AI algorithms to evaluate weather danger, optimize ESG investments, and help sustainable finance projects.

These future directions spotlight the ongoing evolution and potential impact of AI and Fintech at the monetary landscape, paving the manner for persisted innovation, disruption, and transformation inside the industry.

16.16 CONCLUSION

The integration of AI into the Fintech landscape represents a paradigm shift in the financial industry, driving unprecedented levels of efficiency, accessibility, and competitiveness. From personalized financial advice to advanced fraud detection mechanisms, AI-powered solutions are transforming every aspect of finance. However, this alteration isn't always without challenges, along with regulatory complexities, cybersecurity threats, and moral issues surrounding statistics use and algorithmic selection-making. Nonetheless, collaborative efforts between conventional financial establishments and Fintech startups are paving the way for progressive solutions that address these demanding situations even by leveraging the transformative ability of AI. As AI continues to adapt, its effect on Fintech is poised to deepen, heralding a future in which financial offerings are smarter, greater inclusive, and seamlessly integrated into our lives.

BIBLIOGRAPHY

1. "The Evolution of Fintech: A Comprehensive Outlook on AI's Role in the Future," Fintech Weekly, [Online]. Available: https://magazine.fintechweekly.com/magazine/articles/the-evolution-of-fintech-a-comprehensive-outlook-on-ai-s-role-in-the-future.
2. ThisIsHowArtificialGeneralIntelligenceWillDriveFinancial. https://www.weforum.org/agenda/2024/01/ai-is-driving-the-evolution-of-a-more-inclusive-financial-sector-in-latin-america-here-is-how/.
3. AIhasstartedafinancialrevolution-here'show. https://www.weforum.org/agenda/2020/02/how-ai-is-shaping-financial-services/.
4. Mangla,B.(2024,March15). *RevolutionizingFinTech:AI-drivenimpactacrosseveryzone.* Medium. https://bhawnamangla98.medium.com/revolutionizing-fintech-ai-driven-impact-across-every-zone-dbc200bb21ef
5. In the Realm of AI-Driven Financial Evolution, Data Serves as the Bedrock upon which Innovation Thrives. Let's Embark on a Journey through the Pivotal Stages of Data Utilization.
6. Avenga, "5 Natural Language Processing (NLP) Applications in Finance," Avenga, [Online]. Available: https://www.avenga.com/5-nlp-applications-in-finance/.
7. FutureProcessing,"HowIsNLPTransformingFinance,FinTech,andBanking?"[Online]. Available: [https://www.future-processing.com/blog/how-nlp-is-transforming-finance-fintech-and-banking/].

8. Finextra Research, "Natural Language Processing in Fintech World," Finextra. [Online]. Available: https://www.finextra.com/blogposting/20868/natural-language-processing-in-fintech-world. [Accessed: 2-May-2024].
9. Neebal, "The Impact of NLP in Fintech: Natural Language Processing Applications," [Online]. Available:https://www.neebal.com/the-impact-of-nlp-in-fintech-natural-language-processing-applications/.
10. GeeksforGeeks, "Encryption, Its Algorithms And Its Future," [Online]. Available: https://www.geeksforgeeks.org/encryption-its-algorithms-and-its-future/. [Accessed: 29-Jul-2024].
11. JumpCloud, "What Are the Different Types of Access Control?" [Online]. Available: https://jumpcloud.com/blog/different-types-of-access-control.
12. Microsoft, "What Is Threat Detection and Response (TDR)?" [Online]. Available: https://www.microsoft.com/security/blog/2021/07/28/what-is-threat-detection-and-response-tdr/.
13. Investopedia, "Basics of Algorithmic Trading: Concepts and Examples," [Online]. Available: https://www.investopedia.com/terms/a/algorithmic-trading.asp.
14. WallStreetMojo, "Portfolio Optimization – What Is It, Methods, Examples," [Online]. Available: https://www.wallstreetmojo.com/portfolio-optimization/.
15. WallStreetMojo, "Market Analysis – What Is It, Examples, Importance, Methods," [Online]. Available: https://www.wallstreetmojo.com/market-analysis/.
16. TechMagic, "AI in FinTech: Meet the Top 10 Startups Powered by AI," [Online]. Available: https://techmagic.co/blog/ai-in-fintech-top-startups/.
17. Carmatec, "AI in FinTech in 2024: Role, Opportunities and Use Cases," [Online]. Available: https://carmatec.com/blog/ai-in-fintech-2024-role-opportunities-use-cases/.
18. Itransition, "Artificial Intelligence in Fintech: Use Cases and Examples," [Online]. Available: https://www.itransition.com/blog/artificial-intelligence-in-fintech-use-cases-and-examples.
19. Swift, "The KYC Process Explained," [Online]. Available: https://www.swift.com/knowledge/the-kyc-process-explained.
20. Napier, "What is an anti-money laundering (AML) check?" [Online]. Available: https://www.napier.ai/knowledgehub/what-is-an-anti-money-laundering-check.
21. GDPR.eu, "General Data Protection Regulation (GDPR) – Official Legal Text," [Online]. Available: https://gdpr.eu/legal/.
22. GeeksforGeeks, "High Performance Computing," [Online]. Available: https://www.geeksforgeeks.org/high-performance-computing/.
23. Google Cloud, "Cloud Solutions," [Online]. Available: https://cloud.google.com/solutions.
24. AWS, "What is Infrastructure as Code? – IaC Explained," [Online]. Available: https://aws.amazon.com/infrastructure-as-code/.
25. Forbes Advisor, "Best Robo-Advisors," [Online]. Available: https://www.forbes.com/advisor/investing/best-robo-advisors/.
26. Tidio, "15 Best Customer Service Chatbots [Examples & Tools]," [Online]. Available: https://www.tidio.com/blog/best-customer-service-chatbots/.
27. Markettailor, "How to Use Personalized Recommendations to Increase Engagement and Sales," [Online. Available: https://abmatic.ai/blog/45-stats-on-why-personalization-is-important-in-digital-marketing?utm_source=chatgpt.com.

Index

P

R

S

T

V

W

Y

FSC
www.fsc.org
MIX
Papier | Fördert gute Waldnutzung
FSC® C083411

Kolibri 360 GmbH
Ferdinand-Jühlke-Straße 7
99095 Erfurt, Deutschland
produktsicherheit@kolibri360.de